ACADEMIC
READING

Fourth Edition

Kathleen T. McWhorter

Niagara County Community College

Longman

New York San Francisco Boston
London Toronto Sydney Tokyo Singapore Madrid
Mexico City Munich Paris Cape Town Hong Kong Montreal

Senior Acquisitions Editor: **Steven Rigolosi**
Development Editor: **Leslie Taggart**
Marketing Manager: **Melanie Goulet**
Supplements Editor: **Donna Campion**
Production Manager: **Joseph Vella**
Project Coordination, Text Design, and Electronic Page Makeup:
  Thompson Steele, Inc.
Cover Design Manager: **John Callahan**
Cover Designer: **Kay Petronio**
Photo Research: **Photosearch, Inc.**
Manufacturing Buyer: **Roy Pickering**
Printer and Binder: **Maple-Vail Book Manufacturing Group**
Cover Printer: **Phoenix Color Corp.**

For permission to use copyrighted material, grateful acknowledgment is made to the copyright holders on pp. 511–518, which are hereby made part of this copyright page.

Library of Congress Cataloging-in-Publication Data

McWhorter, Kathleen T.
    Academic Reading / Kathleen T. McWhorter.—4th ed.
        p. cm.
    Includes bibliographical references (p.) and index.
    ISBN 0-321-05111-4
        1. Reading (Higher education) 2. Study skills. 3. Reading comprehension. I. Title.

LB2395.3 .M37 2001
428.4'071'1—dc21   00-028851

Please visit our website at http://www.awlonline.com/McWhorter

ISBN 0-321-05111-4

1 2 3 4 5 6 7 8 9 10—MA—03 02 01 00

BRIEF CONTENTS

CONTENTS

DISCIPLINARY REVIEW PANEL

We are grateful to the experienced instructors from across the disciplines who reviewed individual chapters of Part III of *Academic Reading,* Fourth Edition, to ensure that each chapter gives current, accurate, and helpful information. Part III gives specific reading and study strategies for six main disciplinary areas: the social sciences, business, humanities and the arts, mathematics, the natural sciences, and technical and applied fields. We would like to thank the following special reviewers for their assistance in reviewing the chapters devoted to their area of expertise.

Dave
Baker
*Delta
College*

Marvin L.
Bittinger
*Indiana University–
Purdue University*

Josephine
Brankey
*New York
Technical
College*

Ernest T.
Fitzgerald
*Delgado
Community
College*

Diana
Hestwood
*Minneapolis
Community and
Technical
College*

Barbara A.
Klemm
*Broward
Community
College*

Richard
Marius
*Professor
Emeritus,
Harvard
University*

Jannette
Morales
*San Antonio
College*

Victor
Uszerowicz
*Miami-Dade
Community
College*

PREFACE

Each academic discipline has its own subject matter, approach, and methodology. Consequently, reading assignments in each discipline require unique sets of reading skills and strategies. Many students who possess adequate general reading skills have not learned to adapt them to the demands of different academic disciplines. *Academic Reading* is a unique text that focuses on these important discipline-specific reading skills.

APPROACH

Although many texts teach general reading skills, few show students how to apply, modify, and adapt their skills to accommodate the unique features and requirements of various academic disciplines. This text provides a complete review of comprehension and vocabulary skills and general textbook reading strategies; then it discusses ways to apply these strategies to six major academic disciplines.

Academic Reading uses several current, effective methodologies to develop reading skills.

- **Active Reading** For many students, reading is a passive assimilation process: their goal is to acquire as many facts and as much information as possible. The active reading approach used in *Academic Reading* encourages students to interact with the text by predicting, questioning, and evaluating ideas.
- **Levels of Thinking** Using Bloom's taxonomy of cognitive skills as a framework, this book shows students how to apply higher-order thinking skills to their course work.
- **Metacomprehension** Metacomprehension is the reader's awareness of his or her own comprehension processes. Mature and proficient readers exert a great deal of cognitive control over their reading: They analyze reading tasks, select appropriate reading strategies, and monitor the effectiveness of those strategies. This text guides students in developing these metacomprehensive strategies.
- **Academic Thought Patterns** The text describes seven academic thought patterns that are commonly used in various disciplines to

organize and structure ideas. These patterns, presented as organizing schemata, are used to establish order, consistency, and predictability within academic disciplines.

- **Writing As Learning** Although most students regard writing as a means of communication, few are accustomed to using it as a reading aid to help them organize information, focus ideas, recognize relationships, or generate new ideas. This text introduces writing as a vehicle for learning. Techniques such as underlining, outlining, note taking, and cognitive mapping are approached as learning strategies.
- **Learning Style** Not all students learn in the same way. To help students discover their unique learning preferences, the text includes a Learning Style Questionnaire and offers students suggestions for adapting their study methods to suit learning style characteristics.

DISCIPLINE-SPECIFIC READING SKILLS

With the fundamental skills in place, college students are able to develop a diverse repertoire of reading strategies and to select and alternate among them. Some of the discipline-specific reading skills they will develop include the following:

In Social Sciences

- understanding theories in the social sciences
- reading reports of research
- making comparisons and applications

In Business

- reading models
- reviewing case studies
- studying organization charts and flowcharts
- approaching supplemental readings

In Humanities and the Arts

- understanding figurative language
- reading poetry and short stories
- working with literary criticism
- studying visual elements in art

In Mathematics

- understanding mathematical language
- reading sample problems

- verbalizing processes
- reading graphics
- approaching word problems

In Natural Sciences

- previewing before reading
- understanding scientific approaches
- studying sample problems
- learning terminology and notation

In Technical and Applied Fields

- reading illustrations and drawings
- using visualization
- reading technical manuals
- employing problem-solving strategies

CONTENT OVERVIEW

Academic Reading is organized into three units. Chapters within each unit are interchangeable, allowing the instructor to adapt the material to a variety of instructional sequences.

Part 1, Fundamental Reading Strategies, presents fundamental reading strategies that provide the foundation for the remainder of the text. Chapter 1 introduces the key concepts of active reading and comprehension monitoring, and includes a learning style analysis. Chapter 2 presents fundamental comprehension skills and integrates the concept of adjusting rate to meet comprehension demands. Chapter 3 discusses vocabulary: contextual aids, structural analysis, and specialized terminology. Chapter 4 concentrates on the critical reading and thinking strategies necessary to interpret and evaluate text. Reading and evaluating arguments, both inductive and deductive, and identifying errors in logical reasoning are the focus of Chapter 5.

Part 2, Academic Reading Strategies, is concerned with recognizing patterns of general academic thought, learning from textbooks, reading graphics, reading online sources, using writing to learn, and approaching research, reference, and collateral assignments.

Part 3, Strategies for Specific Disciplines, consists of six chapters, each of which focuses on reading strategies for a specific discipline: social sciences, business, humanities and arts, mathematics, natural sciences, and technical fields. Each chapter describes unique characteristics of the discipline, specialized reading techniques, predominant thought patterns, and methods for adapting study techniques.

SPECIAL FEATURES

The following features enhance the text's effectiveness.

- **Learning Objectives** Each chapter begins with a brief list of objectives that establishes its focus and provides students with purposes for reading. The objectives can also be used as a way to review and check retention after reading the chapter.
- **Discipline Overviews** The text provides an introduction to six major academic disciplines. It acquaints the student with the basic subject matter and the basic approach used in those disciplines. For example, the text explains and discusses
  - why social science is a "science"
  - how business focuses on organization and management
  - literature as a focus on ideas
  - why mathematics is a sequential thinking process
  - how the sciences focus on explanations of natural phenomena
  - the importance of application and performance in technical fields
  - Suggestions for adapting study techniques to meet the requirements of each academic discipline are given.

- **Study Tips** Boxed inserts in each chapter offer practical suggestions for studying and learning. Topics include time management, controlling test anxiety, and preparing for exams.
- **Chapter Summaries** Each chapter includes a summary intended to help students review and consolidate chapter content.
- **Reading Selections** Each chapter concludes with one or more reading selections from a college textbook or academically related source to reinforce the skills and strategies presented in the chapter. Each reading is accompanied by a vocabulary review exercise, comprehension questions, critical thinking questions, and an exercise on applying learning/study strategies.
- **Paired Readings** Eight sets of paired readings are included in the text. Each pair provides two viewpoints on a given topic and encourages students to integrate ideas and synthesize sources. Questions to guide students in applying critical thinking skills to make connections between the ideas and approaches of the readings are included.

- **Academic Applications** Exercises labeled "Academic Application" require students to apply their reading skills to textbook or course materials from their other college courses.
- **Exercises for Collaborative Learning** Additional exercises designated "Learning Collaboratively" have been added to provide structured activities in which students can learn from one another as they analyze and apply skills introduced in the chapter.

CHANGES IN THE FOURTH EDITION

Numerous changes and additions have been made in the fourth edition.

- **New Chapter 9, Reading Online** This new chapter recognizes that students need to learn to locate, read, and evaluate electronic sources. The features of Web sites are discussed, and the differences between reading online and print sources are emphasized. Students are shown how to develop new ways of thinking and learning when using electonic sources.
- **New Chapter 5, Reading and Evaluating Arguments** A new chapter on reading and evaluating arguments expands the text's critical reading coverage. The chapter discusses parts of an argument and treats both deductive and inductive arguments. Errors in logical reasoning are also discussed.
- **Disciplinary Review Panel** Professors from each academic discipline represented in Part 3 of the text served as disciplinary review specialists. They were asked to evaluate the chapter for their discipline for accuracy, appropriateness, and usefulness to students. Many reviewers identified current trends in their fields and provided additional advice that was subsequently incorporated into the chapters.
- **Why Study? Feature** To build students' interest and enthusiasm for each academic discipline in Part 3, a "Why Study (*name of discipline*)?" section was added to each of these chapters. Students are led to discover the value, importance, and relevance of the field to their lives and their careers.
- **Learning Style Assessment** The Learning Style Questionnaire has been moved to Chapter 1, and additional material on adapting study strategies to accommodate learning style preferences has been added.
- **New Readings** Twelve new end-of-chapter reading selections have been chosen to provide current, up-to-date coverage of a wide range of academic fields. Numerous in-chapter textbook excerpts have also been replaced or updated.

- **Paired Readings** The number of sets of paired readings has been increased from three in the previous edition to eight in the current edition. The paired readings provide students with additional practice in synthesizing and evaluating sources.
- **Online Research** This activity directs students to Web sites on topics related to the end-of-chapter readings in Part 3, providing further practice in reading and evaluating electronic sources.
- **New Section on the Arts** Chapter 14, formerly "Reading Literature," has been expanded to include a section on the visual arts. This new section approaches the arts as a visual form of expression and presents reasons and techniques for studying and analyzing the arts.

BOOK SPECIFIC ANCILLARY MATERIALS

The Instructor's Manual The Instructor's Manual provides numerous suggestions for using the text, including how to structure the course and how to approach each section of the book. The Instructor's Manual also contains a complete answer key for the text, and a set of overhead projection transparency masters. 0-321-05113-0

Assessment Package/Test Bank An assessment package/test bank accompanies the text. It contains two sets of multiple-choice chapter review quizzes that measure students' knowledge of chapter content. It also contains a set of newly developed mastery tests that measure students' ability to apply concepts, principles, and techniques taught in the chapter. The mastery tests simulate actual academic situations, assignments, and course materials and are designed to be self-scoring, if the instructor so desires. 0-321-05114-9

Manual for Adjunct Faculty To assist adjunct faculty in teaching the course, a *Manual for Adjunct Faculty to Accompany McWhorter Texts* is also available to adopters. It offers instructors additional techniques for classroom management and specific skill instruction. 0-673-97667-X

PowerPoint Slides A series of PowerPoint slides for each chapter can be downloaded free from the Longman Web site at **http://www.awlonline.com/basicskills/mcwhorter**

McWhorter Web site A dedicated Web site to accompany the McWhorter reading and study skills series is available to instructors and students. This Web site includes study tips, electronically scored quizzes and tests, Internet activities and links, a bulletin board, a chat room, and more. Please visit the site at **http://www.awlonline.com/mcwhorter**.

THE LONGMAN DEVELOPMENTAL READING PACKAGE

In addition to the book-specific supplements discussed above, a series of other skills-based supplements is available for both instructors and students. All of these supplements are available either free or at greatly reduced prices.

For Additional Reading and Reference

The Dictionary Deal   Two dictionaries can be shrinkwrapped with this text at a nominal fee. *The New American Webster Handy College Dictionary* is a paperback reference text with more than 100,000 entries. *Merriam Webster's Collegiate Dictionary,* tenth edition, is a hardback reference with a citation file of more than 14.5 million examples of English words drawn from actual use. Contact your local Addison Wesley Longman sales consultant for information on how to order.

Penguin Quality Paperback Titles   A series of Penguin paperbacks is available at a significant discount when shrinkwrapped with this title. Some titles available are: Toni Morrison's *Beloved,* Julia Alvarez's *How the Garcia Girls Lost Their Accents,* Mark Twain's *The Adventures of Huckleberry Finn, Narrative of the Life of Frederick Douglass,* Harriet Beecher Stowe's *Uncle Tom's Cabin,* Dr. Martin Luther King, Jr.'s *Why We Can't Wait,* and plays by Shakespeare, Miller, and Albee. For a complete list of titles or more information on how to order Penguin titles at a discount, please contact your Addison Wesley Longman sales consultant.

The Longman Textbook Reader   This supplement, for use in developmental reading courses, offers five complete chapters from AWL textbooks: computer science, biology, psychology, communications, and business. Each chapter includes additional comprehension quizzes, critical thinking questions, and group activities. Available FREE when packaged with *Academic Reading.* Contact your local Addison Wesley Longman sales consultant for information on how to order this special package.

***The Pocket Reader,* First Edition, and *The Brief Pocket Reader,* First Edition**   These inexpensive volumes contain 80 or 50 brief readings respectively (1–3 pages each) on a variety of themes: writers on writing, nature, women and men, customs and habits, politics, rights and obligations, and coming of age. Also included is an alternate rhetorical table of contents (*The Pocket Reader:* 0-321-07668-0; *The Brief Pocket Reader:* 0-321-07699-9).

Newsweek **Alliance**   Instructors may choose to shrinkwrap a 12-week subscription to *Newsweek* with any Longman text. The price of the subscription is 57 cents per issue (a total of $6.84 for the subscription). Available with the subscription is a free "Interactive Guide to *Newsweek*"— a workbook for students who are using the text. In addition, *Newsweek* provides a wide variety of instructor supplements free to teachers, including maps, Skills Builders, and weekly quizzes. Contact your local Addison Wesley Longman sales consultant for information on how to order *Newsweek* packaged with *Academic Reading.*

Electronic and Online Offerings

Longman Reading Road Trip Multimedia Software, Version 2.0 This innovative and exciting multimedia reading software is available either in CD-ROM format or as a site license. The package takes students on a tour of 15 cities and landmarks throughout the United States. Each of the 15 modules corresponds to a reading or study skill (for example, finding the main idea, understanding patterns of organization, and thinking critically). All modules contain a tour of the location, instruction and tutorial, exercises, interactive feedback, and mastery tests. This second release includes a more streamlined and flexible navigation, along with hundreds of new readings, exercises, and tests. Use ISBN number 0-201-71565-1 to order *Academic Reading* packaged with Free Reading Road Trip 2.0 for your students.

Researching Online, **Third Edition**   A perfect companion for a new age, this indispensable new supplement helps students navigate the Internet. Adapted from *Teaching Online,* the instructor's Internet guide, *Researching Online* speaks directly to students, giving them detailed, step-by-step instructions for performing electronic searches. Available free when shrinkwrapped with this text. Contact your local Addison Wesley Longman sales consultant for information on how to order.

The Longman English Pages Web Site   Both students and instructors can visit our free content-rich Web site for additional reading selections and writing exercises. From the Longman English pages, visitors can conduct a simulated Web search, learn how to write a resume and cover letter, or try their hand at poetry writing. Stop by and visit us at **http://www.awlonline.com/englishpages**.

The Longman Electronic Newsletter Twice a month during the spring and fall, instructors who have subscribed receive a free copy of the Longman Basic Skills Newsletter in their e-mailbox. Written by experienced classroom instructors, the newsletter offers teaching tips, classroom activities, book reviews, and more. To subscribe, visit the Longman Basic Skills Web Site at **http://www.awlonline.com/basicskills,** or send an e-mail to **Basic Skills@awl.com**.

For Instructors

Electronic Test Bank for Reading Available in December 2000, this electronic test bank offers more than 3,000 questions in all areas of reading, including vocabulary, main idea, supporting details, patterns of organization, language, critical thinking, analytical reasoning, inference, point of view, visual aids, and textbook reading. With this easy-to-use CD-ROM, instructors simply choose questions from the electronic test bank, then print out the completed test for distribution (0-321-08179-X).

CLAST Test Package, Fourth Edition These two 40-item objective tests evaluate students' readiness for the CLAST exams. Strategies for teaching CLAST preparedness are included. Free with any Longman English title (Reproducible sheets: 0-321-01950-4; Computerized IBM version: 0-321-01982-2; Computerized Mac version: 0-321-01983-0).

TASP Test Package, Third Edition These 12 practice pre-tests and post-tests assess the same reading and writing skills covered in the TASP examination. Free with any Longman English title (Reproducible sheets: 0-321-01959-8; Computerized IBM version: 0-321-01985-7; Computerized Mac version: 0-321-01984-9).

***Teaching Online: Internet Research, Conversation, and Composition,* Second Edition** Ideal for instructors who have never surfed the Net, this easy-to-follow guide offers basic definitions, numerous examples, and step-by-step information about finding and using Internet sources. Free to adopters (0-321-01957-1).

ACKNOWLEDGMENTS

I wish to acknowledge the contributions of my colleagues and reviewers who have provided valuable advice and suggestions for this and previous editions of *Academic Reading:* Thomas Athey, California State Technical College; Betty Andrews-Tobias, Suffolk Community College; Pamela Bourgeois, California State University, Northridge; Janice Buchner, Suffolk County Community College; Terry Bullock, University of Cincinnati; Marilyn Burke, Austin Community College; Steve Cohen, Norwalk Community Technical College; Diane Cole, Pensacola Junior College, Janet Curtis, Fullerton College; Pat D'Allessio, Dutchess Community College; Susan Deese, University of New Mexico; Cathlene Denny, St. Johns River Community College; J. Ross Eshleman, Wayne State University; Helen Gilbart, St. Petersburg Junior College; Ed Gill, Indiana Vocational Technical College; Brian Holmes, San Jose State University; Jenny Joczik, College of Charleston; Sandra Keith, St. Cloud State University; Kathleen Kiefer, Colorado State University; Terry Kozek, Housatonic Community College; Linda W. Larou, Dutchess Community College; Beverly Lipper, Dutchess Community College; Alice Mackey, Missouri Western State College; Gail Moore, York Technical College; David Murphy, Waubonsee Community College; Karen Nelson, Craven Community College; Michael Newman, Hunter College; Jan Pechenek, Tufts University; Paul Perdew, University of Scranton; Michelle Peterson, Santa Barbara City College; Karen Samson, Chicago State University; Nancy E. Smith, Florida Community College at Jacksonville; Andrew Szilagyi, University of Houston; Betsy Tobias, Suffolk County Community College; Katherine Wellington, Metropolitan State University; Michaeline Wideman, University of Cincinnati; Mary Wolting, Indiana University–Purdue University; Lawrence Ziewaz, Michigan State University.

I am particularly indebted to Leslie Taggart, my developmental editor, for her most valuable advice and guidance. She has contributed knowledge, creativity, and energy, as well as practicality. I also wish to thank Steven Rigolosi, Senior Acquisitions Editor, for his active and enthusiastic role in developing the revision plan and overseeing its implementation.

Kathleen T. McWhorter

PART I

FUNDAMENTAL READING STRATEGIES

STRATEGIES FOR ACTIVE READING

LEARNING OBJECTIVES

- ■ **To understand how reading contributes to college success**
- ■ **To assess your learning style**
- ■ **To build your concentration skills**
- ■ **To develop multilevel thinking skills**
- ■ **To learn to preview and predict before reading**
- ■ **To develop questions to guide your reading**
- ■ **To check your comprehension**

Ask college students to name the ingredients of success in college, and they are likely to say:

"Knowing how to study."

"You have to like school."

"Hard work!"

"Time to study!"

"Motivation!"

Students seldom mention reading as an essential skill, and yet reading is a hidden factor in college success. When you think of college, you may think of attending classes and labs, completing assignments, studying for and taking exams, and writing papers. A closer look, however, reveals that reading is an important part of each of these activities.

Reading stays "behind the scenes" because instructors rarely evaluate it directly. Grades are based on outcomes: that is, how well you express your ideas in papers or how well you do on exams. Yet reading is the primary means by which you acquire your ideas and gather information.

Throughout this text, you will learn numerous ways to use reading as a tool for college success.

READING AND ACADEMIC SUCCESS

Reading involves much more than moving your eyes across lines of print, more than recognizing words, and more than reading sentences. **Reading is thinking.** It is an active process of identifying important ideas and comparing, evaluating, and applying them.

Have you ever gone to a ballgame and watched the fans? Most do not sit and watch passively. Instead, they direct the plays, criticize the calls, encourage the players, and reprimand the coach. They care enough to get actively engaged with the game. Just like interested fans, active readers get involved. They question, challenge, and criticize, as well as understand. Table 1–1 contrasts the active strategies of successful readers with the passive ones of less successful readers.

Throughout the remainder of this chapter, you will discover specific strategies for becoming a more active learner. Not all strategies will work for everyone. Experiment to discover those that work for you.

TABLE 1–1 ACTIVE VERSUS PASSIVE READING	
ACTIVE READERS . . .	**PASSIVE READERS . . .**
Tailor their reading to suit each assignment.	Read all assignments the same way.
Analyze the purpose of an assignment.	Read an assignment *because* it was assigned.
Adjust their speed to suit their purpose.	Read everything at the same speed.
Question ideas in the assignment.	Accept whatever is in print as true.
Compare and connect textbook material with lecture content.	Study lecture notes and textbook separately.
Skim headings to find out what an assignment is about before beginning to read.	Check the length of an assignment and then begin reading.
Make sure they understand what they are reading as they go along.	Read until the assignment is completed.
Read with pencil in hand, highlighting, jotting notes, and marking key vocabulary.	Simply read.
Develop personalized strategies that are particularly effective.	Follow routine, standard methods.

| EXERCISE 1–1 | *Consider each of the following reading assignments. Discuss different ways in which you could get actively involved with them.* |

1. Reading two poems by e.e. cummings for a literature class.
2. Reviewing procedures for your next biology lab.
3. Taking notes on an article in *Time* magazine assigned by your political science instructor.

| EXERCISE 1–2 | *Write a list of active reading strategies you already use. Add to your list several new strategies that you intend to begin using. Compare your list with a classmate's.* |

COLLABORATIVE LEARNING

_____

_____

_____

ASSESSING YOUR LEARNING STYLE

Textbook reading assignments are central to many college classes. Your instructors make daily or weekly assignments, expect you to read the material, learn it, and pass tests on it. Textbook assignments often form the basis of class lectures and discussions. An important part of many college classes, then, consists of completing reading assignments.

Reading and understanding an assignment, however, does not mean you have learned the material. You need to do more than read to learn the content. What else should you do? The answer is not simple.

People differ in how they learn and the methods and strategies they use to learn. These differences can be explained by what is known as *learning style.* Your learning style can begin to explain why some courses are easier for you than others and why you learn better from one instructor than another. Learning style also can explain why certain assignments are easy for you and other learning tasks are difficult.

The following brief Learning Style Questionnaire will help you analyze how you learn and show you how to develop an action plan for learning what you read. Complete and score the questionnaire before continuing with this section.

Learning Style Questionnaire

DIRECTIONS: Each item presents two choices. Select the alternative that best describes you. In cases in which neither choice suits you, select the one that is closer to your preference. Write the letter of your choice in the blank to the left of each item.

Part One

_____ 1. I would prefer to follow a set of
    a. oral directions.
    b. written directions.

_____ 2. I would prefer to
    a. attend a lecture given by a famous psychologist.
    b. read an article written by the psychologist.

_____ 3. When I am introduced to someone, it is easier for me to remember the person's
    a. name.
    b. face.

_____ 4. I find it easier to learn new information using
    a. language (words).
    b. images (pictures).

_____ 5. I prefer classes in which the instructor
    a. lectures and answers questions.
    b. uses films and videos.

_____ 6. To follow current events, I would prefer to
    a. listen to the news on the radio.
    b. read the newspaper.

_____ 7. To learn how to operate a fax machine, I would prefer to
    a. listen to a friend's explanation.
    b. watch a demonstration.

Part Two

_____ 8. I prefer to
    a. work with facts and details.
    b. construct theories and ideas.

_____ 9. I would prefer a job involving
    a. following specific instructions.
    b. reading, writing, and analyzing.

_____ 10. I prefer to
    a. solve math problems using a formula.
    b. discover why the formula works.

_____ 11. I would prefer to write a term paper explaining
     a. how a process works.
     b. a theory.

_____ 12. I prefer tasks that require me to
     a. follow careful, detailed instructions.
     b. use reasoning and critical analysis.

_____ 13. For a criminal justice course, I would prefer to
     a. discover how and when a law can be used.
     b. learn how and why it became law.

_____ 14. To learn more about the operation of a high-speed computer
printer, I would prefer to
     a. work with several types of printers.
     b. understand the principles on which they operate.

Part Three

_____ 15. To solve a math problem, I would prefer to
     a. draw or visualize the problem.
     b. study a sample problem and use it as a model.

_____ 16. To best remember something, I
     a. create a mental picture.
     b. write it down.

_____ 17. Assembling a bicycle from a diagram would be
     a. easy.
     b. challenging.

_____ 18. I prefer classes in which I
     a. handle equipment or work with models.
     b. participate in a class discussion.

_____ 19. To understand and remember how a machine works, I would
     a. draw a diagram.
     b. write notes.

_____ 20. I enjoy
     a. drawing or working with my hands.
     b. speaking, writing, and listening.

_____ 21. If I were trying to locate an office on an unfamiliar campus,
I would prefer
     a. a map.
     b. written directions.

Part Four

_____ 22. For a grade in biology lab, I would prefer to
    a. work with a lab partner.
    b. work alone.

_____ 23. When faced with a difficult personal problem, I prefer to
    a. discuss it with others.
    b. resolve it myself.

_____ 24. Many instructors could improve their classes by
    a. including more discussion and group activities.
    b. allowing students to work on their own more frequently.

_____ 25. When listening to a lecturer or speaker, I respond more to the
    a. person presenting the idea.
    b. ideas themselves.

_____ 26. When on a team project, I prefer to
    a. work with several team members.
    b. divide the tasks and complete those assigned to me.

_____ 27. I prefer to shop and do errands
    a. with friends.
    b. by myself.

_____ 28. A job in a busy office is
    a. more appealing than working alone.
    b. less appealing than working alone.

Part Five

_____ 29. To make decisions, I rely on
    a. my experiences and gut feelings.
    b. facts and objective data.

_____ 30. To complete a task, I
    a. can use whatever is available to get the job done.
    b. must have everything I need at hand.

_____ 31. I prefer to express my ideas and feelings through
    a. music, song, or poetry.
    b. direct, concise language.

_____ 32. I prefer instructors who
    a. allow students to be guided by their own interests.
    b. make their expectations clear and explicit.

_____ 33. I tend to
    a. challenge and question what I hear and read.
    b. accept what I hear and read.

_____ 34. I prefer
    a. essay exams.
    b. objective exams.

_____ 35. In completing an assignment, I prefer to
    a. figure out my own approach.
    b. be told exactly what to do.

To score your questionnaire, record the total number of a's you selected and the total number of b's for each part of the questionnaire. Record your totals in the scoring grid provided below.

Scoring Grid

Part	Total # of Choice "a"	Total # of Choice "b"
One	_____ Auditory	_____ Visual
Two	_____ Applied	_____ Conceptual
Three	_____ Spatial	_____ Verbal
Four	_____ Social	_____ Independent
Five	_____ Creative	_____ Pragmatic

Now, circle your higher score for each part of the questionnaire. The word below the score you circled indicates a strength in your learning style. The next section explains how to interpret your scores.

Interpreting Your Scores

Each of the five parts of the questionnaire identifies one aspect of your learning style. These five aspects are explained below.

Part One: Auditory or Visual Learners This score indicates whether you learn more effectively by listening (auditory) or by seeing (visual). If your auditory score is higher than your visual score, you tend to learn more easily by hearing than by reading. A higher score in visual suggests strengths with visual modes of learning such as reading, studying pictures, reading diagrams, and so forth.

Part Two: Applied or Conceptual Learners   This score describes the types of learning tasks and learning situations you instinctively prefer and find easiest to handle. If you are an applied learner, you prefer tasks that involve real objects and situations. Therefore, practical, real-life examples are ideal for you. If you are a conceptual learner, you prefer to work with language and ideas; you tend to rely less on practical applications for understanding than applied learners.

Part Three: Spatial or Verbal Learners   This score reveals your ability to work with spatial relationships. Spatial learners can visualize or mentally "see" how things work or how they are positioned in space. Their strengths may include drawing, assembling, or repairing things. Verbal or nonspatial learners lack skills in positioning things in space. Instead, they rely on verbal or language skills.

Part Four: Social or Independent Learners   This score reveals whether you like to work alone or with others. If you are a social learner, you prefer to work with others—such as classmates and instructors—closely and directly. You tend to be people-oriented and enjoy personal interaction. If you are an independent learner, you tend to be self-directed or self-motivated as well as goal-oriented.

Part Five: Creative or Pragmatic Learners   This score describes the approach you prefer to take toward learning tasks. Creative learners are imaginative and innovative. They prefer to learn through discovery or experimentation. They are comfortable taking risks and following hunches. Pragmatic learners are practical, logical, and systematic. They seek order and are comfortable following rules.

If you disagree with any part of the Learning Style Questionnaire, go with your own instincts, rather than the questionnaire results. Think of the questionnaire as just a quick assessment, but trust your self-knowledge.

Using Learning Style Effectively

Now that you have completed the Learning Style Questionnaire and know more about *how* you learn, you are ready to develop an action plan for learning what you read. Suppose you have discovered that you are an auditory learner. You still have to read your assignments, which is a visual task.

To learn the assignment, however, you should translate the material into an auditory form. For example, you could repeat aloud, using your own words, information that you want to remember, or you could tape-record key information and play it back. If you are a social learner, you could work with a classmate, the two of you testing each other out loud. Such activities not only shift the presentation of ideas from visual to auditory form but also give you practice in using internal dialogue (see p. 30).

Table 1–2 lists the different types of learning styles and offers suggestions for how students who exhibit each style might learn most effectively from a reading assignment. You can use this table to build an action plan for more effective learning.

1. Circle the five aspects of learning style in which you received the highest scores on the Learning Style Questionnaire. Disregard the others.

2. Read through the suggestions that apply to you.

3. Place a checkmark in front of suggestions that you think will work for you. Choose at least one from each of your five learning styles.

4. List the suggestions that you chose below.

   a. _____

   b. _____

   c. _____

   d. _____

   e. _____

The next step is to experiment with these techniques, one at a time. Use one technique for a while, and then move to the next. Continue using the techniques that seem to work, and work on revising or modifying those that do not. Do not hesitate to experiment with other techniques listed in the table. You may find other techniques that work well for you.

Overcoming Limitations

You should also work on developing learning styles in which you are weak because your learning style is not fixed or unchanging. You can improve areas in which you scored lower. Even though you may be weak in auditory learning, for example, many of your professors will lecture and expect you to take notes. If you work on improving your listening and note-taking skills, you can learn to handle lectures more effectively. Make a conscious effort at improving areas of weakness as well as taking advantage of your strengths.

TABLE 1–2   LEARNING STYLES AND READING/LEARNING STRATEGIES

IF YOUR LEARNING STYLE IS . . .	THEN THE READING/LEARNING STRATEGIES TO USE ARE . . .
Auditory	• Discuss/study with friends. • Talk aloud when studying. • Tape-record self-testing questions and answers.
Visual	• Draw diagrams, charts, and/or tables. • Try to visualize events. • Use films and videos. • Use computer-assisted instruction when available.
Applied	• Think of practical situations to which learning applies. • Associate ideas with their application. • Use case studies, examples, and applications to cue your learning.
Conceptual	• Organize materials. • Use outlining. • Focus on organizational patterns.
Spatial	• Use mapping. • Use outlining. • Draw diagrams; make charts and sketches. • Use visualization.
Verbal	• Translate diagrams and drawings into language. • Record steps, processes, and procedures in words. • Write summaries. • Write your interpretation next to textbook drawings, maps, and graphics.
Social	• Form study groups. • Find a study partner. • Interact with the instructor. • Work with a tutor.
Independent	• Use computer-assisted instruction. • Purchase review workbooks or study guides when available.
Creative	• Ask and answer questions. • Record your own ideas in the margins of textbooks.
Pragmatic	• Study in an organized environment. • Write lists of steps, procedures, and processes. • Paraphrase difficult materials.

BUILDING YOUR CONCENTRATION

Concentration is the ability to focus on the task at hand. Most students find that by improving their concentration, they can reduce their reading time. Building your concentration is a three-part process: eliminating distractions, focusing your attention, and assessing your concentration.

Eliminating Distractions

Activities going on around you can break your concentration. A dog barking, a radio playing, and an overheard conversation are examples of distractions. The first step in improving your concentration is to eliminate distractions. Use the following suggestions in eliminating distractions.

1. *Choose a place conducive to reading.* The spot you select should be as free of distractions and interruptions as possible. If your home or dorm is too busy or noisy, you will be distracted. Study in a quiet place such as student lounge areas or library study areas. Find a place you can associate with studying so that you are ready to concentrate as soon as you sit down. Although your TV chair or your bed may look like a perfect place to study, you already associate them with relaxation and sleep. If you read and work at the same desk or study carrel regularly, you will find that when you sit down you will feel ready to concentrate, and distractions will be less bothersome.

2. *Notice your physical state.* If you are tired, you will have trouble concentrating. If you are hungry, your thoughts will drift toward food. If you feel sluggish and inactive, you may not be able to focus on your work. Try to schedule reading or studying at times when your physical needs are not likely to interfere. If you find that you are hungry, tired, or sluggish while reading, stop and take a break, have a snack, or get up and walk around. If you are physically or mentally exhausted, you may need to stop and find a better time to complete the assignment.

3. *Have necessary materials available.* When you sit down to work, be sure that you have all the needed materials. Surrounding yourself with these tools helps to create a psychological readiness for reading and eliminates the distraction created by breaking off your work to find a book or pen.

4. *Choose your peak periods of attention.* The time of day or night when you read also influences how easy or difficult it is to shut out distractions. You have a natural time limit for how long you can successfully attend to a task; this is your **attention span.** People experience peaks and valleys in their attention spans. Some people are very alert in the early morning, whereas others find they are most focused at midday or in the early evening. To make concentration easier, try to read during the peaks of your attention span. Choose the times of day when you are most alert and when it is easiest to keep your mind on what you are doing. If you are not aware of your own peaks of attention, analyze your reading effectiveness. Over a period of several days, keep track of when you read and study and of how much you accomplish each time. Then look for a pattern.

5. *Keep a list of distractions.* Often, as you are reading or studying, you will be distracted by thoughts of something you must remember to do. If you have a dental appointment scheduled for the next afternoon, you will find that a reminder occasionally flashes through your mind. To help overcome these distractions, keep a list of them. Use a sheet of paper to jot down these mental reminders as they occur. You will find that writing them down on paper temporarily eliminates reminders from your conscious memory.

Focusing Your Attention

Focusing your attention means directing all mental activity to what you are reading. To help focus your attention on the material you are reading, try the following.

1. *Set goals.* Achieving your goals is positive and rewarding; it feels good to accomplish what you set out to do. Before each study or reading session, set specific goals and time limits. Divide large assignments into smaller parts to give yourself the best chance to achieve your goals. Concentrating on these goals and time limits will help you avoid distractions; your attention will remain on your reading. One student set the following reading goals for herself for one evening of study.

Reread Psych lecture notes	15 min.
Read first half Chapter 10—Psych	90 min.
Review Chapter 9—Accounting	30 min.
Read short story—English	30 min.

2. *Reward yourself.* Meeting goals within a time limit is a reward in itself. Other rewards could include watching TV, snacking, or making phone calls. Use these activities as rewards by arranging them to follow periods of reading and studying. For example, you might call a friend after you finish your math problems, or you could plan to rewrite your English composition before watching a favorite TV program.

3. *Begin by reviewing previously read material.* Reviewing the previous assignment will direct your attention to today's work and help you make the "mental switch" from your previous activity to what you are doing now.

4. *Write and underline as you read.* It is easy to let your mind wander while reading, especially if you find the material dull or boring. One way to solve this problem is to involve yourself in your reading by writing or underlining the important ideas in each section. Make marginal notes,

and jot down questions. These activities force you to think: to identify important ideas, to see how they are related, and to evaluate their worth and importance. Refer to Chapter 7 for specific suggestions on each of these techniques.

5. *Approach assignments critically.* Be an active reader. Instead of simply trying to take in large amounts of information, read critically. Seek ideas you question or disagree with. Look for points of view, opinions, and unsupported statements. Try to predict how the author's train of thought is developing. Make connections with what you already know about the subject, with what you have read before, and with what the instructor has said in class. If you can maintain an active, critical point of view, you will minimize distractions.

Assessing Your Concentration

Once you are aware of your concentration level and can recognize when your focus is fading, you can take action to control and improve your concentration. Begin by keeping track, for a half-hour or so, of how many times your mind wanders. Use a piece of paper to make a tally of distractions as they occur. Each time you think about something other than what you are reading, make a mark on the paper. You probably will be surprised at how many times your concentration was broken during the time you were keeping count. Work on decreasing the tally; use this method once a week or so as a check on your concentration. After reading, analyze your performance. Why did you lose your concentration? Was it an external distraction? Did an idea in the text trigger your memory of a related idea? Look for patterns: At what time of day are you most easily distracted? Where are you studying when many distractions occur? What are you studying? Adjust your reading habits to decrease distractions and improve concentration.

EXERCISE 1–3

COLLABORATIVE LEARNING

Make a list of common distractions and problems that interfere with your concentration. Next to each item, note how you can overcome it. Discuss with classmates or your instructor any items for which you have no remedy.

_____

_____

_____

_____

_____

_____

EXERCISE 1–4	*Discuss how each student might improve his or her concentration in the following situations.*

1. A student cannot concentrate because of frequent interruptions by his two preschool children.
2. A student says she cannot concentrate because she is obsessed with a conflict she is having with her parents.
3. A student says he cannot read sociology for longer than a half-hour because he becomes restless and bored.

DEVELOPING LEVELS OF THINKING

Throughout your educational career, your primary task is to **understand** and **recall** information. Consequently, you may not be prepared when your instructors ask you to **apply, analyze, synthesize,** and **evaluate** information.

Table 1–3 describes a hierarchy, or progression, of thinking skills. It was developed by Benjamin Bloom in 1956 and remains widely used among educators in many academic disciplines. You will notice that the progression moves from basic literal understanding to more complex skills that involve synthesis and evaluation.

When they write exams, most college instructors assume that you can operate at each of these levels. Table 1–4 (p. 16) shows a few items from an exam for a course in interpersonal communication. Note how the items demand different levels of thinking.

TABLE 1–3   LEVELS OF THINKING

LEVEL	EXAMPLES
Knowledge: recalling information; repeating information with no changes	Recalling dates; memorizing definitions
Comprehension: understanding ideas; using rules and following directions	Explaining a law; recognizing what is important
Application: applying knowledge to a new situation	Using knowledge of formulas to solve a new physics problem
Analysis: seeing relationships; breaking information into parts; analyzing how things work	Comparing two poems by the same author
Synthesis: putting ideas and information together in a unique way; creating something new	Designing a new computer program
Evaluation: making judgments; assessing the worth of information	Evaluating the effectiveness or value of an argument opposing the death penalty

TABLE 1–4 LEVEL OF THINKING REQUIRED	
TEST ITEM	**LEVEL OF THINKING REQUIRED**
Define nonverbal communication.	Knowledge
Explain how nonverbal communication works.	Comprehension
Describe three instances in which you have observed nonverbal communication.	Application
Study the two pictures projected on the screen in the front of the classroom, and compare the nonverbal messages sent in each.	Analysis
Construct, for an international student visiting your home town, a set of guidelines that will enable him or her to understand local nonverbal communication.	Synthesis
Evaluate an essay whose major premise is "Nonverbal communication skills should be taught formally as part of the educational process."	Evaluation

You don't need to identify the level of thinking that a particular assignment or test item requires. However, you should be able to think and work at each of these levels.

The following passage is taken from a psychology textbook chapter on memory and learning. Read the passage, and study the list that follows.

Some of the oldest data in psychology tell us that retrieval will be improved if practice (encoding) is spread out over time, with rest intervals spaced in between. . . . In fact, this experiment, first performed in 1946, provides such reliable results that it is commonly used as a student project in psychology classes. The task is to write the letters of the alphabet, upside down and from right to left. (If you think that sounds easy, give it a try.)

Subjects are given the opportunity to practice the task under four conditions. The *massed-practice* group works with no breaks between trials. The three *distributed-practice* groups receive the same amount of practice, but get rest intervals interspersed between each 1-minute trial. One group gets a 3- to 5-second break between trials, a second group receives a 30-second rest, and a third group gets a 45-second break between trials.

. . . Subjects in all four groups begin at about the same (poor) level of performance. After 20 minutes of practice, the performance of all the groups shows improvement, but by far, the massed practice (no rest) group does the poorest, and the 45-second rest group does the best.

The conclusion from years of research is that almost without exception, *distributed practice is superior to massed practice.* There are exceptions, however. Some tasks may suffer from having rest intervals inserted in practice time. In general, whenever you must keep track of many things at the same time, you should mass your practice until you have finished whatever you are working on. If, for example, you are working on a complex math problem, you should work it through until you find a solution, whether it's time for a rest break or not. And of course, you should not break up your practice in such a way as to disrupt the meaningfulness of the material you are studying.

—Gerow, *Psychology: An Introduction,* pp. 217–18

Below you can see how you might use each level of thinking to understand and evaluate this passage on memory and learning.

Knowledge	How was the experiment designed?
Comprehension	What did the experiment show about learning?
Application	How can I use distributed practice to plan my study time tonight?
Analysis	Why is distributed practice more effective?
Synthesis	What kind of experiment could I design to test what types of tasks benefit most (and which least) from distributed practice?
Evaluation	How effective is distributed practice?

As mentioned earlier, professors use these levels of thinking in writing exams. An effective way to prepare for an exam, then, is to be sure you have thought about the test material at each level. Do this by predicting possible test questions at each level.

EXERCISE 1–5

Read the following excerpt from an interpersonal communications textbook. Demonstrate your ability to think at various levels by answering the following questions.

A **friendship relationship** is one marked by very close association, contact, or familiarity. Usually a warm friendship has developed as a result of a long association, but this is not always the case. Sometimes friendship develops suddenly. Friendship relationships are very personal or private, and they are often characterized by different types of communication.

People seek friendship relationships for many reasons. These reasons may operate singly or in conjunction with each other. Many overlap. In some situations, with some people, one of these reasons may sustain a relationship, whereas in others, several are likely to operate. The more needs that are fulfilled in a relationship, the more solid the foundation upon which the relationship rests. You seek friendship relationships to fulfill six basic needs: for enjoyment, security, affection, self-esteem, freedom, and equality. They are not necessarily ranked here in order of importance.

Enjoyment is an important, perhaps the most important, need that friendships fulfill. Simply put, friends enjoy each other's company. The "What do you want to do?" syndrome ("I don't know, what do you want to do?") often occurs because neither friend really cares. Just enjoying being together is enough; *doing* something (anything!) is secondary. . . .

Affection relates to a sense of belonging. This could encompass sexual gratification, but does not need to. Affection suggests a moderate feeling toward or emotional attachment to another person. When you feel tender attachment for others or pleasure in being with them, you are experiencing affection. Abraham Maslow labels this "belonging and love needs," placing this need among the basic or essential needs after "psychological" and "safety" needs.

Self-esteem is felt when you are recognized or appreciated by others. Sometimes being with someone enhances your status. Also, if other people attribute a joint identity to your relationship with another person, this may also increase your self-esteem. Self-esteem is affected because such a high premium is often placed on dating and "going steady." Maslow places self-esteem needs only one step higher than affection—as slightly less essential and more optional.

—Weaver, *Understanding Interpersonal Communications*, pp. 423–26

Knowledge and Comprehension

1. Define a friendship relationship.
2. List the six basic needs that friendship relationships fulfill.
3. Explain the meaning of the term *self-esteem*.

Application

4. Name a person with whom you have a friendship that fulfills your need for self-esteem.

Analysis

5. Think of a long-standing friendship. Analyze that friendship by identifying the needs it fulfills.

Synthesis

6. The author states that the six basic needs are not necessarily ranked in order of importance. On the basis of your experience with friendships, list these needs in order of importance to you.

Evaluation

7. Do you agree with the author's statement that a high premium often is placed on dating? Why or why not?

**EXERCISE
1–6**

*Academic
Application*

*Select a one- or two-page section from one of your textbooks. Read the section, and
then write questions that might be asked to test your thinking at each level.*

_____

_____

_____

_____

PREVIEWING AND PREDICTING

Previewing and predicting are skills that will help you to think beyond the
basic levels of knowledge and comprehension. **Previewing** is a means of
familiarizing yourself with the content and organization of an assignment
before you read it. Think of previewing as getting a "sneak preview" of what
a chapter or reading will be about. You can then read the material more
easily and more rapidly.

How to Preview Textbook Assignments

Use the following steps to become familiar with a textbook chapter's content and organization.

1. *Read the chapter title.* The title indicates the topic of the article or
    chapter; the subtitle suggests the specific focus of, or approach to, the
    topic.

2. *Read the introduction or the first paragraph.* The introduction or first para-
    graph serves as a lead-in to the chapter by establishing the overall sub-
    ject, and suggesting how it will be developed.

3. *Read each boldface (dark print) heading.* Headings label the contents of
    each section and announce the major topic of the section.

4. *Read the first sentence under each major heading.* The first sentence often
    states the central thought of the section. If the first sentence seems
    introductory, read the last sentence; often, this sentence states or
    restates the central thought.

5. *Note any typographical aids.* Italics are used to emphasize important ter-
    minology and definitions by distinguishing them from the rest of the
    passage. Material that is numbered 1, 2, 3; lettered a, b, c; or presented
    in list form is also of special importance.

6. *Note any graphic aids.* Graphs, charts, photographs, and tables often suggest what is important in the chapter. Be sure to read the captions of photographs and the legends on graphs, charts, or tables.

7. *Read the last paragraph or summary.* This provides a condensed view of the chapter by outlining the key points of the chapter.

8. *Quickly read any end-of-article or end-of-chapter material.* This might include references, study questions, discussion questions, chapter outlines, or vocabulary lists. If there are study questions, read them through quickly because they tell you what is important to remember in the chapter. If a vocabulary list is included, skim through it to identify the terms you will be learning as you read.

A section of a speech-communication textbook chapter discussing purposes of listening is reprinted here to illustrate how previewing is done. The portions to focus on when previewing are shaded. Read only those portions. After you have finished, test how well your previewing worked by answering the questions in Exercise 1–7.

PURPOSES OF LISTENING

Speakers' motivations for speechmaking vary from situation to situation just as listeners' purposes for paying attention vary. Researchers have identified five types of listening (each serving a different purpose): (a) appreciative, (b) discriminative, (c) therapeutic, (d) comprehension, and (e) critical.

Appreciative Listening

Appreciative listening focuses on something other than the primary message. People who are principally concerned with participating in the experience are appreciative listeners. Some listeners enjoy seeing a famous speaker. Other listeners enjoy the art of good public speaking, pleasing vocal modulation, clever uses of language, impressive phraseology, and the skillful use of supporting materials. Still other listeners simply like to attend special occasions such as inaugurations, dedications, and graduations.

Discriminative Listening

Discriminative listening requires listeners to draw conclusions from the way a message is presented rather than from what is said. In discriminative listening, people seek to understand what the speaker really thinks, believes, or feels. You're engaging in discriminative listening when you draw conclusions about how angry your parents are with you, based not on what they say, but on how they say it. Journalists listening to the way that a message is presented often second-guess the attitudes of national leaders on foreign policy. Performers, of course, can convey emotions such as anger or exhilaration to audiences through their delivery alone. In each of these examples, an important dimension of listening is based on relatively sophisticated inferences drawn from—rather than found in—messages.

Therapeutic Listening

Therapeutic listening is intended to provide emotional support to the speaker. It is more typical of interpersonal than public communication—the therapeutic listener acts as a sounding board for a speaker attempting to talk through a problem, work out a difficult situation, or express deep emotions. Sometimes, however, therapeutic listening occurs in public speaking situations such as when a sports star apologizes for unprofessional behavior, a religious convert describes a soul-saving experience, or a classmate reviews a personal problem and thanks friends for their help in solving it. In therapeutic listening, special social bonding occurs between speaker and listener. Consider the communication of joy that occurs when listeners react to someone who wants to tell others about a new relationship, a new baby, a promotion at work, or an award at school.

Listening for Comprehension

Listening for comprehension occurs when the listener wants to gain additional information or insights provided by the speaker. This is probably the form of listening with which you are most familiar. When you listen to radio or TV news programs, to classroom lectures on the four principal causes of World War II, or to an orientation official previewing your school's new registration process, you're listening to understand—to comprehend information, ideas, and processes.

Critical Listening

Critical listening requires listeners to both interpret and evaluate the message. The most sophisticated kind of listening is critical listening. It demands that auditors go beyond understanding the message to interpreting it, judging its strengths and weaknesses, and assigning it some value. You'll practice this sort of listening in your class. You may also use critical listening as you evaluate commercials, political campaign speeches, advice from career counselors, or arguments offered by controversial talk show guests. When you listen critically, you decide to accept or reject ideas. You may also resolve to act or delay action on the message. . . .

The variety of listening purposes has serious implications for both listeners and speakers. Appreciative listeners are highly selective, watching for metaphors, responding to speaking tones, and searching out memorable phrasings. At the other extreme, critical listeners work hard to catch relevant details, to judge the soundness of competing arguments and to rationally decide whether to accept ideas. Therapeutic listeners decide when to positively reinforce speakers through applause or other signs of approval, and those listening for comprehension distinguish between important and unimportant information. Finally, discriminative listeners search for clues to unspoken ideas or feelings that are relevant to themselves. As you think about your own listening purposes, you'll find yourself adapting your listening behavior to the speaking situation more carefully.

—Gronbeck et. al., *Principles of Speech Communication*, pp. 38–39

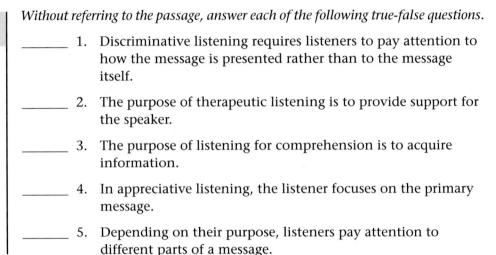

EXERCISE 1–7

Without referring to the passage, answer each of the following true-false questions.

_____ 1. Discriminative listening requires listeners to pay attention to how the message is presented rather than to the message itself.

_____ 2. The purpose of therapeutic listening is to provide support for the speaker.

_____ 3. The purpose of listening for comprehension is to acquire information.

_____ 4. In appreciative listening, the listener focuses on the primary message.

_____ 5. Depending on their purpose, listeners pay attention to different parts of a message.

You probably were able to answer all (or most) of the questions correctly. Previewing, then, does provide you with a great deal of information. If you were to return to the passage from the speech communication textbook and read the entire section, you would find it easier to do than if you hadn't previewed.

When you preview an assignment, use the following hints to get the most out of it.

- Assess the difficulty of the material.
- Discover how it is organized.
- Identify the overall subject.
- Establish what type of material it is (for example, practical, research report, historical background, or a case study).
- Look for logical breaking points where you might divide the assignment into portions, perhaps reserving a portion for a later study session.
- Identify points at which you might stop and review.
- Look for connections between the assignment and class lectures.

Previewing Nontextbook Material

With nontextbook material, you may have to make changes in how you preview. Many articles, essays, and reference books do not have the same features as textbook chapters. They may lack headings or clearly identifiable introductions and summaries. The following hints will help you to preview materials of this sort.

- *Pay close attention to the title;* it may make a statement about the theme or key focus of the article.
- *Identify the author and source of the material.* This information may provide clues about the article's content or focus.
- *Read the first paragraph carefully, searching for a statement of purpose or theme.*
- *If there are no headings, read the first sentence of each paragraph.* The first sentence of the paragraph is often the topic sentence that states the main idea of the paragraph. By reading first sentences, you will encounter most of the key ideas in the article.
- *Pay close attention to the last paragraph.* It probably will not provide a summary, but it usually serves as a conclusion to the article.

Why Previewing Is Effective

Previewing helps you to make decisions about how you will approach the material. On the basis of what you discover about the assignment's organization and content, you can select the reading and study strategies that will be most effective.

Previewing puts your mind in gear and helps you start thinking about the subject.

Also, previewing gives you a mental outline of the chapter's content. It enables you to see how ideas are connected, and, since you know where the author is headed, your reading will be easier than if you had not previewed. Previewing, however, is never a substitute for careful, thorough reading.

EXERCISE 1–8

Select a textbook chapter that you have not read and preview it using the procedure described in this section. When you have finished, answer the following questions.

1. What is its overall subject?
2. What topics (aspects of the subject) does the chapter discuss? List as many as you can recall.
3. How difficult do you expect the chapter to be?
4. How is the subject approached? In other words, is the material practical, theoretical, historical, research-oriented, or procedural?
5. How can you apply this material in your class?

Activating Background Knowledge

After previewing your assignment, you should take a moment to think about what you already know about the topic. Whatever the topic, you probably know *something* about it: This is your background knowledge. For example, a student was about to read an article entitled "Growing Urban Problems" for a sociology class. His first thought was that he knew very little about urban problems because he lived in a rural area. But when he thought of a recent trip to a nearby city, he remembered seeing the homeless people and crowded conditions. This recollection helped him remember reading about drug problems, drive-by shootings, and muggings.

Activating your background knowledge aids your reading in three ways. First, it makes reading easier because you have already thought about the topic. Second, the material is easier to remember because you can connect the new information with what you already know. Third, topics become more interesting if you can link them to your own experiences. Here are some techniques to help you activate your background knowledge.

- *Ask questions, and try to answer them.* If a chapter in your biology text-book entitled "Human Diseases" contains headings such as "Infectious diseases," "Sexually transmitted diseases," "Cancer," and "Vascular diseases," you might ask and try to answer such questions as the following: What kinds of infectious diseases have I seen? What caused them? What do I know about preventing cancer and other diseases?
- *Draw on your own experience.* If a chapter in your business textbook is titled "Advertising: Its Purpose and Design," you might think of several ads you have seen and analyze the purpose of each and how it was constructed.
- *Brainstorm.* Write down everything that comes to mind about the topic. Suppose you're about to read a chapter in your sociology textbook on domestic violence. You might list types of violence—child abuse, rape, and so on. You might write questions such as "What causes child abuse?" and "How can it be prevented?" Alternatively, you might list incidents of domestic violence you have heard or read about. Any of these approaches will help to make the topic interesting.

EXERCISE 1–9

Assume you have just previewed a chapter in your psychology text on psychological disorders. Discover what you already know about psychological disorders by using each of the techniques suggested previously. Then answer the questions that follow.

1. Did you discover you knew more about psychological disorders than you initially thought?
2. Which technique worked best? Why?

Making Predictions

We make predictions about many tasks before we undertake them. We predict how long it will take to drive to a shopping mall, how much dinner will cost at a new restaurant, how long a party will last, or how difficult an exam will be. Prediction helps us organize our time and cope with new situations.

Prediction is an important part of active reading as well. It enables you to approach the material systematically. Also, it helps you read actively because you continually accept or reject your predictions. As you preview, you can predict the development of ideas, the organization of the material, and the author's conclusions. For example, for her philosophy class, a student began to preview an essay titled "Do Computers Have a Right to Life?" From the title, she predicted that the essay would discuss the topic of artificial intelligence: whether computers can "think." Then, as she read the essay, she discovered that this prediction was correct.

When you make predictions, you draw on your background knowledge and experience, making connections between what you already know about the subject and the clues you pick up through previewing. Now, predict the topic and/or point of view of each of the following articles.

"Dangerous Myths about Nuclear Energy"

"Where Darwin Went Wrong on Evolution"

"Why I Am Not a Christian"

Did you predict that the first article would favor the use of nuclear energy, that the second would hold that evolutionary theory is incorrect, and that the third would be concerned with religious beliefs?

In textbook chapters, the boldface headings serve as section "titles" and also are helpful in predicting content and organization. Considered together, chapter headings often suggest the development of ideas through the chapter. For instance, the following headings appeared in a sociology text chapter titled "Energy and the Environment."

The Limits of Fossil Fuels

Nuclear Power: High Promises, Grave Dangers

Conservation: The Hidden "Energy Source"

Solar Power: An Emerging Role

These headings reveal the author's approach to energy resources. We can predict that the chapter will describe the supply of fossil fuels as finite and nuclear power as dangerous; conservation and solar energy will be offered as viable alternatives.

EXERCISE 1–10

Predict the subject and/or point of view of each of the following essays or articles.

1. "Reality as Presented by Television News"
2. "TV Violence—The Shocking New Threat to Society"
3. "Professional Sports: Necessary Violence"

EXERCISE 1–11

Turn to the table of contents in one of your textbooks. Study the headings for two or three chapters you haven't read. Predict the organization or focus of each chapter. Explain which words in the headings helped you make your prediction.

_____

_____

_____

DEVELOPING GUIDE QUESTIONS

Have you ever read an entire page or more and forgotten everything you read? Have you found yourself going from paragraph to paragraph without really thinking about what the writer is saying? Because you are not looking for anything in particular as you read, you do not notice or remember anything specific.

Reading should be a purposeful activity. You should have a reason for reading each piece of material that you pick up. Before you begin reading any article, selection, or chapter, you should know what you want to find out. Your purpose will vary with the situation. For example, you might read a magazine article on child abuse for the purpose of learning more about the general nature and extent of the problem. On the other hand, if you were doing a research paper for a sociology course on the topic of child abuse, your purpose might be quite specific. You would be looking for facts and figures about the causes, effects, and extent of child abuse so you could use this information in your paper.

The easiest way to make certain you are reading purposefully is to use guide questions. These are specific questions that guide or direct your attention to what is important in each chapter section you are reading.

Guide questions are most useful in developing the knowledge and comprehension levels of thinking.

One of the easiest ways to make up guide questions is to turn the chapter title and headings into questions that you will try to answer as you read. Jot them down in the margin of your text, next to each heading, until you get in the habit of forming them. Later, you can form the questions mentally. For instance, for a chapter from a sociology text titled "Methods of Studying Society," you could ask, "What are the methods of studying society?" Then, as you read the chapter, you could look for and underline the answer. Here are three other examples of questions you might ask.

Chapter Title:	"Nine Principles of Communication"
Question:	What are the nine principles of communication?
Essay Title:	"The Real Way to Prevent Nuclear War"
Questions:	How does the essayist think nuclear war can be prevented?
	Are these preventive measures realistic and practical?
Chapter Heading:	"Theories of Color Vision"
Questions:	What are the theories of color vision?
	How do they differ?

Avoid asking guide questions that have one-word answers or that require recall of details. "How," "what," and "why" questions generally are more useful than those beginning with "who," "when," and "where."

EXERCISE 1–12

Write at least one guide question for each of the following headings that appeared in a criminology textbook.

Headings	Questions
Technology and Criminal Justice	_____
Criminalistics: Past, Present, and Future	_____
Justice System Today	_____
Cybercrime: The New White-Collar Crime	_____
Rules of Terrorism	_____
Controlling Terrorism	_____
Technology and Individual Rights	_____

| EXERCISE 1–13 | *Select a chapter from one of your textbooks, and write guide questions for each major heading.* |

Academic Application

_____

_____

_____

_____

CHECKING YOUR COMPREHENSION

You maintain an awareness or "check" on how well you are performing many of your daily activities. In sports such as racquetball, tennis, and bowling, you know if you are playing a poor game; you actually keep score and deliberately try to correct errors and improve your performance. When preparing a favorite food, you often taste as you cook to be sure the recipe will taste the way you want it. When you wash your car, you check to be sure that you have not missed any spots.

A similar type of checking should occur as you read. You need to "keep score" of how effectively you are comprehending and reacting to content. Because reading is a mental process, it is more difficult to check than is bowling or cooking. You may understand certain ideas you read and be confused by others.

Recognizing Comprehension Signals

What happens when you read material you can understand easily? Does it seem that everything "clicks"? Do ideas seem to fit together and make sense? Is that "click" noticeably absent at other times?

Read each of the following excerpts. As you read, be alert to how well you understand each one.

Excerpt I

As you well know, all you have to do to reveal anger is change the way you talk: you may talk louder, faster, and more articulately than usual. You can say exactly the same thing in a fit of anger as in a state of delight and change your meaning by how you say it. You can say "I hate you" to sound angry, teasing, or cruel. Vocal cues are what is lost when your words are written down. The term often used to refer to this quality is paralanguage. As noted before, it includes all the nonlanguage means of vocal expression, such as rate, pitch, and tone. It includes, therefore, what occurs beyond or in addition to the words you speak.

—Weaver, *Understanding Interpersonal Communication*, pp. 226–27

Excerpt 2

Large-quantity waste generators and SQGs must comply with the RCRA regulations, including obtaining an EPA identification (EPA ID) number, proper handling of the waste transport, manifesting the waste (discussed in the next section), and proper record keeping and reporting. Conditionally exempt SQGs do not require EPA ID numbers. Appropriate transport handling requires suitable packaging to prevent leakage and labeling of the packaged waste to identify its characteristics and dangers.

—Nathanson, *Basic Environmental Technology*, p. 351

Did you feel comfortable and confident as you read Excerpt 1? Did the ideas seem to lead from one to another and make sense? How did you feel while reading Excerpt 2? Probably you found it difficult and felt confused. Unfamiliar terms were used, and you could not follow the flow of ideas, so the whole passage didn't make sense.

Table 1–5 lists and compares common signals to assist you in checking your comprehension. Not all the signals appear at the same time, and not all the signals work for everyone. As you study the list, identify those positive signals you sensed as you read the first excerpt about paralanguage. Then identify the negative signals you sensed when reading the excerpt about waste generators.

TABLE 1–5   COMPREHENSION SIGNALS

POSITIVE SIGNALS	NEGATIVE SIGNALS
You feel comfortable and have some knowledge about the topic.	The topic is unfamiliar, yet the author assumes you understand it.
You recognize most words or can figure them out from context.	Many words are unfamiliar.
You can express the main ideas in your own words.	You must reread the main ideas and use the author's language to explain them.
You understand why the material was assigned.	You do not know why the material was assigned and cannot explain why it is important.
You read at a regular, comfortable pace.	You often slow down or reread.
You are able to make connections between ideas.	You are unable to detect relationships; the organization is not apparent.
You are able to see where the author is leading.	You feel as if you are struggling to stay with the author and are unable to predict what will follow.
You understand what is important.	Nothing (or everything) seems important.

Select and read a three- to four-page section of a chapter in one of your textbooks. Be alert for positive and negative comprehension signals as you read. After reading the section, answer the following questions.

1. How would you rate your overall comprehension? What positive signals did you sense? Did you feel any negative signals?
2. Where was your comprehension strongest?
3. Did you feel at any time that you had lost, or were about to lose, comprehension? If so, go back to that part now. What made it difficult to read?

Checking Techniques

At times, signals of poor comprehension do not come through clearly enough. In fact, you may think you understand what you have read until you are questioned in class or take an exam. Only then do you discover that your comprehension is incomplete. Alternatively, you may find that you comprehend material on a factual level, but you cannot apply, analyze, synthesize, or evaluate what you read. Use the following checking techniques to determine whether you really understand what you read.

1. *Use your guide questions.* Earlier in this chapter, you learned how to form guide questions from the boldface headings in your text. Use those questions to check your comprehension while reading. When you finish a boldface-headed section, take a moment to recall your guide questions and answer them mentally or on paper. Your ability to answer your questions will indicate your level of comprehension.

2. *Ask yourself thought-provoking questions.* To be certain that your comprehension is complete and that you are not recalling only superficial factual information, ask yourself questions that require you to think about content. Try to focus on the higher-level thinking skills: application, analysis, synthesis, and evaluation. Here are a few examples:

   Can I apply this information to a real-life situation?

   How does this reading assignment fit with the topics of this week's class lectures?

   How does this material fit with what I already know about the topic?

   Can I identify a principle that this material illustrates?

3. *Use internal dialogue.* Internal dialogue—mentally talking to yourself—is another excellent way to check your reading and learning. Rephrase, in

your own words, the message the author is communicating. If you can't express the ideas in your own words, your understanding is probably incomplete. The following examples of internal dialogue illustrate how the technique is used.

You are reading an essay that argues convincingly that capital punishment does not stop crime. As you finish reading each stage of the argument, you rephrase it in your own words.

While reading a section in a math textbook, you mentally outline the steps to follow in solving a sample problem.

As you finish each boldface section in an anthropology chapter, you summarize the key points in your own words.

This chapter has shown you several active reading techniques, but each takes time and initially may slow you down. Considering all the competing pressures you face, you may be wondering whether you can afford the time to experiment with these techniques. However, each of these techniques will save you time in the long run. You'll learn more while you are reading and will have to spend less time after reading to learn the material.

EXERCISE 1–15

Choose a section from one of your own textbooks. Read it, and check your comprehension by using both guide questions and thought-provoking questions. List your questions on a sheet of paper. List the positive and negative comprehension signals you noted as you read.

EXERCISE 1–16

Select another section from one of your textbooks and experiment with the technique of internal dialogue to check your comprehension. On a sheet of paper, describe the technique you used and evaluate its effectiveness.

College Success

Becoming a successful student requires planning and organization. Here are a few suggestions for ensuring your success.

1. *Organize a place to study.* Select a quiet, comfortable location and study in the same place each day. Be sure to have all your materials (paper, pens, etc.) at hand.

2. *Use a pocket calendar to record due dates for papers and exams.*

3. *Carry a small notebook for recording daily assignments for each course.* Check it each evening before you begin to study.

4. *Get to know someone in each class.* You might enjoy having someone to talk to.

Also, in case you miss a class, you will have someone from whom you can get the assignment and borrow notes.

5. *Attend all classes, whether or not the instructor takes attendance.* Studies show that successful students attend class regularly, whereas unsuccessful students do not.

6. *Get to know your instructors.* Use your instructor's office hours to talk about exams or assignments, ask questions, and discuss ideas for papers.

SUMMARY

Learning style refers to each person's unique way of learning. The Learning Style Questionnaire assesses five aspects of learning style. Active reading plays a critical role in college success. Concentration is among the skills you need to be an active reader. You can improve your concentration by

- eliminating distractions.
- learning to focus your attention.
- assessing your concentration.

Thinking about what you read involves six stages:

- knowledge
- comprehension
- application
- analysis
- synthesis
- evaluation

Previewing helps you become familiar with the chapter's content and organization before reading it. It enables you to

- make predictions.
- anticipate content, development, and organization.

When you create guide questions, you establish a focus and purpose for your reading.

Finally, comprehension checking helps you maintain and evaluate your comprehension.

Psychology

PREREADING QUESTION

Think of a person to whom you are attracted. Why are you attracted to him or her?

Factors Affecting Interpersonal Attraction

Josh R. Gerow

1   Now let's look at some empirical evidence related to attraction. What determines whom you will be attracted to? What factors tend to provide the rewards, or the positive reward/cost ratios, that serve as the basis for strong relationships? Here we'll describe four common principles related to interpersonal attraction.

Reciprocity

2   Our first principle is perhaps the most obvious one. Not surprisingly, we tend to value and like people who like and value us (Backman & Secord, 1959; Curtis & Miller, 1986). Remember that we've already noted, in our discussion of operant conditioning, that the attention of others often can be a powerful reinforcer. This is particularly true if the attention is positive, supportive, and affectionate. Research indicates that the value of someone else caring for us is particularly powerful when that someone initially seemed to have neutral or even negative attitudes toward us (Aronson & Linder, 1965). That is, we are most attracted to people who like us now, but who didn't originally. The logic here is related to attribution. If someone we

Proximity leads to liking, which is why teenagers who go to the same school are likely to form friendships.

meet for the first time expresses nothing but positive feelings and attitudes toward us, we are likely to attribute their reaction internally to the way the person is—rather shallow and the sort who just likes everybody. But if someone at first were to express neutral, or even slightly negative, feelings toward us and then were to become more and more positive, we might have a different, more positive view of their ability to judge others.

Proximity

3   Our second principle suggests that physical closeness, or proximity, tends to produce attraction. Sociologists, as well as your own personal experience, will tell you that people tend to establish friendships (and romances) with others with whom they have grown up, worked, or gone to school. Similarly, social-psychological studies consistently have found that residents of apartments or dormitories tend to become friends with those other residents living closest to them (Festinger et al., 1950). Being around others gives us the opportunity to discover just who can provide those interpersonal rewards we seek in friendship.

mere exposure phenomenon
the tendency to increase our liking of people and things the more we see of them

4   There may be another social-psychological phenomenon at work here called the **mere exposure phenomenon.** Research, pioneered by Robert Zajonc (1968), has shown with a variety of stimuli that liking tends to increase with repeated exposure to stimuli. Examples of this phenomenon are abundant in everyday life. Have you ever bought a CD that you have not heard previously, assuming that you will like it because you have liked all the other CDs this performer made? The first time you listen to your new CD, however, your reaction may be lukewarm at best, and you may be disappointed in your purchase. Not wanting to feel that you've wasted your money, you play the CD a few more times over the next several days. What often happens is that soon you realize that you like this CD after all. The mere exposure effect has occurred, and this commonly happens in our formation of attitudes about other people as well. Apparently, familiarity is apt to breed attraction, not contempt. I also have to add that although there seems to be ample evidence that the mere exposure phenomenon is real, there remains considerable disagreement about *why* familiarity and repeated interactions breed attraction (e.g., Birnbaum & Mellers, 1979; Kunst-Wilson & Zajonc, 1980).

Physical Attractiveness

5   Our physical appearance is one personal characteristic that we cannot easily hide. It is always on display in social situations, and it communicates something about us. People are aware of the role of appearance in nonverbal, interpersonal communication and may spend hours each week doing whatever can be done to improve the way they look.

6   The power of physical attractiveness in the context of dating has been demonstrated experimentally in a classic study directed by Elaine Walster (Walster et al., 1966). University of Minnesota freshmen completed a number of psychological tests as part of an orientation program. The students were then randomly matched for dates to an orientation dance, during which they took a break and evaluated their assigned partners. This study allowed researchers the possibility of uncovering intricate, complex, and subtle facts

about interpersonal attraction, such as which personality traits might tend to mesh in such a way as to produce attraction. As it turned out, none of these complex factors, so carefully controlled for, was important. The effect of physical attractiveness was so powerful that it wiped out all other effects. For both men and women, the more physically attractive their date, the more they liked the person and the more they wanted to go out again with that individual.

7   Numerous studies of physical attractiveness followed this one. Some of these studies simply gave subjects a chance to pick a date from a group of several potential partners (usually using descriptions and pictures). Not surprisingly, subjects almost invariably selected the most attractive person available to be their date (Reis et al., 1980).

8   You may have noticed, however, that in real life we seldom have the opportunity to request a date without at least the possibility of being turned down. When experimental studies began to build in the possibility of rejection, an interesting effect emerged: Subjects stopped picking the most attractive candidate and started selecting partners whose level of physical attractiveness was more similar to their own. This behavior has been called the **matching phenomenon,** and it is an effect that has been verified by naturalistic observation studies (Walster & Walster, 1969).

matching phenomenon
tendency to select partners whose level of physical attractiveness matches our own

Similarity

9   There is a large body of research on the relationship between similarity and attraction, but the findings are consistent, and we can summarize them briefly. Much of this research has been done by Donn Byrne and his colleagues (e.g., Byrne, 1971). It indicates that there is a strong positive relationship between attraction and the proportion of attitudes held in common. Simply put, the more similar another person is to you, the more you will tend to like that person (Buss, 1985; Davis 1985; Rubin, 1973). Sensibly, we also tend to be repelled, or put off, by persons we believe to be dissimilar to us (Rosenbaum, 1986).

10   Perhaps you know a happily married couple for whom this sweeping conclusion does not seem to fit. At least some of their behaviors seem to be quite dissimilar, almost opposite. Perhaps the wife appears to be the one who makes most of the decisions while the husband simply seems to follow orders. It may very well be the case, however, that this apparent lack of similarity in behavior exists only on the surface. There may be an important similarity that makes for a successful marriage here: Both have the same idea of what a marriage should be like—wives decide and husbands obey. In such a case, the observed differences in behavior are reflecting a powerful similarity in the view of the roles of married couples.

—Gerow, *Psychology: An Introduction,* pp. 654–56

VOCABULARY REVIEW

1. For each of the words listed below, use context; prefixes, roots, and suffixes (see Chapter 3); and/or a dictionary to write a brief definition or synonym of the word as it is used in the reading.

    a. empirical (para. 1)_____

    b. reciprocity (para. 2) _____

    c. proximity (para. 3) _____

    d. phenomenon (para. 4)_____

    e. invariably (para. 7) _____

    f. dissimilar (para. 9) _____

2. Underline new specialized terms introduced in the reading.

COMPREHENSION QUESTIONS

1. Write a list of guide questions useful in reading and reviewing this reading.
2. Check your level of comprehension. What positive or negative signals did you sense?
3. What are the four principles discussed in this reading?
4. Explain the mere exposure phenomenon.
5. Explain the matching phenomenon.

THINKING CRITICALLY

1. Think of someone to whom you are attracted. Which of the principles of attraction can account for your attraction?
2. Can you think of other factors not discussed in this reading that may account for interpersonal attraction?
3. Describe an instance in which you experienced the mere exposure phenomenon.
4. Have you observed or experienced the matching phenomenon? If so, describe the situation in which it occurred.

LEARNING/STUDY STRATEGY

For each of the four principles of attraction, the author describes one or more experiments that are related to the principle. To review this research, complete the following study chart.

Principle	Author(s)	Summary of Findings
1. Reciprocity		
2. Proximity		
3. Physical attractiveness		
4. Similarity		

2 | FUNDAMENTAL COMPREHENSION SKILLS

LEARNING OBJECTIVES

- **To identify what is important in a chapter**
- **To learn how to vary your reading rate**
- **To learn how to read selectively**

Many beginning college students are overwhelmed by the amount of required reading. Comments such as "I can't keep up!" and "I'll never get all this read by Friday!" are common.

Other students complain that although they spend large amounts of time reading and studying, they do not earn top grades. The problem may be that they have not comprehended ideas fully. They may not have distinguished main ideas from supporting details and have not grasped the relationships among ideas.

This chapter presents techniques that enable you to read better and more efficiently. There are no easy tricks to becoming a faster reader; textbook reading must always be relatively slow and deliberate. However, if you can learn to locate what is important and then find essential supporting details, your reading will be smoother and faster. You will find, too, that you will learn more as you read, which will enable you to accomplish more as you study and review. The key to success when you are faced with large amounts of reading, then, is selectivity: sorting out what is important and focusing your attention on it.

LOCATING MAIN IDEAS AND SUPPORTING DETAILS

Not all sentences within a paragraph are equally important. In fact, there are three levels of importance:

Most important: the main idea
Less important: primary supporting details
Least important: secondary supporting details

As you read a paragraph, you should be sorting ideas according to their relative importance and paying more attention to some than to others. Here, you will learn how to identify these levels of importance as well as how ideas fit and work together in a paragraph.

Finding the Main Idea

A **paragraph** can be defined as a group of related ideas. The sentences are related to one another and all are about the same person, place, thing, or idea. The common subject or idea is called the **topic**—what the focus of the entire paragraph is about. As you read the following paragraph, you will see that its topic is elections.

> Americans elect more people to office than almost any other society. Each even year, when most elections occur, more than 500,000 public officials are elected to school boards, city councils, county offices, state legislatures, state executive positions, the House of Representatives and the Senate, and of course, every fourth year, the presidency. By contrast with other countries, our elections are drawn-out affairs. Campaigns for even the most local office can be protracted over two or three months and cost a considerable amount of money. Presidential campaigns, including the primary season, last for at least ten months, with some candidates beginning to seek support many months and, as noted earlier, even years before the election.
>
> —Baradat, *Understanding American Democracy*, p. 163

Each sentence of this paragraph discusses or describes elections. To identify the topic of a paragraph, then, ask yourself: *"What or who is the paragraph about?"*

The **main idea** of a paragraph is what the author wants you to know about the topic. It is the broadest, most important idea that the writer develops throughout the paragraph. The entire paragraph explains, develops, and supports this main idea. A question that will guide you in finding the main idea is, *"What key point is the author making about the topic?"* In the above paragraph, the writer's main idea is that elections in America are more numerous and more drawn out than in other countries.

Topic Sentence

Often, but not always, one sentence expresses the main idea. This sentence is called the **topic sentence.**

To find the topic sentence, search for the one general sentence that explains what the writer wants you to know about the topic. A topic sentence is a broad, general statement; the remaining sentences of the paragraph provide details about or explain the topic sentence.

In the following paragraph, the topic is the effects of high temperatures. Read the paragraph to find out what the writer wants you to know about this topic. Look for one sentence that states this.

> Environmental psychologists have also been concerned with the effects that extremely high temperatures have on social interactions, particularly on aggression. There is a common perception that riots and other more common displays of violent behaviors are more frequent during the long, hot days of summer. This observation is largely supported by research evidence (Anderson, 1989; Anderson & Anderson, 1984; Rotton & Frey, 1985). C. A. Anderson (1987, 1989) reported on a series of studies showing that violent crimes are more prevalent in hotter quarters of the year and in hotter years, although nonviolent crimes were less affected. Anderson also concluded that differences in crime rates between cities are better predicted by temperature than by social, demographic (age, race, education), and economic variables. Baron and Ransberger (1978) point out that riots are most likely to occur when the outside temperature is only moderately high, between about 75° and 90° F. But when temperatures get much above 90° F, energy (even for aggression) becomes rapidly depleted, and rioting is less likely to occur.
>
> —Gerow, *Psychology: An Introduction*, p. 553

The paragraph opens with a statement and then proceeds to explain it by citing research. The first sentence of the paragraph functions as a topic sentence, stating the paragraph's main point: High temperatures are associated with aggressive behavior.

The topic sentence can be located anywhere in the paragraph. However, there are several positions where it is most likely to be found.

Topic Sentence First   Most often, the topic sentence is placed first in the paragraph. In this type of paragraph, the author first states his or her main point and then explains it.

> *There is some evidence that colors affect you physiologically.* For example, when subjects are exposed to red light, respiratory movements increase; exposure to blue decreases respiratory movements. Similarly, eye blinks increase in frequency when eyes are exposed to red light and decrease when exposed to blue. This seems consistent with intuitive feelings about blue being more soothing and red being more arousing. After changing a school's walls from orange and white to blue, the blood pressure of the students decreased while their academic performance improved.
>
> —DeVito, *Human Communication*, p. 182

Here, the writer first states that there is evidence of the physiological effects of colors. The rest of the paragraph presents that evidence.

Topic Sentence Last The second most likely place for a topic sentence to appear is last in the paragraph. When using this arrangement, a writer leads up to the main point and then directly states it at the end.

> Is there a relationship between aspects of one's personality and that person's state of physical health? Can psychological evaluations of an individual be used to predict physical as well as psychological disorders? Is there such a thing as a disease-prone personality? *Our response is very tentative, and the data are not all supportive, but for the moment we can say yes, there does seem to be a positive correlation between some personality variables and physical health.*
>
> —Gerow, *Psychology: An Introduction*, p. 700

In this paragraph, the author ponders the relationship between personality and health and concludes with the paragraph's main point: that they are related.

Topic Sentence in the Middle If it is placed neither first nor last, then the topic sentence appears somewhere in the middle of the paragraph. In this arrangement, the sentences before the topic sentence lead up to or introduce the main idea. Those that follow the main idea explain or describe it.

> There are 1,500 species of bacteria and approximately 8,500 species of birds. The carrot family alone has about 3,500 species, and there are 15,000 known species of wild orchids. *Clearly, the task of separating various living things into their proper groups is not an easy task.* Within the insect family, the problem becomes even more complex. For example, there are about 300,000 species of beetles. In fact, certain species are disappearing from the earth before we can even identify and classify them.
>
> —Wallace, *Biology: The World of Life*, p. 283

In this paragraph, the author first gives several examples of living things for which there are numerous species. Then he states his main point: Separating living things into species is not an easy task. The remainder of the paragraph offers an additional example and provides further information.

Topic Sentence First and Last Occasionally, the main idea is stated at the beginning of a paragraph and again at the end, or elsewhere in the paragraph. Writers may use this organization to emphasize an important idea or to explain an idea that needs clarification. At other times, the first and last sentences together express the paragraph's main idea.

Many elderly people have trouble getting the care and treatment they need for their ailments. Most hospitals, designed to handle injuries and acute illness that are common to the young, do not have the facilities or personnel to treat the chronic degenerative diseases of the elderly. Many doctors are also ill-prepared to deal with such problems. As Fred Cottrell points out, "There is a widespread feeling among the aged that most doctors are not interested in them and are reluctant to treat people who are as little likely to contribute to the future as the aged are reputed to." Even with the help of Medicare, the elderly in the United States often have a difficult time getting the health care that they need.

—Coleman and Cressey, *Social Problems,* p. 277

The first and last sentences together explain that many elderly people in the United States have difficulty obtaining needed health care.

EXERCISE 2–1	*Underline the topic sentence(s) of each of the following paragraphs.*

Paragraph 1

Evidence suggests that groups given the right to vote do not immediately exercise that right. In recent elections, young people have not voted at a high rate—always well below 50 percent. Since the passage of the Twenty-sixth Amendment in 1971, the addition of 18- to 20-year-olds to the electorate has contributed to a lower turnout. After the passage of the Nineteenth Amendment in 1920, many women were slow to use their new right. The difference in turnout between men and women has not been significant in recent decades, though. By the 1988 presidential election, it was fairly easy for most Americans to register and vote; yet only about 50 percent turned out to vote. What causes low turnout? How serious is it?

—Keefe et al., *American Democracy,* p. 178

Paragraph 2

. . . language consists of a large number of *symbols.* The symbols that constitute language are commonly referred to as words—labels that we have assigned to concepts, or our mental representations. When we use the word *chair* as a symbol, we don't use it to label just one specific instance of a chair. We use the word as a symbol to represent our concept of chairs. As symbols, words need not stand for real things in the real world. We have words to describe objects or events that cannot be perceived, such as *ghost* or, for that matter, *mind.* With language we can communicate about owls and pussycats in teacups and a four-dimensional, time-warped hyperspace. Words stand for cognitions, or concepts, and we have a great number of them.

—Gerow, *Psychology: An Introduction,* p. 250

Paragraph 3

Body mass is made up of protoplasm, extracellular fluid, bone, and adipose tissue (body fat). One way to determine the amount of adipose tissue is to measure the whole-body density. After the on-land mass of the body is determined, the underwater body mass is obtained by submerging the person in water. Since water helps support the body by giving it buoyancy, the apparent body mass is less in water. A higher percentage of body fat will make a person more buoyant, causing the underwater mass to be even lower. This occurs because fat has a lower density than the rest of the body.

—Timberlake, *Chemistry: An Introduction to General, Organic, and Biological Chemistry*, p. 30

Paragraph 4

Early biologists who studied reflexes, kineses, taxes, and fixed action patterns assumed that these responses are inherited, unlearned, and common to all members of a species. They clearly depend on internal and external factors, but until recently, instinct and learning were considered distinct aspects of behavior. However, in some very clever experiments, Jack Hailman of the University of Wisconsin showed that certain stereotyped behavior patterns require subtle forms of experience for their development. In other words, at least some of the behavior normally called instinct is partly learned.

—Mix et al., *Biology, The Network of Life*, p. 532

Paragraph 5

On election day in 1972, at 5:30 P.M. Pacific Standard Time, NBC television news declared that Richard Nixon had been reelected president. This announcement came several hours before the polls were closed in the western part of the United States. In 1988, polls in a dozen western states were still open when CBS and ABC announced that George Bush had been elected president. These developments point to the continuing controversy over the impact of election night coverage on voter turnout.

—Keefe et al., *American Democracy*, p. 186

Finding an Implied Main Idea

Although most paragraphs do have a topic sentence, some do not. Such paragraphs contain only details or specifics that, taken together, point to the main idea. The main idea, then, is implied but not directly stated. In such paragraphs, you must infer, or reason out, the main idea. This is a process of adding up the details and deciding what they mean together or what main idea they all support or explain. Use the following steps to grasp implied main ideas:

- Identify the topic by asking yourself, "What is the one thing the author is discussing throughout the paragraph?"
- Decide what the writer wants you to know about the topic. Look at each detail and decide what larger idea each explains.
- Express this idea in your own words.

Here is a sample paragraph; use the preceding questions to identify the main idea.

> As recently as 20 years ago, textbooks on child psychology seldom devoted more than a few paragraphs to the behaviors of the neonate—the newborn through the first 2 weeks of life. It seemed as if the neonate did not do much worth writing about. Today, most child psychology texts devote substantially more space to discussing the abilities of newborns. It is unlikely that over the past 20 years neonates have gotten smarter or more able. Rather, psychologists have. They have devised new and clever ways of measuring the abilities and capacities of neonates.
>
> —Gerow, *Psychology: An Introduction*, p. 319

The topic of this paragraph is the neonate. The author's main point is that coverage of neonates in psychology texts has increased as psychologists have learned more about them.

EXERCISE 2–2

Read the following section from an American government textbook and underline the topic sentence in each paragraph. Monitor your comprehension and list positive or negative comprehension signals (see Chapter 1, p. 29) you received while reading. Compare your list with those of other students in the class.

MEDIA RELATIONS WITH GOVERNMENT AND POLITICIANS

Few governments make available to the press the breadth and depth of material that the American media can obtain. An important tool for the press is the **Freedom of Information Act** of 1966. This law requires federal agencies to provide citizens with access to public records upon request. The act exempts material relating to the national security, but it allows citizens to sue the government when disputes arise, thus giving the judiciary the decision about which contested documents shall be made public and which shall remain classified. Accordingly, the Supreme Court in 1989 sharply narrowed the scope of the act by ruling that information gathered by the government during routine operations may be kept secret if the information later becomes part of a criminal investigation. In any event, by gaining access to previously classified documents, the press and many private citizens have uncovered cases of power abuse, attempted intimidation, and government harassment of private citizens.

Formal procedures are, however, not the only sources available to journalists. Among the most controversial leads the press gets are **leaks.** A leak is information unofficially made available to the press. There are many reasons for people in the government to go to the press with information that is supposed to remain confidential. People who oppose the policies of superiors may make secrets public, as apparently was the case with "Deep Throat," the informant Woodward and Bernstein used to unravel the Watergate affair. Disgruntled employees may wish to embarrass superiors, bureaucrats may leak word of impending budget cut proposals so as to alert congressional allies, insecure functionaries may betray confidences to demonstrate that they have access to important information, or someone may just talk too much.

Anyone even casually acquainted with Washington D.C. knows that it thrives on rumor, innuendo, and leaks. The difficulty of keeping information and plans secret has plagued presidents from the beginning of the republic. Indeed, some presidents, such as Nixon and Reagan, became obsessed with the problem. Early in his administration, Reagan tried to place limits on the scope of the Freedom of Information Act and to stay the stream of unauthorized information hemorrhaging from his government. Yet ironically enough, a large number of leaks come deliberately from the administration itself. When the president wants something made public but does not wish to be associated with it, someone in the administration can leak it to the press with the proviso that the source of the item remain anonymous. These kinds of leaks are often referred to as **trial balloons.** By using unattributed leaks, the administration can test public reaction to a change in policy and later be able to deny association with the idea should the public respond negatively.

To this point, we have been examining the media as watchdogs of government, but the media are also often used by public officials to accomplish the officials' ends. **News management** has become an accepted fact of American public life. Any organization of reasonable size, probably including the college you are attending, has a public information office (PIO). A large part of the PIO's task is to feed the press positive stories about the organizations they represent and to practice **damage control** when a negative issue arises. Employed to put the "right spin" on the news, PIO officers are hardly committed to objectivity.

—Baradat, *Understanding American Democracy,* pp. 99–100

Positive signals: _____

_____

_____

Negative signals: _____

_____

_____

EXERCISE
2–3

Academic
Application

Select a two- to three-page excerpt from one of your textbooks and underline the topic sentence of each paragraph.

Recognizing Primary and Secondary Details

Supporting details are those facts, reasons, examples, or statistics that prove or explain the main idea of a paragraph. Though all the details in a paragraph support the main idea, not all details are equally important. As you read, try to identify and pay attention to the most important, primary details. These primary details directly explain the main idea. Secondary, less important details may provide additional information, offer an example, or further explain one of the primary details. You might visualize the structure of a paragraph as follows:

MAIN IDEA
    Primary detail
        Secondary detail
        Secondary detail
    Primary detail
        Secondary detail
    Primary detail

Read the following paragraph. The topic is boxed, the main idea is double-underlined, and primary details are single-underlined.

Our data on the kinds of people who are more likely to read magazines are better than our data on the number who do. Surveys show, not surprisingly, that the amount of magazine reading is highly correlated with education. The more educated people are, the more time they are likely to spend reading magazines. We also know that women tend to read magazines more than men do. This is shown by various kinds of data, including the fact that magazines that appeal primarily to women outsell magazines that appeal primarily to men. It may seem strange or out of date to you for anyone in the 1980s to be talking about men's magazines or women's magazines. However, there is little evidence that the sexual revolution is erasing the clear distinctions between men's and women's tastes in magazines. Men are more likely than women to read magazines that cover news on business and finance, mechanics and science, sports, outdoor life, and those that include photographs of women in various states of undress. Men also have a higher probability of reading the general newsmagazines. Women, on the other hand, are more likely to read magazines with useful household information (recipes, home decor, child care, and gardening) or fashion and beauty information.

—Becker, *Discovering Mass Communication*, p. 159

This paragraph begins with a topic sentence. The primary details present what is known about magazine readership patterns, and the secondary details further explain and offer examples of these patterns.

To determine the importance of a particular detail, decide whether it directly explains the main idea or explains or provides further information about one of the primary details.

**EXERCISE
2–4**

Read the following excerpt from a psychology textbook. For each paragraph, draw a box around the topic sentence and underline the primary details. What types of details did the author provide? When you have finished, evaluate your comprehension by using internal dialogue (see Chapter 1, p. 30) to summarize the key points of the excerpt in your own words.

PSYCHOLOGY AND SPORT

Sport psychology is another new and exciting area of applied psychology. Although it has had a long history in Europe, sport psychology has become an organized focus of attention in this country only within the last 15 to 20 years. **Sport psychology** is "the application of psychological principles to sport and physical activity at all levels of skill development" (Browne & Mahoney, 1984, p. 605). There are many potential applications of psychology to sports and athletes. We'll review just two: analyzing the psychological characteristics of athletes and maximizing athletic performance.

The Psychological Characteristics of Athletes

Psychology's history is filled with research on the measurement of individual differences. Wouldn't it be useful to be able to predict who might become a world-class athlete on the basis of psychological testing? There are physiological differences between athletes and nonathletes—amount of muscle, muscle type, height, weight, lung capacity, and so on. Are there any differences between athletes and nonathletes on personality measures?

Generally, research in this area has been less than satisfactory and results often confirm the obvious. Differences tend to be small, but athletes usually score higher than nonathletes on tests of assertion, dominance, aggression, and need for achievement; they score lower on anxiety level, depression, and fatigue (Browne & Mahoney, 1984; Cox, 1990; Morgan, 1980). This is particularly true when the athletes are at a high skill level. Athletes in some sports, such as hockey and football, are more tolerant of pain than are athletes in other sports, such as golf and bowling (e.g., Ryan & Kovacic, 1966). Tolerance of pain, however, may be more of an outcome (result of their activity) for some athletes than a determinant of success.

This last point raises a problem that has plagued research on the personality of the athlete: Just how shall we define *athlete?* Given the differences among hockey players, golfers, long-distance runners, pocket billiards players, cowboys, bowlers, rock climbers, gymnasts, and so on, it is surprising that research can find *any* significant differences between athletes and nonathletes. In fact, when general trends are sought, they are often not found (e.g., Fisher, 1977).

Maximizing Athletic Performance

Of practical importance to coaches and athletes is the performance of the athlete in competition, and what can be done to maximize that performance.

One area of interest focuses on manipulating the arousal level of the athlete. The athlete in competition surely needs to be aroused and motivated to perform—"psyched up" to his or her best. Psychologists also know that too much arousal can interfere with athletic performance—that optimum levels of arousal can vary as a function of the task at hand. For example, making a long putt in golf requires a low level of arousal, blocking a shot in volleyball requires a slightly higher level, making a tackle in football a higher level, and a bench press in weight lifting requires a very high level of arousal (e.g., Cox, 1990, p. 98). . . . Psychologists can help athletes be sensitive to appropriate levels of arousal while maintaining concentration on the task at hand. This often involves training athletes to be sensitive to such indicators as their own blood pressure, respiration and heart rates, muscle tension and the like (Harris, 1973; Landers, 1982). . . . In a similar vein, psychologists now claim that the so-called home field advantage (Varca, 1980) often may be exaggerated, particularly in important games (Baumeister, 1985; Baumeister & Steinhilber, 1984). The argument is that frenzied, yelling, screaming hometown fans may raise arousal levels of the home team beyond the point of maximum efficiency. The negative effect of fans' reactions is more potent when teams are on offense than when they are playing defense, and it is clearly more potent in end-of-season playoff and championship games.

One sports psychologist, Michael Mahoney, commenting on Olympic athletes, has said, "At this level of competition, the difference between two athletes is 20 percent physical and 80 percent mental" (quoted in Kiester, 1984a, pp. 20–21). To the extent that this observation is accurate, psychologists have tried to help athletes to do their best—to give what is called their peak performance. Mental practice, or "imagery," combined, of course, with physical practice, has proven beneficial (e.g., Smith, 1987). In addition to manipulating acceptable levels of arousal, mental practice is useful in the following:

1. Mentally rehearsing a particular behavioral pattern. (Think about—mentally picture—that golf swing and the flight of the ball before you step up to the tee.)
2. Reducing negative thoughts that may interfere with performance. (Forget about an earlier error and focus on positive experiences, perhaps past victories.)

3. Rehearsing one's role in a team sport. (Mentally practice what you are sup-
    posed to do and when you are supposed to do it in various game situations.)
4. Setting realistic goals. (Don't get tense worrying about a competitor in this
    race, simply try to better your last performance; e.g., Creekmore, 1984;
    Fenker & Lambiotte, 1987; Kiester, 1984a, 1984b; Ogilvie & Howe, 1984; Scott
    & Pelliccioni, 1982; Smith, 1987; Suinn, 1980.)

Obviously, using mental imagery is not a simple matter, nor is it the only way in
which athletes can improve their performances. It's just one technique with which
sports psychologists can help.

—Gerow, *Psychology: An Introduction*, pp. 554–57

ADJUSTING YOUR RATE TO MEET COMPREHENSION DEMANDS

Do you read the newspaper in the same way and at the same speed at which
you read a biology textbook? Do you read an essay for your English class in
the same way and at the same speed at which you read a mystery novel?
Surprisingly, many people do.

If you are an efficient reader, however, you read the newspaper more
quickly and in a different way than you read a biology textbook. Usually,
the newspaper is easier to read, and you have a different purpose for
reading it. Efficient readers adapt their speed and comprehension levels to
suit the material.

To adapt your rate, you need to decide how you will read a given item.
How you will read depends on why you are reading and how much you
need to remember. A number of variables work together. To read efficiently,
you must create a balance among these factors each time you read.

Rate and comprehension are the two main factors that you must keep
in balance; as your reading rate increases, your comprehension may
decrease. Your goal is to achieve a balance that suits the nature of the material and your purpose for reading it. The following steps will help you learn
to vary your reading rate.

1. *Assess the text's difficulty.* Factors such as difficulty of the language,
    length, and organization all affect text difficulty. Usually, longer or
    poorly organized material is more difficult to read than shorter or well-
    organized material. Numerous typographical aids (italics, headings,
    etc.) can make material easier to read. As you preview an assignment,
    notice these features and estimate how difficult the material will be to
    read. There is no rule to use in adjusting your speed to compensate for
    differing degrees of difficulty. Instead, use your judgment to adjust your
    reading rate and style to the material.

2. *Assess your familiarity with and interest in the subject.* Your knowledge of and interest in a subject influence how fast you can read. Material you are interested in or that you know something about will be easier for you to read, and you can increase your speed.

3. *Define your purpose.* The reason you are reading an assignment should influence how you read it. Different situations demand different levels of comprehension and recall. For example, you can read an article in *Time* magazine assigned as a supplementary reading in sociology faster than you can read your sociology text because the magazine assignment does not require as high a level of recall and analysis.

4. *Decide what, if any, follow-up activity is required.* Will you have to pass a multiple-choice exam on the content? Will you be participating in a class discussion? Will you summarize the information in a short paper? The activities that follow your reading determine, in part, the level of comprehension that is required. Passing an exam requires a very high level of reading comprehension, whereas preparing for a class discussion requires a more moderate level of comprehension or retention.

Table 2–1 shows the level of comprehension required for various types of material and gives approximate reading rates appropriate for each level.

TABLE 2–1   LEVELS OF COMPREHENSION

DESIRED LEVEL OF COMPREHENSION	TYPE OF MATERIAL	PURPOSE IN READING	RANGE OF READING RATES
Complete, 100%	Poetry, legal documents, argumentative writing	Analysis, criticism, evaluation	Under 200 wpm
High, 80–100%	Textbooks, manuals, research documents	High comprehension recall for exams, writing research reports, following directions	200–300 wpm
Moderate, 60–80%	Novels, paperbacks, newspapers, magazines	Entertainment enjoyment, general information	300–500 wpm
Selective, below 60%	Reference materials, catalogues, magazines	Overview of material, location of specific facts, review of previously read material	600–800 wpm

| EXERCISE 2–5 | *For each of the following situations, define your purpose and indicate the level of comprehension that seems appropriate.* |

1. Reading the end-of-chapter discussion questions in a business marketing text as part of your chapter preview.

   Purpose: _____

   Comprehension level: _____

2. Reading a critical essay that analyzes a Shakespearean sonnet you are studying in a literature class.

   Purpose: _____

   Comprehension level: _____

3. Reading an encyclopedia entry on poverty to narrow down a term paper assignment to a manageable topic.

   Purpose: _____

   Comprehension level: _____

4. Reading a newspaper article on a recent incident in the Middle East for your political science class.

   Purpose: _____

   Comprehension level: _____

5. Reading an excerpt from a historical novel set in the Civil War period for your American history class.

   Purpose: _____

   Comprehension level: _____

Measure Your Reading Rate

To verify that you are adjusting your reading rate to suit the material and your purpose for reading, measure your reading rate in a variety of situations and make comparisons. The following is an easy method of estimating your reading rate on whatever material you are reading.

1. *After you have chosen a passage in a book or article, count the total number of words in any three lines.* Divide that total by three (3). Round to the nearest whole number. This will give you the average number of words per line.

2. *Count the number of lines in the article or book* (or on one page if it is longer than one page). Multiply the number of words per line by the

total number of lines. This will give you a fairly accurate estimate of the total number of words.

3. *As you read, time yourself.* Record the hour, minute, and second of your starting time (for example, 4:20:18). Start reading when the second hand of the clock reaches 12. Record your finishing time. Subtract your starting time from your finishing time.

4. *Divide the total reading time into the total number of words.* To do this, round the number of seconds to the nearest quarter of a minute and then divide. For example, if your total reading time was 3 minutes and 12 seconds, round it off to $3\frac{1}{4}$, or 3.25, minutes and then divide. Your answer will be your words-per-minute (WPM) score.

Example:

Total number of words on 3 lines: 23

Divide by 3 and round off: $23 \div 3 = 7\frac{2}{3} = 8$

Total number of lines in article: 120

Multiply number of words per line by number of lines:

    8 x 120 = 960 (total words)

Subtract starting time from finishing time: 1:13:28

                                         −1:05:00

                                            8:28

Round to nearest quarter minute: 8.25 minutes

Divide time into total number of words:

$960 \div 8.25 = 116 +$ a fraction (your WPM score)

**EXERCISE
2–6**

Measure how effectively you adjust your reading rate by reading each of the following materials for the purpose stated. Fill in your reading rate in the space provided, and then compare your results with those given in Table 2–1.

1. Material: A legal document (insurance policy, financial aid statement, credit card agreement)

   Purpose: Complete understanding

   Rate: _____

2. Material: A three-page assignment in one of your textbooks

   Purpose: High comprehension; recall for an exam

   Rate: _____

3. Material: An article in a favorite magazine

    Purpose: Moderate comprehension; entertainment

    Rate: _____

Reading Selectively to Improve Your Reading Efficiency

As part of learning how to adjust your reading rate, you should accept the idea that there is nothing sacred about the printed word. Many students erroneously believe that anything that appears in print must be true, valuable, and worth reading. Actually, the importance and value of printed information are affected by whether you need to learn it and whether you can use it in a practical way. Depending on the kind of material and your purpose for reading it, many times you may need to read only some parts and may skip over others. You might read selectively when

1. *You are searching for specific information.* If you are looking up the date of a historical event in your history text, you skip over everything in the chapter except the exact passage that contains the information. This technique of skipping everything except the specific information for which you are looking is called *scanning.*

2. *A high level of comprehension is not needed.* If you are not trying to remember a major portion of the facts and details, then you might concentrate on reading only main ideas. This method of reading only main ideas is called *skimming.*

3. *You are familiar with what you are reading.* In a college chemistry course, for example, you might find that the first few chapters of your text are basic if you have already studied high school chemistry. You could afford to skip basic definitions and the explanations and examples of principles that you already know. Do not, however, decide to skip an entire chapter or even large sections within it; there just may be some new information included. You may find that more exact and detailed definitions are given or that a new approach is taken toward a particular topic.

4. *The material does not match your purpose in reading.* Suppose that, in making an assignment in your physics text, your instructor told you to concentrate only on theories, laws, and principles presented in the chapter. As you begin reading the chapter, you find that the first topic discussed is Newton's law of motion, but the chapter also contains a biographical sketch of Newton giving detailed information about his

life. Because your purpose in reading the chapter is to focus on theories, laws, and principles, it would be appropriate to skip over much of the biographical information.

5. *The writer's style allows you to skip information (portions).* Some writers include many examples of a particular concept or principle. If, after reading two or three examples, you are sure that you understand the idea being explained, quickly glance at the remaining examples. Unless they present a new aspect or different point of view, skip over them. Other writers provide detailed background information before leading into a discussion of the intended topic. If a chapter starts out by summarizing information that was covered in a chapter you just read last week, it is not necessary to read this information again carefully unless you feel you need to review.

EXERCISE 2–7

The following items suggest different reading situations and describe the material to be read. For each item, decide whether you should (a) read the material completely, (b) read parts and skip other parts, or (c) skip most of the material.

1. Your computer science instructor has just returned a test on a chapter on programming in BASIC. She indicates that the class's overall performance on this test was poor and suggests that the chapter be reviewed. You received a grade of 77 on the test. How should you reread this chapter?

2. You have just attended English class, where your instructor discussed Shakespeare's *Richard III*. During his discussion, he made numerous references to Machiavelli's *The Prince*. You have never read this second work but think it's important to know something about it. How would you read it?

3. You are doing research for a sociology term paper on world trends in gender inequality. You are looking for information and statistics on recent income and employment trends. You have located several books from the 1960s on the topic of gender inequality in the United States. How would you read these books?

4. Your American history instructor has assigned each student to read a historical novel for the purpose of getting a realistic picture of what life was like and how people lived during a certain period. As you are reading, you come to a detailed two-page description of decorative glass making in Sandwich, Massachusetts. How should you read these two pages?

5. Your zoology professor has assigned a number of brief outside readings along with the chapters in your regular textbook. He has put them on reserve in the college library for the use of all his classes. This is the only place where they can be used. He did not say whether you would be tested on these readings. How would you read them?

Keeping a Learning Journal

As you begin college, you will encounter many new ideas and meet many new people from whom you will discover new ways of looking at and doing things. You also will begin to explore many new academic fields. A learning journal can be helpful in sorting out your thoughts, ideas, impressions, and reactions. Here are some suggestions for a learning journal.

1. *Keep a journal for each of your most challenging courses.* Many students use a spiral or steno notebook or a separate notebook section for each course.

2. *Date your entries, and reference them to particular chapters or assignments.* Some students find it helpful to record the amount of time spent on each assignment, as well.

3. *Express your reactions to the course in general.* Record your feelings about the overall course content and what you like and don't like about the course. Include ideas that interest you and that you would like to explore further.

4. *Record your impressions about specific assignments.* Include problems you encountered with particular assignments or unique features of them.

5. *Analyze reading and study techniques you have tried.* Include both those that worked and didn't work (and why).

6. *Include new ideas for learning.* Write down changes you made in using various study approaches, and record any new ideas you have encountered for studying the course material.

7. *Enter your reactions to and analysis of exams.* Right after you take an exam, you may have a different impression than when it is returned to you. Comparing these impressions can be useful in improving you exam-taking skills.

8. *Use your journal entries as sources for writing assignments.* They offer excellent starting points for choosing topics of papers and contain information for developing those topics.

SUMMARY

The skills you have learned in this chapter enable you to improve your comprehension, adjust your reading rate, and read selectively.

While you read paragraphs, focus on identifying three types of information:

- the main idea
- primary supporting details
- secondary supporting details

The topic sentence can take several positions:

- first
- last
- in the middle
- first and last

In some paragraphs, the main idea may be implied rather than directly stated. Primary details directly support the main idea, whereas secondary details provide additional information or further explanation of primary details.

Your reading rate should vary to suit the material and your purpose for reading it. Measuring your reading rate can help you assess whether you are reading at the proper rate for good comprehension. You should read selectively when you need only main ideas, a specific fact, or the answer to a question; when you are very familiar with the material; when the material does not match with your purpose; and when the style or type of material is conducive to skipping information.

Economics

PREREADING QUESTION

Have you heard of the age-old system of barter (trading goods you own for those you need)? Is it practical today?

Time Dollars

Ralph Nader

This rich new idea offers hope of solving social problems in an era of fiscal austerity.

1   Action for social change must rest on a new economic base, one that makes it possible for people to meet their own needs while working to rebuild community and revitalize democracy at the grass-roots level.

2   That new economic system is already at work. Some call it "service credits," others term it "care shares"; we call it Time Dollars. It is an organized, inflation-proof currency that can provide as powerful and reliable a reward for decency as the market does for selfishness.

3   It has been tested and it works. Government does not control it. It does not need new laws to make it happen. It can spring up tomorrow in a thousand places. In a period of budget cutbacks and recession, the Time Dollar represents a strategy to generate tremendous resources and to involve thousands of people in the work of overcoming our many social problems.

4   People get many needed services that they couldn't otherwise afford. They pay for them with Time Dollars they've earned by helping others. A teacher tutors a 12-year-old boy in English and he mows her lawn. Elsewhere, a retired secretary types poetry written by a neighbor with multiple sclerosis, and the neighbor repays her by reading the newspaper to the secretary's blind daughter.

5   The mixes and matches are endless. Some 3,000 service credit (work-for-Time-Dollars) volunteers, most of them over 60, are already at work through programs administered by community agencies, schools, local hospitals, and community colleges. That means citizens can begin to address critical needs that otherwise would remain neglected. On this level, Time Dollars simply reward people helping people. Fortunately, the IRS has ruled such exchanges tax exempt because they are not "commercial in nature."

6   But Time Dollars are far more than a tax-exempt barter currency. When strangers start acting like neighbors, and neighbors start acting like extended family, communities are reinvigorated. In an age of mobility, family breakup,

neighborhood decay, and widespread drug-related crime, that is no small achievement. Time Dollars do more than meet human needs; they do more than rebuild trust in a world of many commercial predators. They provide the kind of new economics that can support sustained citizen action on the scale society needs. In these times, many Americans are resigned to the status quo or are too busy paying bills to give the time needed to make democracy work as it could, to hold government officials accountable, and to check corporate lawlessness. Time Dollars could change that.

7   Imagine being able to pay part of your medical bills with Time Dollars earned by attacking sanitation problems and monitoring sources of water pollution that cause hepatitis. That's happening in El Paso. Imagine being able to pay part of your health insurance premiums by giving adult literacy classes or staffing a latchkey program for kids whose only parent has to work. That's happening in Washington, D.C., and Miami. Imagine paying for quality child care by being part of a driver's pool for senior citizens on evenings and weekends. That's happening, too. The Time Dollars system has been used with impressive success for the past four years. Yet many people still do not realize its full potential.

8   The power of the Time Dollars idea stems from four basic truths:

9   The first is that the real wealth of our nation is not money; it is the time of people and willingness of people to use that time helping others. Time Dollars experiments demonstrate that there are substantial and valuable reservoirs of human time that neither the market economy nor volunteerism has tapped.

10   The second truth is that the United States has two economies, the market economy, which the economists all analyze, and the household economy of family, neighborhood, and community. Many of the serious problems our society faces come from the erosion of the family and neighborhood economy. That economy has been taken over by the market economy; many families now pay for services their predecessors used to provide for themselves, from entertainment to companionship, from rearing youngsters to caring for the elderly. For a long time, the decline of that economy was masked by one fact: The unpaid labor of women kept it going. With their massive entry into the job market, the involuntary subsidy that women provided disappeared. Time Dollars may provide an alternative strategy for rebuilding that second, essential economy.

11   The third basic truth underlying Time Dollars is that people respond to rewards other than money. Since society lacks money to reward all the activity it needs and wants, society had better find another reward system. The reward system that Time Dollars provides is unique: It responds to a fundamental human need, the need to be needed and valued. It does so by providing a combination of additional purchasing power with psychological reinforcement. It turns out that the psychological reinforcement, the self-esteem that comes from helping others, may be even more important than additional purchasing

power. If money continues to be the only value that is reinforced in American life, then society will continue to pay a great price in social and civic problems.

12   The fourth truth is that money—even a lot of it—cannot completely substitute for what the family and the neighborhood and community used to provide. It does part of the job; but people must do the rest as citizens, as consumers, and as family members.

13   The Time Dollars concept doesn't fit the usual conservative-liberal categories. It challenges the notion that everything in life is best done by specialists and professionals. It challenges the assumption that money really defines what society can do.

14   The media, congressional debates, economists' predictions, and political oratory all deliver the same grim message: Without more money society must accept more babies dying at birth, more homeless people wandering the streets, more old people alone and abandoned. Global competition, the budget deficit, the S&L bailout, and the price of oil all come first.

15   It amounts to gridlock—moral, fiscal, political. Time Dollars present a new kind of money, a fresh vision, and a way to break gridlock.

—Nader, *Time Dollars*

VOCABULARY REVIEW

1. For each of the words listed below, use context; prefixes, roots, and suffixes (see Chapter 3); and/or a dictionary to write a brief definition or synonym of the word as it is used in the reading.

    a. revitalize (para. 1)_____

    b. reinvigorated (para. 6)_____

    c. predators (para. 6) _____

    d. status quo (para. 6) _____

    e. erosion (para. 10) _____

    f. oratory (para. 14) _____

    g. gridlock (para. 15) _____

2. Underline new specialized terms introduced in the reading.

COMPREHENSION QUESTIONS

1. Underline the topic sentence of each paragraph.
2. Explain how Nader's Time Dollar system works.

3. On what principles ("truths") is the Time Dollar system based?
4. Why is the Time Dollar system needed?

THINKING CRITICALLY

1. Evaluate Ralph Nader's authority to write this article.
2. Does the author present a biased or an objective view of the Time Dollar system?
3. What evidence does Nader offer that this system works? Is the evidence sufficient?
4. Evaluate Nader's four truths. Are they facts, opinions, or assumptions? Does he offer evidence to support them?
5. What additional information would you like to have about the Time Dollar system in order to evaluate its feasibility?
6. What immediate or practical problems do you see in implementing a Time Dollar system?

LEARNING/STUDY STRATEGY

Assume this reading was assigned as a topic for a class discussion by your economics instructor. Reread and annotate the reading in preparation for the class discussion.

3 | ESSENTIAL VOCABULARY SKILLS

LEARNING OBJECTIVES
- To learn techniques for vocabulary development
- To develop skill in using context clues
- To use word parts to expand your vocabulary
- To handle technical and specialized vocabulary

Your vocabulary can be one of your strongest academic assets or one of your worst liabilities. Language is the primary vehicle of thought, expression, and communication. Vocabulary is the basic unit of language. If your vocabulary is limited, your potential for self-expression, effective communication, and adequate comprehension of oral or printed materials also is limited. Conversely, a strong vocabulary can have both immediate (academic) and long-term (career) effects.

TECHNIQUES FOR VOCABULARY DEVELOPMENT

Here are some basic techniques for vocabulary development that can produce immediate results.

Be Selective

An unabridged (most nearly complete) dictionary lists approximately 300,000 words. Be realistic: You'll never learn them all. Your first task, then, is to decide what to learn—that is, to be selective. Some words are more useful to you than others, depending on several factors—the most important being your college major and your career goals. If you are a business administration major and plan to get a job with a major corporation, your working vocabulary should be much different than if you are a biology major planning a career in genetic research.

Use What You Already Know

You may believe that you have one vocabulary and that it is either weak or strong. Actually, you have four different vocabulary levels: reading, writing, listening, and speaking. Although they share a common core of basic, functional words, these levels range widely in both size and content. For example, there are words that you recognize and understand as you read but that you never use in your own writing. Similarly, there are words that you understand when you listen to them but that you do not use when you speak. Probably your listening and reading vocabularies are larger than your speaking and writing vocabularies. In other words, you already know a large number of words, but many of them you do not use. Here are a few examples of words you may know but probably don't use:

conform	contour
congeal	contrite
congenial	cosmic
congenital	cosmopolitan
contort	cosmos

When strengthening your vocabulary, a good place to start is to experiment with words you already know but don't use regularly.

Use New Words You Have Learned

Make a point of using one new word each day, both in speaking and in writing.

Regardless of how much time you spend looking up and recording words, you probably will remember only those that you use fairly soon after you learn them. Forgetting occurs extremely rapidly after learning unless you take action to apply what you have learned.

Acquire the Necessary Tools

To develop a strong vocabulary, you must acquire the necessary tools. These include a dictionary and a thesaurus, as well as access to subject area dictionaries.

Buy a Dictionary   Students commonly ask, "Which dictionary should I buy?" There are several types of dictionaries, each with its own purpose. A pocket or paperback dictionary is an inexpensive, shortened version of a standard desk dictionary. It is small enough to carry with you and costs around $5. Although a pocket dictionary is convenient, its use is also limited. A desk dictionary is more extensive. A pocket edition lists about 50,000 to 60,000 words, whereas a standard desk edition lists up to 150,000 words. Also, the desk edition provides much more information about each word it lists. Desk dictionaries are usually hardbound and cost over $20. Figure 3–1 is a comparison of entries from a pocket and a collegiate desk dictionary.

Figure 3–1   Comparison of Pocket and Collegiate Dictionaries

Pocket Dictionary	*Collegiate Dictionary*
di·lem′ma (di-lem′ə) *n.* a choice between alternatives equally undesirable.	di-lem-ma (dĭ-lĕm′ə) *n.* **1.** A situation that requires a choice between options that are or seem equally unfavorable or mutually exclusive. **2.** *Usage Problem.* A problem that seems to defy a satisfactory solution. **3.** *Logic.* An argument that presents an antagonist with a choice of two or more alternatives, each of which contradicts the original contention and is conclusive. [Late Latin, from Greek *dilemma*, ambiguous proposition : *di-*, two; see DI-¹ + *lēmma*, proposition; see LEMMA] — **dil′em-mat′ic** (dĭl′ə-măt′ĭk) *adj.*
	USAGE NOTE: In its primary sense *dilemma* denotes a situation in which a choice must be made between alternative courses of action or argument. Although citational evidence attests to widespread use of the term meaning simply "problem" or "predicament" and involving no issue of choice, 74 percent of the Usage Panel rejected the sentence *Juvenile drug abuse is the great dilemma of the 1980's.* • It is sometimes claimed that because the *di-* in *dilemma* comes from a Greek prefix meaning "two," the word should be used only when exactly two choices are involved. But 64 percent of the Usage Panel accepts its use for choices among three or more options in the example *Ph.D. students who haven't completed their dissertations by the time their fellowships expire face a difficult dilemma; whether to take out loans to support themselves, to try to work part-time at both a job and their research, or to give up on the degree entirely.*

SOURCE: *The New American Webster Handy College Dictionary* (left) and *The American Heritage Dictionary of the English Language* (right)

Several standard dictionaries are available in both desk and paperback editions. These include *Random House Dictionary of the English Language, Webster's Collegiate Dictionary,* and *The American Heritage Dictionary of the English Language.* A third type of dictionary, the unabridged dictionary, is found in the reference section of the library. The unabridged edition provides the most nearly complete information on each word in the English language.

You should buy a pocket dictionary to carry with you regularly. Use it to check unfamiliar words or unusual spellings. Also, you should purchase a collegiate edition desk dictionary. It is not necessary to have the most up-to-date edition; a used dictionary is just as good and costs considerably less.

A desk dictionary provides complete and varied meanings of words as well as information on word origin and structure. It also contains useful reference information, such as tables of weights and measures, metric equivalents, lists of abbreviations, lists of signs and symbols, a punctuation guide, and information about the mechanics of English and of manuscript form. Biographical and geographical guides also may be included. Electronic dictionaries and dictionaries for phonetic spellers (those who spell the word the way it sounds) are also available.

Use a Thesaurus   A thesaurus is a dictionary of synonyms that groups together words with similar meanings. This type of dictionary is useful for locating a precise descriptive word to fit a particular situation. For example, suppose you are looking for a more precise term for the boldface expression in the following sentence in a term paper you are writing:

> Whether men and women react differently to similar situations is often **talked about** in popular magazine articles.

Figure 3–2 shows a thesaurus entry for the phrase *talk about.*

Figure 3–2   Thesaurus Entry

---

12   discuss, debate, reason, deliberate, deliberate upon, exchange views *or* opinions, talk, talk over, hash over <nonformal>, talk of *or* about, rap <nonformal>, comment upon, reason about, discourse about, consider, treat, dissertate on, handle, deal with, take up, go into, examine, investigate, talk out, analyze, sift, study, canvass, review, pass under review, controvert, ventilate, air, thresh out, reason the point, consider pro and con; kick *or* knock around <nonformal>

Source: *Roget's International Thesaurus*

Right away, you can identify a number of words that are more specific than the phrase *talked about.* The next step is to choose a word from the entry that most closely suggests the meaning you wish to convey. Words such as *debate* and *discuss* would be appropriate. The easiest way to do this is to substitute various choices in your sentence to see which works best; check the dictionary if you are not sure of a word's exact meaning. Many students misuse the thesaurus by choosing words that do not fit the context. Use a word only when you are familiar with all its shades of meaning. Remember, a misused word is often a more serious error than a wordy or an imprecise expression.

The most widely used thesaurus originally was compiled by Peter Mark Roget and is known today as *Roget's Thesaurus;* it is readily available in an inexpensive paperback edition.

**EXERCISE
3–1**

Use a thesaurus to find a more specific or descriptive word to replace the underlined word in each of the following sentences. Revise the sentence, if necessary.

1. The jury made the <u>right</u> decision on the sexual discrimination case.
2. The videotape on the rights of victims shown in my criminal justice class was <u>dull</u>.
3. After completing three exams in one day, Joe seemed <u>tired</u>.
4. Dr. Rodriguez is a <u>good</u> teacher.
5. My friends thought the biology exam was <u>hard</u>.

Use Subject Area Dictionaries

Many academic fields have specialized dictionaries that list most of the important words used in that discipline. These dictionaries give specialized meanings for words and suggest how and when to use the words. For the field of nursing, for instance, there is *Taber's Cyclopedic Medical Dictionary.* Other subject area dictionaries include Henderson's *Dictionary of Biological Terms, The New Grove Dictionary of Music and Musicians,* and *A Dictionary of Economics and Business.*

Find out whether there are subject area dictionaries for the disciplines you are studying. Many such dictionaries are available only in hardback and are likely to be expensive; however, students often find them worth the initial investment. Most libraries have reference copies of many specialized dictionaries.

EXERCISE 3–2

For each of the courses you are taking, find out whether there is a subject area dictionary available. If so, record its title.

Use a System for Learning Vocabulary

One of the most practical systems for expanding your vocabulary is the index card system. It works like this:

1. *Whenever you hear or read a new word that you want to learn, jot it down in the margin of your notes or mark it in the material you are reading.*

2. *Later, write each word on the front of an index card.* Then look up the meaning of each word, and write it on the back. You also might record a phonetic key for the word's pronunciation, if it is a difficult one, or a sample sentence in which the word is used. Sample index cards are shown in Figure 3–3.

3. *Whenever you have a few spare minutes, go through your pack of index cards;* for each card, look at the word on the front and try to recall its meaning on the back. Then check the back of the card to see whether you were correct. If you were unable to recall the meaning or if you confused it with another word, retest yourself. Shuffle the cards after each use.

4. *After you have gone through your pack of cards several times, sort the cards into two piles, separating the words you know from those you have not*

learned. Then, putting the known words aside, concentrate on the words still to be learned.

5. *Once you have mastered all the words, periodically review them to refresh your memory and to keep the words current in your mind.*

6. *Once you have learned the words, use them in your speech and/or writing and evaluate how effectively you have used them.* This step is perhaps the most important of all, because it moves you from the knowledge and comprehension levels of thinking to the application and evaluation levels (see Chapter 1).

This system is effective for several reasons. First, you can accomplish it in your spare time; you can even review your cards while you wait for a bus. Second, the system enables you to spend time learning what you do not know rather than wasting time studying what you already have learned. Finally, the system overcomes a major problem that exists in learning information that appears in list form. When the material is in a fixed order, you tend to learn it in that order and may be unable to recall the items when they appear in isolation or out of order. Shuffling the cards enables you to scramble the order of the words and avoid this problem.

Figure 3–3   Sample Index Cards

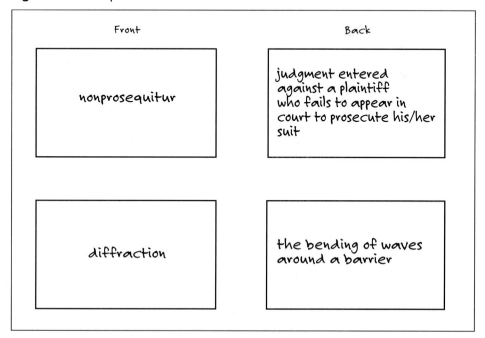

EXERCISE 3–3

Over the next week, prepare a set of 15 to 20 index cards, including new words used by your professor or introduced in your textbook. Include only words you feel you could use in your own speech or writing.

USING CONTEXT CLUES

Although a dictionary is invaluable, it is not practical to look up every new word you encounter. An alternative is to reason out the meaning of an unfamiliar word by using clues in the sentence or paragraph. Read the following paragraph, from which several words have been deleted. Fill them in after you have read the paragraph through once.

> Karl Marx (1818–1883) was born _____ Germany. _____ father, a lawyer, and his _____ were both descended from long lines of rabbis. Marx _____ college and planned _____ practice law, but after becoming involved with a radical antireligious _____, he decided to devote his _____ to philosophy.
>
> —Eshleman et al., *Sociology, An Introduction,* pp. 34–35

Certainly, you had no trouble filling in the missing words. You were able to do this because the paragraph contained enough information or clues about what was missing. Now imagine that instead of blanks, the paragraph contained several unfamiliar words. Often, you can "fill in" the meaning of the unknown words by using clues contained in the paragraph. Use these clues to determine the meanings of the boldface words in the following passage:

> The condition most feared among governments as a cause of war is the power **asymmetry**—that is, an unfavorable tilt in the distribution of power. There is widespread conviction that whatever other **impetuses** to war may be present, a careful equilibration of power between **antagonists** will tend to prevent war, while a disequilibrium will invite aggression....
>
> —Jones, *The Logic of International Relations,* p. 379

Although you may not have been able to define exactly words such as *asymmetry, impetuses,* and *antagonists,* you were able to make a reasonable guess about their meanings. You used the clues contained in the context (surrounding words and phrases) to arrive at the meaning.

Types of Context Clues

Now, let's look at various types of context clues. Each clue requires analysis of the word's context and the ideas that context contains.

Definition or Synonym   Frequently, a writer gives a brief definition or synonym for a word, usually in the same sentence as the word being defined. The definition may be the key idea of the sentence, as in the following examples.

> **Ethology** is the study of the behavior of animals in their natural settings.

At other times, the definition or synonym may be set apart from the key idea of the sentence through the use of commas, dashes, or parentheses.

> Experimental biology includes the study of learning, behavior, memory, perception, and **psychology** (biological bases of behavior).

> Most societies are **patriarchal**—males exert dominant power and authority.

You will find this type of clue used in most introductory college textbooks, especially in the first several chapters in which the "course language" is introduced.

Example Clues   Writers include examples to clarify or illustrate important concepts and ideas. If you are unfamiliar with a word or concept, often you can figure it out by studying the example.

> The use of **nonverbal communication,** such as a smile or gesture, usually reduces the risk of misinterpretation.

From the examples, *smile* and *gesture,* you know that nonverbal communication refers to "body language"—physical movements and facial expressions. Here are two other sentences that contain example clues.

> Collecting **demographic data** on potential consumers, including age, marital status, residency, and income, is an essential part of market research.

> Salary increases, promotions, privileges, and praise are forms of **extrinsic** rewards that motivate behavior.

You may have noticed that the examples in these sentences are signaled by certain words and phrases. *Such as* and *including* are used here. Other common signals are *for instance, to illustrate,* and *for example.*

Contrast Clues   Sometimes, you can determine the meaning of an unknown word from a word or phrase in the context that has an opposite meaning. Note, in the following sentence, how a word opposite in meaning from the boldface word provides a clue to its meaning.

> Despite their seemingly **altruistic** actions, large corporations are self-interested institutions that exist to make profits.

Although you may not know the meaning of *altruistic,* you know it means the opposite of self-interested. The word *despite* suggests this. *Altruistic,* then, means "interested in the welfare of others." Here are two additional sentences containing contrast clues.

> Studies of crowd behavior suggest that people in a crowd lose their personalities and act **impulsively,** rather than making reasoned decisions.

> Polytheism, the worship of more than one god, is common throughout India; however, **monotheism** is the most familiar religion to Americans.

Each of these examples contains a word or phrase that indicates that an opposite or contrasting situation exists. One such signal that was used in the examples is *rather than.* Other signal words that also show a contrasting idea include *but, however, despite, rather, while, yet,* and *nevertheless.*

Inference Clues   Many times, you can figure out the meaning of a word you do not know by using logical reasoning or by drawing on your own knowledge and experience. From the information given in the context, you can infer the meaning of a word you are not familiar with, as in the following sentence.

> Confucius had a **pervasive** influence on all aspects of Chinese life, so much so that every county in China built a temple to him.

If every county in China built a temple to Confucius, you can imagine that his influence was widespread. You can infer, then, that *pervasive* means "spread throughout."

Similarly, in the following example, the general sense of the context provides clues to the meaning of the word.

> In wind instruments such as the trumpet, sound is **emitted** directly by the vibrations of air columns in the instrument.

In this sentence, *emitted* means "sent out."

Sometimes your knowledge and experience can help you figure out an unknown word. Consider, for instance, the following sentence.

> To **simulate** the weightless environment of outer space, astronauts are placed in a specially designed room.

Here, *simulate* means "to give the appearance of."

Limitations of Context Clues

Although context clues generally are useful, they do not always work. There will be words for which the context provides no clues. Also, you should recognize that context clues give you only a general sense of what the word means—not its exact or complete definition. If you've figured a word out from context clues and you feel it is worth learning, mark it and later check its complete meaning in a dictionary.

A final limitation of context is that it suggests the meaning of the word only as it is used in a particular context. Words have multiple meanings; the meaning you infer from a single context gives you only a limited understanding of the word.

**EXERCISE
3–4**

Use context clues to determine the meaning of each word in boldface print. Write a brief definition or synonym in the space provided.

1. People who practice **totemism,** the worship of plants, animals, or objects as gods, usually select for worship objects that are important to the community.

   _____

2. The tone of **percussion** instruments, such as drums and cymbals, depends in part on the geometry of the surface area.

   _____

3. A cult may recruit followers through **deception;** potential followers may not be told what the cult involves or what will be expected of them.

   _____

4. **Euthanasia,** sometimes called mercy killing, is a controversial issue among the families of terminally ill patients.

   _____

5. Establishing a buying **motive,** such as hunger, safety, or prestige, is important in developing an advertising plan for a new product.

   _____

6. Our **paleolithic** ancestors relied on their own body power and the controlled use of fire to get things done. In later Stone Age societies, people used animals for muscle power.

   _____

7. Information, as well as rumors and gossip, is quickly spread through the office **grapevine,** although it is not recognized as an official channel of communication.

_____

8. New hourly employees in the firm are **accountable** to the training director, who, in turn, is accountable in the director of personnel.

_____

9. In one culture, a man may be **ostracized** for having more than one wife, whereas in other cultures, a man with many wives is an admired and respected part of the group.

_____

10. **Homogeneous** groups, such as classes made up entirely of teenagers, social organizations of high-IQ people, and country clubs of wealthy families, have particular roles and functions in our society.

_____

EXERCISE 3–5

Working with a classmate, use context clues to determine the meaning of each word in boldface print in the following passage. Write a brief definition or synonym in the space provided.

ORGANIZATION OF RELIGION

Religious associations take the form of cult, sect, or church depending upon their degree of institutionalization and level of formality. **Cults** represent the most loosely structured and unconventional forms of organization. They consist of small numbers of persons who band together in order to express a new religious cause—a cause often at great **variance** from that of established religion. In Roman times Christians were members of a cult. Today **adherents** of the Reverend Moon's Unification Church—"Moonies"—can be considered [members of] a cult.

Most cults dissipate after a short period of time. They are held together only as long as their charismatic leaders are able to mobilize the loyalty and passion of followers. In order to remain viable, then, religious groups must move to another level of organization: They take the form of either sect or church.

A **sect** is a small religious association that generally appeals to poor, propertyless, or otherwise marginal members of society. As in the case of a cult, the sect frequently supports a cause that places its membership at odds with established religious organizations. Unlike cults, sects usually **emerge** out of established religious orders. Also unlike cults, sects perpetuate themselves over time by developing a loose structure usually consisting of a part-time minister from the congregation who leads a highly involved membership in a number of emotionally charged services. The recent "Born Again" movement in Protestantism is a case in point. On television weekly, the various "Born Again" groups gained enormous popularity in the early and mid–1980s but found themselves **tottering** after the highly publicized scandals of Jim and Tammy Bakker and Jimmy Swaggert in the latter part of the decade.

The most highly structured and conventional religious organization is known as the church. Unlike a sect, a church draws membership from the cultural and economic mainstream of a society. Thus the religious beliefs and rituals of a church generally reflect an acceptance of the **prevailing** social order. Also unlike a sect, a church typically **engages** a specialized and full-time minister (or rabbi) who leads the congregation and socializes new members in religious beliefs and rituals.

—Levin and Spates, *Starting Sociology*, pp. 251–52

1. _____

2. _____

3. _____

4. _____

5. _____

6. _____

7. _____

8. _____

WORD PARTS: THE MULTIPLIER EFFECT

Suppose you want to learn 50 new words. For each word you learn, your vocabulary increases by one word; if you learn all 50, then you've increased your vocabulary by 50 words. The vocabulary of the average young adult is 30,000 words. Adding 50 words is equal to a 0.17 percent increase—negligible at best. You may be thinking, "There must be a better way," and fortunately, there is. If you learn word parts—prefixes, roots, and suffixes (beginnings, middles, and endings of words)—instead of single words, your vocabulary will multiply geometrically rather than increase by one word at a time.

Learning word parts, then, produces a multiplier effect. A single prefix can unlock the meaning of 50 or more words. Think of the prefix *inter-*.

Once you learn that it means "between," you can define many new words. Here are a few examples.

intercede	interscholastic
interconnect	intersperse
interracial	interstellar
interrelate	intertribal
interrupt	intervene

Similarly, knowledge of a single root unlocks numerous word meanings. For instance, knowing that the root *spec* means "to look or see" enables you to understand words such as

inspect	retrospect
inspector	retrospection
introspection	spectator
introspective	speculate
perspective	speculation

Learning word parts is a much more efficient means of building vocabulary than learning single words. The following sections list common prefixes, roots, and suffixes and provide practice in learning them. Before you begin to learn specific word parts, study the following guidelines.

1. In most cases, a word is built on at least one root.

2. Words can have more than one prefix, root, or suffix.
   a. Words can be made up of two or more roots (geo-logy).
   b. Some words have two prefixes (in-sub-ordination).
   c. Some words have two suffixes (beauti-ful-ly).

3. Words do not always have both a prefix and a suffix.
   a. Some words have neither a prefix nor a suffix (read).
   b. Others have a suffix but no prefix (read-ing).
   c. Others have a prefix but no suffix (pre-read).

4. Roots may change in spelling as they are combined with suffixes (arid, arable).

5. Sometimes, you may identify a group of letters as a prefix or root but find that it does not carry the meaning of the prefix or root. For example, in the word *internal*, the letters *i-n-t-e-r* should not be confused with the prefix *inter-*, which means "between." Similarly, the letters *m-i-s* in the word *missile* are part of the root and are not the prefix *mis-*, which means "wrong or bad."

Prefixes

Prefixes appear at the beginning of many English words and alter the meaning of the root to which they are connected. Table 3–1 (p. 76) groups 36 common prefixes according to meaning.

Learning word parts is particularly useful for science courses. Many scientific words are built from a common core of prefixes, roots, and suffixes. Chapter 16 offers several examples on page 469.

EXERCISE 3–6

Using the list of common prefixes in Table 3–1 (p. 76), write the meaning of each of the following words in boldface print. If you are unfamiliar with the root, check its meaning in a dictionary.

1. a **multinational** corporation_____

2. **antisocial** behavior_____

3. **inefficient** study habits_____

4. **postglacial** period_____

5. **unspecialized** training _____

6. housing **subdivision** _____

7. **redefine** one's goals _____

8. a **semifinalist**_____

9. **retroactive** policies _____

10. a sudden **transformation** _____

EXERCISE 3–7

Select two classmates and, working as a team, create as many words as you can that begin with one of the following prefixes. Record your findings and compare them with those of other classroom teams.

1   pre-
2. de-
3. mis-

Roots

Roots carry the basic or core meaning of a word. Hundreds of root words are used to build words in the English language. Table 3–2 (p. 77) lists 30 of the most common and most useful roots.

TABLE 3–1   COMMON PREFIXES

PREFIX	MEANING	EXAMPLE
Amount or Number		
bi-	two	bimonthly
deci-	ten	decimal
centi-	hundred	centigrade
equi-	equal	equidistant
micro-	small	microscope
milli-	thousand	milligram
mono-	one	monocle
multi-	many	multipurpose
poly-	many	polygon
semi-	half	semicircle
tri-	three	triangle
uni-	one	unicycle
Negative		
a-	not	asymmetrical
anti-	against	antiwar
contra-	against, opposite	contradict
dis-	apart, away, not	disagree
in-/il-/ir-/im-	not	illogical
mis-	wrongly	misunderstood
non-	not	nonfiction
un-	not	unpopular
pseudo-	false	pseudoscientific
Direction, Location, or Placement		
circum-	around	circumference
com-/col-/con-	with, together	compile
de-	away, from	depart
ex-/extra-	from, out of, former	ex-wife
hyper-	over, excessive	hyperactive
inter-	between	interpersonal
intro-/intra-	within, into, in	introduction
post-	after	posttest
pre-	before	premarital
re-	back, again	review
retro-	backward	retrospect
sub-	under, below	submarine
super-	above, extra	supercharge
tele-	far	telescope
trans-	across, over	transcontinental

TABLE 3–2   COMMON ROOTS

ROOT	MEANING	EXAMPLE
aud/audit	hear	audible
aster/astro	star	astronaut
bio	life	biology
cap	take, seize	captive
chron(o)	time	chronology
corp	body	corpse
cred	believe	incredible
dict/dic	tell, say	predict
duc/duct	lead	introduce
fact/fac	made, do	factory
graph	write	telegraph
geo	earth	geophysics
log/logo/logy	study, thought	psychology
mit/miss	send	dismiss
mort/mor	die, death	immortal
path	feeling	sympathy
phono	sound, voice	telephone
photo	light	photosensitive
port	carry	transport
scop	seeing	microscope
scrib/script	write	inscription
sen/sent	feel	insensitive
spec/spic/spect	look, see	retrospect
tend/tent/tens	stretch or strain	tension
terr/terre	land, earth	territory
theo	god	theology
ven/vent	come	convention
vert/vers	turn	invert
vis/vid	see	invisible
voc	call	vocation

EXERCISE 3–8

Use the list of common roots in Table 3–2 (above) to determine the meanings of the following words in boldface print. Write a brief definition or synonym of each, checking a dictionary, if necessary.

1. **bioethical** issues _____

2. **terrestrial** life _____

3. to **desensitize** _____

4. to study **astronomy** _____

5. **synchronize** your watches _____

6. **visualize** the problem_____

7. a religious **missionary** _____

8. **biographical** data_____

9. a **geology** course_____

10. **pathological** behavior_____

Suffixes

Suffixes are word endings that often change the part of speech of a word. For example, adding the suffix -*y* to the noun *cloud* produces the adjective *cloudy.* Accompanying the change in part of speech is a shift in meaning.

Often, several different words can be formed from a single root word with the addition of different suffixes. Some examples follow.

Root: class
root + suffix = class-ify, class-ification, class-ic
Root: right
root + suffix = right-ly, right-ful, right-ist, right-eous

If you know the meaning of the root word and the ways in which different suffixes affect the meaning of the root word, you will be able to understand a word's meaning when a suffix is added. A list of common suffixes and their meanings appears in Table 3–3.

EXERCISE 3–9

For each of the words listed, add a suffix so that the word will complete the sentence. Write the new word in the space provided.

1. *behavior*

   _____ therapy attempts to change habits and illnesses by altering people's responses to stimuli.

2. *atom*

   Uranium, when bombarded with neutrons, explodes and produces a heat reaction known as _____ energy.

3. *advertise*

   One important purpose of an _____ is to inform potential customers about the service or product and familiarize the public with the brand name.

TABLE 3–3   COMMON SUFFIXES

SUFFIX	EXAMPLE
State, Condition, or Quality	
-able	touchable
-ance	assistance
-ation	confrontation
-ence	reference
-ible	tangible
-ion	discussion
-ity	superiority
-ive	permissive
-ment	amazement
-ness	kindness
-ous	jealous
-ty	loyalty
-y	creamy
"One Who"	
-ee	tutee
-eer	engineer
-er	teacher
-ist	activist
-or	advisor
Pertaining to or Referring to	
-al	autumnal
-ship	friendship
-hood	brotherhood
-ward	homeward

4. *uniform*

   The _____ of a law requires that it must be applied to all relevant groups without bias.

5. *evolution*

   Darwin's theory of natural selection tied the survival of a species to its _____ fitness—its ability to survive and reproduce.

6. *compete*

   When food sources are not large enough to support all the organisms in a habitat, environmental _____ occurs.

7. *religion*

   During the Age of Reason in American history, _____ revivals swept the nation.

8. *perform*

   Perhaps an administrator's most important duty is establishing conditions conducive to high employee motivation, which results in better job _____.

9. *effective*

   A critical factor in evaluating a piece of literature or art is its _____ —how strongly and clearly the artist's message has been conveyed to the audience.

10. *theory*

    _____ have spent decades studying the theory of relativity.

EXERCISE 3–10

Use your knowledge of context clues and word parts to determine the meaning of each word in boldface print. On a separate sheet of paper, write a brief definition of each word that fits its use in the sentence.

1. GLOBAL TECHNOLOGY

The advancement of technology is a **global** issue. The United States has been known as a world leader in the advancement of technology. To remain **competitive,** however, global research and development strategies must respond to changes in transportation, communication, information technology, and **merged** national markets. Intellectual capital is the critical resource in the global economy. The ability to **generate,** access, and rapidly use new knowledge and **convert** it (technology transfer) into marketable quality products and processes is the key to competitive advantage.

The **diffusion** of technological capabilities and expansion of the technically trained work force worldwide have strengthened the competitive position of industrialized countries and **enabled** many more to enter the marketplace. As a result, **dominance** by the United States in nearly all high-tech markets is being challenged.

In many countries, government-sponsored programs have reduced the costs and risks associated with technological development by **assuring** long-term financial commitment. Airbus Industrie, for example, is a cross-national European consortium that has developed and produced airplanes through support of its partner companies in the form of repayable loans.

—Kinnear et al., *Principles of Marketing,* pp. 57–58

2. LINGUISTIC ANTHROPOLOGY

While all organisms have some way of communicating, and some animals, such as porpoises and chimpanzees, have highly developed means of communicating, humans have evolved a unique and extremely complex system. Without it, human culture as we know it would be impossible. The field of **linguistic anthropology** focuses on this aspect of human life. It is, in turn, divided into a number of **subfields.**

Descriptive linguistics deals with how languages are constructed and how the various parts (sound and grammar) are **interrelated** to form coherent systems of communication. Historical linguistics concerns the **evolution** of language—how languages grow and change. Sociolinguistics studies the relationship between language and social factors, such as class, ethnicity, age, and gender. Finally, a topic of interest to many anthropological linguists is language and culture, which examines the ways that language affects how we think and, *conversely,* how our beliefs and values might influence our linguistic patterns.

—Howard, *Contemporary Cultural Anthropology,* pp. 12–13

LEARNING SPECIALIZED AND SCIENTIFIC VOCABULARY

You probably have noticed that each sport and hobby has its own language—a specialized set of words with specific meanings. Baseball players and fans talk about no-hitters, home runs, errors, and runs batted in. Each academic discipline, too, has its own set of specialized words. These terms enable specialists to give accurate and concise descriptions of events, principles, concepts, problems, and occurrences.

One of the first tasks that you face in a new course is to learn its specialized language. This task is especially important in introductory courses where the subject is new and unfamiliar to you. In an introductory computer science course, for instance, you often start by learning how a computer functions. From that point, many new terms are introduced: *bit, byte, field, numeric characters, character positions, statements, coding, format,* and so forth.

In science courses, new terminology is especially important. Hundreds of new scientific terms are introduced in each course. For specific suggestions on learning scientific terminology, refer to Chapter 16, pages 356–58.

Specialized Terminology in Class Lectures

Often, the first few class lectures in a course are devoted to acquainting students with the nature and scope of the field and to introducing its specialized language. Many instructors devote considerable time to presenting the language of the course carefully and explicitly. Be sure to record each new term accurately for later review and study. Good lecturers give you clues to what terms and definitions are important to record. Some instructors make a habit of writing new words on the chalkboard; others may speak very slowly so that you can record definitions. Still other instructors may repeat a word and its definition several times or offer several variations of the word's meaning. As a part of your note-taking system, develop a consistent way of easily identifying new terms and definitions recorded in your notes. For instance, you might circle or draw a box around each new term or write "def." in the margin.

EXERCISE 3–11

Estimate the number of new terms that each of your instructors introduced during the first several weeks for each of your courses. Now check the accuracy of your estimates by reviewing the first two weeks of your class notes and the first several chapters of the textbook for each course you are taking. How many new terms and definitions were included for each course? Most students underestimate. Did you?

Specialized Terminology in Textbooks

The first few chapters in a textbook are generally introductory, too. They are written to familiarize you with the subject and acquaint you with its specialized language. In one economics textbook, 34 new terms were introduced in the first two chapters (40 pages). In the first two chapters (28 pages) of a chemistry book, 56 specialized words were introduced.

Textbook authors use various means to emphasize new terminology. In some texts, new vocabulary is printed in italics, boldface type, or colored print. Other texts indicate new terms in the margin of each page. Still the most common means of emphasis, however, is the "New Terminology" or "Vocabulary" list that appears at the beginning or end of each chapter. Many texts also include a glossary of key terms at the back of the book.

EXERCISE 3–12

Review the first chapter from two of your texts and then answer the following questions.

1. How many new terms are introduced in each?
2. If your texts contain glossaries, are all of these new terms listed?
3. Are most new words technical terms, or are they words in everyday use to which a specialized meaning is attached?
4. How does each textbook author call your attention to these new terms?

Learning Core Prefixes, Roots, and Suffixes

Terminology in a particular academic discipline often uses a core of common prefixes, roots, and suffixes. For example, in the field of human anatomy and physiology, the prefix *endo-* means "inner" and the root *derma* refers to "skin." Thus the word endoderm refers to the inner layer of cells in the skin. Numerous other words are formed by using the root *derma* in conjunction with a suffix.

As you are learning new terminology for each course, make a point of noticing recurring prefixes, roots, and suffixes. Compile a list of these word parts and their meanings, along with several examples of each one. A partial sample list for anthropology follows.

PREFIXES	MEANINGS	EXAMPLES
bi-	two	bipedalism
anti-	against	antibody
poly-	many	polygyny

ROOTS		
terra	earth, ground	territory
gene	unit of chromosomes	genotype
anthropo	human	anthropoid

SUFFIXES		
-us	one who	Australopithecus
-cene	era or epoch	Pleistocene
-cide	killing of	infanticide

EXERCISE 3–13

Academic Application

For one of your courses, identify five commonly used prefixes, roots, and suffixes. If you have difficulty, review the glossary of the text to discover commonly used word parts.

Developing a Course Master File

For each course you are taking, set up a master file that includes new terminology to be learned and a list of essential prefixes, roots, and suffixes. Also include a list of frequently used signs, abbreviations, and symbols and their meanings.

In the sciences, numerous symbols are used in formulas. You'll save time and avoid frequent interruptions if you learn these symbols right away rather than having to refer to the text to translate each sign or symbol. Your course master file can be a big help in this effort.

An abbreviated version of a course master file for a course in American politics is shown in Figure 3–4.

Because each course is different, your course master file will change for each course you're taking. Check with the Learning Lab or Academic Skills Center at your college; it may offer lists of common prefixes and roots.

Figure 3–4   Sample Course Master File

New Terminology

Cabinet	Group of presidential advisors made up of secretaries who head government departments and the attorney general.
Deficit	An excess of government expenditures over federal revenues.
Bill	A proposed law that must be passed by Congress and signed by the President to become a law.

Prefixes, Roots, Suffixes

Prefix	*Meaning*	*Example*
anti-	against	antitrust
bi-	two	bicameral
sub-	under	subgovernments

Root	*Meaning*	*Example*
pol	political	policy
employ	to provide work	unemployment
pluri	many	pluralist

Suffix	*Meaning*	*Example*
-ism	a quality, doctrine, theory, or principle	capitalism
-ive	state, condition, or quality	progressive
-al	referring to	presidential

Abbreviations

CIA	Central Intelligence Agency
PAC	political action committee
FTC	Federal Trade Commission
CPI	Consumer Price Index
FEC	Federal Election Committee

EXERCISE 3–14

Begin preparing a master file for one of your courses. Using both your text and your lecture notes, begin with the first chapter and list new terms, prefixes, roots, and suffixes, as well as symbols and abbreviations.

STUDY Tips · Procrastination

When your work load increases, it is tempting to put things off. Here are some suggestions to help you overcome or control procrastination.

1. *Clear your desk.* Move everything from your desk except materials for the task at hand. With nothing else in front of you, you are more likely to start working and less likely to be distracted from your task while working.

2. *Give yourself five minutes to start.* If you are having difficulty beginning a task, tell yourself that you will work on it for just five minutes. Often, once you start working, your motivation and interest will build, and you will want to continue working.

3. *Divide the task into manageable parts.* Complicated tasks are often difficult to start because they seem so long and unmanageable. Before beginning such tasks, spend a few minutes organizing and planning. Divide each task into parts, and list what you need to do and in what order.

4. *Start somewhere, no matter where.* If you are having difficulty getting started, do something rather than sit and stare, regardless of how trivial it may seem. If you are having trouble writing a paper from rough draft notes, for example, start by recopying the notes. Suddenly, you'll find yourself rearranging and rephrasing them, and you'll be well on your way toward writing a draft.

5. *Recognize when you need more information.* Sometimes, procrastination is a signal that you lack skills or information. You may be avoiding a task because you're not sure how to do it. You may not understand why you use a certain procedure to solve a type of math problem, for example, so you feel reluctant to do math homework. Or selecting a term paper topic may be difficult if you aren't certain of the purpose or expected length of the paper. Overcome such stumbling blocks by discussing them with classmates or with your professor.

SUMMARY

This chapter focused on basic techniques of vocabulary development. Some basic tools for vocabulary development are

- pocket and collegiate dictionaries
- a thesaurus
- subject area dictionaries
- the index card system

Often, you can determine the meaning of unfamiliar words by examining the context in which they appear. Four common types of context clues are

- definition or synonym
- example
- contrast
- inference

If you learn common word parts (prefixes, roots, and suffixes), you can unlock the meaning of thousands of words.

Each academic discipline has its own set of specialized and technical vocabulary. Aids to mastering specialized terminology include

- subject area dictionaries
- core prefixes, roots, and suffixes
- a course master file

INTERPERSONAL COMMUNICATION

PREREADING QUESTIONS

1. Do people always understand what you are saying?
2. Why does miscommunication occur?

WHAT WORDS CAN AND CANNOT DO

Richard L. Weaver, III

1   If we see a series of stones lying across a stream, we know they will help us get to the other side. But our experience with such stones tells us that some of the stones may be loose or covered with slime and could cause us to slip. Like these stones, words can help us to reach our goals, or they can cause us to stumble and fall. Let's look at some characteristics of language that affect our interpersonal communication.

2   When we talk to people, we often assume too quickly that we are being understood. If we tell people we are going to put on some music, we probably don't think about whether they are expecting to hear the kind of music we intend to play—we just turn it on. But think about the word *music* and how many different interpretations there are of it. (See Figure 2.)

Figure 2   One word may have many different interpretations.

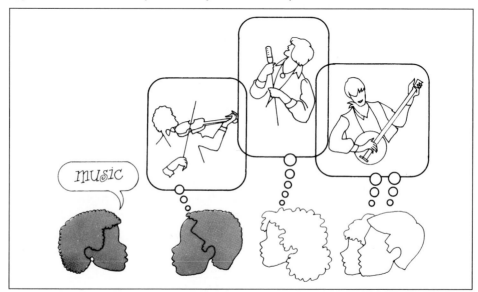

3   We depend on context and on nonverbal cues to give us the meaning of words. If we say we are going to put on some music, our friends may be able to predict from knowing our taste and from nonverbal cues (our mood) what we might play. But they have a good chance of being wrong. In our daily conversation, we use about 2,000 words. Of those 2,000, the 500 we use most often have more than 14,000 dictionary definitions. Think of the possibilities for confusion! The problem of figuring out what a person means by a certain word is compounded by the fact that even dictionary meanings change, and new words are constantly being added to the language.

4   **Denotative meanings.** *The* **denotative meaning** *of a word is its dictionary definition.* Dictionaries provide alternatives; we still must choose from those alternatives. The choice of what is "appropriate" or "inappropriate" is left to the user.

5   Some words have relatively stable meanings. If several people were to define a particular word special to their discipline, they would probably use about the same definition—an agreed-upon interpretation. To lawyers, the word *estoppel* has one precise, denotative meaning. Doctors would probably agree upon the definition of *myocardial infarction.* People in many disciplines depend on certain words having precise, unchanging meanings in order to carry on their work. There is little likelihood of confusion with denotative meanings because there is a direct relationship between the word and what it describes. Connotative meanings, on the other hand, depend a lot more than denotative meanings on our subjective thought processes. (See Figure 3.)

6   **Connotative meanings.** *The* **connotative meaning** *of a word is the associations and overtones people bring to it.* Dictionary definitions would probably not help our friends predict the kind of music we would play or what we mean by "music." But their experience with us and with music will give them a clue as to what we mean. If "music" connotes the same thing to us and to our friends, there's less chance of misunderstanding.

7   When we hear a word, the thoughts and feelings we have about that word and about the person using it determine what that word ultimately means to

CONSIDER THIS

The belief that sitting down and talking will ensure mutual understanding and solve problems is based on the assumption that we can say what we mean, and that what we say will be understood as we mean it.

—Deborah Tannen, *That's Not What I Meant!* (New York: William Morrow and Company, Inc., 1986), p. 124.

Figure 3 Connotative meanings may depend a great deal on the perceiver's experience.

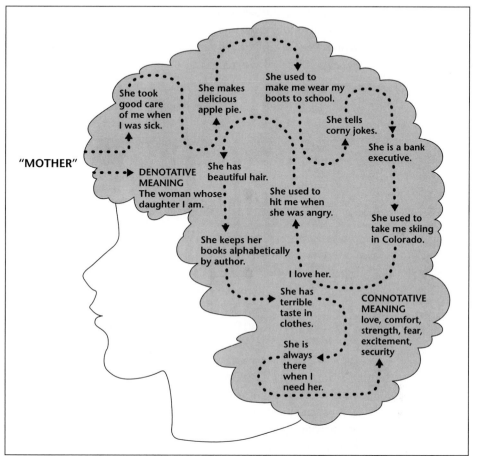

us. This is the word's *connotative* meaning. Connotative meanings change with our experience. Just as we experience something different in every second of life that we live, so does everyone else. And no two of these experiences are identical! It's no wonder there are infinitely many connotations for every word we use. Figure 3 illustrates the process through which words may accumulate their connotative meanings.

8   If a word creates pretty much the same reaction in a majority of people, the word is said to have a general connotation. Actually, the more general the connotation of a word, the more likely that meaning will become the dictionary meaning because most people will agree on what that word represents. The more general the connotation of a word, the less likely people are to misunderstand it.

9   Problems in interpersonal communication increase as we use words with many connotative meanings. Because these meanings are so tied to the particular feelings, thoughts, and ideas of other people, we have a bigger chance of being misunderstood when we use them. On the other hand, richly connotative words give our language power. Note, for example, the differences between the following lists of words:

freedom	book
justice	piano
love	tree
liberty	teacher
music	fire

The words in the left column have many connotations; the words in the right column are more strictly denotative. "The teacher put the book on the piano" is an unambiguous statement. The sentence, "The love of freedom burns like a white flame in all of us" can be interpreted in numerous ways.

10   What does all this have to do with our use of words? First, we should recognize that words evoke sometimes unpredictable reactions in others. We should try to anticipate the reactions of others to our words as much as we can. For example, if we are talking to an art major, we may cause confusion or even produce a hostile response if we use the psychology-major jargon we have picked up. If we anticipate this negative reaction, we'll leave the jargon in the psychology classroom.

11   Second, most words have both denotative and connotative meanings, and we should recognize that these meanings vary from person to person. People will react to words according to the meaning *they* give them. An effective communicator tries to recognize different reactions and to adapt to them. Remember as you communicate that meanings do *not* reside in the words themselves. *Meanings are in the minds of the people who use and hear the words. That is the essence of the transactional view of communication.*

—Weaver, *Understanding Interpersonal Communication*, pp. 230–33

VOCABULARY REVIEW

1. For each of the words listed below, use context; prefixes, roots, and suffixes; and/or a dictionary to write a brief definition or synonym of the word as it is used in the reading.

    a. nonverbal (para. 3) _____

    b. denotative (para. 4) _____

    c. connotative (para. 6) _____

    d. unambiguous (para. 9)_____

    e. jargon (para. 10) _____

    f. transactional (para. 11) _____

2. Underline new specialized terms introduced in the reading.

COMPREHENSION QUESTIONS

1. Explain the differences between denotative and connotative meanings.
2. Why do professions use words with agreed-upon denotative meanings?
3. According to this author, what are the causes of miscommunication?

THINKING CRITICALLY

1. Make a list of words with numerous connotations.
2. Give an example of a word whose connotative meaning changes with the speaker's experience.
3. International students often have difficulty understanding the connotations of English words. Why?
4. This reading focuses on miscommunication in speech. Do similar miscommunications occur in reading and writing? If so, do they stem from the same causes?
5. Do you think more or fewer misunderstandings occur in reading and writing than in speaking? Justify your answer.
6. Are there other causes of miscommunication not discussed in the reading? If so, what are they?

LEARNING/STUDY STRATEGY

Summarize the most important information in this reading.

4 | CRITICAL READING STRATEGIES

LEARNING OBJECTIVES

- ■ **To make inferences and understand implied meanings**
- ■ **To assess an author's ideas**
- ■ **To react to ideas presented**
- ■ **To synthesize and compare sources**

In college you will be reading many new kinds of material: research articles, essays, critiques, reports, and analyses. Your instructors expect you to be able to do much more than understand and remember the basic content. They often demand that you read critically—interpreting, evaluating, and reacting to assigned readings. To meet these expectations, you'll need to make solid inferences, annotate as you read, analyze and evaluate what you have read, and draw comparisons among several works.

INTERPRET IMPLIED MEANING

So far, we have been concerned primarily with the literal meanings of writing. You have been shown techniques to help you to understand what the author says and retain the literal, factual content. However, you often need to go beyond what authors *say* and to be concerned with what they *mean.* Look at the photograph on page 93, which appeared in a psychology textbook. What do you think is happening here? Where is it happening? What are the feelings of the participants?

To answer these questions, you had to use any information you could get from the photo and make guesses based on it. The facial expressions, body language, clothing, and other objects present in this photo implied or hinted at the emotions of those involved, the event that is occurring, and the locale of that event. This process of drawing conclusions, as you did, from these implied meanings is called "making an inference."

Make Inferences from the Given Facts

An inference is a reasoned guess about what you don't know made on the basis of what you do know. Inferences are common in our everyday lives.

When you enter an expressway and see a long, slow-moving line of traffic, you might predict that there is an accident or roadwork ahead. When you see a puddle of water under the kitchen sink, you can infer that you have a plumbing problem. The inferences you make may not always be correct, even though you based them on the available information. The water under the sink might have been the result of a spill. The traffic you encountered on the expressway might be normal for that time of day, but you didn't know it because you aren't normally on the road then. An inference is only the best guess you can make in a situation, given the information you have.

Inferences from Written Material

When you read the material associated with your college courses, you need to make inferences frequently. Writers do not always present their ideas directly. Instead, they often leave it to you to add up and think beyond the facts they present. You are expected to reason out, or infer, the meaning an author intended (but did not say) on the basis of what he or she did say. In a sense, the inferences you make act as bridges between what is said and what is not said but is meant.

There are several reasons why textbook authors and other writers require you to make inferences. Often, information is left out because it would make the message too long or would divert you from the central point. Sometimes an author assumes the readers know enough to fill in the omitted ideas. Other times, the writer believes that you will get more meaning or enjoyment from engaging in the thought process required in making an inference. Finally, some writers leave out pertinent information in order to make it easier to influence you to draw a desired conclusion, especially if you might have challenged the details had they been included. You can see, then, that making solid inferences is an important first step toward reading critically.

How to Make Inferences

Each inference you make depends on the situation, the facts provided, and your own knowledge and experience. Here are a few guidelines to help you see beyond the factual level and make solid inferences.

Know the Literal Meaning Be sure you have a firm grasp of the literal meaning. You must understand the stated ideas and facts before you can move to higher levels of thinking, which include inference making. You should recognize the topic, main idea, key details, and organizational pattern of each paragraph you have read.

Notice Details As you are reading, pay particular attention to details that are unusual or stand out. Often, such details will offer you clues to help you make inferences. Ask yourself

- What is unusual or striking about this piece of information?
- Why is it included here?

Read the following excerpt, which is taken from a business marketing textbook, and try to mark details that are unusual or striking.

MARKETING IN ACTION

Dressing Up the Basics in Idaho

In almost any grocery store across the United States, consumers can purchase ten pounds of Idaho-grown potatoes for less than $2.00. Despite this fact, Rolland Jones Potatoes, Incorporated, has been extremely successful selling a "baker's dozen" of Idaho potatoes for $18.95. The potatoes are wrapped in a decorative box that uses Easter grass.

The Baker's Dozen of Idaho potatoes is only one example of a growing phenomenon. Laura Hobbs, marketing specialist for the Idaho Department of Agriculture, reports that more than 200 Idaho farms produce specialty or value-added products. These goods typically consist of basic farm commodities that have been "dressed-up" with packaging. Consumers can choose from these products: microwave popcorn that comes on the cob and pops right off the cob, a bag of complete chili ingredients that makers claim won't cause embarrassing side-effects, and chocolate-covered "Couch Potato Chips."

Idaho farmers are supported by two groups, the Idaho Specialty Foods Association and Buy Idaho, whose goals are to help producers market and promote unique items. With the help of the groups, Idaho farmers are getting quite savvy. The marketers have discovered, for example, that packaging certain items together can increase their attractiveness. Hagerman's Rose Creek Winery found that sales of its wines soared when they were packaged in gift baskets with jars of Sun Valley brand mustard.

According to Hobbs, consumers attracted to the unique packaging provide a market for an endless variety of products, all of which are standard commodities transformed into new products through packaging. The value added through the unique packaging also provides opportunities to charge prices in ranges far above the prices of standard products—like $18.95 for 12 potatoes!

—Kinnear et al., *Principles of Marketing*, p. 301

Did you mark details such as the price of $18.95 for potatoes, corn that pops right off the cob, and chocolate-covered potato chips?

Add Up the Facts   Consider all of the facts taken together. To help you do this, ask yourself such questions as the following:

- What is the writer trying to suggest from this set of facts?
- What do all these facts and ideas seem to point toward or add up to?
- Why did the author include these facts and details?

Making an inference is somewhat like assembling a complicated jigsaw puzzle, in which you try to make all the pieces fit together to form a recognizable picture. Answering these questions will require you to add together all the individual pieces of information, which will enable you to arrive at an inference.

When you add up the facts in the article "Dressing Up the Basics in Idaho," you realize that the writer is suggesting that people are willing to pay much more than a product is worth if it is specially packaged.

Be Alert to Clues   Writers often provide you with numerous hints that can point you toward accurate inferences. An awareness of word choices, details included (and omitted), ideas emphasized, and direct commentary can help you determine a textbook author's attitude toward the topic at hand. In the foregoing excerpt, the authors offer clues that reveal their attitude toward increased prices for special packaging. Terms such as *dressed-up* and the exclamation point at the end of the last sentence suggest that the authors realize that the products mentioned are not worth their price.

In addition to these clues, writers of fiction also provide hints in their descriptions of characters and actions and through the conversations of their characters.

Consider the Author's Purpose   Also study the author's purpose for writing. If an author's purpose is to convince you to purchase a particular product, as in an advertisement, as you begin reading you already have a clear idea of the types of inferences the writer hopes you will make. For instance, here is a magazine ad for a stereo system.

> If you're in the market for true surround sound, a prematched system is a good way to get it. The components in our system are built for each other by our audio engineers. You can be assured of high performance and sound quality.

Verify Your Inference   Once you have made an inference, check that it is accurate. Look back at the stated facts to be sure that you have sufficient evidence to support the inference. Also, be certain that you have not overlooked other equally plausible or more plausible inferences that could be drawn from the same set of facts.

| **EXERCISE 4–1** | *Read each of the following statements. Place a checkmark in front of each of the sentences that follow that is a reasonable inference that can be made from the statement.* |

1. Political candidates must now include the Internet in their campaign plans.

    _____ a. Political candidates may host online chats to assess voter opinion.

    _____ b. Informal debates between candidates may be conducted online.

    _____ c. Internet campaigning will drastically increase overall campaign expenditures.

    _____ d. Television campaigning is likely to remain the same.

2. Half of the public education classrooms in the United States are now hooked up to the Internet.

    _____ a. Children are more computer literate than their parents.

    _____ b. Students now have access to current world news and happenings.

    _____ c. Books are no longer considered the sole source of information on a subject.

    _____ d. Teachers have become better teachers now that they have Internet access.

3. The Internet can make doctors more efficient through the use of new software and databases that make patient diagnosis more accurate.

_____ a. The cost of in-person medical care is likely to decrease.

_____ b. Doctors may be able to identify patients with serious illness sooner.

_____ c. Doctors are likely to pay less attention to their patients' descriptions of symptoms.

_____ d. Information on the symptoms and treatment of rare illnesses is more readily available.

EXERCISE 4–2

Read the following paragraph. A number of statements follow it; each statement is an inference. Label each inference as either

PA—Probably accurate—there is substantial evidence in the paragraph to support the statement.

IE—Insufficient evidence—there is little or no evidence in the paragraph to support the statement.

> While working for a wholesale firm, traveling to country stores by horse and buggy, Aaron Montgomery Ward conceived the idea of selling directly to country people by mail. He opened his business in 1872 with a one-page list of items that cost one dollar each. People could later order goods through a distributed catalog and the store would ship the merchandise cash on delivery (COD). The idea was slow to catch on because people were suspicious of a strange name. However, in 1875 Ward announced the startling policy of "satisfaction guaranteed or your money back." Contrasting with the former retailing principle of caveat emptor (Latin for "buyer beware"), this policy set off a boom in Ward's business.
>
> —Frings, *Fashion: From Concepts to Consumer,* p. 11

_____ 1. Aaron Ward had experience in sales before he began his own business.

_____ 2. Country people were targeted because they do not have access to stores in cities.

_____ 3. Ward's mistake was to give every item on the list the same price.

_____ 4. Other stores in operation at the time did not offer money back guarantees.

_____ 5. Other mail order business quickly followed Ward's success.

Read the following passages, and then answer the questions. The answers are not directly stated in the passage; you will have to make inferences in order to answer them.

Passage A "Is Laughter the Best Medicine?"

Lucy went to the hospital to visit Emma, a neighbor who had broken her hip. The first thing Lucy saw when the elevator door opened at the third floor was a clown, with an enormous orange nose, dancing down the hall, pushing a colorfully decorated cart. The clown stopped in front of Lucy, bowed, and then somersaulted to the nurses' station. A cluster of patients cheered. Most of them were in wheelchairs or on crutches. Upon asking for directions, Lucy learned that Emma was in the "humor room," where the film *Blazing Saddles* was about to start.

Since writer Norman Cousins's widely publicized recovery from a debilitating and usually incurable disease of the connective tissue, humor has gained new respectability in hospital wards around the country. Cousins, the long-time editor of the *Saturday Review*, with the cooperation of his physician, supplemented his regular medical therapy with a steady diet of Marx brothers movies and *Candid Camera* film clips. Although he never claimed that laughter alone effected his cure, Cousins is best remembered for his passionate support of the notion that, if negative emotions can cause distress, then humor and positive emotions can enhance the healing process (Cousins, 1979, 1989).

—Zimbardo and Gerrig, *Psychology and Life,* p. 501

1. What is the purpose of the story about Lucy and Emma?
2. What is a "humor room"?
3. What type of movie is *Blazing Saddles?*
4. Answer the question asked in the title.

Passage B "Oprah Winfrey—A Woman for All Seasons"

Oprah Winfrey—actress, talk-show host, and businesswoman—epitomizes the opportunities for America's women entrepreneurs. From welfare child to multimillionaire, Ms. Winfrey—resourceful, assertive, always self-assured, and yet unpretentious—has climbed the socioeconomic ladder by turning apparent failure into opportunities and then capitalizing on them.

With no playmates, Oprah entertained herself by "playacting" with objects such as corncob dolls, chickens, and cows. Her grandmother, a harsh disciplinarian, taught Oprah to read by age 2-$\frac{1}{2}$, and as a result of speaking at a rural church, her oratory talents began to emerge.

At age 6, Winfrey was sent to live with her mother and two half-brothers in a Milwaukee ghetto. While in Milwaukee, Winfrey, known as "the Little Speaker," was often invited to recite poetry at social gatherings, and her speaking skills continued to develop. At age 12, during a visit to her father in Nashville, she was paid $500 for a speech she gave to a church. It was then that she prophetically announced what she wanted to do for a living: "get paid to talk."

Her mother, working as a maid and drawing available welfare to make ends meet, left Oprah with little or no parental supervision and eventually sent her to live with her father in Nashville. There Oprah found the stability and discipline she so desperately needed. "My father saved my life," Winfrey reminisces. Her father—like her grandmother—a strict disciplinarian, obsessed with properly educating his daughter, forced her to memorize 20 new vocabulary words a week and turn in a weekly book report. His guidance and her hard work soon paid off, as she began to excel in school and other areas.

—Mosely et al., *Management: Leadership in Action,* p. 555

1. What is the author's attitude toward Winfrey?
2. What is the author's attitude toward strict discipline for children?
3. Is the author optimistic about business opportunities for women? How do you know?
4. What factors contributed to Winfrey's success?

ASSESS THE AUTHOR'S IDEAS

When you read actively and critically, you take very little for granted. You carefully evaluate what you are reading by asking the following questions.

Is the Author a Qualified Expert?

Not everything that appears in print is accurate and competently reported. Also, there are varying levels of expertise within a field. Consequently, you must assess whether the material you are reading is written by an expert in the field who can knowledgeably and accurately discuss the topic. For example, a sociologist who has studied the criminal justice system is not necessarily an expert on problems of immigrant populations. A scientist who specializes in genetics cannot write authoritatively about the greenhouse effect. In some materials, the author's credentials are footnoted or summarized at the end of the work. In journal articles, the author's college or university affiliation is often included. Authors also may establish their expertise or experience in the field within the material itself.

EXERCISE 4–4

Working together with a classmate, discuss and identify who (title or job description) would be considered a qualified expert on each of the following topics.

a. the side effects of a prescription drug
b. building code laws for an apartment building
c. controlling test anxiety

d. immigration laws
e. influence of television violence on children

What Are the Facts, and What Are the Opinions?

Facts are statements that can be tested as true or false—they are verifiable pieces of information. *Opinions* are statements that express feelings, attitudes, or beliefs that are neither true nor false. Here are a few examples of each.

Facts
Birth rates declined from 1960 to 1979.
The proportion of married women in the work force has steadily increased in the past 40 years.

Opinions
A drastic change is soon to occur in family structure.
Parenthood is the most rewarding human experience.

There is also what is known as informed opinion or testimony—the opinion of an expert or authority. Ralph Nader represents expert opinion on consumer rights, for example. Textbook authors, too, offer informed opinions, especially when they interpret events, summarize research, or evaluate trends. In the following paragraph, the author of a sociology textbook on marriage and the family interprets recent studies on sexuality.

> Recent studies of the history of sexuality in Western society have revealed that dramatic changes have taken place in beliefs and behavior. Among the most striking contrasts with our own times are the acceptance of bisexuality among men in ancient times and the disapproval of sexual pleasure in marriage for many centuries of the Christian era. The new studies also reveal that the sexual culture of any particular place and time is a complex mixture of expressive and repressive codes.
> —Skolnick, *The Intimate Environment,* p. 224

As you read a work, it is essential to distinguish between fact and opinion. Factual statements from reliable sources can be accepted and used in drawing conclusions, building arguments, and supporting ideas. Opinions, however, are one person's point of view that you are free to accept or reject.

**EXERCISE
4–5**

Read each of the following statements and identify whether it sounds like fact (F), opinion (O), or informed opinion (IO).

_____   1. Most Americans feel strongly about the gun control issue.

_____ 2. Mosquitoes can transmit a disease known as encephalitis.

_____ 3. By 2005, more than 500 million people will use the Internet.

_____ 4. Marine biologists use the Internet in researching and identifying plant and animal species.

_____ 5. Computer users often feel guilty and blame themselves when their computer fails or performs an illegal operation.

_____ 6. Borders is the biggest music retailer on the Internet.

_____ 7. James Gleick, a well-known author who writes about technology, notes that networked digital devices set the pace of change in the computer field.

_____ 8. An increasing number of private citizens have their own web sites.

_____ 9. Personal web sites give people a sense of power and importance.

_____ 10. Capron, an author of a textbook on computers, says Internet traffic jams can be expected, creating slow response times in sending and receiving messages.

What Is the Author's Purpose?

As you read an article, ask yourself, "Why did the author write this?" In academic reading, you will most often find that the author's purpose is either to inform (present information) or to persuade. For example, an essay on state aid to private colleges may present information on current levels of funding, it may argue for an increased or decreased level of funding, or it may address both topics. You need to know which is the author's primary purpose because that information will determine how you read and what critical questions you ask.

**EXERCISE
4–6**

Based on the title of each of the following essays, predict whether the author's purpose is to inform or persuade.

1. Changing Habits: How shopping online is different.
2. I got straight A's, but I wasn't happy.
3. Animals can't speak: We must speak for them!
4. Guns don't kill people; people kill people.
5. What the Bible says about the end of the world.

Does the Author Support His or Her Generalizations?

A generalization is a reasoned statement about an entire group based on known information about part of the group. It requires a leap from what is known to a conclusion about the unknown. The key to evaluating generalizations is to evaluate the type, quality, and amount of evidence given to support them. Each of the following statements is a generalization.

Most college students are undecided about future career goals.

Fast food lacks nutritional value.

Foreign cars outperform similar American models.

EXERCISE 4–7

Read each of the following statements and place a check mark before each generalization.

_____ 1. The Internet is changing America.

_____ 2. Influenza causes severe epidemics every two years.

_____ 3. Most drug cases start with busts of small, local dealers and move to a search of their suppliers.

_____ 4. Attending college is essential for economic success and advancement.

_____ 5. Colds are caused by viruses, not bacteria, not cold weather, and not improper diet.

EXERCISE 4–8

Review "Psychology And Sport," which appears on page 48 in Chapter 2. Working with a classmate, locate and underline generalizations the author makes. For each generalization, discuss whether the author provides adequate evidence to support the generalization.

What Assumptions Is the Author Making?

An assumption is an idea or principle the writer accepts as true and makes no effort to prove or substantiate. Usually, it is a beginning or premise on which he or she bases the remainder of the work. For example, an author may assume that television encourages violent behavior in children and proceed to argue for restrictions on TV watching. Or a writer may assume that abortion is morally wrong and suggest legal restrictions on how and when abortions are performed.

**EXERCISE
4–9**

Read each of the following statements and then place a checkmark before those choices that are assumptions made by the writer of the statement.

1. Cosmetics should not be tested on animals, since they may cause pain, injury, or even death.

   _____ a. Animals have the right to avoid pain and suffering.

   _____ b. Cosmetics should be tested on people.

   _____ c. Animals should be anesthetized before research is conducted.

2. Teachers aides lack advanced college degrees: therefore, they are unable to teach children effectively.

   _____ a. Teachers aides should obtain advanced degrees.

   _____ b. Advanced college degrees are needed in order to teach effectively.

   _____ c. Teachers who hold advanced degrees are not necessarily effective teachers.

3. Border states in the U.S. must take action to curb illegal immigration; otherwise, state funds will be quickly exhausted.

   _____ a. The writer opposes using state funds to help illegal immigrants.

   _____ b. Illegal immigrants must enter the U.S. legally to receive state aid.

   _____ c. State funding guidelines should be revised.

Is the Author Biased?

If an author is biased, he or she is partial to one point of view or one side of a controversial issue. The author's language and selection of facts provide clues about his or her bias.

In the following excerpt from a biology text, the author's choice of words (see underlining) and sarcastic comment in parentheses reveal his attitude toward seal hunters.

> Greenpeace is an organization dedicated to the preservation of the sea and its great mammals, notably whales, dolphins, and seals. Its ethic is <u>nonviolent</u> but its <u>aggressiveness</u> in protecting our oceans and the life in them is becoming legendary.
>
> Greenpeace volunteers routinely place their lives in <u>danger</u> in many ways, such as by riding along the backs of whales in inflatable zodiacs, keeping themselves between the animal and the harpoons of ships giving <u>chase</u>. They have pulled

alongside Dutch ships to stop the <u>dumping</u> of <u>dangerous toxins</u> into the sea. They have placed their zodiacs directly in the paths of ships <u>disrupting delicate</u> breeding grounds of the sea with soundings and have forced some to turn away or even abandon their efforts. They have confronted hostile sealers on northern ice floes to try to stop them from <u>bludgeoning</u> the baby seals in the birthing grounds, skinning them on the spot, and leaving the mother sniffing at the <u>glistening red corpse</u> of her baby as its skin is <u>stacked</u> aboard the ship on the way to warm the <u>backs of very fashionable people</u> who gather where the bartender knows their favorite drink. (The mother seal would be <u>proud</u> to know that her dead baby had nearly impressed some bartender.) They have petitioned the International Whaling Commission to establish rules and enact bans.

—Wallace, *Biology: The World of Life,* p. 754

EXERCISE 4–10

Read each of the following statements, and place a checkmark in front of each that reveals bias.

_____ 1. The feminist movement is no longer oppressed by men; it is oppressed by feminism itself.

_____ 2. Approximately 60% of men feel they are above average in their level of self-confidence.

_____ 3. Racist and sexist speech on the Internet should be prohibited.

_____ 4. There is a marked increase in volunteerism among college students.

_____ 5. Women's fashion magazines portray an ideal woman and create guilt and anxiety for those who cannot measure up to the ideal.

How Strong Are the Data and Evidence?

Many writers who express their opinions, state viewpoints, or make generalizations provide data or evidence to support their ideas. Your task as a critical reader is to weigh and evaluate the quality of this evidence. You must examine the evidence and assess its adequacy. You should be concerned with two factors: the type of evidence being presented and the relevance of that evidence. Various types of evidence include

- Personal experience or observation
- Statistical data
- Examples, descriptions of particular events, or illustrative situations
- Analogies (comparisons with similar situations)

- Historical documentation
- Experimental evidence

Each type of evidence must be weighed in relation to the statement it supports. Acceptable evidence should directly, clearly, and indisputably support the case or issue in question.

EXERCISE 4–11

For each of the following statements, discuss the type or types of evidence that you would need in order to support and evaluate the statement.

1. Individuals must accept primary responsibility for the health and safety of their babies.
2. Apologizing is often seen as a sign of weakness, especially among men.
3. There has been a steady increase in illegal immigration over the past 50 years.
4. More college women than college men agree that abortions should be legal.
5. Car advertisements sell fantasy experiences, not means of transportation.

EXERCISE 4–12

The following brief excerpt is taken from an article titled "Trash Troubles" that appeared in the periodical World and I, in November 1998. Using the guidelines for evaluating writing, answer the questions that follow.

TRASH TROUBLES

Our accumulating piles of solid waste threaten to ruin our environment, pointing to the urgent need for not only better disposal methods but also strategies to lower the rate of waste generation.

As our ship surges forward, we notice a mound jutting up ahead, directly in our path. Like an iceberg, a much larger mass is hidden beneath the surface. If we keep running the vessel at current speed, we may have a major problem on our hands.

No, this not the Titanic. The ship we're on is our consumer-goods-dependent lifestyle that creates as much as a ton of solid waste per person each year. And the peak ahead is but the tip of a massive "wasteberg" that is 95 percent hidden from view: For every ton of trash we generate, there is an underlying loss of another 19 tons of industrial, agricultural, mining, and transportation wastes, building up into a mound that threatens to shatter our future.

The wasteberg entails a formidable economic and environmental challenge. For most local governments, solid waste management ranks behind only schools and highways as the major budget item. Improperly managed solid waste eats up dollars while polluting water supplies, threatening neighborhoods, and squandering natural resources.

So how is this odyssey progressing? Are we about to capsize on the wasteberg and drown, or can we successfully circumnavigate the threat? Better yet, can we shrink the wasteberg?

Circumnavigating the Wasteberg

The simplest way to steer around the wasteberg is to try to isolate wastes from their surrounding environment. This has been the major approach worldwide—solid waste management has usually meant solid waste disposal. Around the world, many nations have chosen incineration as the preferred way to dispose of solid waste. This is particularly the case where landfill sites are scarce. Japan, for example, has around 2,800 municipal incinerators that reduce solid wastes to ashes. In the United States, though, incineration has fallen strongly out of favor. Despite significant improvements in the technology, concerns that the incineration process may release toxic pollutants such as dioxins have brought this once-popular technology to near-obsolescence.

Shrinking the Wasteberg

For every pound of trash that goes into the waste basket, another 19 are released elsewhere in the environment—in forms ranging from industrial byproducts to fertilizer runoff to wasted energy. Thus if we reduce our generation of solid waste, the "leverage effect" is enormous: Each ton of trash kept out of the dump means that 19 tons of waste, along with related environmental impacts and the dollar cost of producing it, are avoided.

There are three major approaches to narrowing the waste stream: reducing, redesigning, and recycling. All require vigorous participation by both producers and consumers.

Reducing. Producers reduce waste through offering products that are less wasteful. Consumers reduce waste by using less of the product and using materials longer.

Redesigning. Producers offer alternative products that have a lower environmental impact than traditional ones, while continuing to meet given needs.

Recycling. Producers make reusable products, utilizing waste materials in manufacturing these goods. Consumers reuse the products and collect the materials to recycle out of the waste stream and back to the producers.

—Purcell, "Trash Troubles" in *The World and I*, p. 190

1. The author, Arthur H. Purcell, is the founder and director of the Resource Policy Institute, the author of *The Waste Watchers*, and a commentator for America Public Radio's "Marketplace." Evaluate his authority to discuss this topic.

2. Is the article primarily fact, opinion, or expert opinion? Support your answer with examples.
3. What is the author's purpose?
4. Does the author make generalizations? If so, underline several examples. Are the generalizations supported by evidence?
5. What assumptions does the author make?
6. Is the author biased?
7. Evaluate the types and adequacy of the evidence the author provides.

EXERCISE 4–13

Working with another classmate as a team, review the reading "Factors Affecting Interpersonal Attraction," which appears on page 34 in Chapter 1, and answer questions 2 through 7 in Exercise 4–12.

REACT TO THE IDEAS PRESENTED

An important part of reading critically is to react to the author's ideas. You may agree, disagree, question, challenge, or seek further information, for example. To do so, begin by writing down your reactions while and after you read. Then, once you have finished, review your notes and evaluate the writer's ideas.

Annotate As You Read

If you were reading the classified ads in a newspaper in search of an apartment to rent, you probably would mark certain ads. Then, when you phoned for more information, you might make notes about each apartment. These notes would be useful when you decided which apartments were worth visiting.

Similarly, in other types of reading, making notes—*annotating*—is a useful strategy. Annotating is a means of keeping track of your impressions, ideas, reactions, and questions as you read. Reviewing your annotations will help you form a final impression of the work. If a writing assignment accompanies the reading, your annotations will serve as an excellent source of ideas for a paper. This reading strategy is discussed in more detail in Chapter 10.

There are no fixed rules about how or what to annotate. In general, try to mark or note any ideas about the work that come to mind as you read or reread. Underline or highlight within the work and use the margins to write your notes. Your annotations might include

- Questions
- Generalizations, assumptions, and other features listed above
- Key points
- Ideas with which you disagree
- Good or poor supporting data or examples
- Inconsistencies
- Key terms or definitions
- Contrasting points of view
- Key arguments
- Words with strong connotations
- Figures of speech (images that reveal the writer's feelings)

A sample annotation is shown in the following passage on the meaning of color. Read it carefully, noticing the types of markings and annotations that were made.

COLOR AND EMOTIONS

the issue or question

The research in color preference led to a spin-off area of research, that of color and emotional response or moods. Researchers asked whether a reliable mood-color association exists and <u>whether color could influence one's emotional state</u>.

would like reference to these studies

Well-controlled research studies have shown that a definite color-mood tone association exists, although the color-mood association differed widely among people participating in the study. In fact, the studies showed all colors to be associated with all moods in varying degrees of strength. Although certain colors are more strongly associated with a given mood or emotion, there was evidence to

does not state nature and strength of evidence

suggest a <u>one-to-one relationship between a given color and a given emotion</u>. What seemed to make the difference was how strongly a person associated a particular color with a particular mood or emotion.

What evidence? describe?

Colors have been stereotyped by the public when it comes to emotions. In spite of <u>physical evidence</u> to the contrary, most people continue to equate red tones with excitement and activity and blue tones with passivity and tranquillity in color-mood association research. This is a learned behavior. From the time we are very young we learn to associate red with fire engines, stop lights, and danger signals that cause us to form an alert or danger association with red. Further, the red, orange, and yellow tones in fire further cause association between those colors and heat and kinetic energy. We have seen how cultural biases that are a part of our language further support the red equals excitement myth. These subconscious messages clearly affect the response to red. Blue tones, being associated with cool streams, the sky, and the ocean, continue to be equated with calm and tranquillity. This, too, is a learned response with which we are subtly surrounded from early childhood. <u>In understanding color, it is important to differentiate between these culturally learned color associations and true biological responses.</u>

What are the biological ones ——

Research on the emotional aspects of color <u>has for the most part resulted in a gross oversimplification</u> of a very involved process. Unfortunately, this oversimplification has been promoted heavily in the popular press. The design community too has jumped on the bandwagon, often making sweeping statements about color that are totally unsupported by anything but myth or personal belief. For example, one book refers to blue as "communicating cool, comfort, protective, calming, although may be slightly depressing if other colors are dark; associated with bad taste." There is of course no basis for these statements except as the personal opinion of the author, but too often these <u>personal opinions</u> become accepted as fact.

How ——

Clothing design? interior design? building design? —which one?

Could be expert opinion, depending on qualifications of author ——

Colors do not contain any inherent emotional triggers. Rather, it is more likely that our changing moods and emotions caused by our own physiological and psychological makeup at the moment interact with color to create preferences and associations that we then link to the color-emotion response itself.

Summary

—Fehrman and Fehrman, *Color: The Secret Influence*, p. 83–84

Analyze and Evaluate Ideas

After you have read (and perhaps reread) the work and made annotations, the final step is to review your annotations and, thereby, to arrive at some conclusions and final impressions of the work. This is a creative as well as a logical process that involves looking for patterns and trends, noticing contrasts, thinking about the author's intentions, analyzing the effects of stylistic features, and determining the significance of the work. You might think of it as a process similar to evaluating a film after you have seen it or discussing a controversial television documentary. Your overall purpose is analysis: to arrive at an overall interpretation and evaluation of the work.

When analyzing a work, it may be helpful to write lists of words, issues, problems, and questions to discover patterns and evaluate the author's bias. Use the following questions to guide your analysis.

- What did the author intend to accomplish?
- How effectively did he or she accomplish this?
- What questions does the work raise and answer?
- What questions are ignored or left unanswered?
- What contributions to your course content and objectives does this work make?
- How does this work fit with your course textbook?
- How worthwhile is the material? What are its strengths and weaknesses?

**EXERCISE
4–14**

Preview, read, and annotate the following essay titled "The Barbarity of Meat." Assume it is one of several articles your health and nutrition instructor assigned for a class discussion on vegetarianism. Pose several guide questions to focus your reading. Annotate as you read. Then analyze and evaluate the reading using the questions listed on p. 111.

THE BARBARITY OF MEAT

The food industry downplays the connection between steak and cows

If, as some authors suggest, eating meat is indeed an important statement of human power, it might seem strange that we are apparently becoming progressively more uncomfortable with reminders of its animal origins. Consumer attitudes today are in a state of flux, not least for this reason. Whereas once it was sufficient simply to display whole animals and pieces of meat, the packing of the product is now a more delicate task. Most of us prefer not to think too directly about where our meat has come from, and unwelcome reminders can be distinctly off-putting. As one consumer put it, "I don't like it when you see . . . veins and things coming out of the meat . . . because it always reminds me of my own insides in a funny sort of a way. I suppose it's the idea of, like, blood flowing [that] makes you realize that this slab of meat was once a bit of functioning body, a bit like your own."

Meat marketing has responded accordingly, to assuage customers' sensitivity to the nature of the product. Nowadays, the consumer need never encounter animal flesh in its vulgar, undressed state. Instead it will come cooked and reshaped, in a sesame bun or an exotically flavored sauce, as a turkey roll or as chicken nuggets, in a crumb coating or a vacuum package, with not a hint of blood in sight. More and more butchers' windows sport fresh green vegetables, fragrant herbs, and perhaps a stir-fry mixture. A deliberate process of disguising the source of animal foods has gained momentum in the 20th century, reacting to our evident unease with the idea of eating dead animals: Said one butcher, "I deplore deliveries being carried into the front of my shop on the neck of a van driver—especially if they are not wrapped. . . . I can think of little more guaranteed to turn pedestrians off buying meat than the sight of pigs' heads flopping about as he struggles past them with the carcass."

The number of independent butchers' shops has declined considerably in recent years. Supermarkets have clearly derived particular competitive advantage from presenting meat in conspicuously hygienic conditions with all preparation completed out of sight. Often only the best cuts are displayed; bones, guts, and skin are nowhere to be seen. The hermetically sealed package is effectively dissociated from the animal to which its contents once belonged, a service that is clearly winning customers.

The names we give to the flesh of the main meat animals are another device whereby we reduce the unpleasant impact of having to acknowledge their identity. We do not eat cow, we eat beef; we do not eat pig, we eat pork; we do not eat deer, we eat venison. It is as if we cannot bear to utter the name of the beast whose death we have ordained.

To some, our willingness to consume meat as well as the many other assorted products of the animal industry, but apparent unwillingness to slaughter the beasts for ourselves or even to acknowledge our complicity in that process, is a matter for moral reproof. Said one critic, "I think the meat industry is very dishonest. The people are not allowed to be aware of what's going on. To them meat is wrapped up in cellophane in supermarkets; it's very divorced from the animal that it's coming from. . . . People don't go down on the factory farm to see what's really going on down there. I think if a lot of people did do that or [went] to the slaughterhouse to see how the meat is produced, then a lot of them would become vegetarians."

There is some evidence to support this belief. Many first-generation vegetarians and semivegetarians directly trace their abstinence to occasions when, for one reason or another, they were brought face to face with the connection between the meat on their plate and once-living animals. The particular incident related by any individual—be it the sight of carcasses being carried into a butcher's shop, or an encounter with vegetarian polemicism, or a visit to a slaughterhouse on daily business, or merely an unusually vivid flight of imagination—is of minor importance. What matters is that many people, when confronted with this ethical perplexity, seemingly prefer to forgo meat altogether rather than to condone the treatment of animals on their path from birth to plate. And equally important, perhaps, is how new this rebellion is, or rather how rapid its development has been in recent history.

—Fiddes, *Meat: A Natural Symbol,* p. 100–101

1. Does the author establish his authority on the subject of vegetarianism?
2. Is the article primarily fact or opinion? Justify your answer.
3. What is the author's purpose? How effectively does he accomplish it?
4. What generalizations does the author make?
5. What assumptions about people and human behavior does the author make?
6. Summarize the evidence the author offers in support of his main points.
7. Does the author anticipate and address objections to his argument? If so, what are the objections and how does he refute them?
8. What questions might be raised during a class discussion of this essay?

EXERCISE
4–15

Use the reading "An Open Letter to the Nation's Drug Czar" at the end of this chapter to complete this exercise. Work with a classmate to answer the following questions.

1. Identify the author's thesis or main point.
2. Is the authority of the author evident? Why?
3. Is the article primarily fact or opinion?
4. Does the author make any assumptions? What are they?
5. How does the author support his main points?

SYNTHESIZE AND COMPARE SOURCES

The first step in making a comparison of several works or different sections within the same work is to read, annotate, and analyze each text. Once you have studied each carefully, you are ready to discover the similarities and differences among them. Compare the works on the basis of such factors as

- Overall theme or position
- Types and quality of supporting evidence
- Degree of bias shown in each work
- Authority of each author
- Author's purpose
- Points of agreement and disagreement
- How each work approached the subject
- Effectiveness of each work in persuading or educating you
- Types of arguments used
- Style
- Intended audience

Make notes as you study each work, both in the margins of the works themselves and on separate pieces of paper. Then study your annotations and notes, looking for similarities and differences. Try to put into your own words what you discover. When you write about the two works, rather than just thinking about them, it forces you to clarify your ideas.

Ask questions such as these.

- On what do the sources agree?
- On what do the sources disagree?
- How do they differ?
- Are the viewpoints toward the subject similar or different?
- Does each source provide supporting evidence for major points?

To initiate a discussion on the issue of computer privacy, a business professor distributed two excerpts from articles on the topic. In preparation for the discussion, the instructor asked the class to read both accounts and be prepared to discuss them in class. One student read and annotated each selection as shown below.

Account 1

The advent of e-commerce is, however inadvertently, endangering privacy. Companies have long boasted about the efficiency, convenience and personalized service that distinguish commerce online. But that promise hinges on the merchants' intimate knowledge of their customers' tastes and behavior. For starters, *types of information collected* — they know who their customers are, where they live and their credit-card numbers. And the more someone buys, the more the seller finds out about him: likes bourbon and trash novels; sends someone not his wife flowers every Wednesday.

Any web-site operator can reconstruct a visitor's every move on his site: what pages he viewed, what information he entered and the Internet service he uses. Privacy advocates warn that most online companies won't fight subpoenas seeking *does not tell us what to do about the problem* — access to those logs. Security guru Richard Smith, founder of Phar Lap Software, likens Web sites to VCRs "constantly recording when you come in, who you talked to and maybe what you talked about."

—Sandberg, "Losing Your Good Name Online," *Newsweek,* September 20, 1999, p. 57

Account 2

exchange of personal information — We live in an information age, and data is one of the currencies of our time. Businesses and government agencies spend billions of dollars every year to collect and exchange information about you and me. More than 15,000 specialized mar-*marketing databases* — keting databases contain 2 billion consumer names, along with a surprising amount of personal information. The typical American consumer is on 25 marketing lists. *organization* — Many of these lists are organized by characteristics like age, income, religion, political affiliation, and even sexual preference—and they're bought and sold every day.

Marketing databases are only the tip of the iceberg. Credit and banking infor-*businesses and agencies that collect information* — mation, tax records, health data, insurance records, political contributions, voter registration, credit card purchases, warranty registrations, magazine and newsletter subscriptions, phone calls, passport registration, airline reservations, automobile registrations, arrests, Internet explorations—they're all recorded in computers, and we have little or no control over what happens to most of these records once they're collected.

—Beekman, *Computer Confleunce: Exploring Tomorrow's Technology,* p. 204

Then the student made notes and wrote the following paragraph.

Paragraph

Sandberg discusses the types of information that can be collected from e-commerce and focuses on personal data collected by online merchants and from Web sites. Beekman states that information that is collected becomes part of a database and explains that other businesses and agencies collect information, as well. Both emphasize that privacy may be endangered.

Assume you are taking a business retailing course. Your instructor has asked you to read each of the following brief descriptions of how Jeff Bezos, founder of Amazon.com, an online bookstore, founded his business. Using information from both articles, write a paragraph summarizing how Bezos began his company.

Statement 1

A leading contender [in online retailing] is the 35-year old son of a Cuban immigrant, Jeffrey P. Bezos, founder and CEO of Amazon.com Inc.—the upstart Internet company that boasts 4.5 million customers in 160 countries. Bezos stands alone against his prime adversary, the very well financed Barnes & Noble Corporation, a behemoth on the brutish playing fields of bookselling. The media have often made comparisons to David and Goliath. But in this showdown, it's no longer easy to tell who is David and who is Goliath.

Bezos concocted the right formula for on-line selling when he chose books as the product to move. In less than four years, he has risen from Wall Street wunderkind to become one of cyberdom's kings of the world. In 1994, Bezos quit his job as a hedge fund manager to stake a claim on the wild frontier of Internet retailing, or "e-tailing." He moved to Seattle and started his business in a rented garage with loans from investment bankers, family, friends, and venture capitalists.

Since its debut on the World Wide Web in July 1995, Amazon.com has become the model to watch—and to envy. Soon after the site appeared, chat group participants praised its availability of product and user-friendly style. Paradoxically, in the nonhuman realm of cyberspace, it is the very pedestrian experience of word of mouth that Amazon executives regard as a major reason for its success.

What Amazon also did early on was spend millions of dollars on advertising in such publications as *The New York Times Review of Books*. It also invested in banner links that touted the site in the "hot corner" of browsers. The huge amounts of money spent—$6.1 million in 1996—stirred excitement in the business world and evoked highly positive press. The advertising blitz helped the company reap $16 million in revenue, much of which went into refining the site.

—Martinez, "Lord of the Jungle," *Hispanic Magazine*, January/February 1999

Statement 2

Bezos's idea was simple: as the Internet extended its reach, an efficient retailer could do away with the bricks and mortar (hereafter referred to as B&M) of physical stores and serve customers better because the Net allows sellers direct contact with buyers. All at a potential profit margin the B&M guys can't match. If a chain of 1,000 stores wants to double sales, Bezos says, it has to open *another* thousand stores, with all the land and manpower costs that that entails. But once an online operation gets past the fixed cost of its Web site and distribution channel, it can handle bigger sales with very few extra expenses. "You can offer both the lowest prices and the highest service level," he says, "which is impossible in the physical-world environment."

These concepts came together in 1994 after the Florida-born Bezos left a job as a financial strategist and flew to Ft. Worth, Texas, to pick up his father's 1988 Blazer. As his wife, MacKenzie, drove, Bezos hammered out his business plan on a laptop. The destination was Seattle, which offered an ideal employment pool of overeducated slackers.

Bezos's business plan originally met with skepticism, and even its author had doubts. "The big problem was not whether the technology would work," he says, "but whether customers would want to shop this way." He spent a year of planning before he opened the site, figuring out what would push book buyers into the digital age. His prime goals: providng a wide selection, good prices and an effortless experience.

Fortunately, Internet users then were early-adopter types, ready to take the virtual bungee jump into the new world of e-commerce. And as the Internet population grew, and increasingly resembled the country's overall demographic, word-of-mouth spread. In the last two years Amazon's customer list has grown from 2 million to 11 million.

—Levy, "Wired for the Bottom Line," *Newsweek*, September 20, 1999, p. 44

Managing Your Study Time

As college students, many of you struggle to divide your time among classes, study, job responsibilities, and friends and family. Effective planning and time management are essential for you to maintain a workable balance. Here are a few suggestions for managing your study time effectively.

1. *Develop a weekly study plan.* Allocate time for reading, reviewing, doing homework, and studying for exams. Select several specific times each week for working on each of your courses.

2. *As a rule of thumb, reserve two study hours for each hour you spend in class.*

3. *Use peak periods of concentration.* Everyone has high and low periods of concentration and attention. First, determine when these occur for you; then reserve peak times for intensive study and use less efficient times for more routine tasks such as recopying

an assignment or collecting information in the library.

4. *Study difficult subjects first.* While it is tempting to get easy tasks and short little assignments out of the way first, do not give in to this approach. When you start studying, your mind is fresh and alert and you are at your peak of concentration. This is the time you are best equipped to handle difficult subjects.

5. *Schedule study for a particular course close to the time when you attend class.* Plan to study the evening before the class meets and soon after the class meeting. For example, if a class meets on Tuesday morning, plan to study Monday evening and Tuesday afternoon or evening. By studying close to class time, you will find it easier to relate class lectures and discussions to what you are reading and studying, to see connections, and to reinforce your learning.

(continued)

6. *Include short breaks in your study time.* Take a break before you begin studying each new subject. Your mind needs time to refocus so that you can switch from one set of facts, problems, and issues to another. You should also take short breaks when you are working on just one assignment for a long period of time. A 10-minute break after 50 to 60 minutes of study is reasonable.

SUMMARY

Critical reading involves interpreting, evaluating, and reacting to ideas.

An inference is a reasoned guess about what you do not know on the basis of what you do know. To make inferences as you read,

- know the literal meaning
- notice details
- add up the facts
- be alert for clues
- verify your inference

To assess an author's ideas, ask the following questions.

- Is the author a qualified expert?
- What are the facts and what are the opinions?
- What is the author's purpose?
- Does the author support his or her generalizations?
- What assumptions is the author making?
- Is the author biased?
- How strong are the data and evidence?

To react to an author's ideas, annotate during and after reading, and analyze the ideas using the following questions.

- What did the author intend to accomplish?
- How effectively did he or she accomplish this?
- What questions does the work raise and answer?
- What questions are ignored or left unanswered?
- What contributions to your course content and objectives does this work make?
- How does this work fit with your course textbook?
- How worthwhile is the material? What are its strengths and weaknesses?

To compare and synthesize several works, focus on similarities and differences among them.

Sociology/Contemporary Issues

PREREADING QUESTIONS

1. Can you predict two arguments the author might use to support his view that drugs should not be legalized?
2. What kinds of questions might the author reasonably pose regarding drug legalization?
3. Do you believe drugs should be legalized?

Why Drug Legalization Should Be Opposed

Representative Charles B. Rangel

1　In my view, the very idea of legalizing drugs in this country is counterproductive. Many well-meaning drug legalization advocates disagree with me, but their arguments are not convincing. The questions that I asked them twenty years ago remain unanswered. Would all drugs be legalized? If not, why? Would consumers be allowed to purchase an unlimited supply? Are we prepared to pay the medical costs for illnesses that are spawned by excessive drug use? Who would be allowed to sell drugs? Would an illegal market still exist? Would surgeons, bus drivers, teachers, military personnel, engineers, and airline pilots be allowed to use drugs?

2　Drug legalization threatens to undermine our society. The argument about the economic costs associated with the drug war is a selfish argument that coincides with the short-sighted planning that we have been using with other social policies. With any legalization of drugs, related problems would not go away; they would only intensify. If we legalize, we will be paying much more than the $30 billion per year we now spend on direct health care costs associated with illegal drug use.

3　Drug legalization is not as simple as opening a chain of friendly neighborhood "drug" stores. While I agree that some drugs might be beneficial for medicinal purposes, this value should not be exploited to suggest that drugs should be legalized. Great Britain's experience with prescription heroin should provide a warning. Until 1968, British doctors were freely allowed to prescribe drugs to addicts for medicinal purposes. Due to the lack of rigorous controls, some serious problems became associated with this policy. Doctors supplied drugs to non-addicts, and addicts supplied legally obtained drugs to the general population resulting in an increased rate of addiction. There is plenty of evidence to show that drug legalization has not worked in other countries that have tried it. The United States cannot afford such experiments when the data shows that drug legalization policies are failing in other countries.

4   In minority communities, legalization of drugs would be a nightmare. It would be a clear signal that America has no interest in removing the root causes of drug abuse: a sense of hopelessness that stems from poverty, unemployment, inadequate training, and blight. Legalization of drugs would officially sanction the total annihilation of communities already at risk. Instead of advocating drug legalization, we should focus our efforts on rebuilding schools, strengthening our teachers, improving housing, and providing job skills to young people.

5   The issue should not be whether or not drugs should be legalized. Rather, we need to focus on changing the way the war on drugs is being fought. The real problems are our emphasis on incarceration, including mandatory minimum sentences, the unfair application of drug laws, the disparity in sentencing between crack cocaine and powder cocaine, and the failure to concentrate on the root causes of drug abuse. These shortcomings in our drug policy should not become a license for legalization. Many critics of the drug war have the knowledge and skills to improve our national drug control policy. Instead of supporting the Drug Czar, they use their resources to blast all efforts to eradicate drugs in this country. It is a shame that many educated and prominent people suggest that the only dangerous thing about drugs is that they are illegal.

6   If we are truly honest, we must confess that we have never fought the war on drugs as we have fought other adversaries. The promotion of drug legalization further complicates the issue. We must continue our efforts to stop the flow of illegal drugs into our country. Most importantly, we need to remove the root causes of drug abuse and increase our focus in the areas of prevention and treatment through education. Rather than holding up the white flag and allowing drugs to take over our country, we must continue to focus on drug demand as well as supply if we are to remain a free and productive society.

—Rangel, *Criminal Justice Ethics*, Vol. 17, No. 2., Summer/Fall 1998, p. 2

VOCABULARY REVIEW

1. For each of the words listed below, use context; prefixes, roots, and suffixes; and/or a dictionary to write a brief definition or synonym of the word as it is used in the reading.

    a. advocates (para. 1) _____

   b. spawned (para. 1) _____

   c. undermine (para. 2) _____

   d. exploited (para. 3)_____

   e. blight (para. 4) _____

   f. sanction (para. 4) _____

   g. annihilation (para. 4)_____

   h. incarceration (para. 5) _____

   i. disparity (para. 5) _____

   j. eradicate (para. 5) _____

2. Underline new specialized terms introduced in the reading.

COMPREHENSION QUESTIONS

1. Identify three reasons why the author is opposed to legalizing drugs.
2. What effect does the author believe drug legalization would have?
3. What cue words in the first paragraph suggest the author may have a bias?
4. Does the author propose an alternate solution for the drug problem? If so, what is that solution?
5. What does the author imply when he states that "[drug] legalization is not as simple as opening a chain of friendly neighborhood 'drug' stores?"
6. According to the author, why did legalizing heroin in Great Britain by making it a prescription drug fail?

THINKING CRITICALLY

1. What is the author's purpose in writing this essay?
2. What do you believe is the strongest argument the author uses to support his position? Why is this a strong argument?
3. The author states that there is "plenty of evidence to show that drug legalization has not worked in other countries . . ." Other than with information about Great Britain, does the author support this statement? How does this weaken or strengthen the author's argument?
4. The author believes that we will be paying much more money in health care costs if we legalize drugs. Do you agree or disagree? Why?

5. The author states that legalizing drugs "will undermine our society." Does he support this with generalizations or specific facts? Explain.

6. In general, do you think the author is essentially biased or essentially objective in presenting his arguments? On what do you base your assessment?

LEARNING/STUDY STRATEGY

Annotate the reading by highlighting why the author is opposed to legalizing drugs. Then record your ideas and reactions to these arguments.

Sociology/Contemporary Issues

PREREADING QUESTIONS

1. Has the current drug policy failed? Why do you think so?
2. Can you speculate on why the author believes it has failed?
3. Can you predict what the author will suggest the Office of Drug Policy do instead?

An Open Letter to the Nation's Drug Czar

Judge James P. Gray

General Barry McCaffrey
Director, Office of Drug Policy
The White House

Dear Gen. McCaffrey:

1   Our great country is reeling from wounds which we have been inflicting upon ourselves because of our current failed drug policy. It is clear that we are not in better shape today than we were five years ago regarding drug use and abuse and all of the crime and misery which accompany them, and, unless we change our approach, we can have no legitimate expectation that we will be in better shape next year than we are today. However, we will not pursue change until we realize, as a country, that it is all right to talk about this issue—and that just because we talk about the possibility of changing our drug policy does not mean that we condone drug use or abuse.

2   Change for the better starts with a leader who has a proven record of honesty, dedication, experience, and results—one who will be able to discuss realities without effectively being labeled as "soft" on crime or criminals. Our country desperately needs a person in authority who will not be afraid to take a fresh and objective look at our most basic assumptions and recommend changes based upon the evidence. Our country needs you.

3   You are known to be an intelligent, non-political, dedicated public servant who is in that position of authority and respect. If you would speak about our country's futile efforts to eradicate the growing of these dangerous drugs in, and the shipping of them from, various foreign countries, people in and out of our government will listen.

4   If you would quote the Rand Corporation study of June, 1994, which concluded that drug treatment is seven times more effective than drug prosecution

even for heavy drug users and 11 times more effective than interdiction at our country's borders, people will begin to realize why we are going broke trying to incarcerate our way out of this pervasive and multi-faceted problem.

5   If you would acknowledge that no one in law enforcement will even tell us with a straight face that we seize more than 10 percent of the illegal drugs in our society and that the more candid estimate is that we seize only about five percent, our people will begin to understand that each seizure of a ton of cocaine in not a victory, but is instead merely a symptom of the depth of the problem.

6   Our citizens and taxpayers will then realize that for every ton of cocaine we seize, we easily fail to seize between nine and 19 tons. In the War on Drugs, victory is now literally being viewed as slowing down the pace of defeat.

7   Our present policy has made cocaine the most lucrative crop in the history of mankind. It has made marijuana the most lucrative crop in my home state of California, easily outdistancing the second leading crop, which is corn.

8   Our present policy is directly responsible for the material and demonstrable reduction of our cherished liberties under the Bill of Rights.

9   Our present policy is directly funneling tens of billions of dollars per year into organized crime, with all of its accompanying violence and corruption, both in our country and around the world.

10   Our present policy is directly causing our children in the inner cities and virtually everywhere else to have drug dealers as their role models, instead of people like you who have gotten their education and who have worked hard to be successful.

11   Our present policy has directly spawned a cycle of hostility by the incarceration of vastly disproportionate numbers of our minority groups.

12   And our present policy is directly responsible for medical doctors being unable to prescribe appropriate medications for their patients who are either in pain or are suffering from a number of devastating diseases. We all understand the necessity of holding people accountable for their actions. However, our citizens recognize that what we are doing in the critical area of drug policy is not working. They are frustrated because their ostensible leaders are afraid to discuss the subject openly.

13   As a result, thousands of Americans such as Dr. Milton Friedman, former Secretary of State George Shultz, Mayor Kurt Schmoke of Baltimore, and former San Jose Chief of Police Joseph McNamara have signed a resolution calling for the investigation of change by a neutral commission. This resolution actually was passed by Congress and signed into law by President Clinton as a part of the recent crime bill; however, it has been widely ignored since that time. The signatories include a formidable list of judges; civic, business, and religious leaders; probation officers and prison officials; medical doctors; teachers; and

counselors. There is wide support for the investigation of change—our present policy simply will not stand scrutiny. However, our country needs a credible person in government like you to step forward and legitimize the discussion.

14   We do not ask you to support any particular method or approach for addressing the drug problem. We simply ask you to agree that there are fundamental problems with our current policy and that both our government and our citizens need better to understand the history and social forces which drive this problem, and our options for the future. We need to investigate the possibility of change. Education and the honest exchange of information are the only ways we will begin to reduce the continuing harm wrought by these dangerous drugs in our country. Accordingly, we ask you publicly to join us in a non-partisan and non-political search for the truth. If you would do this, you simply could not provide our country and all of its people with a greater or more lasting service.

Sincerely,
Judge James P. Gray*
*Judge Gray is a judge in the Superior Court of California in Orange County.

—Gray, In *The Orange County Register*, August 12, 1996

VOCABULARY REVIEW

1. For each of the words listed below, use context; prefixes, roots, and suffixes; and/or a dictionary to write a brief definition or synonym of the word as it is used in the reading.

    a. condone (para. 1) _____

    b. interdiction (para. 4) _____

    c. pervasive (para. 4) _____

    d. demonstrable (para. 7) _____

    e. disproportionate (para. 7) _____

    f. ostensible (para. 12) _____

    g. signatories (para. 13) _____

    h. scrutiny (para. 13) _____

    i. wrought (para. 14) _____

    j. non-partisan (para. 14) _____

2. Underline new specialized terms introduced in the reading.

COMPREHENSION QUESTIONS

1. Is the author in favor of legalizing drugs as a solution to the problem? How can you tell?
2. What were the implications of the Rand Corporation study of June 1994?
3. What is the author's purpose in telling General McCaffrey that he is "known to be an intelligent, non-political, dedicated public servant?"
4. What is it that the author really wants General McCaffrey to do? What in the reading leads you to believe this?
5. What does the author believe will cause the government to listen to McCaffrey? (See paragraph 3.)

THINKING CRITICALLY

1. At the end of the first paragraph, the author makes it clear that he does not necessarily "condone drug use." What evidence in the selection indicates that he does or does not condone drug use?
2. What is the author implying when he says that we are trying to "incarcerate our way out of this pervasive and multi-faceted problem?"
3. Why is seizing 5–10% of the illegal drugs in this country not perceived as a victory by the author?
4. What is the first indication the reader has that the author believes Americans' civil rights have been violated?
5. The author states that the present drug policy "has made cocaine the most lucrative crop in the history of mankind." Is this a statement of fact or opinion? How can you tell?
6. The author blames the current drug policy for the country's drug problem. How does the author support this statement?

LEARNING/STUDY STRATEGY

Annotate the reading by listing the author's beliefs about what he wants the office of Drug Policy to do to try to solve the current drug problem. Then record your reactions to these ideas.

THINKING ABOUT THE PAIRED READINGS

INTEGRATING IDEAS

1. How do the authors' purposes differ in these two readings?
2. Which reading is more objective? Why? (What about this reading makes it more objective?)

3. In which selection does the author better support his ideas? Give an example of this.
4. Do you think both sources are equally credible? Why or why not?
5. Apart from the fact that one reading is written in letter form, what is the major difference in style between these two readings? How does this difference affect the reader in assessing which reading is more persuasive?
6. Is there a common overall theme in each of the two readings? If so, what is that theme and who expresses it more clearly?

GENERATING NEW IDEAS

1. Using one quote from each source, write a 1–2 page paper stating whether you believe drugs should be legalized.
2. Make a list of the strengths and weaknesses of each selection.

5 | READING AND EVALUATING ARGUMENTS

LEARNING OBJECTIVES
- **To recognize the elements of an argument**
- **To recognize types of arguments**
- **To evaluate arguments**
- **To recognize errors in logical reasoning**

An argument between people can be an angry exchange of ideas and feelings. Family members might argue over household chores or use of the family car. Workers may argue over policies and procedures on the job. To be effective, however, an argument should be logical and should present well-thought-out ideas. It may involve emotion, but a sound argument is never simply a sudden, unplanned release of emotions and feelings.

An argument, then, always presents logical reasons and evidence to support a viewpoint. In a government course, you might read arguments for or against free speech; in a literature class, you may read a piece of literary criticism that argues for or against the value of a particular poem, debates its significance, or rejects a particular interpretation.

Here is a brief argument. As you read, notice that the argument offers reasons to support the viewpoint that college student activity fees should not be used to support political student organizations.

FEES FUND FORUM FOR IDEAS

The University of Wisconsin case before the Supreme Court today presents the crucial question of whether the First Amendment rights of students are offended by a policy under which mandatory student activities fees are used in part by a college or university to support organizations that engage in political speech. The same question might have been raised in regard to student tuition payments, since tuition revenues are used to support a broad range of college programs, not just the particular academic program in which the student happens to be enrolled.

The First Amendment is not offended if student fees are used on a neutral basis to support a broad array of student organizations. Such funding does not compel speech or association connected with any particular viewpoint or activity. Instead, it creates an essential forum for the free exchange of ideas and perspectives.

The very idea of a university is to create a marketplace of ideas. The aim is to expose students to a broad range of viewpoints, including the political and ideological.

This happens, not just in student activities, but also in classrooms—in courses of history, literature, political science, economics, sociology, philosophy and virtually every discipline.

It happens in auditoriums—when guest lecturers speak on ethics, contemporary problems, civil rights and the like.

And it happens in extracurricular activities—in connection with student government, student newspapers and student organizations as in the case in question.

It is inevitable that some members of the campus community will encounter speech and ideas they find unfamiliar, even abhorrent. Learning to assess and respond to new and different ideas is an important part of the education process.

Universities have a vital interest in the protections offered by the First Amendment. Educational institutions dependent on the courts or others to approve or sanction ideas and activities are no longer free. Students and faculty will suffer, but it is a free society that loses.

—Ikenberry, "Today's Debate: Politics and Student Fees," *USA Today*, November 9, 1999

PARTS OF AN ARGUMENT

An argument has three essential parts. First, an argument must address an **issue**—a problem or controversy about which people disagree. Abortion, gun control, animal rights, capital punishment, drug legalization are all examples of issues. Second, an argument must take a position on an issue. This position is called a **claim.** An argument may claim that capital punishment should be outlawed or that medical use of marijuana should be legalized. Finally, an argument offers **support** for the claim. Support consists of reasons and evidence that the claim is reasonable and should be accepted. An argument may also include a fourth part—a **refutation.** A refutation considers opposing viewpoints and may attempt to disprove or discredit them.

In the argument above, the issue is the use of college student fees to support political student organizations. Notice that the first sentence of the argument clearly identifies the issue. Ikenberry's claim is that such student fees are not a violation of First Amendment rights. He states this claim in the second paragraph. The remainder of the argument is devoted to reasons in support of the claim. The primary reason Ikenberry offers in favor of free speech is that it creates a marketplace of ideas that is central to a university. Ikenberry recognizes the opposing viewpoint in paragraph 7, noting that some speech and ideas expressed may be abhorrent. He refutes this objection by arguing that students need to learn how to assess and respond to ideas different from their own.

Types of Claims

The claim is the position or stand the writer takes on the issue. You might think of it as his or her viewpoint. Here are a few sample claims on the issue of animal rights.

> Animals should have none of the rights that humans do.

> Animals have limited rights: freedom from pain and suffering.

> Animals should be afforded the same rights as humans.

There are three common types of claims. A **claim of fact** is a statement that can be proven or verified by observation or research, as in the following example.

> Within ten years, destruction of rain forests will cause hundreds of plant and animal species to become extinct.

A **claim of value** states that one thing or idea is better or more desirable than another. Issues of right versus wrong or acceptable versus unacceptable lead to claims of value. The following claim of value asserts that mandatory community service is appropriate.

> Requiring community service in high school will produce more community-aware graduates.

A **claim of policy** suggests what should or ought to be done to solve a problem. Ikenberry in "Fees Fund Forum for Ideas" makes a claim of policy; he feels students' fees should be allowed to support political groups. Here is another example.

> To reduce school violence, more gun and metal detectors should be installed in public schools.

EXERCISE 5–1

Identify whether each of the following is a claim of fact (F), claim of value (V), or claim of policy (P), and label each.

_____ 1. Mandatory jail sentences should be imposed for drivers convicted of more than one drunk driving violation.

_____ 2. Student government elections were largely ignored by the student body due to student satisfaction with current policies and leadership.

_____ 3. Marijuana use and abuse continues to escalate in American society.

_____ 4. A mandatory dress code should be implemented in public schools.

_____ 5. Killing deer and other large animals for sport is wrong.

EXERCISE 5–2

For two of the following issues, write two claims about the issue. For each issue, try to write two different types of claims.

1. Same sex marriages
2. Violence in schools
3. Privacy on the Internet
4. Drug testing in the workplace

Types of Support

Three common types of support are reasons, evidence, and emotional appeals. A **reason** is a general statement that supports a claim. It explains why the writer's viewpoint is reasonable and should be accepted. In "Fees Fund Forum for Ideas," Ikenberry's primary reason for arguing that student fees be allowed to support political organizations is that such free exchange of ideas is essential to the university.

Evidence consists of facts, statistics, experiences, comparisons, and examples that demonstrate why the claim is valid. Ikenberry in "Fees Fund Forum for Ideas" offers facts that demonstrate that a marketplace of ideas already occurs elsewhere throughout the university, in classrooms, auditoriums, and in student newspapers. He also makes a comparison. He compares the issue of fees to that of student tuition payments.

Emotional appeals are ideas that are targeted toward needs or values that readers are likely to care about. Needs include physiological needs (food, drink, shelter) and psychological needs (sense of belonging, sense of accomplishment, sense of self-worth, sense of competency). An argument favoring gun control, for example, may appeal to a reader's need for safety, while an argument favoring restrictions on sharing personal or financial information may appeal to a reader's need for privacy and financial security.

Ikenberry in "Fees Fund Forum for Ideas" appeals to a reader's sense of freedom—to be able to discuss and evaluate ideas openly.

EXERCISE 5–3

For each of the following brief arguments, identify the type(s) of evidence used to support it.

1. Many students have part-time jobs that require them to work late afternoons and evenings during the week. These students are unable to use the library during the week. Therefore, library hours should be extended to weekends.
2. Because parents have the right to determine their children's sexual attitudes, sex education should take place in the home, not at school.
3. No one should be forced to inhale unpleasant or harmful substances. That's why the ban on cigarette smoking in public places was put into effect in our state. Why shouldn't there be a law to prevent people from wearing strong colognes or perfumes, especially in restaurants since the sense of smell is important to taste?

INDUCTIVE AND DEDUCTIVE ARGUMENTS

Two types of arguments—inductive and deductive—are common. An **inductive argument** reaches a general conclusion from observed specifics. For example, by observing the performance of a large number of athletes, you could conclude that athletes possess physical stamina. A **deductive argument,** on the other hand, begins with a general statement, known as a major premise and moves toward a more specific statement,

Figure 5–1 Inductive and Deductive Arguments

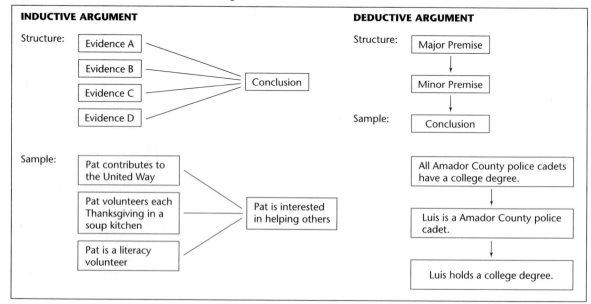

known as the minor premise. For example, from the major premise that "Athletes possess physical stamina," you can reason that because Anthony is an athlete (the minor premise), he must possess physical stamina.

Both types of arguments begin with statements that are assumed to be correct. Basically, both follow a general pattern of "If that is so, then this is so . . ." At times, an argument may be more complex, involving several steps—"If that is so, and this happens, then this should be done." You can visualize each type of argument as shown in Figure 5–1.

EXERCISE 5–4

For each of the following inductive arguments, supply the missing pieces.

1. Evidence: Prof. Hong wear jeans and flannel shirts to class.
   Evidence: Prof. Hutchinson wears kakhi pants and running shoes when he lectures.

   Evidence: _____

   Conclusion: Professors on this campus dress casually for class.

2. Evidence: Many people walk down the street talking on their cellular phones.
   Evidence: Most families own at least two cellular phones.
   Evidence: In restaurants and in shopping malls people can be observed using their cellular phones.

   Conclusion: _____

EXERCISE 5–5

For each of the following deductive arguments, supply the conclusion.

1. Major Premise: All students with yearly averages above 3.5 are offered a summer internship.
   Minor Premise: Jacqueline has a yearly average of 3.7.

   Conclusion: _____

2. Major Premise: Most elementary school children are absent from school due to illness.
   Minor Premise: Quinne, a second grade student, was absent yesterday.

   Conclusion: _____

STRATEGIES FOR READING AN ARGUMENT

Arguments need to be read slowly and carefully. Count on reading an argument more than once. The first time you read it, try to get an overview of its three essential elements: issue, claim, and support. Then reread it more carefully to closely follow the author's line of reasoning and to identify and evaluate the evidence provided.

Think Before You Read

1. *What does the title suggest? Before you read,* preview the essay (see p. 22) and ask yourself what the title suggests about the issue and claim or support. Ikenberry's title, for example, suggests his primary reason for urging that fees be allowed to subsidize political groups.

EXERCISE 5–6

For each of the following titles, predict the issue and claim the essay addresses.

1. "A Former Smoker Cheers New Legislation"
2. "Overflowing, Overcrowded Jails: New Solutions"
3. "The Right to Die My Way"
4. "The Effects of Unchecked Immigration"
5. "Indecent Proposal: Internet Censorship"

2. *Who is the author, and what are his or her qualifications?* Check to see if you recognize the author, and if so, evaluate whether he or she is qualified to write about the issue. For example, an article written by professional golfer Tiger Woods would be an authoritative source on the issue of ethics in professional golf. If the same argument were written by a state senator or a medical doctor, it would have less credibility. The specific qualifications of the author have a bearing on the worth of the evidence provided.

3. *What is the date of publication?* Checking the date will prompt you to consider whether new, even possibly contradictory, evidence has recently developed.

4. *What do I already know about the issue?* Try brainstorming using a two-column list. Label one "pro" and the other "con," and list as many ideas as you can in each column. By thinking about the issue on your own, you are less likely to be swayed by the writer's appeals and more likely to think and evaluate the reasons and evidence objectively.

EXERCISE 5–7

Preview but do not *read the following argument. (For previewing guidelines, see p. 19.) Complete the activities that follow. Read the argument after you have finished the next section "Reading Actively."*

CONSIDER METHODS THAT KEEP DOCTOR-PATIENT RELATIONSHIP INTACT

Pity the poor HMOs. Having signed up millions of patients with promises of generous prescription drug coverage, they are now getting hit with big drug bills.

So many are turning to a cost-control method that quietly discourages doctors from prescribing the drugs patients need.

The device is called "capitation." And it works by getting doctors to accept a financial stake in reducing patients' use of prescriptions.

The trend, which was reported last week in *USA Today,* is on the upswing. It's now used by about a third of HMOs, up from 24% in 1996, according to an industry report.

As a result, hundreds of thousands of HMO members may find it more difficult to obtain needed prescriptions. Others may find access to drug treatments effectively blocked at the doctor's door.

Here's how the arrangements work: HMOs pay doctors a fixed amount per patient for prescription drug costs. Say $9 a month. If a doctor's total prescriptions come in above that amount, he pays the HMO the difference. One California clinic had to pony up $1.6 million to insurers last year. But when costs stay below $9, the doctor keeps the extra.

The idea of giving doctors financial incentives to deny patients care isn't new—or without controversy.

HMOs have long employed capitation in contracts with doctors to encourage more prudent treatment of patients. This made sense as a way to counter the old system of fee-for-service medicine, in which doctors could essentially reward themselves by loading up treatments and tests. The result was billions spent each year on needless health care.

But pitting doctor against patient in the cost-control battle raises risks for patients. If the spending caps are too tight, doctors might deny patients needed treatments just to keep their own bank accounts healthy.

For that reason, half the states in the country ban health plans from offering doctors financial incentives to deny care. Most federal proposals in patient rights bills would do the same at the national level.

Applying these crude financial incentives to prescription drugs is much riskier, since there may be little room for doctors to cut drug costs without denying needed therapies to patients.

Unlike other medical treatments, nobody argues that, outside of antibiotics, drugs are vastly overused.

Nor do doctors have a big financial incentive to overprescribe. And the HMO industry already uses several other cost-control measures, such as generic substitution and restricted lists of plan-approved drugs.

More worrisome, however, is that those most in need are put at the greatest risk. The costliest drugs are those used to treat heart diseases and central nervous system disorders—which together make up 40% of all drug spending—along with expensive new drug therapies. If doctors are going to keep within strict drug budgets, those are the obvious targets for savings.

There are more effective ways to encourage wise use of medicines while leaving the doctor-patient relationship intact. Increasing the costs shared by patients, for instance, has proven to make patients more sensitive to the price of their drug treatments.

The amount paid by patients might be a little higher. Better that, though, than the devious tactic of promising them a benefit while rewarding doctors who with-hold it.

—*USA Today*, September 27, 1999, p. 18a

1. What does the title suggest about the issue, claim, or evidence?
2. What do you already know about the issue? Brainstorm a two-column "Pro-Con" list.

Read Actively

When reading arguments, it is especially important to read actively. For general suggestions on active reading, see Chapter 1. Use the following specific strategies for reading arguments:

1. *Read once for an initial impression.* Don't focus on specifics; instead, try to get a general feel for the argument.

2. *Read the argument several more times.* First identify the specific claim the writer is making and start to identify the reasons and evidence that support it. Read the argument again to examine whether the writer acknowledges or refutes opposing viewpoints.

3. *Annotate as you read.* Record your thoughts; note ideas you agree with, those you disagree with, questions that come to mind, additional reasons or evidence overlooked by the author, and the counter arguments not addressed by the author.

4. *Highlight key terms.* Often, an argument depends on how certain terms are defined. In an argument on the destruction of forests, for example, what does "destruction" mean? Does it mean building homes within a forest, or does it refer to clearing the land for timber or to create a housing subdivision? Highlight both the key terms and the definitions the author provides.

5. *Diagram or map to analyze structure.* Because many arguments are complex, you may find it helpful to diagram or map them. By mapping the

Figure 5–2   The Structure of an Argument

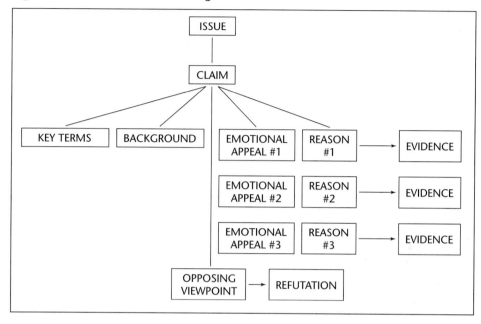

argument you may discover unsubstantiated ideas, reasons for which evidence is not provided, or an imbalance between reasons and emotional appeals. Use the format shown in Figure 5–2 to help you analyze an argument's structure. Figure 5–3 on p. 136 shows you how the argument presented in "Consider Methods That Keep Doctor-Patient Relationship Intact" on pages 133–134 is mapped.

STRATEGIES FOR EVALUATING ARGUMENTS

Once you have understood the article by identifying what is asserted and how it is asserted, the next step is to evaluate the soundness, correctness, and worth of the argument. Specifically, you must evaluate evidence, both type and relevancy, definitions of terms, cause-effect relationships, value systems, and recognition of counter arguments.

Types of Evidence

The validity of an inductive argument rests, in part, on the soundness and correctness of the evidence provided to draw the conclusion. The validity of a deductive argument, on the other hand, rests on the accuracy and correctness of the premises on which the argument is based. Evaluating each type of argument involves assessing the accuracy and correctness of statements

Figure 5–3   A Map of an Argument

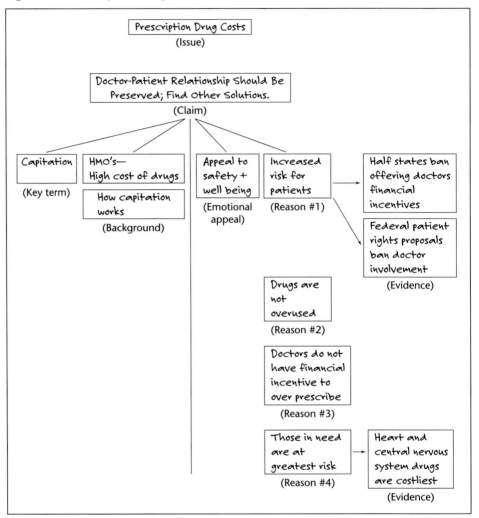

on which the argument is based. Often, writers provide evidence to substantiate their observations or premises. As a critical reader, your task is to assess whether the evidence is sufficient to support the claim. Here are some suggestions for evaluating each type of evidence.

Personal Experience

Writers often substantiate their ideas through experience and observation. Although a writer's personal account of a situation may provide an interesting perspective on an issue, personal experience should not be accepted as proof. The observer may be biased or may have exaggerated or incorrectly perceived a situation.

Examples

Examples are descriptions of particular situations that are used to illustrate or explain a principle, concept, or idea. To explain what aggressive behavior is, your psychology instructor may offer several examples: fighting, punching, and kicking. Examples should not be used by themselves to prove the concept or idea they illustrate, as is done in the following sample.

> The American judicial system treats those who are called for jury duty unfairly. It is clear from my sister's experience that the system has little regard for the needs of those called as jurors. My sister was required to report for jury duty the week she was on vacation. She spent the entire week in a crowded, stuffy room waiting to be called to sit on a jury and never was called.

The writer's sister's experience may be atypical, or not representative, of what most jurors experience.

Statistics

Many people are impressed by statistics—the reporting of figures, percentages, averages, and so forth—and assume they are irrefutable proof. Actually, statistics can be misused, misinterpreted, or used selectively to give other than the most objective, accurate picture of a situation. Suppose you read that magazine *X* has increased its readership by 50 percent while magazine *Y* made only a 10 percent increase. From this statistic, some readers might assume that magazine *X* has a wider readership than *Y*. However, if provided with complete information, you can see that this is not true. The missing, but crucial, statistic is the total readership of each magazine before the increase. If web site *X* had 20,000 visits, and increased it by 50 percent, its visits would total 30,000. However, if web site *Y's* visits was already 50,000, a 10 percent increase (bringing the new total to 55,000) would still give it the larger visitation despite the fact that it made the smaller increase. Approach statistical evidence with a critical, questioning attitude.

Comparisons and Analogies

Comparisons or analogies (extended comparisons) serve as illustrations and are often used in argument. Their reliability depends on how closely the comparison corresponds or how similar it is to the situation to which it is being compared. For example, Martin Luther King, in his famous letter from the Birmingham jail, compared nonviolent protesters to a robbed man. To evaluate this comparison, you would need to consider how the two are similar and how they are different.

Relevancy and Sufficiency of Evidence

Once you have identified the evidence used to support an argument, the next step is to decide whether there is enough of the right kind of evidence to lead you to accept the writer's claim. This is always a matter of judgment; there are no easy rules to follow. You must determine whether the evidence provided directly supports the claim and whether sufficient evidence has been provided.

Suppose you are reading an article in your campus newspaper that states Freshman Composition should not be required of all students at your college. As evidence, the student includes the following.

> Composition does not prepare us for the job market. Besides, the reading assignments have no relevancy to modern times.

This reason provides neither adequate nor sufficient evidence. The writer does nothing to substantiate his statements of irrelevancy of the course to the job market or modern times. For the argument to be regarded seriously, the writer would need to provide facts, statistics, expert opinion, or other forms of documentation.

EXERCISE 5–8

Reread the argument "Consider Methods that Keep Doctor-Patient Relationship Intact" on p. 133, paying particular attention to the type(s) of evidence used. Then answer the questions that follow.

1. What type(s) of evidence is used?
2. Is the evidence convincing?
3. Is there sufficient evidence?
4. What other types of evidence could have been used to strengthen the argument?

Definition of Terms

A clear and effective argument carefully defines key terms and uses them consistently. For example, an essay arguing for or against animal rights should state what is meant by the term, describe or define those rights, and use that definition through the entire argument.

The following two paragraphs are taken from two different argumentative essays on pornography. Notice how in the first paragraph the author carefully defines what he means by pornography before proceeding with his argument, whereas in the second the term is not clearly defined.

PARAGRAPH 1—CAREFUL DEFINITION

There is unquestionably more pornography available today than 15 years ago. However, is it legitimate to assume that more is worse? Pornography is speech, words, and pictures about sexuality. No one would consider an increase in the level of speech about religion or politics to be a completely negative development. What makes speech about sexuality different?[5]

—Lynn, "Pornography's Many Forms: Not All Bad," *Los Angeles Times*, May 23, 1985

PARAGRAPH 2—VAGUE DEFINITION

If we are not talking about writing laws, defining pornography doesn't pose as serious a problem. We do have different tastes. Maybe some of mine come from my middle-class background (my mother wouldn't think so!). I don't like bodies presented without heads, particularly female bodies. The motive may sometimes be the protection of the individual, but the impression is decapitation, and I also happen to be someone who is attracted to people's faces. This is a matter of taste.[6]

—Rule, "Pornography Is a Social Disease," *The Body Politic*, January/February 1984

Cause-Effect Relationships

Arguments are often built around the assumption of a cause-effect relationship. For example, an argument supporting gun control legislation may claim that ready availability of guns contributes to an increased number of shootings. This argument implies that availability of guns causes increased use. If the writer provides no evidence that this cause-effect relationship exists, you should question the accuracy of the statement.

Implied or Stated Value System

An argument often implies or rests on a value system (a structure of what the writer feels is right, wrong, worthwhile, and important). However, everyone possesses a personal value system, and although our culture promotes many major points of agreement (murder is wrong, human life is worthwhile, and so forth), it also allows points of departure. One person may think telling lies is always wrong; another person may say it depends on the circumstances. Some people have a value system based on religious beliefs; others may not share those beliefs.

In evaluating an argument, look for value judgments and then decide whether the judgments are consistent with and acceptable to your personal value system. Here are a few examples of value judgment statements.

1. Abortion is wrong.

2. Financial aid for college should be available to everyone regardless of income.

3. Capital punishment violates human rights.

Recognizing and Refuting Opposing Viewpoints

Many arguments recognize opposing viewpoints. For example, Ikenberry in his argument on college activity fees recognizes that some speech and ideas expressed may be objectionable. Many arguments also attempt to refute (explain why the opposing viewpoint is wrong, flawed, or unacceptable). Basically, it is a process of finding weaknesses in the opponent's argument. One way this can be done is to question the accuracy, relevancy, or sufficiency of the opponent's evidence. Another way is to disagree with the opponent's reasons. Ikenberry refutes the reason that speech may be abhorrent by arguing that objectionable speech will allow students to learn to evaluate ideas different from their own.

When reading arguments that address opposing viewpoints, ask yourself the following questions.

- Does the author address opposing viewpoints clearly and fairly?
- Does the author refute the opposing viewpoint with logic and relevant evidence?

Unfair Emotional Appeals

Emotional appeals attempt to involve or excite readers by appealing to their emotions, thereby controlling the reader's attitude toward the subject. Several types of emotional appeals are described below.

1. *Emotionally Charged or Biased Language.* By using words that create an emotional response, writers establish positive or negative feelings. For example, an advertisement for a new line of fragrances promises to "indulge," "refresh," "nourish," and "pamper" the user. An ad for an automobile uses phrases such as "limousine comfort," "European styling," and "animal sleekness" to interest and excite readers.

2. *False Authority.* False authority involves using the opinion or action of a well-known or famous person. We have all seen athletes endorsing

underwear or movie stars selling shampoo. This type of appeal works on the notion that people admire celebrities and strive to be like them, respect their opinion, and are willing to accept their viewpoint.

3. *Association.* An emotional appeal also is made by associating a product, idea, or position with others that are already accepted or highly regarded. Patriotism is already valued, so to call a product All-American in an advertisement is an appeal to the emotions. A car being named a Cougar to remind you of a fast, sleek animal, a cigarette ad picturing a scenic waterfall, or a speaker standing in front of an American flag are other examples.

4. *Appeal to "Common Folk."* Some people distrust those who are well-educated, wealthy, highly artistic, or in other ways distinctly different from the average person. An emotional appeal to this group is made by selling a product or idea by indicating that it is originated from, held by, or bought by ordinary citizens. A commercial may advertise a product by showing its use in an average household. A politician may describe her background and education to suggest that she is like everyone else; a salesperson may dress in styles similar to his clients.

5. *Ad Hominem.* An argument that attacks the holder of an opposing viewpoint rather than his or her viewpoint, is known as *ad hominem,* or an attack on the man. For example, the statement, "How could a woman who does not even hold a college degree criticize a judicial decision?" attacks the woman's level of education, not her viewpoint.

6. *"Join the Crowd" Appeal.* The appeal to do, believe, or buy what everyone else is doing, believing, or buying is known as crowd appeal or the bandwagon appeal. Commercials that proclaim their product as the "#1 bestselling car in America" are appealing to this motive. Essays that cite opinion polls on a controversial issue in support of a position—"68% of Americans favor capital punishment"—are also using this appeal.

ERRORS IN LOGICAL REASONING

Errors in reasoning, often called logical fallacies, are common in arguments. These errors invalidate the argument or render it flawed. Several common errors in logic are described next.

Circular Reasoning

Also known as begging the question, this error involves using part of the conclusion as evidence to support it. Here are two examples.

> Cruel medical experimentation on defenseless animals is inhumane.

> Female police officers should not be sent to crime scenes because apprehending criminals is a man's job.

In circular reasoning, because no evidence is given to support the claim, there is no reason to accept the conclusion.

Hasty Generalization

This fallacy means that the conclusion has been derived from insufficient evidence. Here is one example: You taste three tangerines and each is sour, so you conclude that all tangerines are sour. Here is another: By observing one performance of a musical group, you conclude the group is unfit to perform.

Non Sequitur ("It Does Not Follow")

The false establishment of cause-effect is known as a *non sequitur*. To say, for example, that "Because my doctor is young, I'm sure she'll be a good doctor" is a *non sequitur* because youth does not cause good medical practice. Here is another example: "Arturio Alvarez is the best choice for state senator because he is an ordinary citizen." Being an ordinary citizen will not necessarily make someone an effective state senator.

False Cause

The false cause fallacy is the incorrect assumption that two events that follow each other in time are casually related. Suppose you opened an umbrella and then tripped on an uneven sidewalk. If you said you tripped because you opened the umbrella, you would be assuming false cause.

Either-Or Fallacy

This fallacy assumes that an issue is only two sided, or that there are only two choices or alternatives for a particular situation. In other words, there is no middle ground. Consider the issue of censorship of violence on television. An either-or fallacy is to assume that violence on TV must either be allowed or banned. This fallacy does not recognize other alternatives such as limiting access through viewing hours, restricting certain types of violence, and so forth.

EXERCISE
5–9

Identify the logical fallacy in each of the following statements.

1. All African American students in my biology class earned A grades, so African Americans must excel in life sciences.
2. If you are not for nuclear arms control, then you're against protecting our future.
3. My sister cannot do mathematical computations or balance her checkbook because she has math anxiety.
4. A well-known mayor, noting a decline in the crime rate in the four largest cities in his state, quickly announced that his new "get-tough on criminals" publicity campaign was successful and took credit for the decline.
5. I always order a fruit pastry for dessert because I am allergic to chocolate.

EXERCISE
5–10

Read the following pair of arguments on college course notes on the Web that appeared in USA Today and answer the questions that follow.

Argument 1

NET NOTES TRUMP BORING LECTURE

Our View: E-world tool helps ease frustrations of mass college classes.

Quick, a test: You're a freshman and you're running late for Psych 101. You could drag yourself over to the lecture hall and strain to hear the tiny professorial speck down at the lectern impart Wisdom.

Or you could click on www.StudentU.com and download the speck's course notes for free.

Over the past week, StudentU.com has begun publishing notes for big, introductory classes at 85 campuses nationwide—mostly those with student bodies over 25,000. What's more, the site gets up to 1 million hits daily.

The phenomenon is exposing a rift between those who embrace the Web and those in the college community who view Net notes as a way for students to cheat the system.

A few hundred professors across the country have been wired for years, posting lecture notes, practice exams and reading lists on Web pages that they link to the World Lecture Hall (www.utexas.edu). But many of their colleagues disapprove of using Net notes to help the record 14.8 million students attending four-year institutions this fall.

Among the gripes: Students who substitute attendance with Net notes "miss the opportunity for exchange, for questioning, for that puzzled look that immediately informs the professor that a fuller explanation of a point is needed." That's according to Bill Cooper, president of the University of Richmond.

Other scholarly objections include the view that with their lectures, professors build students' character. To click on Net notes is to click on Plato's Academy, the Socratic method, Oxford and traditions of liberal education.

Such arguments could come only from sheltered idealists who've never tried to read the chalkboard from 20 yards away. Students at larger schools aren't likely to see 500-seat lectures as any sort of valuable tradition at all.

Certainly, the assigned reading is valuable. As are discussions. And in smaller seminars, students may get that "opportunity for exchange." But the uninspiring mass lecture is hardly a sine qua non.

So students who download notes are right. The notes are adding value to the assembly line of undergraduate education, where grad students and minor lights, not earth-shattering geniuses, lecture, and where traded paper notes long have been the order of the day.

New economy to the ivory tower: Net notes will help students learn. They're not a form of cheating, like the frat-house essay file. Nor are they some robbery of high-caliber, original thinking. Rather, they represent the natural convergence of student demand and the Internet's unique, fascinating supply.

Any professor worth his weight in learning curves should be on notice: Resistance to StudentU.com and its ilk is futile. Survival belongs to professors who see the value of Net notes—or better yet, post notes of their own.

—"Today's Debate: Course Notes on Web," *USA Today,* September 15, 1999, p. 15A

Argument 2

WEB CAN'T SUPPLY CLASS CONTEXT

Opposing View: Net sites threaten integrity of higher education.

By Peter Wood

If Oran Wolf, the entrepreneur who created the new Web site StudentU.com has his way, college students everywhere will soon have free access to class notes for courses taught in 85 American colleges and universities.

Ostensibly, this is a service to students who miss a class or who wish to supplement their notes. But in reality, it's another technological assault on the integrity of higher education.

In the form Wolf gives them, the notes impoverish students' learning. His notes are bound to distract at least some students from the close attention they need to pay to their teachers—and to the process of taking their own notes. What's missing on the Web site is the governing context of a class.

Eating a meal is not the same as reading the menu; hearing about a movie is not the same as seeing it. "You had to be there" applies just as well to class. Notes are a weak substitute. But the Internet somehow seems to undermine common sense in higher education.

Wolf's marketing venture is only one example. Term-paper mills, which help students cheat their way to college degrees, flourish on-line. More and more students are relying on the "research" they can pursue by Web browsing and are skipping the serious inquiry that demands hours in the library. And almost every day a new "virtual college" offering on-line degrees establishes its Web domain.

College professors are looking for the best ways to harness new technology to enhance college study. But bad uses of the Internet proliferate, seriously impairing the education of a whole generation of students. Some Internet abuses are probably illegal and certainly unethical. The Internet notoriously makes protecting intellectual property harder, just as it makes plagiarism and sloppy research easier.

But the greatest danger the Internet poses to higher education is that it teaches students they don't have to be there. Down this road lies the virtual university where remote transactions replace the in-person teacher altogether.

That's a recipe for superficial learning, and it's exactly where the Internet is going.

Peter Wood is a professor of anthropology and the associate provost of Boston University.

—"Today's Debate: Course Notes on Web," *USA Today,* September 15, 1999, p. 15A

For Each Argument:

1. Identify the claim.
2. Outline the primary reasons used to support the claim.
3. What types of evidence are used?
4. Evaluate the adequacy and sufficiency of the evidence.
5. What emotional appeals are used?
6. Does the author recognize or refute counter arguments?

Comparing the Arguments:

1. Compare the types of evidence used.
2. Which argument did you find more convincing? Why?
3. What further information would be useful in assessing the issue?

Working with Classmates: Group Projects

Many assignments and class activities involve working with a small group of classmates. For example, a sociology instructor might divide the class into groups and ask each group to brainstorm solutions to the economic or social problems of the elderly. Group presentations may be required in a business course, or groups in your American history class might be asked to research a topic.

Group projects are intended to enable students to learn from one another by viewing each other's thinking processes and by evaluating each other's ideas and approaches. Use the following suggestions to help your group to function effectively:

1. *Select alert, energetic classmates if you are permitted to choose group members.*

2. *Be an active, responsible participant.* Accept your share of the work and expect others to do the same. Approach the activity with a serious attitude, rather than joking or complaining about the assignment. This will establish a serious tone and cut down on wasted time.

3. *Because organization and direction are essential for productivity, every group needs a leader.* Unless some other competent group member immediately assumes leadership, take a leadership role. While leadership may require more work, you will be in control. As the group's leader, you will need to direct the group in analyzing the assignment, organizing a plan of action, distributing work assignments, planning, and if the project is long term, establishing deadlines.

4. *Suggest that specific tasks be assigned to each group member and that the group agree upon task deadlines.*

5. *Take advantage of individual strengths and weaknesses.* For instance, a person who seems indifferent or is easily distracted should not be assigned the task of recording the group's findings. The most organized, outgoing member might be assigned the task of making an oral report to the class.

If your group is not functioning effectively or if one or more members are not doing their share, take action. Communicate directly, but try not to alienate or anger group members.

SUMMARY

An argument presents logical reasons and evidence in support of a particular viewpoint.

An argument has three essential parts:

- The issue—a problem or controversy about which people disagree
- The claim—the position the writer takes on the issue.
- Support—the reasons and evidence that suggest the claim is reasonable and should be accepted

Some arguments include a refutation which considers opposing viewpoints and may attempt to disprove or discredit them.

There are three types of claims:

- A claim of fact is a statement than can be verified through observation or research.
- A claim of value states that one thing or idea is better or more desirable than another.
- A claim of policy suggests what should or ought to be done to solve a problem.

There are three common types of support: reasons, evidence, and emotional appeals.

Two types of arguments are inductive and deductive:

- Inductive arguments reach a general conclusion from observed specifics.
- Deductive argument begins with a general statement (major premise), moves toward a more specific statement (minor premise), reaches a conclusion.

The chapter presents strategies for reading and evaluating arguments.

Six types of emotional appeals are emotionally charged language, false authority, association, appeal to "common folk," *Ad hominem,* and "join the crowd" appeal.

Errors in logical reasoning include circular reasoning, hasty generalization, *Non Sequitur,* false cause, and either-or fallacy.

EDUCATION

PREREADING QUESTIONS

1. What is meant by the voucher system?
2. What kind of schools do you think can benefit most from a voucher system?

SCHOOL BOARDS DOING LITTLE TO CLOSE GAP BETWEEN WHITES, MINORITIES

1   Surrounded by housing projects in downtown Pensacola, Fla., A.A. Dixon Elementary School is ground zero in the growing national debate over school vouchers. If the "critically low-performing" school fails to shape up, parents should be given vouchers so their children can ship out, says Gov. Jeb Bush. In Pennsylvania, Gov. Tim Ridge made a similar vow earlier this month: We'll help failing schools improve, but while that happens parents should receive vouchers good for any public or private school in the state. Such voucher plans, now spreading nationally, often emerge lacking critical details. Vouchers to where, for instance?

2   At A.A. Dixon, most parents lack phones, let alone cars. Most couldn't get their kids to private schools even if they found one to take them, according to Dixon's principal, Judith Ladner. Dixon students already can pick another public school, but they can't get to one. Many of her students haven't even been to the beach, just 15 miles away. Further, it's not at all clear that kids most in need would ever be helped. Dixon's 5-year-olds arrive for kindergarten with the school readiness of 3-year-olds. Single mothers barely edge single grand-mothers as the dominant head of households. Traditional two-parent families make up about 8% of the population.

3   The educational establishment and teachers unions regularly point to such difficulties as reasons to plead for more time, to put off radical alternatives such as vouchers. But as valid as their concerns about vouchers are, the broader reality is this: Few school districts have made progress of their own against those problems, and with Republican governors who favor vouchers increasingly taking over the education debate, they're running out of time.

4   While the establishment's criticism is loud, its record is mostly feeble. Since 1990, the gap separating white students from black and Latino students has only widened. By the time those children reach eighth grade, nearly half can't

handle subtraction problems or any multiplication or division beyond simple one-digit calculations. Yet it's not clear that urban school boards are getting the message. When urban residents are asked about their schools, only about half say the schools are succeeding. Ask the same question of urban school board members, and nearly three-fourths think they are succeeding, according to a poll released last week. This is occurring even as public educators have arrows added to their quivers.

5   Public school choice is one, but as at Dixon, it often is not a real choice. Charter schools offer another promising tool, though one too new to fully assess. And in a few scattered areas, more familiar methods are bearing fruit. In Houston and El Paso, for instance, state accountability laws, which demand that all students of all races make progress, are paying off. Some urban schools are turning in test scores that resemble suburban schools, and the state has made fast progress in national tests. But the simple fact that such success stories are scarce drives the voucher movement.

6   Vouchers still have much to prove. They risk leaving the most needy behind. They drain resources from public schools. And when used at religious schools, they raise difficult questions about separation of church and state. They are not the first option to consider. But they have two virtues: They haven't failed yet. And there are some encouraging signs that competition can improve public education. Unless public educators grasp the power of that message and improve their record soon, it is they who will be left behind.

—*USA Today*, March 22, 1999, p. 22A

VOCABULARY REVIEW

1. For each of the words listed below, use context; prefixes, roots, and suffixes; and/or a dictionary to write a brief definition or synonym or the word as it is used in the reading.

a. voucher (para. 1) _____

b. dominant (para. 2) _____

c. radical (para. 3) _____

d. feeble (para. 4) _____

e. quivers (para. 4) _____

f. charter schools (para. 5) _____

g. assess (para. 5) _____

h. accountability (para. 5) _____

i. virtues (para. 6) _____

2. Underline new specialized terms introduced in the reading.

COMPREHENSION QUESTIONS

1. What is the major issue in this article?
2. What is the author's claim?
3. Describe the socioeconomic setting of A.A. Dixon Elementary School.
4. Give one reason why the parents of children attending A.A. Dixon Elementary School would not be able to send their children to another school even if a voucher system were in place.
5. What one piece of evidence does the reading give in support of accountability laws?
6. The author acknowledges three arguments against the voucher system. Summarize each.
7. The author gives two reasons for considering the voucher system as an option. What are they?

THINKING CRITICALLY

1. What is the author's purpose in writing this article?
2. Whom do you think is the intended audience for this article?
3. Does the author use an emotional appeal in formulating any of his arguments? Defend your answer.
4. What other kinds of information would help you determine whether the voucher system is a useful alternative?

LEARNING/STUDY STRATEGY

Using the model shown in Figure 5–2, diagram the structure of the argument.

EDUCATION

PREREADING QUESTIONS

1. In what ways could school vouchers by the wrong choice for public education?
2. Are there other alternatives to improving our school system?

SCHOOL VOUCHERS: THE WRONG CHOICE FOR PUBLIC EDUCATION

1   Most Americans believe that improving our system of education should be a top priority for government at the local, state and Federal levels. Legislators, school boards, education professionals parent groups and community organizations are attempting to implement innovative ideas to rescue children from failing school systems, particularly in inner-city neighborhoods. Many such groups champion voucher programs. The standard program proposed in dozens of states across the country would distribute monetary vouchers (typically valued between $2,500–$5,000) to parents of school-age children, usually in troubled inner-city school districts. Parents could then use the vouchers towards the cost of tuition at private schools—including those dedicated to religious indoctrination.

2   Superficially, school vouchers might seem a relatively benign way to increase the options poor parents have for educating their children. In fact, vouchers pose a serious threat to values that are vital to the health of American democracy. These programs subvert the constitutional principle of separation of church and state and threaten to undermine our system of public education.

VOUCHERS ARE . . . CONSTITUTIONALLY SUSPECT

3   Proponents of vouchers are asking Americans to do something contrary to the very ideals upon which this country was founded. Thomas Jefferson, one of the architects of religious freedom in America, said, "To compel a man to furnish contributions of money for the propagation of opinions which he disbelieves . . . is sinful and tyrannical." Yet voucher programs would do just that; they would force citizens—Christians, Jews, Muslims and atheists—to pay for the religious indoctrination of schoolchildren at schools with narrow parochial agendas. In

many areas, 80 percent of vouchers would be used in schools whose central mission is religious training. In most such schools, religion permeates the classroom, the lunchroom, even the football practice field. Channeling public money to these institutions flies in the face of the constitutional mandate of separation of church and state.

4   Supreme Court precedent supports this view. Over 50 years ago, the High Court said that the Establishment Clause requires that "[n]o tax in any amount large or small . . . be levied to support any religious activities or institutions." In 1997, the Court refused to abandon this principle, reaffirming the proposition that the government may not fund the "inculcation of religious beliefs." The Supreme Court has also held unconstitutional government programs that have the effect of advancing religion or of excessively entangling government with religion.

5   While the High Court has not yet heard a case on vouchers, it has struck down education programs that allow parents of parochial school students to recover a portion of their educational expenses from the state. And the Court has found unconstitutional any government aid that accrues to parochial schools in a way that might assist those schools in their sectarian missions. For example, it has held unconstitutional programs in which the state paid for certain secular instruction taking place in pervasively sectarian schools when such instruction was provided by the regular employees of those schools. Federal appeals courts have even prohibited the government from lending instructional materials to parochial schools. By subsidizing the tuition paid to schools dedicated to religious indoctrination, voucher programs violate the separation of church and state.

6   Still, the Constitution leaves substantial room for government programs that result in indirect benefits to religious institutions. For example, the Court has upheld programs that allow parents of children who attend sectarian schools to deduct the cost of tuition from their total income for tax purposes. Further, the Court has not struck down programs like the G.I. Bill, which pays the educational expenses of veterans of the armed forces even if they attend pervasively sectarian universities or divinity schools. These programs, though, are a far cry from the voucher initiatives that would direct public school-children—and tax revenue earmarked for public education—to overwhelmingly religious institutions.

VOUCHERS . . . UNDERMINE PUBLIC SCHOOLS

7   Implementation of voucher programs sends a clear message that we are giving up on public education. Undoubtedly, vouchers would help some students. But the glory of the American system of public education is that it is for *all* children, regardless of their religion, their academic talents or their ability to pay a fee.

This policy of inclusiveness has made pubic schools the backbone of American democracy.

8   Private schools are allowed to discriminate on a variety of grounds. These institutions regularly reject applicants because of low achievement, discipline problems, and sometimes for no reason at all. Further, some private schools promote agendas antithetical to the American ideal. Under a system of vouchers, it may be difficult to prevent schools run by extremist groups like the Nation of Islam or the Ku Klux Klan from receiving public funds to subsidize their racist and anti-Semitic agendas. Indeed, the proud legacy of *Brown v. Board of Education* may be tossed away as tax dollars are siphoned off to deliberately segregated schools.

9   Proponents of vouchers argue that these programs would allow poor students to attend good schools previously only available to the middle class. The facts tell a different story. A $2,500 voucher supplement may make the difference for some families, giving them just enough to cover the tuition at at private school (with some schools charging over $10,000 per year, they would still have to pay several thousand dollars). But voucher programs offer nothing of value to families who cannot come up with the rest of the money to cover tuition costs.

10   In many cases, voucher programs will offer students the choice between attending their current public school or attending a school run by the local church. Not all students benefit from a religious school atmosphere—even when the religion being taught is their own. For these students, voucher programs offer only one option: to remain in a public school that is likely to deteriorate even further.

11   As our country becomes increasingly diverse, the public school system stands out as an institution that unifies Americans. Under voucher programs, our educational system—and our country—would become even more Balkanized than it already is. With the help of taxpayers' dollars, private schools would be filled with well-to-do and middle-class students and a handful of the best, most motivated students from inner cities. Some public schools would be left with fewer dollars to teach the poorest of the poor and other students who, for one reason or another, were not private school material. Such a scenario can hardly benefit public education.

12   Finally, as an empirical matter, reports on the effectiveness of voucher programs have been mixed. Initial reports on Cleveland's voucher program, published by the American Federation of Teachers, suggest that is has been less effective than proponents argue. Milwaukee's program has resulted in a huge budget shortfall, leaving the public schools scrambling for funds. While some studies suggest that vouchers are good for public schools, there is, as yet, little evidence that they ultimately improve the quality of public education for those who need it most.

VOUCHERS ARE . . . NOT UNIVERSALLY POPULAR

13   When offered the opportunity to vote on voucher-like programs, the public has consistently rejected them; voters in 19 states have rejected such proposals in referendum ballots. In the November 1998 election, for example, Colorado voters rejected a proposed constitutional amendment that would have allowed parochial schools to receive public funds through a complicated tuition tax-credit scheme. Indeed, voters have rejected all but one of the tuition voucher proposals put to the ballot since the first such vote over 30 years ago.

14   Voucher proposals have also made little progress in legislatures across the country. While 20 states have introduced voucher bills, only two have been put into law. Congress has considered several voucher plans for the District of Columbia, but none has been enacted.

15   A recent pool conducted by the Joint Center for Political and Economic Studies demonstrates that support for vouchers has declined over the last year. Published in October 1998, the Poll revealed that support for school vouchers declined from 57.3 percent to 48.1 percent among Blacks, and from 47 to 41.3 percent among whites. Overall, 50.2 percent of Americans now oppose voucher programs; only 42 percent support them.

CONCLUSION

16   School voucher programs undermine two great American traditions: universal public education and the separation of church and state. Instead of embracing vouchers, communities across the country should dedicate themselves to finding solutions that will be available to every American schoolchild and that take into account the important legacy of the First Amendment.

—Anti-Defamation League Website (http://www.adl.org)

VOCABULARY REVIEW

1.   For each of the words listed below, use context; prefixes, roots, and suffixes; and/or a dictionary to write a brief definition or synonym or the word as it is used in the reading.

a.   indoctrination (para. 1) _____

b.   benign (para. 2) _____

c.   subvert (para. 2) _____

d.   compel (para. 3) _____

e. propagation (para. 3) _____

f. tyrannical (para. 3) _____

g. mandate (para. 3) _____

h. inculcation (para. 4) _____

i. parochial (para. 5)_____

j. sectarian (para. 5) _____

k. subsidized (para. 5) _____

l. inclusiveness (para. 7) _____

m. antithetical (para. 8)_____

n. legacy (para. 8)_____

o. Balkanized (para. 11) _____

p. empirical (para. 12)_____

2. Underline new specialized terms introduced in the reading.

COMPREHENSION QUESTIONS

1. What is the author's claim?
2. Give two reasons the author offers in support of this claim.
3. How has the Supreme Court demonstrated support of parents sending their children to parochial schools?
4. Describe the Supreme Court's decisions concerning parochial schools.
5. Why does the author quote Thomas Jefferson, and what effect does this have?
6. In what ways might the voucher system undermine public education?

THINKING CRITICALLY

1. In what way does the author use emotional appeals to foster his argument?
2. Identify one assumption the author makes.
3. Does the author refute opposing viewpoints? If so, which one(s)?
4. Is the section titled "Vouchers Are Not Universally Popular" relevant to the author's claim?
5. In what way might the essay seem biased?

LEARNING/STUDY STRATEGIES

1. Using the model shown in Figure 5–2, diagram the structure of the argument.
2. For each reason given in support of the author's claim, write a counter argument.

THINKING ABOUT THE PAIRED READINGS

INTEGRATING IDEAS

1. When comparing the two articles, does one seem less biased and more objective than the other? If so, why?
2. Which of the two articles is more detailed?
3. Which reading did you find more convincing? Why?
4. Based on this reading, what further information would you like to have in order to take a position on the issue?

GENERATING NEW IDEAS

1. Write a paper on the voucher issue using one or both readings to support your viewpoint.
2. Write a letter to your congressional representative or senator urging him or her to either promote or reject school vouchers.

PART 2

ACADEMIC READING STRATEGIES

6 | PATTERNS OF ACADEMIC THOUGHT

LEARNING OBJECTIVES
- ■ **To recognize common academic thought patterns**
- ■ **To use thought patterns to focus your reading**

This term, you probably are taking courses in several different disciplines. You may study psychology, anatomy and physiology, mathematics, and English composition all in one semester. During one day, you may read a poem, solve math problems, and study early developments in psychology. These diverse tasks seem difficult to master because you treat each course differently from every other. Consequently, you are forced to shift gears for each course, developing new approaches and strategies.

What few students realize is that a biologist and a psychologist, for example, think about and approach their subject matter in similar ways. Both carefully define terms, examine causes and effects, study similarities and differences, describe sequences of events, classify information, solve problems, and enumerate characteristics. The subject matter and language they use differ, but their approaches to the material are basically the same. Regardless of their field of expertise, researchers, textbook authors, and your professors use standard approaches, or patterns of thought, to organize and express their ideas. The more familiar you become with these patterns, the easier your reading assignments will be.

PATTERNS: A FOCUS FOR READING

Let's begin by trying a few learning experiments.

Experiment 1. Supply the missing numbers in the following numeric sequence.

1, 5, 7, 8, 12, 14, 15, _____, _____, _____

Experiment 2. Study each of the following drawings briefly, and then continue reading.

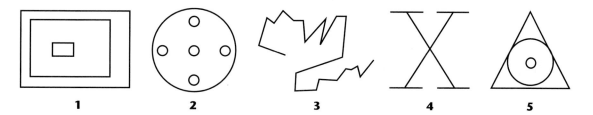

1   2   3   4   5

Next, close the book and quickly sketch each of the preceding drawings.

Now let's analyze your performance. In the first experiment, the last three digits are 19, 21, and 22. If you were correct, you realized the numbers increased successively by 4, by 2, and by 1, and then the pattern repeated. Now supply the next three numbers. Did you get 26, 28, and 29? It is an easy task now that you know the pattern. Reconstructing the entire sequence from memory also is a simple task now that you know the pattern.

For the second experiment, you probably sketched some or all of drawings 1, 2, 4, and 5 correctly. But did you get drawing 3 correct? Probably not. Why? Drawing 3 is irregular and had no pattern.

From these experiments, you can see that patterns make certain tasks easier to complete and that they facilitate your memory and recall. Patterns exist for ideas as well; we will refer to them as **thought patterns.**

Familiarity with these basic thought patterns will enable you to approach all of your courses more effectively. You will find textbook chapters easier to read if you can identify the thought pattern(s) by which they are organized. The same patterns also are used by your professors as they lecture. Lectures will be easier to follow and your notes will be better organized if you can identify these patterns.

Commonly used academic thought patterns include

Definition

Classification

Order or sequence

Cause and effect

Comparison and contrast

Listing/enumeration

These patterns can work for you in several ways.

1. *Patterns provide a focus for reading by enabling you to anticipate the author's thought development.* For example, from a heading or topic sentence

alone, you often can predict the thought pattern that the section or paragraph will follow. When you encounter "Types of Government Spending," you might expect to read about how government spending is divided or classified. Or suppose you read the following topic sentence: "Vaporization, or evaporation as it is also called, is the change from a liquid to a gas." Here, you would anticipate vaporization to be further defined in the paragraph. If your professor announced, "Today we'll consider the impact of stress upon health," then you could expect the speaker to use a cause-and-effect pattern of development.

2. *Patterns help you remember and recall what you read.* Information that is grouped, chunked, or organized is easier to store than single, unrelated bits of information. Also, the manner in which information is stored in memory influences the ease with which it is retrieved. Thought patterns provide a vehicle for organizing information, and they function as retrieval clues for subsequent recall.

3. *Patterns are useful in your own writing;* they help you organize and express your ideas in a more coherent, comprehensible form. As you write essay exam answers, class assignments, or term papers, thought patterns will provide a base or structure around which you can effectively develop ideas.

The following section describes each thought pattern listed above. In subsequent chapters, you will see how these patterns are used in specific academic disciplines.

ACADEMIC THOUGHT PATTERNS

Definition

Each academic discipline has its own specialized vocabulary (see Chapter 3). One of the primary purposes of introductory textbooks is to introduce students to this new language. Consequently, definition is a commonly used pattern throughout most introductory-level texts.

Suppose you were asked to define the word *comedian* for someone unfamiliar with the term. First, you would probably say that a comedian is a person who entertains. Then you might distinguish a comedian from other types of entertainers by saying that a comedian is an entertainer who tells jokes and makes others laugh. Finally, you might mention, by way of example, the names of several well-known comedians who have appeared on television. Although you may have presented it informally, your definition would have followed the standard, classic pattern. The first part of your definition tells what general class or group the term belongs to (entertainers). The second part tells what distinguishes the term from other items in the same class or category. The third part includes further explanation, characteristics, examples, or applications.

Here are two additional examples.

Term	General Class	Distinguishing Characteristics
Stress	Physiological reaction	A response to a perceived threat
Mutant	Organism	Carries a gene that has undergone a change

See how the term *genetics* is defined in the following paragraph, and notice how the term and the general class are presented in the first sentence. The remainder of the paragraph presents the distinguishing characteristics.

> Genetics is the scientific study of heredity, the transmission of characteristics from parents to offspring. Genetics explains why offspring resemble their parents and also why they are not identical to them. Genetics is a subject that has considerable economic, medical, and social significance and is partly the basis for the modern theory of evolution. Because of its importance, genetics has been a topic of central interest in the study of life for centuries. Modern concepts in genetics are fundamentally different, however, from earlier ones.
>
> —Mix et al., *Biology: The Network of Life*, p. 262

Writers often provide clues that signal the thought pattern being used. These signals may occur within single sentences or as transitions or connections between sentences. (Clue words that occur in phrases are italicized here to help you spot them.) Examples of clue words or phrases used for the definition pattern are shown below.

CLUE WORDS
genetics *is* . . .
bureaucracy *means* . . .
patronage *refers to* . . .
aggression *can be defined as* . . .
deficit is *another term* that . . .
balance of power *also means* . . .

EXERCISE 6–1

The following paragraph offers definitions of the terms family *and* home. *Read the paragraph and, for each of the definitions, identify the general class and distinguishing characteristics. Underline clue words that signal the definition pattern.*

The French satirist and social reformer Voltaire (1694–1778) once defined the family as a "group of people who cannot stand the sight of each other but are forced to live under the same roof." The American poet Robert Frost (1875–1963) in his narrative poem *Death of the Hired Man* has one character observe, "Home is the place where, when you have to go there, They have to take you in." Whether home and family prove burdensome depends upon one's maturity level, emotional stability, and willingness to work on the difficulties which arise from close relationships. Most would agree, however, that there are few households which glide serenely along on a perpetually even keel.

—Janaro and Altshuler, *The Art of Being Human*, p. 334–35

EXERCISE 6–2

Using the pattern described above, work with a classmate to write a two-part definition for each of the following terms.

1. Robot
2. Age discrimination
3. Fiction
4. Adolescence
5. Phobia

Classification

If you were asked to describe types of computers, you might mention mainframes, minicomputers, and microcomputers. By dividing a broad topic into its major categories, you are using a pattern known as **classification.**

This pattern is widely used in many academic subjects. For example, a psychology text might explain human needs by classifying them into two categories: primary and secondary. In a chemistry textbook, various compounds may be grouped and discussed according to common characteristics, such as the presence of hydrogen or oxygen. The classification pattern divides a topic into parts, on the basis of common or shared characteristics.

Here are a few examples of topics and the classifications or categories into which each might be divided.

Movies: comedy, horror, mystery

Motives: achievement, power, affiliation, competency

Plant: leaves, stem, roots

Note how the paragraph that follows classifies the various types of cancers.

The name of the cancer is derived from the type of tissue in which it develops. Carcinoma (carc = cancer; omo = tumor) refers to a malignant tumor consisting of epithelial cells. A tumor that develops from a gland is called an adenosarcoma (adeno = gland). Sarcoma is a general term for any cancer arising from connective tissue. Osteogenic sarcomas (osteo = bone; genic = origin), the most frequent type of childhood cancer, destroy normal bone tissue and eventually spread to other areas of the body. Myelomas (myelos = marrow) are malignant tumors, occurring in middle-aged and older people, that interfere with the blood-cell-producing function of bone marrow and cause anemia. *Chondrosarcomas* (chondro = cartilage) are cancerous growths of cartilage.

—Tortora, *Introduction to the Human Body,* p. 56

Examples of clue words and phrases that indicate the classification pattern follow.

CLUE WORDS

There are *several kinds* of chemical bonding . . .
There are *numerous types of* . . .
Reproduction can be *classified as* . . .
the human skeleton is *composed of* . . .
muscles *comprise* . . .
one type of communication . . .
another type of communication . . .
finally, there is . . .

EXERCISE 6–3

The following passage discusses the classification of bones. Read the passage and answer the questions that follow.

TYPES OF BONES

The bones of the body may be classified into four principal types on the basis of shape: long, short, flat, and irregular. **Long bones** have greater length than width and consist of a shaft and extremities (ends). They are slightly curved for strength. Long bones consist mostly of compact bone (dense bone with few spaces) but also contain considerable amounts of spongy bone (bone with large spaces). The details of compact and spongy bone are discussed shortly. Long bones include bones of the thighs, legs, toes, arms, forearms, and fingers. Figure 6–1a shows the parts of a long bone.

Short bones are somewhat cube-shaped and nearly equal in length and width. They are spongy except at the surface where there is a thin layer of compact bone. Short bones include the wrist and ankle bones.

Flat bones are generally thin and composed of two more or less parallel plates of compact bone enclosing a layer of spongy bone. Flat bones afford considerable protection and provide extensive areas for muscle attachment. Flat bones include the cranial bones, the sternum (breastbone), ribs, and the scapulas (shoulder blades).

Irregular bones have complex shapes and cannot be grouped into any of the three categories just described. They also vary in the amount of spongy and compact bone present. Such bones include the vertebrae (backbones) and certain facial bones.

—Tortora, *Introduction to the Human Body*, p. 100

1. What are the four principal types of bones?
2. What is the basis of classification (how are they divided)?
3. Underline clue words that signal the classification pattern.

EXERCISE 6–4

Divide each of the topics listed below into several groups or categories.

1. Foods _____

2 Cars_____

3. Arts _____

4. Laws _____

5. Pollutants _____

Order or Sequence

If you were asked to summarize what you did today, you probably would mention key events in the order in which they occurred. In describing how to write a particular computer program, you would detail the process step by step. If asked to list what you feel are your accomplishments so far this week, you might present them in order of importance, listing your most important accomplishment first. In each case, you are presenting information in a particular sequence or order. Each of these examples illustrates a form of the thought pattern known as **order,** or **sequence.** Let's look at several types of order.

Chronology   Chronological order refers to the sequence in which events occur in time. This pattern is essential in the academic disciplines concerned with the interpretation of events in the past. History, government, and anthropology are prime examples. In various forms of literature, chronological order is evident; the narrative form, used in novels, short stories, and narrative essays, relies on chronological order.

The following paragraph uses chronology to describe how full-scale intervention in Vietnam began.

The pretext for full-scale intervention in Vietnam came in late July 1964. On July 30, South Vietnamese PT (patrol torpedo) boats attacked bases in the Gulf of Tonkin inside North Vietnamese waters. Simultaneously, the *Maddox,* an American destroyer, steamed into the area to disrupt North Vietnamese communication facilities. On August 2, possibly seeing the two separate missions as a combined maneuver against them, the North Vietnamese sent out several PT boats to attack the destroyer. The *Maddox* fired, sinking one of the attackers, then radioed the news to Washington. Johnson ordered another ship into the bay. On August 3 both destroyers reported another attack, although somewhat later, the commander of the *Maddox* radioed that he was not sure. Nonetheless, the president ordered American planes to retaliate by bombing inside North Vietnam.

—Wilson et al., *The Pursuit of Liberty: A History of the American People,* p. 493

Examples of clue words and phrases that indicate chronological order include

CLUE WORDS
in ancient times . . .
at the start of the battle . . .
on September 12 . . .
the *first* primate species . . .
later efforts . . .

Other clue words are

then, before, during, by the time, while, afterward, as, after, thereafter, meanwhile, at that point

Process   In disciplines that focus on procedures, steps, or stages by which actions are accomplished, the **process** pattern is often employed. These subjects include mathematics, natural and life sciences, computer science, and engineering. The pattern is similar to chronology, in that the steps or stages follow each other in time. Clues and signals often used in conjunction with this pattern are similar to those used for chronological order.

Note how this pattern is used in a paragraph explaining what occurs in the brain during sleep.

Let us track your brain waves through the night. As you prepare to go to bed, an EEG records that your brain waves are moving along at a rate of about 14 cycles per second (cps). Once you are comfortably in bed, you begin to relax and your brain waves slow down to a rate of about 8 to 12 cps. When you fall asleep, you enter your *sleep cycle,* each of whose stages shows a distinct EEG pattern. In Stage 1 sleep, the EEG shows brain waves of about 3 to 7 cps. During Stage 2, the EEG is characterized by *sleep spindles,* minute bursts of electrical activity of 12 to 16 cps. In the next two stages (3 and 4) of sleep, you enter into a very deep state of relaxed sleep. Your brain waves slow to about 1 to 2 cps, and your breathing and heart rate decrease. In a final stage, the electrical activity of your brain increases; your EEG looks very similar to those recorded during stages 1 and 2. It is during this stage that you will experience REM sleep, and you will begin to dream.

—Zimbardo and Gerrig, *Psychology and Life*, p. 115

Order of Importance This pattern of ideas sometimes expresses order of priority or preference. Ideas are arranged in one of two ways: from most to least important, or from least to most important. In the following paragraph, the causes of the downward trend in the standard of living are arranged in order of importance.

The United States' downward trend in standard of living has many different causes, of which only a few major ones can be identified here. Most important is probably deindustrialization, the massive loss of manufacturing jobs as many U.S. corporations move their production to poor, labor-cheap countries. But deindustrialization hurts mostly low-skilled manufacturing workers. Most of the well-educated, high-skilled employees in service industries are left unscathed. Deindustrialization alone is therefore not enough to explain the economic decline. Another major factor is the great increase in consumption and decrease in savings. Like their government, people spend more than they earn and become deeply in debt. Those who do practice thrift still have an average rate of savings significantly lower than in countries with fast-growing economies. The habits of high consumption and low saving may have resulted from the great affluence after the Second World War up until the early 1970s (Harrison, 1992).

—Thio, *Sociology*, p. 255

Order of importance is used in almost every field of study. Commonly used clues that suggest this pattern include

CLUE WORDS
is *less* essential than . . .
more revealing is . . .
of *primary* interest is . . .

Other clue words are

first, next, last, most important, primarily, secondarily

Spatial Order Information organized according to its physical location, or position or order in space, exhibits a pattern known as **spatial order.** Spatial order is used in academic disciplines in which physical descriptions are important. These include numerous technical fields, engineering, and the biological sciences.

You can see how the following description of a particular type of blood circulation relies on spatial relationships.

> Pulmonary circulation conducts blood between the heart and the lungs. Oxygen-poor, CO_2-laden blood returns through two large veins (venae cavae) from tissues within the body, enters the right atrium, and is then moved into the right ventricle of the heart. From there, it is pumped into the pulmonary artery, which divides into two branches, each leading to one of the lungs. In the lung, the arteries undergo extensive branching, giving rise to vast networks of capillaries where gas exchange takes place, with blood becoming oxygenated while CO_2 is discharged. Oxygen-rich blood then returns to the heart via the pulmonary veins.
>
> —Mix et al., *Biology: The Network of Life*, pp. 663–64

Diagramming is of the utmost importance in working with this pattern; often, a diagram accompanies text material. For example, a diagram makes the functions of the various parts of the human brain easier to understand. Lecturers often refer to a visual aid or chalkboard drawing when providing spatial descriptions. Examples of clue words and phrases that indicate spatial order follow.

CLUE WORDS
the *left side* of the brain . . .
the *lower* portion . . .
the *outer* covering . . .
beneath the surface . . .

Other clue words are

next to, beside, to the left, in the center, externally

EXERCISE 6–5

The following paragraph uses the spatial pattern to describe skeletal muscle tissue. Read the paragraph and answer the questions below.

> **Skeletal muscle tissue** is named for its location—attached to bones. Skeletal muscle tissue is also *voluntary* because it can be made to contract by conscious control. A single skeletal muscle fiber (cell) is cylindrical and appears *striated* (striped) under a microscope; when organized in a tissue, the fibers are parallel to each other. Each muscle fiber has a plasma membrane, the **sarcolemma,** surrounding the cytoplasm, or **sarcoplasm.** Skeletal muscle fibers are multinucleate (more than one nucleus), and the nuclei are near the sarcolemma.
>
> —Tortora, *Introduction to the Human Body,* p. 77

1. Briefly describe skeletal muscle tissue.
2. Underline the new terminology that is mentioned in this paragraph.

EXERCISE 6–6 *Read each of the following opening sentences from a textbook reading assignment, and anticipate whether the material will be developed using chronology, process, order of importance, or spatial order. Then underline the portion(s) of the sentence that suggest(s) the pattern you choose.*

1. Several statistical procedures are used to track the changes in the divorce rate.

   _____

2. The immune system's ability to defend against an almost infinite variety of antigens depends on a process called clonal selection.[1]

   _____

3. We have no idea how many individuals comprised the human species in our earliest days, and we don't know much more about our numbers in recent times.[2]

   _____

4. There are sources of information about corporations that might help an investor evaluate them. One of the most useful is the *Value Line Investment Survey.*

   _____

5. Human development begins at conception, when the father's sperm cell unites with the mother's ovum.[3]

   _____

6. In the human digestive system, the breakdown of food particles begins in the mouth, where chewing breaks food apart and increases the surface area on which enzymes can act.[4]

   _____

7. The two atrioventricular (AV) valves, one located at each atrial-ventricular junction, prevent backflow into the atria when the ventricles are contracting.[5]

   _____

8. One of the most significant benefits of family therapy is the strengthening of the family unit.

   _____

9. The spinal cord is located within the spinal column; it looks like a section of rope or twine.

   _____

10. The transition from medieval to modern societies occurred from approximately 1400 to 1800.

Cause and Effect

The **cause-and-effect** pattern expresses a relationship between two or more actions, events, or occurrences that are connected in time. The relationship differs, however, from chronological order in that one event leads to another by *causing* it. Information that is organized in terms of the cause-and-effect pattern may

explain causes, sources, reasons, motives, and action

explain the effect, result, or consequence of a particular action

explain both causes and effects

Cause and effect is clearly illustrated by the following passage, which gives the sources of fashions or the reasons why fashions occur.

> Why do fashions occur in the first place? One reason is that some cultures, like ours, *value change:* what is new is good, even better. Thus, in many modern societies clothing styles change yearly, while people in traditional societies may wear the same style for generations. A second reason is that many industries promote quick changes in fashion to increase sales. A third reason is that fashions usually trickle down from the top. A new style may occasionally originate from lower-status groups, as blue jeans did. But most fashions come from upper-class people who like to adopt some style or artifact as a badge of their status. But they cannot monopolize most status symbols for long. Their style is adopted by the middle class, maybe copied or modified for use by lower-status groups, offering many people the prestige of possessing a high-status symbol.
>
> —Thio, *Sociology*, p. 534

The cause-and-effect pattern is used extensively in many academic fields. All disciplines that ask the question "Why" employ the cause-and-effect thought pattern. It is widely used in the sciences, technologies, and social sciences.

Many statements expressing cause-and-effect relationships appear in direct order, with the cause stated first and the effect following: "When demand for a product increases, prices rise." However, reverse order is sometimes used, as in the following statement: "Prices rise when a product's demand increases."

**EXERCISE
6–7**

Identify the cause and the effect in each of the following statements. Circle the cause and underline the effect.

1. Most nutritionists agree that long-term weight loss involves a combination of moderate dieting (say, eating 200 to 500 fewer calories a day than your body requires) and moderate exercise, both of which usually involve some behavior modification.[6]
2. When the body loses fluids, the kidneys stimulate the production of a hormone that activates the thirst drive.
3. Anorexia nervosa—a type of self-starvation—may be caused, in part, by our culture's emphasis on thinness.
4. The decrease in tensions between the former Soviet Union and the Western world has made it possible for the UN to become much more active than in the past.[7]
5. A computer program is easy or difficult to run, depending in part on the data entry system you choose.

The cause-and-effect pattern is not limited to an expression of a simple one-cause, one-effect relationship. There may be multiple causes, or multiple effects, or both multiple causes and multiple effects. For example, both slippery road conditions and your failure to buy snow tires (causes) may contribute to your car's sliding into the ditch (effect).

In other instances, a chain of causes or effects may occur. For instance, failing to set your alarm clock may force you to miss your 8:00 A.M. class, which in turn may cause you not to submit your term paper on time, which may result in a grade penalty. Clue words or phrases that suggest the cause-and-effect pattern follow.

CLUE WORDS

stress *causes* . . .
aggression *creates* . . .
depression *leads to* . . .
forethought *yields* . . .
mental retardation *stems from* . . .
life changes *produce* . . .
hostility *breeds* . . .
avoidance *results in* . . .

Other clue words are

therefore, consequently, hence, for this reason, since

**EXERCISE
6–8**

Determine whether each of the following statements expresses single or multiple causes and single or multiple effects. Circle each cause; underline each effect.

1. Heavy drinking (three drinks or more per day) significantly increases the chance of having smaller babies with retarded physical growth, poor coordination, poor muscle tone, intellectual retardation, and other problems, collectively referred to as fetal alcohol syndrome (FAS).[8]

_____

2. Psychogenic amnesia—a severe and often permanent memory loss—results in disorientation and the inability to draw on past experiences.

_____

3. Social loafing, the tendency to work less when part of larger groups, may account for declining worker productivity and corporate profits in rapidly expanding businesses.

_____

4. The world price of an internationally traded product may be influenced greatly, or only slightly, by the demand and supply coming from any one country.[9]

_____

5. Insulin's main effect is to lower blood sugar levels, but it also influences protein and fat metabolism.[10]

_____

EXERCISE 6–9

The following paragraph is organized using the cause-and-effect pattern. Read the paragraph and answer the questions that follow.

All objects continually radiate energy. Why, then, doesn't the temperature of all objects continually decrease? The answer is that all objects also continually absorb radiant energy. If an object is radiating more energy than it is absorbing, its temperature does decrease; but if an object is absorbing more energy than it is emitting, its temperature increases. An object that is warmer than its surroundings emits more energy than it receives, and therefore it cools; an object colder than its surroundings is a net gainer of energy, and its temperature therefore increases. An object whose temperature is constant, then, emits as much radiant energy as it receives. If it receives none, it will radiate away all its available energy, and its temperature will approach absolute zero.

—Hewitt, *Conceptual Physics*, p. 272

1. Explain why not all objects that radiate energy drop in temperature.
2. What happens to an object that radiates energy but does not absorb any?
3. Underline clue words that signal the cause-and-effect pattern.

Comparison and Contrast

The **comparison** thought pattern is used to emphasize or discuss similarities between or among ideas, theories, concepts, or events, whereas the **contrast** pattern emphasizes differences. When a speaker or writer is concerned with both similarities and differences, a combination pattern is used. The comparison-and-contrast pattern is widely used in the social sciences, where different groups, societies, cultures, or behaviors are studied. Literature courses may require comparisons among poets, among literary works, or among stylistic features. A business course may examine various management styles, compare organizational structures, or contrast retailing plans.

A contrast is shown in the following paragraph, which describes the purchasing processes of small and large businesses.

> Small businesses are likely to have less formal purchasing processes. A small retail grocer might, for example, purchase a computer system after visiting a few suppliers to compare prices and features, while a large grocery store chain might collect bids from a specified number of vendors and then evaluate those bids on pre-established criteria. Usually, fewer individuals are involved in the decision-making process for a small business. The owner of the small business, for example, may make all decisions, and a larger business may operate with a buying committee of several people.
>
> —Kinnear et al., *Principles of Marketing*, p. 218

Depending on whether a speaker or writer is concerned with similarities, differences, or both similarities and differences, the pattern might be organized in different ways. Suppose a professor of American literature is comparing two American poets, Whitman and Frost. Each of the following organizations is possible.

1. *Compare and then contrast the two.* That is, first discuss how Frost's poetry and Whitman's poetry are similar, and then discuss how they are different.

2. *Discuss by author.* For example, discuss the characteristics of Whitman's poetry; then discuss the characteristics of Frost's poetry; then summarize their similarities and differences.

3. *Discuss by characteristic.* For example, first discuss the two poets' use of metaphor, next discuss their use of rhyme, and then discuss their common themes.

Examples of clue words and phrases that reflect these patterns follow.

CLUE WORDS: Contrast

unlike Whitman, Frost . . .

less wordy than Whitman . . .

contrasted with Whitman, Frost . . .

Frost *differs from* . . .

Other contrast clue words are

in contrast, however, on the other hand, as opposed to, whereas

CLUE WORDS: Comparison

similarities between Frost and Whitman . . .

Frost is *as* powerful *as* . . .

like Frost, Whitman . . .

both Frost and Whitman . . .

Frost *resembles* Whitman in that . . .

Other comparison clue words are

in a like manner, similarly, likewise, correspondingly, in the same way

EXERCISE 6–10

The following paragraph uses the comparison-and-contrast pattern. Read the paragraph and then answer the questions below.

> When considering the relationship of Congress and the president, the basic differences of the two branches must be kept in mind. Members of Congress are elected from narrower constituencies than is the president. The people usually expect the president to address general concerns such as foreign policy and economic prosperity, while Congresspersons are asked to solve individual problems. There are structural differences as well. Congress is a body composed of hundreds of independent people, each with a different power base, and it is divided along partisan lines. Thus, it is difficult for Congress to act quickly or to project unity and clear policy statements.
>
> —Baradat, *Understanding American Democracy,* p. 300

1. What two branches of the government are discussed?
2. Explain how these two branches are similar and/or different.
3. Underline clue words that signal the comparison-and-contrast pattern.

EXERCISE 6–11

Read each of the following opening sentences from a textbook reading assignment and predict whether a comparison, contrast, or combination pattern will be used.

1. In Rembrandt's *Self-Portrait* and Frank Auerbach's *Head of Michael Podro,* the artists' responsiveness to both the reality of their subjects and the physical nature of paint and painting is clearly visible.[11]

   _____

2. The Enlightenment celebrated the power of reason; however, an opposite reaction, Romanticism, soon followed.[12]

   _____

3. The small group develops in much the same way that a conversation develops.[13]

   _____

4. Think of the hardware in a computer system as the kitchen in a short-order restaurant: It's equipped to produce whatever output a customer (user) requests, but it sits idle until an order (command) is placed.[14]

   _____

5. One important conceptual issue that arises frequently in economics is the distinction between stock and flow variables.[15]

   _____

EXERCISE 6–12

Write five sentences that express either a comparison or a contrast relationship. Exchange your sentences with a classmate, asking him or her to identify the pattern used.

Listing/Enumeration

If asked to evaluate a film you saw, you might describe the characters, plot, and technical effects. These details about the film could be arranged in any order; each detail provides further information about the film, but they have no specific relationship to one another. This arrangement of ideas is known as **listing** or **enumeration**—giving bits of information on a topic by stating them one after the other. Often, there is no particular method of arrangement for those details.

The following list of managers' difficulties in problem solving could have been presented in any order without altering the meaning of the paragraph.

Although accurate identification of a problem is essential before the problem can be solved, this stage of decision making creates many difficulties for managers. Sometimes managers' preconceptions of the problem prevent them from seeing the situation as it actually is. They produce an answer before the proper question has ever been asked. In other cases, managers overlook truly significant issues by focusing on unimportant matters. Also, managers may mistakenly analyze problems in terms of symptoms rather than underlying causes.

—Pride et al., *Business*, p. 189

This pattern is widely used in college textbooks in most academic disciplines. In its loosest form, the pattern may be simply a list of items: factors that influence light emission, characteristics of a particular poet, a description of an atom, a list of characteristics that define poverty.

Somewhat tighter is the use of listing to explain, support, or provide evidence. Support may be in the form of facts, statistics, or examples. For instance, the statement "The incidence of white collar crime has dramatically increased over the past 10 years" would be followed by facts and statistics documenting the increase. The clue words or phrases used for this pattern include the following.

CLUE WORDS
one aspect of relativity . . .
a second feature of relativity . . .
also, relativity . . .
there are several characteristics of . . .
(1) . . . , (2) . . . , and (3) . . . ,
(a) . . . , (b) . . . , and (c) . . . ,

Other clue words are

in addition; first, second, third, finally, another

EXERCISE 6–13

The following paragraph uses the listing pattern. Read the paragraph and answer the questions below.

By far the most important committees in Congress are the standing committees. Currently 16 standing committees in the Senate and 22 in the House receive the bills that are introduced in Congress. The standing committees are assigned subject-matter jurisdiction by the rules of their respective house, and their titles reflect their general area of expertise. Hence, we have the Senate Finance Committee, the House Agriculture Committee, the Senate Budget Committee, the House Judiciary Committee, and so on. The authority of the standing committees includes the power to study legislation, to subpoena witnesses or information, to remand bills to subcommittees, to vote bills dead, to table bills (putting them aside, thus allowing them to die quietly at the end of the congressional term), to amend bills, to write bills (amending a bill or writing an entirely new version of a bill is called **marking-up**), or to report the bill to the floor.

—Baradat, *Understanding American Democracy*, p. 202

1. What is the topic of the paragraph?
2. What types of information does this paragraph list?

EXERCISE 6–14

Identify and circle the topics listed below that might be developed by using the listing pattern.

1. The Impact of Budget on Crime Prevention
2. The Aims of Legal Punishment
3. America: A Drugged Society?
4. Varieties of Theft
5. Homicide and Assault: The Current Picture

Mixed Patterns

Thought patterns are often combined. In describing a process, a writer may also give reasons why each step must be followed in the prescribed order. A lecturer may define a concept by comparing it to something similar or familiar. Suppose an essay in your political science textbook opens by stating, "The distinction between 'power' and 'power potential' is an important one in considering the balance of power." You might expect a definition pattern (where the two terms are defined), but you also might anticipate that the essay would discuss the difference between the two terms (contrast pattern).

EXERCISE 6–15

For each of the following topic sentences, anticipate what thought pattern(s) the paragraph is likely to exhibit. Record your prediction in the space provided. Underline the word(s) that suggest the pattern(s) you chose.

1. Another form of learning that does not fit neatly into the mold of classical or operant conditioning is learning through insight.

   _____

2. GNP (gross national product) is an economic measure that considers the total value of goods and services that a country produces during a given year.

   _____

3. Diseases of the heart and blood vessels—cardiovascular diseases—are the leading cause of death in the United States today.[16]

   _____

4. Impulse conduction in neurons has been compared to electrical impulses in, say, a copper wire, but the analogy is not a good one.[17]

5. The body's first line of defense against infection consists of several kinds of nonspecific resistance, so named because they do not distinguish one invader from another.[18]

6. Research suggests that obsessive-compulsive disorder has a biological basis.[19]

7. Nervous systems consist of two major types of cells: neurons (nerve cells), which are specialized for carrying signals from one location in the body to another, and supporting cells, which protect, insulate, and reinforce neurons.[20]

8. Both Neoclassicism and Romanticism had their beginnings in rebellion.[21]

9. Some astute observers have noted that when we find ourselves in an energy crunch, as when Iraq invaded Kuwait and threatened the Saudi oil fields in 1990, the first response of our national leaders is to act to insure our continued access to Middle East oil.[22]

10. Before the twentieth century, most of the population of Latin America resembled the populations of antiquity, with high birthrates offset by high death rates.[23]

EXERCISE 6–16

Academic Application

Choose a one- or two-page section of one of your textbooks and determine the pattern of each major paragraph. Then identify the overall pattern of the section as a whole.

EXERCISE 6–17

Turn to the table of contents of this text. Predict the thought pattern(s) that any five of the readings will follow. Ask a classmate to confirm or disagree with the patterns you identified.

APPLYING ACADEMIC THOUGHT PATTERNS

Now that you are familiar with the six basic thought patterns, you are ready to use these valuable structures to organize your learning and shape your thinking. Patterns give ideas shape or form, thereby making them more readily comprehensible. Look for these patterns as you read, listen for them in lectures, and use them in completing assignments and writing papers.

Subsequent chapters in this text will demonstrate the use of patterns in specific learning situations and in specific academic disciplines. Although it is not within the scope of this text, you also will discover that academic thought patterns are useful in organizing and answering essay questions and writing term papers.

STUDY Tips   **Taking Lecture Notes**

In many courses, your instructor will lecture, and you will need to take accurate notes for study and review. Use the following suggestions to take effective notes.

1. *Read the textbook material on which the lecture will be based* before *attending the lecture.*

2. *Listen carefully to the lecturer's opening comments;* they often reveal the purpose, focus, or organization of the lecture.

3. *Focus on ideas, not facts.* Do not try to record everything the lecturer says.

4. *Discover the thought pattern(s) on which the lecture is based.*

5. *Record the main ideas and enough details and examples so that the ideas will make sense later.*

6. *Record the organization of the lecture.* Use an indentation system to show the relative importance of ideas.

(continued)

7. *Leave plenty of blank space as you take notes;* you may want to fill in missed or additional information later.

8. *Use an abbreviation system* for commonly used words (psy = psychology, w/ = with, etc.) to save time.

9. *Review your notes as soon as possible* after the lecture, filling in missing or additional information. This review will also help you remember the lecture.

SUMMARY

Recognition of an author's or speaker's thought pattern aids comprehension and recall and also allows you to anticipate idea development. Six thought patterns are common.

- *Definition.* An object or idea is explained by describing the general class or group to which it belongs and then specifying how it differs from others in the same group (distinguishing characteristics).
- *Classification.* Classification divides a topic into parts or categories on the basis of common or shared characteristics.
- *Order or sequence.* There are four forms of the order or sequence pattern. Chronology refers to the arrangement of events in time; process focuses on the order in which procedures or steps are accomplished; order of importance expresses priority or preference; and spatial order refers to physical location, position, or order.
- *Cause and effect.* Causal relationships between two or more events or actions are shown with this pattern. Causes may be implied or directly stated, and often multiple causes and/or multiple effects are evident.
- *Comparison and contrast.* This pattern emphasizes similarities and/or differences among ideas, concepts, people, or events.
- *Listing/enumeration.* This pattern is a means of presenting pertinent information about or in support of a topic, either step by step or with no inherent order.

BIOLOGY

PREREADING QUESTIONS

1. What thought pattern(s) do you anticipate this reading will use?
2. What do you already know about right-brain and left-brain dominance?

THE HUMAN BRAIN

Robert A. Wallace

1   Now we come to the rather interesting notion of the human brain talking about itself. Perhaps it is because of this strange twist that we encounter so many endless accolades about this great organ. Let's begin with some basic descriptions.

2   The human brain is divided into three parts: the hindbrain, the midbrain, and the forebrain. The **hindbrain** consists of the medulla, the cerebellum, and the pons. The hindbrain is sometimes called the "old brain" because it evolved first. These structures still dominate the brain of some animals, as we have seen. The **midbrain,** logically enough, is the area between the forebrain and hindbrain and connects the two. The **forebrain,** or "new brain," consists of the two cerebral hemispheres and certain internal structures.

THE HINDBRAIN
The Medulla

3   As a rough generality, the more subconscious, or mechanical, processes are directed by the more posterior parts of the brain. For example, the hindmost part, the **medulla,** is specialized as a control center for such basic functions as breathing, digestion, and heartbeat. In addition, it is an important center of control for certain charming activities such as swallowing, vomiting, and sneezing. As we have already seen, it connects the spinal cord and the more anterior parts of the brain.

The Cerebellum and Pons

4   Above the medulla and more toward the back of the head is the **cerebellum,** which is concerned with balance, equilibrium, and coordination. Do you suppose there might be differences between athletes and nonathletes in this part of the brain? (Apparently there are, but the differences are slight.) Do you think this "lower" center of the brain is subject to modification through learning?

Figure 6   The human brain in surface view (a) and in sagittal section (b). Note that there is so much regularity in the convolutions that some have been named.

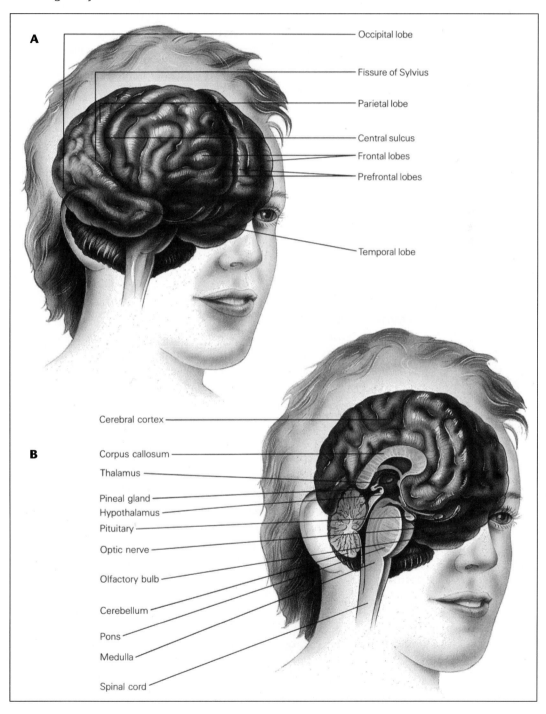

(Can you improve your coordination through practice?) The **pons,** which is the portion of the brainstem just above the medulla, acts as a bridge connecting certain parts of the brain. For instance, it connects the cerebellum and the cerebral cortex, accenting the relationship between the cerebellar part of the hindbrain and the more "conscious" centers of the forebrain.

THE MIDBRAIN

5   The **midbrain** connects the hindbrain and forebrain by numerous tracts. In addition, certain parts of the midbrain receive sensory input from the eyes and ears. In vertebrates, sound is processed here before being sent to the forebrain. The midbrain has a more complex role in fishes and amphibians than in reptiles, birds, and mammals because in the latter group, many of its functions are taken over by the forebrain.

THE FOREBRAIN

The Thalamus and Reticular System

6   The thalamus and hypothalamus are located at the base of the forebrain. The **thalamus** is rather unpoetically called the "great relay station" of the brain. It consists of densely packed clusters of nervous cells that presumably connect the various parts of the brain—between the forebrain and the hindbrain, between different parts of the forebrain, and between parts of the sensory system and the cerebral cortex.

7   The thalamus contains a peculiar neural structure called the **reticular system,** an area of interconnected neurons that are almost feltlike in appearance. The reticular system runs through the medulla, pons, and thalamus and extends upward to the cerebral cortex. The role of the reticular system is still a bit mysterious, but several interesting facts are known about it. For example, it bugs your brain. Every afferent and efferent pathway to and from the brain sends side branches to the reticular system as it passes through the thalamus. So all the brain's incoming and outgoing communications are "trapped." Also, these reticular neurons are rather unspecific. That is, the same neuron may respond to stimuli from, say, the hand, foot, ear, or eye. It has been suggested that the reticular system serves to activate the appropriate parts of the brain upon receiving a stimulus. In other words, the reticular system activates the part of the brain that is needed for the particular task at hand. If there is no incoming stimuli—no need for conscious activity—the system sends fewer signals, quieting the brain. You may have noticed it is much easier to fall asleep lying on a soft bed in a quiet, darkened room than on a pool table in a disco. With the quietness, the reticular system receives fewer messages and the brain is lulled rather than aroused. On those nights when you have the "big eye" and just can't

sleep, the cause may be continued (possibly spontaneous) firing of reticular neurons.

8   The reticular system may also regulate which impulses are allowed to register in your brain. When you are engrossed in a television program, you may not notice that someone has entered the room. But when you are engaged in even more absorbing activities, it might take a general stimulus on the order of an earthquake to distract you. Such filtering and selective depression of stimuli apparently takes place in the reticular system.

The Hypothalamus

9   The **hypothalamus** is a small body, densely packed with cells. It helps regulate the internal environment as well as some aspects of behavior. For example, the hypothalamus helps to control heart rate, blood pressure, and body temperature. It also plays a part in the regulation of the pituitary gland, as we learned earlier. And it controls such basic drives as hunger, thirst, and sex. So now you know what to blame for all your problems. Experimental electrical stimulation of various centers in the hypothalamus can cause a cat to act hungry, angry, cold, hot, benign, or horny.

The Cerebrum

10   For many people the word *brain* conjures up an image of two large, deeply convoluted gray lobes. What they have in mind, of course, is the outside layer of the two cerebral hemispheres, the dominant physical aspect of the human brain. The **cerebrum** is present in all vertebrates, but it assumes particular importance in humans. In some animals, it is essentially an elaborate refinement that implements behavior that could be performed to some degree without it. It has a far greater importance in other animals.

HEMISPHERES AND LOBES

11   The human cerebrum consists of two hemispheres, the left and the right, each of these being divided into four lobes. At the back is the **occipital lobe,** which receives and analyzes visual information.

12   The **temporal lobe** is at the side of the brain. It roughly resembles the thumb on a boxing glove, and it is bounded anteriorly by the fissure of Sylvius. The temporal lobe shares in the processing of visual information, but its main function is auditory reception.

13   The **frontal lobe** is right where you would expect to find it—at the front of the cerebrum, just behind the forehead. This is the part that people hit with the heel of the palm when they suddenly remember what they forgot. One part of the frontal lobe is the center for the regulation of precise voluntary movement. Another part functions importantly in the use of language, and damage here results in speech impairment.

14   The area at the very front of the frontal lobe is called the **prefron area,** if you follow that. Whereas it was once believed that this area was the seat of intellect, it is now apparent that its principal function is sorting out information and ordering stimuli. In other words, it places information and stimuli into their proper context. The gentle touch of a mate or the sight of a hand protruding from the bathtub drain might both serve as stimuli, but they would be sorted differently by the prefrontal area. Up until a few years ago, parts of the frontal lobe were surgically removed in efforts to bring the behavior of certain aberrant individuals more into line with what psychologists had decided was the norm. The operation was called a frontal lobotomy, and it resulted in passive and unimaginative individuals. Fortunately, the practice has been largely discontinued, largely because chemical treatments now meet the same objectives.

15   The **parietal lobe** lies directly behind the frontal lobe and is separated from it by the central sulcus. This lobe receives stimuli from the skin receptors, and it helps to process information regarding bodily position. Even if you can't see your feet right now, you have some idea of where they are thanks to neurons in the parietal lobe. Damage to the parietal lobe may produce numbness and may cause a person to perceive his or her own body as wildly distorted and to be unable to perceive spatial relationships in the environment.

TWO BRAINS, TWO MINDS?

16   The best way to begin a banal conversation a few years ago was, "What sign are you?" Today, though, sophisticates may lead with, "Are you right-brained or left-brained?" Some of the findings of one of the most fascinating branches of neural research have indeed filtered into the public consciousness.

17   The question is based on information that has been accumulating since the middle of the last century when A. L. Wigam, a British physician, performed autopsies on men who had led somewhat normal lives with only half a brain. That is, one hemisphere had been destroyed by accident or other trauma. The question then arose, since we only need half a brain, then why do we have two? At first it was assumed that this was another case where nature had built in redundancy, or backup, in a critical system.

18   Brain research has revealed a fascinating fact: the hemispheres are not duplicates at all, but structures with quite different specializations. To oversimplify, the left hemisphere is the center of logical, stepwise reasoning, of mathematics and language. It processes information in a fragmentary, sequential manner, sorting out the parts of questions and dealing with each quite rationally. (*Star Trek's* Spock was definitely left-brained.) The right brain, on the other hand, is the center of awareness for music and art. Imagination swells from this lobe and it sees things in their entirety (holistically), often solving problems through insight, as it compares relationships.

19   The flexibility of the two hemispheres has been shown when one is damaged and the other takes over its role. Such flexibility, by the way, may be greater in left-handers than in right-handers. It seems that the brain centers of south-paws are generally more diffuse, less localized, with functions more equally dispersed between the two hemispheres. Brain damage to left-handers may produce different symptoms than right-handers with similar injuries.

20   The two halves of the brain are connected by a great, broad tract of nerve fibers, about 4 inches wide, called the **corpus callosum.** Information from each half can be communicated to the other half via the corpus callosum. Thus, special abilities of the two parts of the brain can be integrated and allow us to solve problems, perform tasks, and appreciate life's offerings by a grand union of complex and differing abilities.

21   Or maybe not. Evidence indicates that usually one hemisphere is dominant and inordinately influences how we approach life. Furthermore, some researchers argue that the hemispheres compete with each other for our attention. Such arguments, at this point, quickly extend beyond science and enter the realm of philosophy.

—Wallace, *Biology: The World of Life*, pp. 604–14

VOCABULARY REVIEW

1. For each of the words listed below, use context; prefixes, roots, and suffixes; and/or a dictionary to write a brief definition or synonym of the word as it is used in the reading.

    a. afferent (para. 7) _____

    b. efferent (para. 7) _____

    c. banal (para. 16) _____

    d. redundancy (para. 17) _____

    e. specializations (para. 18)_____

    f. fragmentary (para. 18) _____

    g. realm (para. 21) _____

2. Underline new specialized terms introduced in the reading.

COMPREHENSION QUESTIONS

1. Which area of the brain is responsible for each of the following functions?

    a. balance and coordination_____

      b. regulation of heart rate _____

      c. vision _____

      d. hearing_____

      e. sorting out information_____

2. Describe the specializations of the right brain and of the left brain.
3. Explain what happens when one brain hemisphere is damaged.
4. Why do left-handed people have more flexibility between hemi-spheres than right-handed people?
5. Identify the overall thought pattern(s) used in this reading.
6. Underline clue words that signal the overall pattern(s).

THINKING CRITICALLY

1. If the author of the reading were present, what questions would you like to ask him about right-brain or left-brain dominance or brain functioning?
2. Why does the author defer the argument in paragraph 21 to a philosopher?
3. Are you right- or left-brained? That is, which hemisphere dominates your thinking and behavior?

LEARNING/STUDY STRATEGY

Draw a sketch of the brain. Label its parts.

Psychology

PREREADING QUESTIONS

1. Are certain types of people more creative than others? Which ones?
2. What conditions do you think promote creativity?

Route to Creativity: Following Bliss or Dots?

Natalie Angier

1   To the roster of favorite oxymorons that includes "jumbo shrimp," "military intelligence" and "healthy tan," a new report proposes a tart addition: "artistic freedom." By the reckoning of three Israeli researchers, nothing imprisons the mind more thoroughly, nothing stifles inventiveness and artistry more brutally, than too much freedom, too much wiggle room for the imagination. Instead, they argue, the real source of productive creativity may lie in art's supposed bugaboos: rules, structure, even the occasional editor or two.

2   In an essay in the current issue of the journal *Science,* Dr. Jacob Goldenberg, Dr. David Mazursky and Dr. Sorin Solomon of Hebrew University in Jerusalem describe an algorithm, or formula, for creating new advertisements that is surprisingly simple, yet unnervingly effective. When they fed the algorithm into a computer, it generated advertising concepts judged more original and appealing than equivalent advertisements spawned by a group of humans who were told, in essence, to "follow their bliss."

3   The computer program demonstrates graphically what many creative people know intuitively: the land of the imagination is a country like any other, with laws, rituals and a tireless police corps that must be obeyed if one hopes to retain citizenship there. Creativity, by this measure, is not some mystical, inchoate process, beyond analysis and delineation, but rather is composed of a series of distinct subroutines, which can be rallied repeatedly to churn out ideas that seem the opposite of routine. The notion of creative thinking as amenable to parsing and replication is both cheering and disheartening: cheering because it means that just about anybody can learn to do it at least passably well, and disheartening for showing, once again, that even genius is so much meat in motion.

4   For their part, the researchers were interested less in philosophical matters than in practicality, in coming up with better techniques for stimulating creative thinking. They focused on advertising as a business that demands chronic novelty. In their report, they describe experiments in which they deconstructed

renowned advertisements and found that they often followed specific formulas, which they term templates.

5   One of the commonest templates they found is the so-called replacement template. For example, they considered a Nike ad, in which a group of firemen are standing around in a rescue pose, looking up as though someone was about to jump from a burning building into their net. In lieu of a net is a giant Nike sneaker, with copy boasting of how the new Nike walking shoes are "very safe places to land." In this advertisement, the sneaker replaces an object whose most salient characteristic is "cushioning." Indeed, the life net cushions a person from death itself. Similarly, a series for Bally shoes shows various objects that symbolize freedom—a beach, clouds in the sky—in the shape of a foot, the implication being that the wearing of Bally shoes frees the wearer from cares, the rat race, bunions.

6   The researchers then translated principles of the replacement template into a simple program, and had a computer create concepts designed to pitch different products. The computer did not generate real ads with all the visual flourishes, but simply came up with descriptions. The researchers also asked people outside advertising and untrained in the replacement algorithm or other creativity techniques, to generate hypothetical ads for the same products. When shown to judges, both advertising professionals and outsiders, the advertisements from the computer were invariably ranked higher in creativity and originality than those from the laypeople. In fact, the computer's ads were rated with genuine ones from major magazines, and virtually on par with ones that had won major awards.

7   In one case, the computer, asked to design a campaign promoting the coming of the World Cup tennis tournament to Jerusalem, conceived of the notion of picturing Jerusalem's famed Temple Mountain mosque with a tennis ball texture. The untrained humans could come up with nothing more thrilling than an image of Jerusalem's Old Wall and ad copy announcing the tournament.

8   When asked to hawk the on-time performance of an airline, the computer program suggested an image of a cuckoo clock, with the emerging cuckoo in the shape of a plane. A human proposal: a picture of a family running through the airport while one of the parents screams: "Let's run, this airline is right on time."

9   Dr. Goldenberg and Dr. Mazursky, who are in the school of business, and Dr. Solomon, of the physics department, designed the program to counter a hoary principle in creativity theory that the most original ideas are born of utter freedom, a shifting of paradigms, a circling of the square, a streaming of consciousness, a squelching of the internal editor. Instead, they argue, their work on templates indicates that constraining options and focusing thought in a specific, rigorous and discerning direction may yield comparatively fresher results. "To suspend criticism and think any idea is possible or good may ultimately be destructive to creativity," said Dr. Goldenberg.

10   The researchers emphasized that their work has scant relevance to the science of artificial intelligence, and that they have no interest in proving computers to be potentially more creative than humans, HAL[1] with a beret and ponytail. Instead, they are seeking to mimic the way people solve problems or create ideas, and then describe the process thematically. When taught the algorithms, they said, lay humans will match and often outperform the machine. "Humans can criticize themselves, and computers can't," said Dr. Mazursky. "As Oscar Wilde said, imagination is imitative—the real innovation lies in criticism."

11   The researchers also said that the algorithms they designed for advertising would not necessarily work outside the domain of advertising. "We are not studying just creativity, but creativity in specific contexts," said Dr. Mazursky.

12   Some people in the creativity business found the new paper enlightening and amusing, and said it jibed with the premises of their approach to changing the mind's light bulb. "Limits can be a powerful motivator," said Roger von Oech, a creativity consultant for businesses and author of a classic in the field, "A Whack on the Side of the Head," published in its third edition last year by Warner Books. "If you're given a really tight deadline and a small budget, you'll probably be more resourceful than if you have a ton of time and a limitless budget. Skyscrapers weren't invented by people with a lot of land, but by those who had to figure out how to build more offices on tight and incredibly expensive real estate." Von Oech paraphrased Stephen Sondheim, who said that if someone asked him to write a song about the sea, he would be at sea himself; but ask him to write a ballad about a woman in a red dress in a lounge at three in the morning and falling off the bar stool in drunken sorrow, and he is inspired.

13   Von Oech says that in his corporate seminars and training sessions, he gives his clients very specific tasks. Most of them are centered on humor, his belief being that, as he puts, "there's a close relationship between the ha-ha of humor and the ah-ha of discovery." For example, he asks people to come up with offbeat mottoes for themselves or their companies, and he has stimulated some beauties. From the Bank of America group: "Bank of America: Where you're never alone until you need a loan." From Microsoft: "We're arrogant, and we should be."

14   But other creativity researchers called the new Science paper something of an artful dodge. "It wasn't very profound, and it didn't thrill me," said Dr. Mark A. Runco, editor of Creativity Research Journal and a professor of child and adolescent studies at California State University in Fullerton. "For one thing, I'm not sure it was a fair test. Who are these judges of creativity? People aren't very good at judging creative ideas. Not even creative people are good at it." The poet Goethe, Dr. Runco pointed out, thought his study of optics to be his most

[1]HAL is the rebellious computer that takes over the space flight in the movie *2001: A Space Odyssey*.

important contribution to humanity, but today people read his poetry, not his science papers. Beethoven judged as his greatest composition a piece of music that practically nobody listens to anymore.

15   Nor was it fair to have given the human subjects complete freedom without any structure or template, he said. "I can't think of anyone who would think that a completely open task or environment would be most conducive to creativity," Dr. Runco said. Instead, he explained, most researchers in creativity studies are seeking to understand the balance and interdynamics between structure and openness.

16   Joyce Wycoff, the founder of Innovation Network, a professional association of creativity consultants, and author of "Mind Mapping" (Putnam, 1991), believes the key to creativity is "structure, but structure with permeability." Another essential factor, she said, is energy. "People are never out of idea," she said, "but they may run out of energy." And in this arena, alas, the computer will always have us beat.

—Angier, "Route to Creativity: Following Bliss or Dots?"
The New York Times, September 1999

VOCABULARY REVIEW

1. For each of the words listed below, use context; prefixes, roots, and suffixes; and/or a dictionary to write a brief definition or synonym of the word as it is used in the reading.

a. reckoning (para. 1) _____

b. stifles (para. 1) _____

c. spawned (para. 2) _____

d. inchoate (para. 3) _____

e. delineation (para. 3) _____

f. amenable (para. 3) _____

g. deconstructed (para. 4) _____

h. salient (para. 4) _____

i. hypothetical (para. 6) _____

j. conceived (para. 7) _____

k. constraining (para. 9) _____

l. domain (para. 11) _____

m. jibed (para. 12)_____

n. conducive (para. 15)_____

2. Underline new specialized terms introduced in the reading.

COMPREHENSION QUESTIONS

1. What did the experiments with the computer program demonstrate about creativity?
2. What does the author mean when she says, "Creativity . . . is not some mystical, inchoate process, beyond analysis and delineation, but rather is composed of a series of distinct subroutines. . . ."?
3. What were the researchers—Drs. Goldenberg, Mazursky, and Solomon—primarily interested in?
4. What did the researchers discover about advertisements written by computers versus those written by people?
5. What did they conclude about how the most original ideas are formed?
6. According to Dr. Mazursky, what advantage do humans have over computers in the creative thinking process?
7. What faults have other creativity researchers found with the research published in *Science?*
8. What thought patterns are used in this reading?

THINKING CRITICALLY

1. Explain why the term *artistic freedom* (para. 1) is an oxymoron (a phrase that contains contradictory terms).
2. Would the researchers likely agree or disagree with the following statement: "You are either born with creative talent or you are not."? Explain your reasons.
3. Should Drs. Goldenberg, Mazursky, and Solomon be regarded as qualified experts on the subject of creativity?
4. If you were asked to write a creative advertisement for a specific brand of cereal such as Rice Krispies or Honeycombs, what might be a good way to start, according to this article?
5. What further research would need to be done to answer the objections raised by other researchers about how this study was conducted?
6. Explain whether you agree or disagree that creativity occurs best within a specific framework and time or budgetary restrictions. Give several examples from your own experience.

LEARNING/STUDY STRATEGY

Write a summary of the research findings present in the article in *Science*.

THINKING ABOUT THE PAIRED READINGS

INTEGRATING IDEAS

1. What is the purpose of each reading?
2. In what ways are these readings similar, and how are they different?
3. Which reading was easier to read? Explain your reasons.
4. Assume you are preparing for an essay exam. How would you study each reading? How would your strategies differ?

GENERATING NEW IDEAS

1. Identify one famous historical figure and write a one-page paper describing whether and how that person is left- or right-brained.
2. Based on the article "Route to Creativity: Following Bliss or Dots?" write a list of practical advice (do's and don'ts) for a friend faced with a creative task such as composing a song, writing a story, or creating a sculpture. In other words, what should he or she do to stimulate creative thinking?

7 | LEARNING FROM TEXTBOOKS

LEARNING OBJECTIVES

- **To become familiar with standard textbook format**
- **To use textbook features to facilitate learning**
- **To devise systematic approaches for textbook study**
- **To learn systematic retention and recall techniques**

In many college courses, the textbook is your primary source of information. Each term you will spend hours reading, reviewing, and studying textbooks. Class lectures are often coordinated with reading assignments in the course text, written assignments require you to apply or evaluate ideas and concepts presented in the textbook, and term papers explore topics introduced in the text.

This chapter presents strategies for using textbooks as efficiently as possible. It describes the standard format, identifies features that aid learning, discusses systematic approaches to textbook study, and presents recall and retention strategies.

TEXTBOOK FORMAT

When you first examine a textbook, it may seem like an overwhelming collection of facts and ideas. However, textbooks are highly organized, well-structured sources of information. They follow specific patterns of organization and are uniform and predictable in format and style. Once you become familiar with these structures, you will come to regard textbooks as easy-to-use resources and valuable guides to learning.

Preface

A textbook usually begins with an opening statement called a preface, in which the author describes the text. The preface often specifies

- Structure or organization of the book
- Major points of emphasis
- Distinctive features
- Author's reasons for writing the text
- Intended audience
- Special learning features
- Author's qualifications
- References or authorities consulted when writing

Reading the preface gives you a firsthand impression of the author and his or her attitudes toward the text. Think of it as a chance to get a glimpse of the author as a person.

Some authors include, instead of or in addition to a preface, an introduction titled "To the Student." Written specifically for you, it contains information similar to that in a preface. The author may also include an introduction directed "To the Instructor." Although it may often be quite technical, discussing teaching methodologies and theoretical issues, it may contain some material of interest to students as well. Figure 7–1 shows an excerpt from the preface of a computer science text. Marginal annotation and underlining have been added to call your attention to its contents.

EXERCISE 7–1

Read or reread the preface in Academic Reading and in one of your other textbooks. Using the list above as a guide, list on your own paper the types of information each preface provides.

Table of Contents

The table of contents is one of the first things a professor looks at to evaluate a book. It is also one of the first things you should look at after you have purchased a textbook. The table of contents is an outline of the textbook's main topics and subtopics. It shows the organization of the text and indicates the interrelations among the topics. You can easily identify predominant thought patterns used throughout the text.

Besides using the table of contents to preview a text's overall content and organization, be sure to refer to it before reading particular chapters. Although chapters are organized as separate units, they are related. To

Figure 7–1   Excerpt From a Preface

What is Computer Confluence?

book is part of a multimedia package

Computer Confluence is more than a textbook; it's <u>the confluence of three information sources:</u> an illustrated textbook, a multimedia CD-ROM, and a timely World Wide Web site on the Internet. This integrated learning package takes advantage of the unique strengths of three media types:

advantages of textbooks

- *Computer Confluence,* the text. In spite of the talk about a paperless future, a <u>book's user interface still has many advantages:</u> You can read it under a tree or on the subway, you can bend the corners and scribble in the margins, you can study the words and pictures for hours without suffering from eyestrain or backache. A well-written text can serve as a learning tool, a reference work, a study guide, and even a source of motivation and inspiration. A textbook is no substitute for a good teacher, but a good textbook can almost always make a good teacher better. This book, which started out as *Computer Currents* in 1994, has served as an information-age guidebook for thousands of students through its first two editions.

CD-ROM uses

- *Computer Confluence,* the CD-ROM. A CD-ROM may not be as warm and friendly as a good book, but it <u>can deliver video, audio, animation, and other dynamic media that can't be printed on paper.</u> A well-designed CD-ROM can encourage exploration through interactivity. The *Computer Confluence* CD-ROM supplements and reinforces the material in the book with state-of-the-art 3-D animation, audio, and video. It also includes a software sampler for hands-on experimentation and interactive study materials that provide student feedback.

Web site uses

- *Computer Confluence,* the Web site (http://www.computerconfluence.com). The information in computer books and CD-ROMs has a short shelf life. The Internet makes it possible to publish <u>up-to-the-minute news</u> and information regularly and <u>link that information to other sources around the world.</u> The Internet can also serve as a <u>communication conduit for on-line discussion and research.</u> An extensive collection of timely, media-rich Web pages keeps the information in *Computer Confluence* current. The pages include late-breaking news, multimedia tidbits, and links to the most important computer and information technology sites, all organized by chapter and topic. The Web site also includes discussion areas where students, instructors, and authors can meet on-line. Students can also visit the Web site to take practice quizzes and submit answers to on-line exercises.

Computer Confluence presents computers and information technology on three levels:

Levels of thinking on which the book focuses

- <u>Explanations:</u> *Computer Confluence* clearly explains what a computer is and what it can (and can't) do; it explains the basics of information technology clearly and concisely.
- <u>Applications:</u> *Computer Confluence* clearly illustrates how computers and networks can be used as practical tools to accomplish a wide variety of tasks and solve a wide variety of problems.
- <u>Implications:</u> *Computer Confluence* puts computers in a human context, illustrating how information technology affects our lives, our world, and our future.

Who Is Computer Confluence For?

intended audience

Computer Confluence: Exploring Tomorrow's Technology is designed especially for the introductory computer class for both nonmajors and majors. *Computer Confluence* is also appropriate for introductory computer science classes, discipline-specific computer courses offered through other departments, high school courses, and adult education courses. *Computer Confluence* can also serve as a self-study guide for anyone who's motivated to understand the changing technological landscape ...

How is Computer Confluence Organized?

The book consists of 16 chapters organized into five broad sections:

overall organization: 5 key topics

1. *Approaching Computers: Hardward and Software Fundamentals*
2. *Using Computers: Essential Applications*
3. *Exploring with Computers: Networks and Gateways*
4. *Mastering Computers: Issues, Algorithms, and Intelligence*
5. *Living with Computers: Information Age Implications*

(continued)

<table>
<tr>
<td>content review
of each part</td>
<td>Part 1 provides the basics: a brief historical perspective, a nontechnical discussion of computer and Internet basics, an an overview of hardware and software options. These chapters quickly introduce key concepts that recur throughout the book, putting the student on solid ground for understanding future chapters. Part 2 covers the most important and widely used computer applications, including word processing, spreadsheets, graphics, multimedia tools, and databases. These applications, like those in Parts 3 and 4, are presented in terms of concepts and trends rather than keystrokes. Part 3 explores the world of networks, from simple interoffice LANs to the massive global infrastructure that's evolving from the Internet. Part 4 begins with a discussion of information technology risks and related ethical issues; it then explores the process and the problems of creating software, including the curious field of computer science known as artificial intelligence. Part 5 explores the far-reaching impact of computers on our work, our schools, our homes, our society, and our future.</td>
</tr>
<tr>
<td>focus of
the text</td>
<td>Throughout the five parts, the book's focus gradually flows from the concrete to the controversial and from the present to the future. Individual chapters have a similarly expanding focus. After a brief introduction, each chapter flows from concrete concepts that provide grounding for beginners toward abstract, future-oriented questions and ideas.</td>
</tr>
<tr>
<td>instructional
aides</td>
<td>Each chapter includes instructional aids to help students master the material quickly. Key terms are highlighted in boldface type for quick reference; secondary terms are italicized. Terms are defined in context, in a glossary at the end of the text, and in the CD-ROM's hypertext glossary. Each chapter begins with a list of objectives and ends with a chapter summary; a list of key terms; collections of review questions, discussion questions, and projects; and an annotated list of sources and resources for students who want more information or intellectual stimulation.</td>
</tr>
</table>

Source: Beekman, *Computer Confluence,* pp. xix–xxi

understand a given chapter, note what topics immediately precede and what topics follow it.

Recent textbooks may include a brief table of contents listing only unit and chapter titles, followed by a complete table of contents that lists subheadings and various learning aids contained within each chapter. The brief table of contents is most useful for assessing the overall content and structure of the entire text, whereas the complete one is more helpful when you are studying individual chapters.

In the brief table of contents excerpted from a sociology textbook shown in Figure 7–2, you can see that the text approaches the study of sociology by first examining the sociological perspective, followed by the basic concepts of the social framework. It then considers how people are differentiated and treated unequally, the institutions that society creates, and finally, the causes and results of social change. The thought pattern used to organize the textbook's contents is *classification.*

Figure 7–3 on p. 198 is an excerpt from the detailed table of contents that appears in the same textbook. The chapter discusses how socialization occurs. The predominant thought pattern is evident: *order* and *sequence.* Both process and chronological sequence patterns are evident in individual chapter sections, as marked on the figure.

Figure 7–2   Brief Table of Contents

Source: Thompson and Hickey, *Society in Focus,* p. vii

**EXERCISE
7–2**

Turn to the table of contents of one of your textbooks. Choose a unit or part that you have not read but that will be assigned soon. Predict and list on your own paper the thought pattern(s) of as many sections of the chapters as possible. Then, when you read the chapter, confirm or reject each of your predictions.

Figure 7–3   Detailed Table of Contents

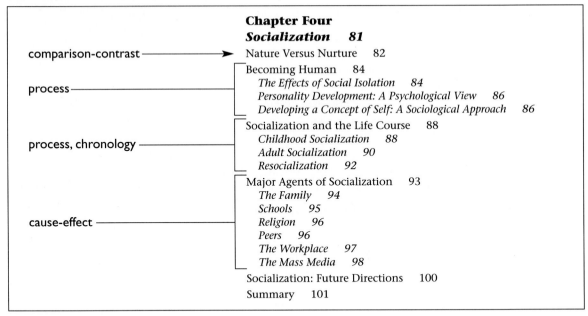

Source: Thompson and Hickey, *Society in Focus,* p. ix–x

Appendix

The appendix of a textbook contains supplementary information that does not fit within the framework of the chapters. Often, the appendix offers valuable aids. For example, one physics text contains five appendices:

Appendix A. Systems of Measurement

Appendix B. More About Motion

Appendix C. Graphing

Appendix D. More About Vectors

Appendix E. Exponential Growth and Doubling Time[1]

The textbook includes these appendixes for the reader's convenience, and the text refers to each one frequently.

Glossary

A glossary is an alphabetical listing of new vocabulary words that are used in the text. The meaning of each word is also included. Located in the back of the text, the glossary serves as a mini-dictionary. To make it even more convenient to use, take some paper clips and attach them to the first page of the glossary in each of your texts. The paper clips will enable you to turn directly to the glossary without hunting and fumbling.

The glossary is easier to use than a regular dictionary. As you know, many words have several meanings, and regular dictionaries list all of the most common meanings. To find the meaning of a word in a dictionary, you have to sort through all the meanings until you find one that suits the way the word is used in the text. A glossary, on the other hand, lists only one meaning—the meaning intended by the author of your text.

The glossary can serve as a useful study aid, particularly at the end of a course when you have completed the text. The glossary is actually a list of words that you should have learned. The easiest way to check whether you have learned these new terms is to go through each column of the glossary, covering up the meanings with an index card or folded sheet of paper. Read each word and try to write a definition for it or just make up the definition mentally. Then uncover the meaning and see whether you were correct. Keep track of the terms you miss, and study them later.

Index

At the end of most texts, you will find an alphabetical subject index that lists topics covered in the text along with page references. Although its primary function is to enable you to locate information on a specific topic, it can also be used as a study aid for final exams. If you have covered most or all of the chapters in the text, then you should be familiar with each topic indexed. For example, suppose the index of an economics textbook includes the following.

Saving, 487
    desired, equilibrium national income and, 497–499
    domestic, economic development and, 751
    marginal propensity to save and, 490–491
    national, 518–519
    private, 511
    public, 511–512
    short- and long-run effects of, 728–729

To review for an exam, you can look at each index entry and test your recall. In the economics textbook example you would ask yourself, "What is the equilibrium national income? How does it relate to desired saving? What is the difference between national and public saving? What are the effects of saving?" and so forth.

Some texts also include a name index that enables you to locate references to individuals mentioned in the text.

The checklist in Figure 7–4 is provided to help you quickly assess a textbook's content and organization.

EXERCISE 7–3

Use the checklist in Figure 7–4 to analyze the content and organization of one of your textbooks. Check each item that describes your textbook.

Figure 7–4   Textbook Checklist

Preface

- ■ States the purpose of the text
- ■ Indicates intended audience
- ■ Explains book organization
- ■ Includes author's credentials
- ■ Describes distinctive features
- ■ Discusses major points of emphasis
- ■ Describes learning aids

Table of Contents

- ■ Includes brief table of contents
- ■ Groups chapters into parts or sections
- ■ Indicates thought pattern(s) throughout the text

Appendix

- ■ Offers useful tables and charts
- ■ Includes supplementary documents
- ■ Describes background or reference material

Glossary

- ■ Includes definitions of special terms
- ■ Provides pronunciation guide, as well as word meanings

Index

- ■ Includes subject index
- ■ Offers separate name index

TEXTBOOK LEARNING FEATURES

Most college textbooks are written by professors who are experienced teachers. They understand how students learn, and they know which topics and concepts usually cause students difficulty. Their purpose in writing is not only to present information but also to help students learn actively. Consequently, most textbooks contain numerous learning aids: chapter previews, marginal notes, special-interest boxes or inserts, review questions, lists of key terms, summaries, and references. A textbook is a guide to learning—a source that directs your attention, shows you what is important, and enables you to read actively. Learning will be easier if you use the textbook's learning aids to best advantage.

Chapter Preview

Research indicates that if readers have some knowledge of the content and organization of material *before* they begin to read it, their comprehension and recall increase. Consequently, numerous textbooks begin each chapter with some kind of preview. There are several common forms.

Chapter Objectives Some texts list the objectives of each chapter beneath its title, as is done in this book. The objectives help to focus your attention on important ideas and concepts. They usually are listed in the order in which the topics appear in the chapter, presenting an abbreviated outline of the main topics.

Chapter Outline Other texts provide a brief outline of each chapter's contents. Formed from the headings and subheadings used throughout the chapter, the outline reflects both the content and the organization of the chapter. A sample outline from a psychology text is shown in Figure 7–5 on p. 202. As you study a chapter outline, pay attention to the sequence and progression of topics and look for thought patterns.

Chapter Overview Some textbook authors provide a preview section in which they state what the chapter is about, explain why certain topics are important, focus the reader's attention on key issues, or indicate how the chapter is related to other chapters in the book. Overviews may be labeled "Chapter Preview," "Overview," a less obvious title such as "Memo," or, as in the sample shown in Figure 7–6 on p. 203 (taken from a biology text), with no title at all, but presented on the opening page of the chapter following the objectives.

Each type of preview can be used to activate and monitor your learning before you begin, while you are reading, and after you finish the chapter.

Figure 7–5 Chapter Outline

CHAPTER THIRTEEN

Development over the Life Span

From Conception to the First Year
Prenatal Development
The Infant's World

Cognitive Development
The Ability to Think
The Ability to Speak

Gender Development

Moral Development
Moral Judgments: Reasoning About Morality
Moral Emotions: Acquiring Empathy, Guilt, and Shame
Moral Action: Learning to Behave Morally

Adolescence
The Physiology of Adolescence
The Psychology of Adolescence

Adulthood
The Biological Clock
The Social Clock

Are Adults Prisoners of Childhood?

Think About It: Puzzles of Psychology
How Long Should We Prolong Life?

Taking Psychology with You
Bringing Up Baby

Source: Wade and Tavris, *Psychology,* p. 491

Before reading
- Use the chapter preview to activate your prior knowledge on the subject. Recall what you already know about the subject by trying to anticipate the chapter's main points.
- Use chapter previews to predict the predominant thought patterns.
- Use previews to anticipate which portions or sections of the chapter will be the most difficult or challenging.

While reading
- Use the preview as a guide to what is important to learn.
- Mark or underline key information mentioned in the preview.

Figure 7–6 Chapter Overview

All the known field mice in the universe must live on whatever this planet can provide for them. They run little risk of depleting their planet's resources, however, because their needs are few—a warm hole, a little food, and a little social acceptance. It's a good thing for them that their requirements are so few, because they have only the resources that their planet can provide. Should they deplete or foul those resources, they would be in a bit of a fix, because *that's all there is.* The point is not too subtle, is it? We share the planet with the field mice. And our resources, too, are limited. But their gentle touch on the great, delicate globe is far from our sledgehammer impact.

In this chapter, we will review the state of some of the resources and energy necessary to life and try to see just how our impact is influenced by something very ephemeral and hard to pin down—our values. We will approach the question of whether our behavior and values could or should be based on our access to the Earth's resources and energy. And how have we treated our heritage?

We will consider the Earth's resources to be in one of two categories, renewable and nonrenewable. **Renewable resources** are those that do not exist in set amounts—they can be reused or replenished at least as fast as we use them. If we cut a pine tree, we can grow another one (assuming that the topsoil didn't wash away because we cut the first one). **Nonrenewable resources** are those that exist in set amounts on the planet and cannot be replenished. Once used, they are gone, or they are changed so much that they are difficult to recover in their original form. The two gallons of gasoline your auto consumed on your date last night is an example.

Source: Wallace, *Biology: The World of Life,* p. 535

After reading
- Use the preview to monitor your comprehension.
- Test your ability to recall key information.
- Immediately review any material you were unable to recall.

EXERCISE 7–4

Refer to the chapter outline in Figure 7–5 to answer the following questions.

1. What predominant thought pattern(s) do you predict the chapter will use? Why?

   _____

2. Which section do you feel will be the most difficult to read and learn? Justify your choice.

   _____

3. What guide questions could you ask to guide your reading?

   _____

EXERCISE 7–5

Refer to the chapter overview in Figure 7–6 to answer the following questions.

1. What do you know about the connections between resources, energy, and human life? Activate your prior knowledge by listing several issues or problems associated with this topic.

   _____

2. What predominant thought pattern(s) do you predict the chapter will use?

   _____

3. Besides listing the topics that will be covered in this chapter, what does the author do to focus attention on the key issues?

   _____

Marginal Notations

Textbooks used to have wide, empty margins that were useful to students for jotting notes. Recently, some textbook authors have taken advantage of this available space to offer comments on the text; pose questions based on the text; provide illustrations, examples, and drawings; or identify key vocabulary. Figure 7–7, excerpted from a psychology text, illustrates one type of marginal notation.

In the excerpt, brief definitions of key terms are given in the margin next to the sentence in which the term is first introduced.

Refer to marginal notes once you have read the text to which they correspond. Use them to review and monitor your comprehension, as well. If the marginal notes are in the form of questions, then you should go through the chapter, section by section, answering each question. Test your ability to define each term in your own words.

EXERCISE 7–6

Read the excerpt and marginal notations in Figure 7–7. Monitor your comprehension by writing your own definitions of theory and personality without reference to the figure. Compare your definitions with those given in the notations.

Special-Interest Inserts

Many textbooks contain, within or at the end of the chapter, brief articles, essays, or commentaries that provide a practical perspective or an application of the topic under discussion. Typically, these inserts are set apart from the text by using boxes or shaded or colored print. Usually, too, the insert titles suggest their function. They might be called "Focus," "Counterpoint," or "Today's Problems." In a chapter on drug abuse, a sociology textbook

Figure 7–7   Marginal Annotations

Theories of Personality

The major task of this Topic is to describe some of the theories of personality. We'll organize this discussion of specific personality theories into four basic approaches. But, before we do, let's see what we mean by *theory* and *personality* in this context.

theory   *an organized collection of ultimately testable ideas used to explain a particular subject matter*

A theory is a series of assumptions; in our particular case, these assumptions are about people and their personalities. The ideas or assumptions that constitute a theory are based on observations, and are reasonably and logically related to each other. The ideas of a theory should lead, through reason, to specific, testable hypotheses. In short, a **theory** is an organized collection of testable ideas used to explain a particular subject matter.

personality   *those affects, behaviors, and cognitions that characterize a person in a variety of situations*

What, then, is personality? Few terms have been as difficult to define. Actually, each of the theoretical approaches we will study in this Topic generates its own definition of personality. We'll say that **personality** includes the affects, behaviors, and cognitions of people that characterize them in a number of situations over time. (Here again is our *ABC* mnemonic from Topic 1A.) Personality also includes those dimensions we can use to judge people to be different from one another. So, with personality theories we are looking for ways that allow us to describe how people remain the same over time and circumstances, and to describe differences we know exist among people (R. F. Baumeister, 1987). Note that personality somehow resides *inside* the person; it's something a person brings to his or her interactions with the environment. Here's another way of saying the same thing: "Personality refers to the enduring, inner characteristics of individuals that organize their behaviors" (Derlega et al., 1991, p. 2).

Source: Gerow, *Psychology: An Introduction*, p. 324

might include a vivid narrative of the life of a drug addict. An economics text might describe specific situations in which key concepts are applied. When reading and studying chapters that offer article inserts, try the following approach.

- Read the insert *after* you have read the text material on the page.
- Determine the purpose of the insert, and mark in the margin the concept or principle to which the insert refers.
- When reviewing for exams, especially essay exams, quickly review the chapter inserts, especially if your instructor has emphasized them.

EXERCISE 7–7

Read the insert shown in Figure 7–8 on p. 206, which is taken from a child development text chapter. Then answer the following questions using your own paper.

1. What aspect of child development does the research of Whitehurst and his colleagues investigate?
2. Summarize the findings of this research.

3. How useful do you feel this information would be in preparing for an exam?

4. Does Whitehurst's research help you understand the practical applications of child development? If so, how?

Review Questions

Some textbook chapters conclude with a set of review questions. Read through these questions *before* you read the chapter. They serve as a list of what is important in the chapter. Usually, the questions are listed in the order in which they appear in the chapter, forming an outline of important topics.

Figure 7–8   Special-Interest Insert

Research Report
The Importance of Reading to the Child

One intriguing piece of evidence showing the importance of the child's environment in early language learning comes from a series of studies by G. J. Whitehurst and his colleagues. In their first study (Whitehurst et al., 1988), they trained some parents to read picture books to their toddlers and to interact with them in a special way during the reading, a pattern called *dialogic* reading. Specifically, they were trained to use questions that could not be answered just by pointing. So a mother reading *Winnie the Pooh* might say, "There's Eeyore. What's happening to him?" Or the parent might ask, pointing to some object shown in a book, "What's the name of that?" or ask a question about some character in a story, such as "Do you think the kitty will get into trouble?" Other parents were encouraged to read to the child but were given no special instructions. After a month, the children in the experimental group had shown a larger gain in vocabulary than had the children in the comparison group.

Whitehurst has now replicated this study in day-care centers for poor children in both Mexico and New York City (Valdez-Menchaca & Whitehurst, 1992; Whitehurst et al., 1994) and in a large number of Head Start classrooms (Whitehurst et al., 1995). In the Mexican study, one teacher in a day-care center was trained in dialogic reading. She then spent 10 minutes each day for six or seven weeks reading with each of ten 2-year-olds. A comparison group of children in the same day-care center spent an equivalent amount of time with the same teacher each day but was given arts and crafts instruction rather than reading. At the end of the intervention, the children who had been read to had higher vocabulary scores on a variety of standardized tests and used more complex grammar when talking in a special test conversation with another adult.

In Whitehurst's U.S. day-care and Head Start studies, children were read to in this special way either by their teacher or by both their mother and the teacher, while control group children experienced normal interactions with day-care workers or teachers. In both studies, the children who had participated in dialogic reading gained in vocabulary significantly more than did the control group children, and the effect appears to last.

Similarly, Catherine Crain-Thoreson and Philip Dale (1995) found that they could significantly increase language skills in language-delayed children by teaching either parents or teachers to read to them in this special way.

The fact that we now have evidence of the same types of effects in two different cultures, with two different languages, with both teachers and parents, with both poor and middle-class children, and with language-delayed children, strengthens the argument that richer, interactive language between adult and child is one important ingredient in fostering the child's language growth.

Source: Bee, *The Developing Child*, p. 236

As you read and locate answers to the questions in the text, be sure to underline or mark them. Review questions are a useful—but by no means sufficient—review. These questions often test only factual recall of specific information. They seldom require you to pull together ideas and compare them, assess causes, or react to the information presented. Read the review questions again *after* you finish the chapter and use them to test your recall.

Lists of Key Terms

Lists of key terms are often found at the end of each chapter. Usually, only specialized terms that are introduced for the first time in that chapter are included. Glancing through the list before reading the chapter will familiarize you with these terms and make reading go more smoothly.

Chapter Summaries

The end-of-chapter summary is useful both before and after you read a chapter. Before reading, the summary familiarizes you with the chapter's basic organization and content. After reading the chapter, it provides an excellent review and helps you to tie together, or consolidate, the major points.

Suggested Readings or References

Many authors provide a list of suggested readings at the end of each chapter or section. This list refers you to additional sources that provide more information on topics discussed in the chapter. References given in this list provide a useful starting point when you are researching a topic discussed in the chapter.

The evaluation list shown in Figure 7–9 on p. 208 will enable you to assess quickly the learning aids that a chapter provides.

Texts Without Learning Features

Instructors are always careful to select textbooks that help their students learn. However, not all textbooks have all the features described in this section. For instance, one of your texts may not include a list of key terms, and another may lack marginal annotations. When a text lacks a feature that you find particularly helpful, construct the feature yourself. Prepare your own list of key terms; write your own marginal annotations. If your text lacks special-interest boxes that discuss how the material can be applied, take a few moments to think of your own applications. You will find that writing your own features will be at least as helpful as using those supplied by the textbook author.

Figure 7–9 Evaluation List

- Chapter preview
  Are thought patterns evident?
  How could the preview be used for review?

- Marginal notes
  How can the notes be used for study and review?

- Special-interest inserts
  How are inserts related to chapter content?
  How much emphasis should be given to the inserts?

- Review questions
  Do the questions provide an outline of chapter content? (Compare them to chapter headings.)
  What types of thinking do the questions require? Are they primarily factual, or do they require critical thinking?

- Key terms
  How many words are already familiar?
  How difficult do you predict the chapter will be?

- Chapter summary
  Does the summary list the main topics the chapter will cover?
  Is a thought pattern evident?

- Suggested readings
  What types of sources are listed?
  To which topics do they refer?

EXERCISE 7–8

Use the evaluation list shown in Figure 7–9 to analyze how the author of one of your current textbooks guides your learning. Write a brief critique of the textbook, including both strengths and weaknesses.

SYSTEMATIC APPROACHES TO TEXTBOOK READING

Throughout this text, you have learned numerous strategies and techniques to improve your textbook reading skills, and you may ask how you can combine them most effectively. Several systems have been developed that integrate these techniques into a step-by-step procedure for learning as you read. In this book, we focus on one particularly useful system.

The SQ3R Reading/Study System

Developed in the 1940s, the SQ3R system has been used successfully for many years and has proved effective in increasing retention of information. It is especially useful for textbooks and other highly factual, well-organized materials. Basically, SQ3R is a way of learning as you read. Its name is taken from the first letter of each step. First we will summarize the steps, and then we will apply the system to a sample selection.

Survey   Become familiar with the overall content and organization of the material. You already have learned this technique and know it as previewing.

Question   Formulate questions about the material that you expect to be able to answer as you read. As you read each successive heading, turn it into a question. This step is similar to establishing guide questions, a topic discussed in Chapter 1.

Read   As you read each section, actively search for the answers to your guide questions. When you find the answers, underline or mark the portions of the text that concisely state the information.

Recite   Probably the most important part of the system, "recite" means that after each section or after each major heading, you should stop, look away from the page, and try to remember the answer to your question. If you are unable to remember, look back at the page and reread the material. Then test yourself again by looking away from the page and "reciting" the answer to your question. This step is a form of comprehension and retention assessment that enables you to catch and correct weak or incomplete comprehension or recall. Here, you are operating primarily at the knowledge and understanding levels of thinking.

Review   Immediately after you have finished reading, go back through the material again, reading titles, introductions, summaries, headings, and graphic material. As you read each heading, recall your question and test yourself to see whether you still can remember the answer. If you cannot, reread that section. Once you are satisfied that you have understood and recalled key information, move toward the higher-level thinking skills. Consider applications, analyze, synthesize, and evaluate the material. Ask questions. Some students like to add a fourth "R" step—for "React."

Now, to get a clear picture of how the steps in the SQ3R method work together to produce an efficient approach to reading/study, let's apply the method to a textbook reading. Suppose you have been assigned the article at the bottom of this page on nonverbal communication for a communication class. Follow each of the SQ3R steps in reading this section.

Survey Preview the article, noting introductions, headings, first sentences, and typographical clues. Refer to Chapter 1, page 19, for more information on previewing. From this prereading, you should have a good idea of what information this article will convey and should know the general conclusions the authors draw about the subject.

Question Now, using the headings as a starting point, develop several questions to which you expect to find answers in the article. Think of these as guide questions (see Chapter 1, page 26). You might ask such questions as:

What are the major types of nonverbal cues?

What are spatial cues?

What messages are communicated at each of the four distances?

Read Now read the selection through. Keep your questions in mind. Stop at the end of each major section and proceed to the next step.

Recite After each section, stop reading and check to see whether you can recall the answer to the corresponding question.

Review When you have finished reading the entire article, take a few minutes to reread the headings, recall your questions, and write answers to your questions to see how well you can remember the answers.

TYPES OF NONVERBAL CUES

You now have a definition of nonverbal communication, you know how much nonverbal communication counts, you understand the characteristics most nonverbal cues share, and you know the functions and forms, so it is time to examine the types of nonverbal cues. In this section, spatial cues, visual cues, vocal cues, touch, time, and silence will be discussed.

Spatial Cues
Spatial cues are the distances we choose to stand or sit from others. Each of us carries with us something called informal space. We might think of this as a bubble; we occupy the center of the bubble. This bubble expands or contracts depending on varying conditions and circumstances such as these:

- Age and sex of those involved.
- Cultural and ethnic background of the participants.

- Topic or subject matter.
- Setting for the interaction.
- Physical characteristics of the participants (size or shape).
- Attitudinal and emotional orientation of partners.
- Characteristics of the interpersonal relationship (like friendship).
- Personality characteristics of those involved.

In his book *The Silent Language,* Edward T. Hall, a cultural anthropologist, identifies the distances that people assume when they talk with others. He calls these distances intimate, personal, social, and public. In many cases, the adjustments that occur in these distances result from some of the factors listed above.

Intimate distance. At an **intimate distance** (0 to 18 inches), you often use a soft or barely audible whisper to share intimate or confidential information. Physical contact becomes easy at this distance. This is the distance we use for physical comforting, lovemaking, and physical fighting, among other things.

Personal distance. Hall identified the range of 18 inches to 4 feet as **personal distance.** When you disclose yourself to someone, you are likely to do it within this distance. The topics you discuss at this range may be somewhat confidential and usually are personal and mutually involving. At personal distance you are still able to touch another if you want to. This is likely to be the distance between people conversing at a party, between classmates in a casual conversation, or within many work relationships. This distance assumes a well-established acquaintanceship. It is probably the most comfortable distance for free exchange of feedback.

Social distance. When you are talking at a normal level with another person, sharing concerns that are not of a personal nature, you usually use the **social distance** (4 to 12 feet). Many of your on-the-job conversations take place at this distance. Seating arrangements in living rooms may be based on "conversation groups" of chairs placed at a distance of 4 to 7 feet from each other. Hall calls 4 to 7 feet the close phase of social distance; from 7 to 12 feet is the far phase of social distance.

The greater the distance, the more formal the business or social discourse conducted is likely to be. Often, the desks of important people are broad enough to hold visitors at a distance of 7 to 12 feet. Eye contact at this distance becomes more important to the flow of communication; without visual contact one party is likely to feel shut out and the conversation may come to a halt.

Public distance. **Public distance** (12 feet and farther) is well outside the range for close involvement with another person. It is impractical for interpersonal communication. You are limited to what you can see and hear at that distance; topics for conversation are relatively impersonal and formal; and most of the communication that occurs is in the public-speaking style, with subjects planned in advance and limited opportunities for feedback. . . .

—Weaver, *Understanding Interpersonal Communications,* pp. 215–18

How SQ3R Improves Your Reading Efficiency

The SQ3R system improves your reading efficiency in three ways. It increases your comprehension, it enhances your recall, and it saves you valuable time by encouraging you to learn as you read.

Your comprehension is most directly improved by the Survey and Question steps. By surveying or prereading, you acquire an overview of the material that serves as an outline to follow as you read. In the Question step, you are focusing your attention and identifying what is important to look for as you read.

Your recall of the material is improved through the Recite and Review steps. By testing yourself while reading and immediately after you finish, you build a systematic review pattern that provides the repetition needed to promote learning and recall.

Finally, because you are learning as you are reading, you will save time later when you are ready to study the material for an exam. Since you already have learned the material through recitation and review, you will find that you need much less time to prepare for an exam. Instead of learning the material for the first time, you can spend the time reviewing. You also will have time to consider applications, to pull the material together, to analyze it, and to evaluate its usefulness.

Adapting the SQ3R System

To make the best use of SQ3R, you must adapt the procedure to fit the material you are studying. You also must adjust the system to suit how you learn and to fit the kind of learning that is expected.

Adapting SQ3R to Suit the Material   Your texts and other required readings vary greatly from course to course. To accommodate this variation, use the SQ3R system as a base or model. Then add, vary, or rearrange the steps to fit the material.

For example, when working with a mathematics text, you might add a Study the Sample Problems step in which you analyze the problem-solving process. When reading an essay, short story, or poem for a literature class, add a React step in which you analyze various features of the writing, including the writer's style, tone, purpose, and point of view (see Chapter 14). For textbooks with a great deal of factual information to learn, you might add Underline, Take Notes, or Outline steps.

Adapting SQ3R to Suit Your Learning Style   Throughout your school experience, you probably have found that some learning techniques work better for you than others. Just as everyone's personality is unique, so is everyone's learning style. Refer to the Learning Style Questionnaire discussed in Chapter 1, page 4.

Try to use knowledge of your learning style to develop your own reading/study system. Experiment with various study methods and adapt the SQ3R system accordingly. For instance, if writing outlines helps you recall information, then replace the Recite step with an Outline step, and make the Review step a Review of Outline step. Or if you have discovered that you learn well by listening, replace the Recite and Review steps with Tape Record and Listen steps, in which you dictate and record information to be learned and review by listening to the tape.

There are numerous possibilities for developing your own reading/study system. The best approach is to test variations until you find the most effective system.

EXERCISE 7–9

Get together with other students taking the same course (or courses within the same discipline or department). Discuss and prepare a list of modifications to the SQ3R system that would be appropriate for your course's content and learning requirements.

EXERCISE 7–10

Use the SQ3R system to read one of the readings included in this text. Write your questions on a separate sheet, and underline your answers in the reading selection.

EXERCISE 7–11

Apply the SQ3R system to a chapter in one of your other textbooks. List your questions on a separate sheet, and underline the answers in your textbook. Evaluate the effectiveness of your approach and decide on any modifications needed.

RETENTION AND RECALL STRATEGIES

Although the SQ3R system is an effective means of improving both comprehension and recall, it cannot ensure complete retention by itself. Periodic review, pattern recognition, association, visualization, mnemonic devices, and the use of writing also are helpful in learning and retaining the text material.

Periodic Review

Immediate review is effective and increases your ability to recall information, but it is not sufficient for remembering material for long periods of time. To remember facts and ideas permanently, you will need to review them periodically, going back and refreshing your recall on a regular basis. For example, suppose you are reading a chapter on criminal behavior in your sociology text, and a midterm exam is scheduled in four weeks. If you read the chapter, reviewed it immediately afterward, and then did nothing with it until the exam a month later, you would not remember enough to score well. To achieve a good grade, you need to review the chapter periodically. You might review the chapter once several days after reading it, again a week later, and once again a week before the exam. Then, when the time comes to study the chapter for the exam, you will find that you are still basically familiar with the chapter's content and you will not need to spend valuable study time becoming reacquainted with the material. Instead, studying will be a matter of learning specifics and organizing particular information into a format that will be easily remembered during the exam. You also will have time to consider how to apply what you have learned—a higher-level thinking skill.

Pattern Recognition

When you read about academic thought patterns in Chapter 6, you learned that it is easier to remember information that has a pattern or structure than it is to remember material that is randomly arranged. Now that you are familiar with the six basic academic thought patterns, you can learn to use these patterns to help you organize ideas.

In some chapters, the patterns will be clearly evident. In others, as well as in articles and essays, a pattern may not be as obvious. You may find it necessary to outline the material or rearrange it into a more meaningful pattern. Chapter 10 describes techniques for organizing information.

Association of Ideas

Association is a useful way to remember new facts and ideas. It involves connecting information that is new and unfamiliar to facts and ideas you already know. For instance, if you are reading a management text for a business class and are trying to remember a list of the characteristics of successful entrepreneurs, you might try to associate each characteristic with a person you know who exhibits that trait.

Using association involves stretching your memory to see what the new information has in common with what you already know. When you find a connection between the known and the unknown, you can retrieve from your memory the new information along with the old.

Visualization

Visualizing, or creating a mental picture of what you have read, often aids recall. The effectiveness of this technique definitely depends on the type of material you are reading. When you are reading descriptive writing in which the writer intends to create a mental picture, visualization is an easy task. When you are reading about events, people, processes, or procedures, visualization is again relatively simple. However, visualization of abstract ideas, theories, philosophies, and concepts may not be possible. Instead, you may need to create in your mind, or on paper, a visual picture of the *relationship* between ideas. For example, suppose you are reading about the invasion of privacy and learn that there are arguments for and against the storage of personal data on each citizen in large computer banks. You might create a visual image of two lists: advantages and disadvantages.

Mnemonic Devices

Memory tricks and devices, often called mnemonics, are useful in helping you recall lists of factual information. You might use a rhyme, such as "Thirty days hath September, April, June, and November. . . ." Another device involves making up a word or phrase in which each letter represents an item you are trying to remember. If you remember the name Roy G. Biv, for example, you will be able to recall the colors in the light spectrum: *r*ed, *o*range, *y*ellow, *g*reen, *b*lue, *i*ndigo, *v*iolet.

Use of Writing to Enhance Learning

Your senses of sight, hearing, and touch all can be used to help you remember what you read. Most of the time, you use just one sense—sight—as you read. However, if you are able to use more than one sense, you will find that recall is easier. Activities such as underlining, highlighting, note taking, and outlining involve your sense of touch and enable you to reinforce your learning. These activities also force you to organize and consolidate information. Chapter 10 discusses each of these techniques in detail.

EXERCISE 7–12

Five study/learning situations follow. Decide which of the aids to retention described in this section—periodic review, pattern recognition, association, visualization, mnemonic devices, and the use of writing—might be useful in each situation, and list the aids after each item. Explain why each would be helpful.

1. In a sociology course, you are assigned to read about and remember the causes of child abuse.

   _____

2. You are learning to simplify radicals in a mathematics class.

   _____

3. You are studying mitosis, the multistage process of cell division, in a biology class.

   _____

4. In economics, you are studying the law of demand. The law states, "The price of a product and the amount purchased are inversely related: if the price rises, the quantity demanded falls; if the price falls, the quantity demanded increases."

   _____

5. You are studying the similarities and differences between plant and animal cells for a biology class.

   _____

 Learning Strategies

For each of your courses, you will need to learn many facts, ideas, and concepts. Use the following suggestions to learn most efficiently.

1. *Apply the principle of spaced study.* It is more effective to space, or spread out, study sessions than to study in one or two large blocks of time.

2. *Use immediate review.* As soon as you finish reading or studying, take a few minutes to look back through the material, recalling key points and rereading notes or summaries. If you review immediately after study, you will increase the amount you remember.

3. *Review frequently.* In order to retain information over time, it is necessary to review periodically. Although you are learning new material each week, reserve time to reread notes, underlining, and chapter summaries of previously covered material.

4. *Associate new information with previously learned information.* Call to mind what you already know about a topic before you begin to read or study.

5. *Use numerous sensory channels by incorporating writing, speaking, and listening into your study.* For example, consider tape recording and playing back your history notes or writing a summary sheet of key formulas for a math course.

SUMMARY

Textbooks contain numerous features to enable you to read, study, and learn as efficiently as possible.

- Preface and table of contents provide keys to the overall organization.
- Appendix, glossary, and index organize and supplement the content.

Numerous learning aids are featured within a textbook chapter:

- chapter previews
- marginal notes
- special-interest inserts
- review questions
- lists of key terms
- references

You can read your textbook most effectively if you use a systematic approach that integrates prereading and postreading. The SQ3R system is a five-step process:

- survey
- question
- read
- recite
- review

Additional strategies to ensure retention and recall are

- periodic review
- pattern recognition
- association
- visualization
- use of mnemonic devices
- use of writing

BIOLOGY

PREREADING QUESTIONS

1. How would you define thinking?
2. Do you believe animals can think?

DO ANIMALS THINK?

Michael C. Mix, Paul Farber, and Keith I. King

1   Scientists have investigated the human organism from a mechanistic viewpoint for over a century. Their underlying assumption has been that humans could be viewed as elegant chemical machines that follow predictable natural laws. This approach has had stunning success. We know a great deal about the human body, we can design drugs to alleviate various ailments, and we can counter numerous conditions that cause suffering or death. Although science can tell us a great deal about our physical condition by treating the human body as a machine, no one doubts that humans, unlike machines, are conscious creatures. Our own consciousness is evident. What about animals?

2   To those of us who have pets, such as dogs or cats, it is difficult to think of them as machines without self-awareness—as entities more akin to our washing machines, personal computers, and blow-dryers than to our family members and friends (see Figure I). Can it be that our clever dog, Cassie, that "comforts" us when we are down, leaps with "joy" when we return from work, and has "outsmarted" the neighbor's dog that used to "steal" her food, is simply a genetically programmed automaton? Or that ZiZi, our neighbor's cat, that would seemingly "favor" starvation to dry cat food and that, if not a connoisseur of lasagna, is known to "prefer"—very definitely—smoked salmon to canned tuna, is, in her behavior, just reflecting an idiosyncratic program rather than expressing a conscious preference?

3   Until shortly after World War I, it seemed obvious to scientists that animals had feelings and that they could think. Charles Darwin believed that female birds showed aesthetic preferences in their choice of mates and that sexual selection was strongly influenced by it.

4   Many writings done in the late nineteenth century on the animal mind, however, were uncritical and highly anthropomorphic. Human desires, fears, and attitudes were attributed to animals, and numerous stories were accepted without any careful attempts at verification. It is not surprising, then, that when we read this literature today, much of it seems comical.

Figure 1   (A) Can this animal think? (B) Do pet tricks reflect thinking ability?

5   Psychologists in the 1920s reacted strongly to this uncritical literature and took the position that it was not possible to verify whether or not animals could think. They concluded that the question of animals' thinking was not a meaningful topic for science because it could not be tested experimentally. Instead, psychologists focused on the observable behavior of animals. They argued that in establishing a scientific psychology, it was irrelevant whether animals thought. They intended to establish scientific laws about how animals learn and behave that could be verified by other scientists. To psychologists like James Watson or B. F. Skinner, the private mind of the animal, if it existed, was closed to human investigation.

6   Ethologists who studied animal behavior, for the most part, were equally dismissive about probing the inner world of animals. A few workers were interested in how the world might "look" to animals, which have different sense organs than humans, but the primary thrust of ethology was in documenting repeatable patterns of behavior and in comparing these patterns with the object of establishing evolutionary connections.

7   Modern animal behavior draws on knowledge derived from psychology, ethology, and an ever-growing body of research in the fields of genetics, ecology, neurophysiology, and neuroanatomy. Until recently, all of these areas of research had been far removed from discussions of animal thought or animal awareness.

8   A well-known investigator of animal behavior, Donald Griffin of Rockefeller University, argues that neglecting animal awareness and thinking is not only an

overreaction to the naive acceptance of undocumented animal stories but also a blind spot that retards advances in the scientific understanding of animal behavior. Griffin believes that mental experiences in animals could have an adaptive value—the better an animal understands its environment, the better it can adjust its behavior to survive and reproduce in it. He is also interested in animal communication, which he feels can sometimes be used to convey information about objects or events that are distant in time or space. This form of information may suggest awareness.

9   In support of his ideas, Griffin cites various behaviors that seem to involve accurate evaluation in complex environments. For example, he refers to a classic study on the prey selection of wagtails, a type of bird found in southern England. These birds feed on fly eggs and on a number of small insects. Each day they must make several choices on where to hunt, when to move on to hunt in another area, and whether to join a flock or hunt alone. Scientists who study these wagtails have shown that they hunt with great proficiency. Although proficiency is not necessarily an indicator of awareness, Griffin argues that in cases where accurate evaluation of a changing and complex environment occurs, it is reasonable to consider that the animal is consciously thinking about what it is doing. Cooperative hunting by lions and the cultural transmission of behavior such as the potato washing done by Japanese macaques, both described in this chapter, and insight learning, described in Chapter 28, are other examples of behaviors that suggest to Griffin and others that animals are aware and can think.

10   At present, Griffin and analysts who agree with him are in the minority in the scientific community. How can the question of animal thinking be resolved? One way is to attempt to design experiments that might give an indication one way or the other. Psychologists in the early twentieth century were very outspoken in their rejection of animal consciousness, claiming that testing for it was impossible. Griffin has proposed that some tests may be possible and that evidence can be gathered to support his position. He argues that once we have a better understanding of the electrical signals that are correlated with conscious thinking in humans, we could search for equivalents in animals. If none were found, that would suggest that his hypothesis of animal awareness is false. The strongest supporting evidence of Griffith's hypothesis involves cases in which animal communication is active and specialized, information is exchanged, and the receiving animal responds interactively. To Griffin, such cases are compelling examples of conscious and intentional acts.

11   It is too early to tell what researchers of animal behavior will conclude about animal awareness. Further research on interesting phenomena, such as animal communication, will ultimately provide the results necessary for formulating a scientific conclusion. Until then, we are confident that people will continue to discuss the world with their dogs and cats.

—Mix et al., *Biology: The Network of Life*, pp. 551–52

VOCABULARY REVIEW

1. For each of the words listed below, use context; prefixes, roots, and suffixes; and/or a dictionary to write a brief definition or synonym of the word as it is used in the reading.

   a   entities (para. 2)_____

   b. connoisseur (para. 2) _____

   c. anthropomorphic (para. 4)_____

   d. ethologists (para. 6) _____

   e. dismissive (para. 6) _____

2. Underline new specialized terms introduced in the reading.

COMPREHENSION QUESTIONS

1. Why did psychologists in the 1920s declare that the question of animal thinking was not meaningful?
2. How do ethologists approach the study of animal behavior?
3. What evidence does Donald Griffin offer in support of animals' ability to think?
4. Explain what Griffin means by "adaptive value" (para. 8).
5. What types of additional evidence are needed to change the opinion of the scientific community?
6. What learning features does this excerpt include?

THINKING CRITICALLY

1. What does the last sentence of the reading suggest about humans?
2. Does the reading contain any clues about the author's answer to the question of whether animals can think?
3. Evaluate the evidence offered by Griffin. Do you feel it is sufficient and convincing?

LEARNING/STUDY STRATEGIES

1. Write a brief set of notes for the reading. (Refer to pages 300–302 for suggestions on note taking.)
2. What thought pattern(s) is (are) evident in the reading?
3. What retention or recall strategies would be helpful in learning this material?
4. Did you use SQ3R when reading the material? If so, how did you find it helpful?

Biology

PREREADING QUESTIONS

1. Do you think parrots are capable of communicating through the use of words?
2. What thought patterns do you anticipate this reading will use?

The Subject Is Alex

Kenn Kaufman

1   At first sight Alex appears out of place, somebody's pet brought in for the day and plopped down in a corner of the modern research laboratory at the University of Arizona. But the impression is wrong. Alex is the research. An African Grey, *Psittacus Erithacus,* he lacks the gaudy greens and yellows of many species. Despite his silky sheen and crimson tail feathers, he seems duller than the average parrot. Perched on the back of a metal folding chair with newspapers unceremoniously spread underneath, he shifts his feet nervously and turns an owlish eye toward anyone who approaches.

2   "Alex, how many?" A researcher holds up a purple metal key and a larger green plastic key. The parrot stares, turning his head slowly: The questions hangs for fifteen silent seconds. Why expect an answer? Doesn't "to parrot" mean "to mimic mindlessly."? But then the parrot says, "Two."

3   The same two keys are held up with a different question. "Which is *bigger?*" Again the parrot stares, pauses, then says, "Green key." Next is a wooden Popsicle stick. "What matter?" Again the long pause, again a correct answer: "Wood."

4   Getting the stick as a reward, Alex splinters it in his massive beak. It's strange to watch this bird perform—especially strange for anyone with a background in traditional science. For years the assumption had been that "talking" birds are nothing but mimics, attaching no meaning to their "words." But this parrot seems to crush that assumption as easily as he crushes Popsicle sticks. Alex is impressive—and so is the scientist who trained him.

5   Irene Pepperberg was well on her way to earning a Ph.D. in chemical physics from Harvard when, in 1973, her professional interest began to shift toward animals. The *Nova* programs on public service television provided the spark: It was the first time, she says, that TV had shown wild animals as they really were and had suggested scientific studies of them were worthwhile. Especially compelling were programs on animal communication: voices of birds attempts to teach sign language to chimpanzees. "Suddenly," Pepperberg says,

"mathematical modeling of the reaction pathways of molecules seemed a lot less exciting than trying to understand communication in animals."

6   "Most people felt that the brain structure of birds wouldn't allow for much intelligence," she says, "or that the striatal area in birds couldn't handle information as well as the cortex in mammals. But a different brain type didn't have to be fundamentally inferior. Birds had done well in experiments with problem-solving based on numbers. Otto Koehler had ravens, jackdaws and Grey parrots that could match numbers of spots up to eight. Pastore's canaries could pick out the third item from a series. Logler had an African Grey parrot trained on numbers up to eight.

7   "In all these tests the birds 'responded' by picking a certain item. There was no vocal response. In the 1940's and 1950's a psychologist named Mowrer tried to teach parrots to use words for objects, and that effort failed. But I thought it should be possible to teach a bird to use at least a few vocal labels. The vocal behavior of birds is such a rich subject. Some individual marsh wrens, for example, will use hundreds of different songs, and a lot is known about how some birds learn their songs in different context—suggesting that they attach some meaning to the sounds. So why not see if those meanings could be attached to specific objects?"

8   Her Ph.D. word complete, Pepperberg wound up in Indiana on the academic periphery of Purdue University. Her husband had a job there; she did not. But Purdue agreed to let her use lab space if she would raise the funds for her research. She designed her own study and, in June 1977, bought Alex, a thirteen-month-old grey parrot chosen at random in a Chicago pet store.

9   "The Grey parrot was the logical species," she says, "It had done so well with numbers in Logler's tests. Besides, if you think about wild parrots, they live in social groups. Most are in tropical forests, where the foliage is dense, and they might need complex vocal signals to stay in touch."

10   Pepperberg's logic sounds simple in retrospect. At the outset, however, launching her study was far from easy. She wrote grant proposals, but no one was interested in funding an offbeat "talking bird" experiment. So she scraped up used equipment, enlisted volunteer help, and endured the mild putdowns of other scientists.

11   Within a few months it appeared Alex was catching on; within a couple of years it was beyond doubt. In a paper entitled "Functional Vocalizations by an African Grey Parrot" published in 1981, Pepperberg reported Alex could identify more than thirty objects by name, shape, and color; he had averaged 80 percent accuracy over some two hundred tests. This was a breakthrough, the first solid evidence that a bird could attach meanings to sounds, labels to objects. But the experiments went on from there.

12   "OKAY, ALEX, BACK to the chair." It's a rule of the lab: On the counter top, the floor, or someone's shoulder, Alex can clown around or request whatever he wants, but when he sits on the back of the metal chair, he has to work.

"Alex, what's this?" "Rrrock!" says Alex. Irene Pepperberg hands him the rock, which he turns over in his bill a couple of times before dropping it on the floor.

13   Next question: "What color?" Alex eyes the blue toy truck and reaches for it. Pepperberg pulls it away. "No. Tell me what color?" Alex pauses and then says, "Want a nut." Pepperberg speaks sharply and turns away: "No! Bad parrot! Pay attention. What color?" Finally he gets it out ("Blhoo"), and gets to play with the truck.

14   Then he has a request of his own: "Want pah-ah." "Better!" says Pepperberg "Say it better." Alex tries again. "Want pah-ssdah." "Okay, that's pretty good," says Pepperberg, and hands him a piece of raw pasta. He crunches it hard, sending a shower of fragments to join the accumulation of crushed shredded-wheat squares, Popsicle sticks, and grapes on the newspaper below.

15   Then Pepperberg holds up three spools of different sizes and color. "Which is smaller?" Show Alex a paper triangle and ask, "What shape?" and he'll say, "Three-corner." Show him five Popsicle sticks dyed red and ask, "What color?" and he'll say, "Rose." Then ask, "How many?" and he'll say, "Five." He is clearly responding to the question itself, as well as to the objects. He understands "different" and "same" and can answer questions about relationships: Show him a blue-dyed cork and blue key and ask, "What's the same?" he will answer, "Color." Show him two identical squares of rawhide and ask, "What's different?" and he will say, "None." Substitute a pentagon for one square, and he will answer, "Shape."

16   To do these things Alex must understand the questions. analyze several qualities, compare them, and search his vocabulary; he is processing information on several levels. None of this is simple memorization. On questions of size or color or shape, "different" or "same," Alex scores slightly *better* with new objects than with familiar ones; novelty seems to focus his attention.

17   It's an incredible performance for a bird. But Alex did not reach this level by accident. Every detail of his training and testing has been carefully considered.

18   For example, Alex regularly nuzzles and scratches with Pepperberg and all the student assistants. This is essential. The parrot is highly social and needs this interplay. If it felt no bond with researchers, it would never cooperate. On the other hand major problems could result if the bird felt a strong "pair bond" with one person—parrots can be violently jealous about their "mates." Thus, assistants were brought in to interact with Alex from the beginning.

19   Alex does not seem to know the meaning of "bad parrot" or "good parrott" or "pay attention" but tones of approval and disapproval are enough to influence him. Another factor to reinforce learning: appropriate rewards. Past experiments with birds had rewarded "correct behavior" with food. But when Alex names an object correctly he is rewarded with the object itself; he may examine it, scratch himself with it, or chew it for several minutes before he loses interest and drops it.

20   The language training rests on a technique developed by German biologist Dietmar Todt, who found the Grey parrot learned phrases most quickly from two trainers: One formed a bond with the parrot; the other acted as both "rival" and model. For the parrot to gain the attention of its "mate," it learned to mimic simple phrases used repeatedly by the model/rival. In Pepperberg's study no one person took the role of Alex's mate. Trainers took turns "training" each other to name objects while Alex watched and listened; eventually he joined in.

21   The initial aim was to teach Alex to use words for objects, something no bird had been proven to do before. Next the focus moved to categories of color and shape, to numbers, to concepts such as similarity and difference. At every stage Alex was subjected to rigorous tests. The results had to be above question—beyond any suggestion the bird was receiving cues from the researchers. Tests were administered by students who had not taken part in the training. Pepperberg kept score of Alex's answers but sat with her back turned, unable to see the objects being presented. Each response had to be clear enough to be understood. Alex would get no hints, no leniency.

22   But as the tests became more complex, Alex continued to score around 80 percent accuracy in his answers, far above what would have been possible by chance alone. Carefully documenting the parrot's progress, Pepperberg published one scientific paper after another.

23   Researchers trying to open two-way communication with animals are caught in the crossfire of a controversy that has been running for decades. On one side are the strict behaviorists, who suggest that animals have no real thought processes, no consciousness, no awareness of their own actions. At the other extreme are those who maintain that animals may indeed be thinking and that science should inquire what they are thinking about. Joining this far-reaching debate are psychologists, linguists, and philosophers who ask: What is awareness? What is language? Do things like "belief" and "desire" really exist, even in humans?

24   The arguments continue, but the study of animal minds—now dignified with the name "cognitive ethology"—is gaining stature as a legitimate field. Researchers have managed to open limited dialogues with various mammals: chimpanzees, gorillas, orangutans, dolphins, sea lions. And joining this cast of "smart" mammals on stage is one Grey parrot. "We haven't gone as far as the chimpanzee or marine mammal studies," says Pepperberg. "But up to this point Alex has performed as well as the chimps or dolphins." No other researcher has taken bird communication to this level.

25   For Pepperberg the Grey parrot was a calculated choice as a promising study species. But parrots also represent the endangered wildlife of the tropics. "There are more than three hundred parrot species," she says, "mostly in the tropics, and nearly one-fourth of those could be considered endangered in the

wild. These are intelligent, adaptable birds, and they could probably survive alongside 21st Century humanity given a chance. But the cage-bird trade doesn't give them a chance." She favors legislation now being considered that would ban the import of wild birds. "Wild-caught parrots make inferior pets, and a shocking number of wild parrots die in transport. If someone really has the time to devote to a pet parrot, the only responsible approach is to buy one that has been raised by a reputable breeder.

26   "If my research could affect public awareness," she concludes, "I'd like people to realize that a parrot is not just a bundle of bright feathers. A parrot is a creature with mental capabilities beyond what we would have guessed—a creature that deserves respect. As civilized beings, we can't go on blithely destroying the habitat and populations of wild parrots."

—Kaufman, "The Subject Is Alex," *Audubon Magazine*, September–October, 1991

VOCABULARY REVIEW

1. For each of the words listed below, use context; prefixes, roots, and suffixes; and/or a dictionary to write a brief definition or synonym of the word as it is used in the reading.

    a. mimic (para. 2) _____

    b. compelling (para. 5) _____

    c. periphery (para. 8) _____

    d. retrospect (para. 10) _____

    e. reinforce (para.19)_____

    f. rival (para. 20) _____

    g. leniency (para. 21) _____

    h. calculated (para. 25) _____

    i. blithely (para. 26) _____

2. Underline new specialized terms introduced in the reading.

COMPREHENSION QUESTIONS

1. How did Pepperberg become interested in studying communication with parrots?
2. Why did Pepperberg choose to study parrots instead of other animals?
3. What kinds of thinking does Alex demonstrate when answering questions asked by Pepperberg?

4. Describe the methods Pepperberg uses to teach Alex.
5. Explain the controversy among scientists about two-way communication with animals.

THINKING CRITICALLY

1. What is Pepperberg's attitude toward the capture and sale of wild parrots?
2. Do you think that Pepperberg's work with Alex establishes that parrots can think? If not, what further information or experiments are needed to answer the question: "Do Animals Think?"
3. What does Pepperberg think about keeping parrots as pets?
4. What kinds of information is Alex able to learn?

LEARNING/STUDY STRATEGIES

1. What thought pattern is used throughout this reading?
2. Write a set of notes that would be useful if you were writing a research paper that argues that animals can think.

THINKING ABOUT THE PAIRED READINGS

INTEGRATING IDEAS

1. Compare the position each reading takes on whether animals can think.
2. Compare the organization of the two readings.
3. Compare the purpose of each of the readings. What is each intended to accomplish?

GENERATING NEW IDEAS

1. Design an experiment that would evaluate whether an animal could think. Explain what you would have the animal do and how you would determine whether thought occurred.
2. If you were to write a research paper on animal intelligence, what further information would you need to write that paper? Explain what sources you would consult and what information you would need.

8 | READING GRAPHICS

LEARNING OBJECTIVES
- **To develop reading strategies for graphics**
- **To learn to read different types of graphs**

Many college textbooks include graphics such as maps, diagrams, charts, tables, or graphs. Some students find graphics intimidating, mainly because they have not learned how to approach them. All graphic devices serve the same primary functions. First, graphics summarize and condense written information, making it easier to comprehend and retain. In this respect, graphics actually save you time by eliminating lengthy written explanations. To illustrate, first study the table in Figure 8–1. Then read the paragraph that begins to present the factual information contained in the table.

Which would you rather read, the table or the paragraph? The paragraph is dull, routine reading, whereas the table presents the same information concisely and in a more interesting format. The table also makes it easier to understand the relationship between individual bits of information. A glance at the table tells you that 19.1 percent of adolescent boys engaged in three problem behaviors, compared to 2.6 percent of girls. (Locating this information would be much more difficult if it were presented only in paragraph form.) By providing a visual picture of the information, graphics also make relationships, trends, and patterns easier to grasp.

It is tempting to skip over the graphic aids included in textbooks. Stopping to study a graph or chart takes time and may seem to interrupt your flow of reading. Because graphics do not present information in words (there are no statements to underline or remember), you may think they are unimportant. Actually, graphics often are more important than the paragraphs that surround them. They are included to call your attention to, emphasize, and concisely describe a relationship.

Figure 8–1

Co-Occurrence of Three Serious Problem Behaviors Among Adolescent Girls and Boys

NUMBER OF SERIOUS PROBLEM BEHAVIORS	FEMALES	MALES
None	57.4%	21.9%
One		
Sex	15.5	26.6
Substance use	7.9	2.8
Total	23.4	29.4
Two		
Sex/substance use	14.0	27.0
Substance use/assault	2.6	2.5
Total	16.6	29.5
Three		
Sex/substance use/assault	2.6	19.1

Paragraph:

57.4 percent of females exhibited no serious problem behaviors, 23.4 percent engaged in one (sex or substance use), 16.6 percent reported serious engagement in two problem behaviors, and 2.6 percent had been involved in all three. The males in the sample were more generally involved than females in problem behaviors, but 21.9 percent had not engaged seriously in any of the three problem behaviors. About 29 percent of the males had engaged seriously in one problem behavior (primarily sex), nearly 30 percent had engaged in two (primarily sex combined with substance use), and 19.1 percent had engaged in all three.

Source: Conger and Galambos, *Adolescence and Youth,* pp. 296–97

HOW TO READ GRAPHICS

Here are some general suggestions that will help you get the most out of graphic elements in the material you read.

1. *Read the title or caption.* The title tells you what situation or relationship is being described.

2. *Determine how the graphic is organized.* If you are working with a table, note the column headings. For a graph, note what is marked on the vertical and horizontal axes.

3. *Note any symbols and abbreviations used.*

4. *Determine the scale or unit of measurement.* Note how the variables are measured. For example, does a graph show expenditures in dollars, thousands of dollars, or millions of dollars?

5. *Identify the trend(s), pattern(s), or relationship(s) the graphic is intended to show.* The following sections will discuss this step in greater detail.

6. *Read any footnotes.* Footnotes, printed at the bottom of a graph or chart, indicate how the data were collected, explain what certain numbers or headings mean, or describe the statistical procedures used.

7. *Check the source.* The source of data is usually cited at the bottom of the graph or chart. Unless the information was collected by the author, you are likely to find listed a research journal or publication from which the data were taken. Identifying the source is helpful in assessing the reliability of the data.

TYPES OF GRAPHICS

All graphics describe some type of relationship. Not coincidentally, these relationships correspond to the thought patterns we examined in Chapter 6.

Tables: Comparison and Classification of Information

Sociologists, psychologists, scientists, economists, and business analysts frequently use tables to organize and present statistical evidence. A table is an organized display of factual information, usually numbers or statistics. Its purpose is to classify information so that comparisons can be made between or among data.

Take a few minutes now to study Figure 8–2, using the suggestions listed above. Then use the following steps to analyze the table.

1. *Determine how the data are classified, or divided.* This table classifies sources of sound according to level of intensity. Note that the relative sound intensity and the effects of prolonged exposure are also included.

2. *Make comparisons and look for trends.* This step involves surveying the rows and columns, noting how each entry compares with the others.

Be sure to compare columns and rows, noting both similarities and differences and focusing on trends. In Figure 8–2, you might compare the relative intensities of several common sounds to which you are exposed.

3. *Draw conclusions.* Decide what the data show. You can conclude from Figure 8–2 that prolonged exposure to some sounds is dangerous. Often you will find clues, and sometimes direct statements, in the paragraphs that correspond to the table. The portion of the text that refers you to the table often makes a general statement about what the table is intended to highlight.

Once you have drawn your conclusions, stop, think, and react. For example, you might consider what the data in Figure 8–2 suggest about your daily activities.

Figure 8–2   Interpreting a Table

The Intensity of Some Common Sounds

SOUND SOURCE EXPOSURE	DECIBELS (dbA)	RELATIVE SOUND INTENSITY	EFFECT ON HEARING (PROLONGED EXPOSURE)
	0*	1	Audibility threshold
Breathing	10	10	
Whisper, rustling leaves	20	100	Very quiet
Quiet rural nighttime	30	1000	
Library, soft music	40	10,000	
Normal conversation	50	100,000	Quiet
Average office	60	1,000,000	
Vacuum cleaner	70	10,000,000	Annoying
Garbage disposal	80	100,000,000	Possible hearing damage
City traffic, diesel truck	90	1,000,000,000	Hearing damage (8 hours or more exposure)
Garbage truck, chain saw	100	10,000,000,000	Serious hearing damage (8 hours or more exposure
Live rock band; portable stereo held close to ear	110	100,000,000,000	
Siren (close range); jet takeoff (200 yds)	120	1,000,000,000,000	Hearing pain threshold
Crack of gunfire	130	10,000,000,000,000	
Aircraft carrier deck	140	100,000,000,000,000	Eardrum ruptures
Jet takeoff (close range)	150	1,000,000,000,000,000	

* The threshold of hearing is 0 decibels because the scale is logarithmic, and the logarithm of 1 is 0.

Source: Byer and Shainberg, *Living Well: Health in Your Hands,* p. 788

| EXERCISE 8–1 | *Study the table shown in Figure 8–3, and answer the accompanying questions.* |

1. What is the subject of the table?_____

2. Describe how the data are organized. _____

3. Which racial group will experience the largest percentage increase in population between 1980 and 2000? Which group will experience the least? _____

4. In 2000, what percentage of the population will be Hispanic?_____

5. Which racial group will experience the greatest increase in number between 1980 and 2000?_____

Graphs: Relationships Among Variables

Graphs depict the relationship between two or more variables such as price and demand or expenditures over time. Put simply, they are pictures of relationships between two or more sets of information. As you read and study in various academic disciplines, you will encounter many variations of a few basic types of graphs.

Linear Graphs   In linear graphs, information is plotted along a vertical and a horizontal axis, with one or more variables plotted on each. The resulting graph makes it easy to see the relationship between the variables. A sample linear graph is shown in Figure 8–4. The line graph compares the growth of federal expenditures in four categories from 1967 to 1997.

Figure 8–3   Interpreting a Table

Composition of the Population by Race

| | POPULATION (IN MILLIONS) | | | PERCENT INCREASE | PERCENT DISTRIBUTION | |
	1980	1990	2000	1980–2000	1980	2000
White	195	210	221	13	86	83
Black	27	31	35	31	12	13
Hispanic	15	20	25	73	6	9
	227	249	267	18	104	105

Note: Figures do not add up exactly to totals because of the omission of minorities such as American Indian, Eskimo, and Asian, and because about half of Hispanics are also counted as white.

SOURCE: U.S. Census Bureau, Current Population Reports, Series P-25, 1988

Source: Kinnear et al., *Principles of Marketing,* p. 120

Figure 8–4 A Sample Linear Graph

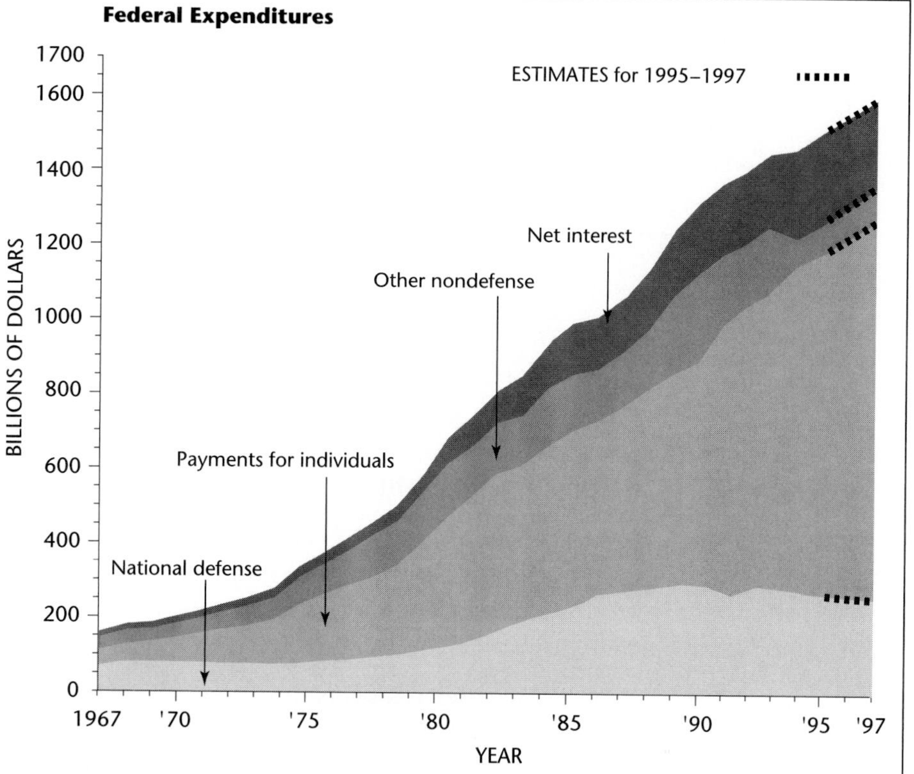

Federal Expenditures

ESTIMATES for 1995–1997 ▪▪▪▪▪

Net interest

Other nondefense

Payments for individuals

National defense

BILLINGS OF DOLLARS

1700
1600
1400
1200
1000
800
600
400
200
0

1967   '70   '75   '80   '85   '90   '95 '97

YEAR

Source: *Budget of the United States Government, Fiscal Year 1996: Historical Tables* (Washington, DC: U.S. Government Printing office, 1995), 85-88.

Source: Edwards et al., *Government in America,* p. 369

In addition to yearly comparisons, the graph also enables you to determine the general trend or pattern among the variables. Generally, this graph shows a slight, steady increase in spending for national defense and a dramatic increase in other expenditure categories.

A graph can show one of three general relationships: positive, inverse, or independent. Each of these is shown in Figure 8–5 (p. 234).

1. *Positive relationships.* When both variables increase or decrease simultaneously, the relationship is positive and is shown on a graph by an upwardly sloping line. In Figure 8–5, Graph A shows the relation between how long a student studied and his or her exam grade. As the study time increases, so does the exam grade.

2. *Inverse relationships.* Inverse relationships occur when one variable increases while the other decreases, as shown in Graph B. Here, as the

Figure 8–5 Relationships Shown by Graphs

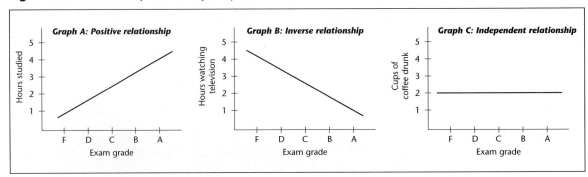

exam grade increases, the amount of time spent watching TV decreases. The inverse relationship is shown by the line or curve that slopes downward and to the right of the point of origin.

3. *Independent relationships.* When the variables have no effect on or relationship to one another, the graph looks like Graph C. There, you can see that the amount of coffee drunk while studying has no effect on exam grades.

From these three relationships, you can see that linear graphs may suggest a cause-and-effect relationship between the variables. However, do not assume that simply because two variables both change, one is acting on the other. Two events may occur at the same time but have no relation to one another. For example, your grades may improve during a semester in which you modify your diet, but the change in diet did not cause your grades to improve. Once you have determined the trend and the nature of the relationship that a linear graph describes, be sure to jot these down in the margin next to the graph. These notes will save you time as you review the chapter.

EXERCISE 8–2

What type of relationship (positive, inverse, or independent) would each of the following linear graphs show?

1. In a graph that plots the way effective use of study time is related to semester grade point average, what type of relationship would you expect?_____

_____

_____

2. In a graph that plots the way time spent reading is related to time spent playing tennis, what relationship would you predict?_____

_____

3. What type of relationship would be shown by a graph that plots the way time checking a dictionary for unknown words is related to reading speed? _____

_____

EXERCISE 8–3

Study the graph shown in Figure 8–6, and answer the following questions.

1. What is the purpose of this graph?
2. What type of relationship (positive, inverse, or independent) does this graph show between the value of exports and imports and years?
3. What trends does this graph reveal about U.S. exports and imports?
4. During what time periods were there the least and the greatest differences between exports and imports?

Figure 8–6   Interpreting a Linear Graph

Source: U.S. Bureau of the Census, *Statistical Abstract of the United States, 1994* (Washington, DC: U.S. Government Printing Office, 1994), 818.

Source: Edwards et al., *Government in America*, p. 523

Figure 8–7   Sample Circle Graph

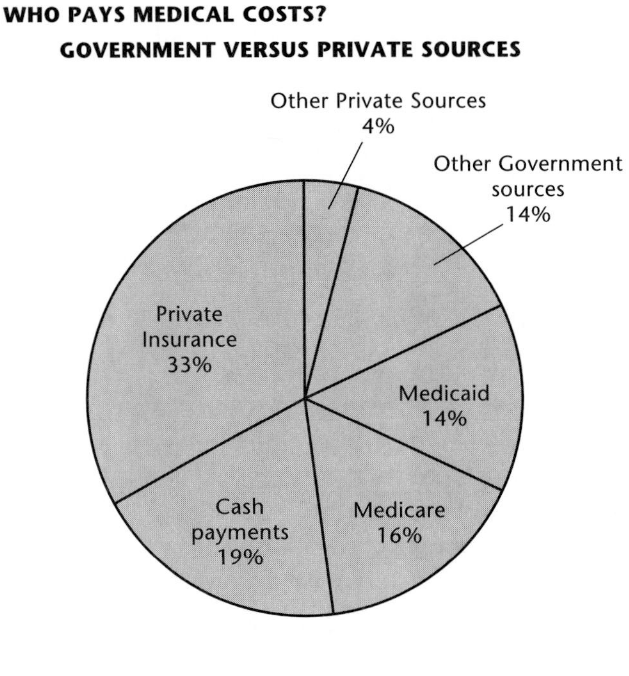

WHO PAYS MEDICAL COSTS?
GOVERNMENT VERSUS PRIVATE SOURCES

Other Private Sources
4%

Other Government
sources
14%

Private
Insurance
33%

Medicaid
14%

Cash
payments
19%

Medicare
16%

Source: U.S. Bureau of the Census, *Statistical Abstract of the United States,
1994* (Washington, DC: U.S. Government Printing Office, 1994), 110.

Source: Edwards et al., *Government in America,* p. 488

Circle Graphs   A circle graph, also called a pie chart, is used to show the relationships of parts to the whole or to show how given parts of a unit have been divided or classified. Figure 8–7 is a circle graph that shows the sources of payment of medical costs. In this graph, payments are divided into six categories.

Circle graphs often are used to emphasize proportions or to show the relative size or importance of various parts. You can see from this graph that private insurance is the greatest source of medical payments, and that other private sources make up the smallest identified source.

**EXERCISE
8–4**

Study the circle graphs shown in Figure 8–8, and answer the accompanying questions.

1.   What are these circle graphs intended to show?

_____

2. Where does the largest portion of the federal dollar come from?

    _____

3. Where does the largest portion go?

    _____

4. What percent of the federal government dollar comes from borrowing?

    _____

5. What percent is spent on interest?

    _____

Figure 8–8   Comparing Circle Graphs

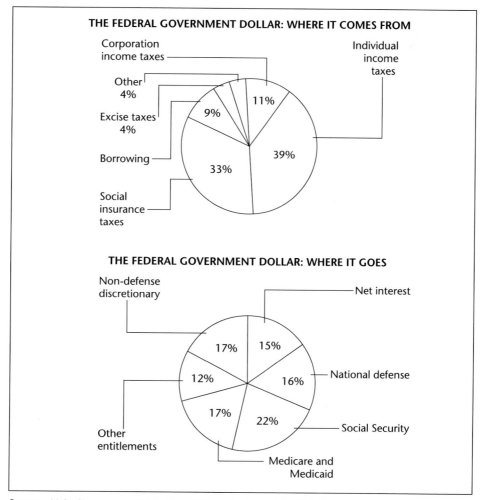

Source: U.S. Government Printing Office, *Budget of the U.S. Government, Fiscal Year 1997.*

Figure 8–9 Sample Bar Graph

Source: Bureau of Labor Statistics,1994

Source: Thio, *Sociology,* p. 450

Bar Graphs A bar graph is often used to make comparisons between quantities or amounts. The horizontal scale often measures time and the vertical scale quantity. A sample bar graph is shown in Figure 8–9. It gives the numbers of strikes that occurred in the years 1969 through 1994.

| EXERCISE 8–5 | *Study the bar graph shown in Figure 8–9, and answer the questions below.* |

1. What is the purpose of the graph? _____

   _____

2. The greatest number of strikes occurred in what year(s)?_____

3. What year(s) had the fewest strikes? _____

4. In which year(s) were there 300 or more strikes? _____

   _____

Diagrams: Explanations of Processes

Diagrams are often included in technical and scientific as well as business and economic texts to explain processes. Diagrams are intended to help you see relationships between parts and understand sequences. Figure 8–10,

Figure 8–10   Sample Diagram

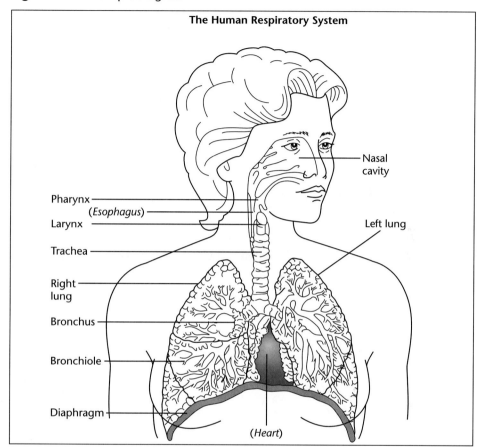

The Human Respiratory System

Nasal cavity

Pharynx

(*Esophagus*)

Larynx

Left lung

Trachea

Right lung

Bronchus

Bronchiole

Diaphragm

(*Heart*)

Source: Campbell et al., *Biology Concepts and Connections,* p. 444

which is taken from a biology textbook, shows the organs of the human respiratory system.

Reading diagrams differs from reading other types of graphics in that diagrams often correspond to fairly large segments of text. This means you have to switch back and forth frequently between the text and the diagram to determine what part of the process each paragraph is discussing.

Because diagrams of processes and the corresponding text are often difficult, complicated, or highly technical, plan to read these sections more than once. Use the first reading to grasp the overall process. In subsequent readings, focus on the details of the process, examining each step and understanding how the process unfolds.

One of the best ways to study a diagram is to redraw it without referring to the original, including as much detail as possible. Redrawing is a true test of whether you understand the process you have diagrammed.

Alternatively, you can test your understanding and recall of the process illustrated in a diagram by explaining it step by step in writing, using your own words.

| EXERCISE 8–6 | *Study the diagram in Figure 8–11, which shows how the AIDS virus spreads in the bloodstream. Then answer the questions that follow.* |

1. What type of cell does the AIDS virus attack?

   _____

2. Why doesn't the host cell reject the AIDS virus?

   _____

   _____

3. Explain how the AIDS virus spreads beyond the first cell it attacks.

   _____

   _____

Photographs: A Visual Impression

Photographs are often considered an art form, but they serve some of the same purposes as other graphics: They are used in textbooks in place of verbal descriptions to present information. Photographs are also used to spark your interest and, often, to draw out an emotional response or impression. Study the photograph shown in Figure 8–12 on p. 242.

This photograph appears on a page of a biology textbook chapter titled "Resources, Energy and Human Life." The photograph of Diane Fossey, a scientist who studied gorilla behavior, reveals the trusting relationship she established with gorillas. Use the following steps to understand photographs.

1. Read the caption to discover the subject and context of the photograph.

2. If the photo is referred to in the text, read the text before studying the photograph. What details are emphasized? What conclusions are drawn?

3. Study the photograph. What is your first overall impression? What details did you notice first? Answering these questions will lead you to discover the purpose of the photograph.

Figure 8–11   Sample Diagram

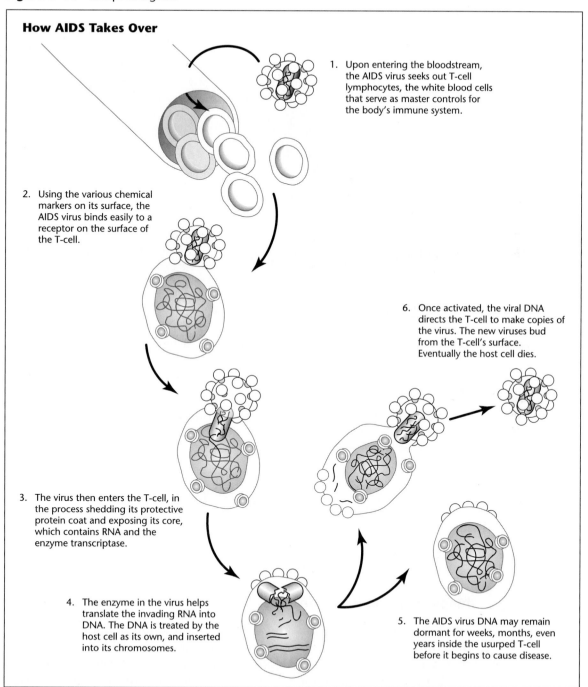

How AIDS Takes Over

1. Upon entering the bloodstream, the AIDS virus seeks out T-cell lymphocytes, the white blood cells that serve as master controls for the body's immune system.

2. Using the various chemical markers on its surface, the AIDS virus binds easily to a receptor on the surface of the T-cell.

6. Once activated, the viral DNA directs the T-cell to make copies of the virus. The new viruses bud from the T-cell's surface. Eventually the host cell dies.

3. The virus then enters the T-cell, in the process shedding its protective protein coat and exposing its core, which contains RNA and the enzyme transcriptase.

4. The enzyme in the virus helps translate the invading RNA into DNA. The DNA is treated by the host cell as its own, and inserted into its chromosomes.

5. The AIDS virus DNA may remain dormant for weeks, months, even years inside the usurped T-cell before it begins to cause disease.

Source: Wallace, *Biology: The World of Life,* p. 567

Figure 8–12   Sample Photograph

Much of what we know in science is due to simple observation. Diane Fossey told us a great deal about mountain gorillas by being able to move among them. The arrogant, tough, and dedicated Fossey was instrumental in protecting these shy beasts from poachers (who sell gorilla hands to wealthy Europeans to be used for ashtrays) until she was killed by an assailant in her mountain cabin.

Source: Wallace, *Biology: The World of Life,* p. 38 (text); Peter Weit, Corbis/Sygma (photo)

EXERCISE 8–7

Study the photograph shown in Figure 8–13. Then answer the questions below.

1. What emotional reaction does this photograph create?

   _____

   _____

2. Why would it be included in a sociology textbook chapter titled "Third World Problems"?

   _____

   _____

Maps: Physical Relationships

Maps describe relationships and provide information about location and direction. They are commonly found in geography and history texts, and they also appear in ecology, biology, and anthropology texts. Most of us think of maps as describing distances and locations, but maps are also used to describe placement of geographical and ecological features such as areas of pollution, areas of population density, or political data (voting districts).

Figure 8–13   Interpreting a Photograph

Source: Charles Caratini, Corbis/Sygma

When reading maps, use the following steps:

1. Read the caption. This identifies the subject of the map.

2. Use the legend or key to identify the symbols or codes used.

3. Note distance scales.

4. Study the map, looking for trends or key points. Often, the text that accompanies the map states the key points that the map illustrates.

5. Try to visualize, or create a mental picture of, the map.

6. As a learning and study aid, write, in your own words, a statement of what the map shows.

Now refer to the map shown in Figure 8–14 on p. 244, which is taken from a biology textbook.

This map shows the number of different species of trees located in North America. The caption notes trends and explains that diversity is affected by changes in longitude and latitude.

Figure 8–14 Sample Map

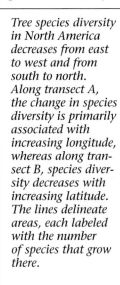
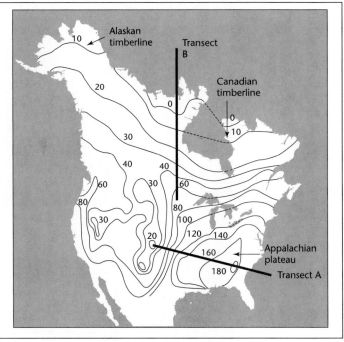

Tree species diversity in North America decreases from east to west and from south to north. Along transect A, the change in species diversity is primarily associated with increasing longitude, whereas along transect B, species diversity decreases with increasing latitude. The lines delineate areas, each labeled with the number of species that grow there.

Alaskan timberline
Transect B
Canadian timberline
Appalachian plateau
Transect A

Source: Mix et al., *Biology: The Network of Life,* p. 128

EXERCISE 8–8

Study the map shown in Figure 8–15, and answer the following questions.

1. What is the purpose of the map?
2. What country has the lowest rate of HIV infection among males?
3. In what area is the largest number of people infected with HIV?
4. How does the rate of HIV infection among males in the United States compare with that of the other countries represented in this map?

EXERCISE 8–9

Use the following statistics to construct a graphic that organizes some or all of the information on population growth. Exchange your creation with a classmate, and offer each other ideas for improvement.

1. In 1970, the world population was 3,632 million.
2. In 1990, the world population was 5,320 million.
3. In 1970, the population of Africa was 344 million.
4. In 1990, the population of Africa was 660 million.
5. In 1970, the population of Asia was 2,045 million.

6. In 1990, the population of Asia was 3,111 million.
7. In 1970, the population of Europe was 462 million.
8. In 1990, the population of Europe was 499 million.

EXERCISE 8-10

Select two different graphic devices used in a textbook chapter you have read recently, and answer the following questions about each.

1. What is the subject of the graphic?
2. What is its purpose?
3. If it presents data, how is it organized? If it is a diagram or photo, how does it achieve its purpose?
4. What is its source, and how recent is it?

Figure 8–15   Sample Map

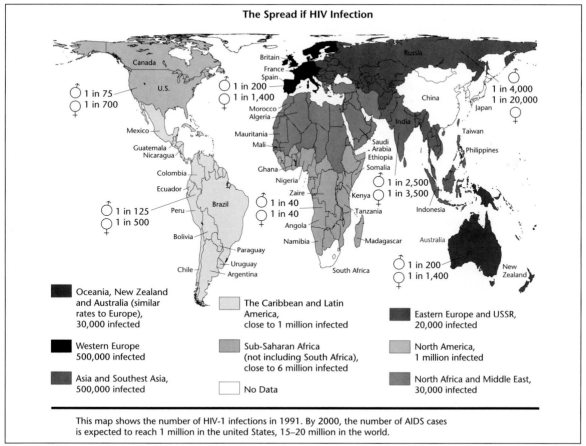

Source: Mix et al., *Biology: The Network of Life,* p. 784

Managing Stress

College is a new and challenging experience, and new and challenging experiences tend to produce stress. Consequently, stress is a common problem that many college students must face.

Common Symptoms
worn-out feeling
queasiness, indigestion
short-temperedness
listlessness
headaches
feeling rushed
difficulty concentrating
weight loss

How to Reduce Stress

1. *Eliminate stressors.* Identify possible sources of stress, and work toward eliminating them. If a part-time job is stressful, for instance, quit or find another that is less stressful. If a math course is creating stress, take action: Go to the learning lab or math lab for assistance or inquire about tutoring.

2. *Establish a daily routine.* To eliminate daily hassles and make daily tasks as simple as possible, establish a daily routine. A routine eliminates the need to make numerous small decisions, thereby giving you a sense of "smooth sailing."

3. *Accentuate your accomplishments.* When you feel pressured, stop and review what you have already accomplished that day and that week. This review will give you confidence that you can handle the work load. A positive attitude goes a long way in overcoming stress.

4. *Eat nutritious meals.*

5. *Get physical exercise.* Exercise often releases tension, promotes a general feeling of wellness, and improves self-concept. Many students report that as little as 30 minutes of exercise produces immediate relaxation and helps them to place daily events in perspective.

6. *Get adequate amounts of sleep.*

7. *Seek knowledgeable advice.* If stress becomes an insurmountable problem, seek assistance from the student counseling center. The office may offer workshops in stress-reduction techniques such as relaxation or biofeedback training.

8. *Get involved with campus activities.* Some students become so involved with their course work that they do little else but study or worry about studying. In fact, they feel guilty or stressed when they are not studying. Be sure to allow some time in each day to relax and have fun. Campus activities provide a valuable means of releasing tension and taking your mind off your work.

SUMMARY

Graphics summarize and condense information and emphasize or clarify relationships. It is important to remember to do the following things when reading graphics.

- Read the caption.
- Determine the organization of the graphic.
- Note symbols, abbreviations, and/or scales.
- Identify trends or patterns.
- Study footnotes.
- Check the source of information.

Several types of graphics are described.

- Tables are used to compare and classify data or information.
- Graphs depict relationships among variables.
- Diagrams present visual representations of processes or sequences.
- Photographs provide visual impressions and often provoke an emotional response.
- Maps are used to describe physical relationships.

AMERICAN GOVERNMENT

PREREADING QUESTIONS

1. Do you believe your vote makes a difference in national elections? Why or why not?
2. Do you think that by participating in your community, you are being politically active?

HOW AMERICANS PARTICIPATE IN POLITICS

George P. Edwards, Martin P. Wattenberg, and Robert L. Lineberry

1   In politics, as in many other aspects of life, the squeaky wheel gets the grease. The way citizens "squeak" in politics is by participation. Americans have many avenues of political participation open to them.

- Mrs. Jones of Iowa City goes to a neighbor's living room to attend her local precinct's presidential caucus.
- Tipper Gore, wife of Vice President Al Gore, testifies before a Senate committee to express her view that warning labels should be put on record albums that contain vulgar language.
- Protesters against ethnic cleansing n Bosnia gather outside the United Nations in New York to urge international intervention.
- Parents in Alabama file a lawsuit to oppose textbooks that, in their opinion, promote "secular humanism."
- Mr. Smith, a Social Security recipient, writes to his senator to express his concern about a possible cut in his cost-of-living benefits.
- Over one hundred million people vote in a presidential election.

2   All of these activities are types of political participation. **Political participation** encompasses the many activities used by citizens to influence the selection of political leaders or the policies they pursue. Participation can be overt or subtle. The mass protests throughout Eastern Europe in the fall of 1989 were an avalanche of political participation, yet quietly writing a letter to your congressperson is also participating. Political participation can be violent or peaceful, organized or individual, casual or consuming.

3   Generally, the United States has a participatory political culture. Citizens express pride in their nation: Eighty-seven percent say they are very proud to be Americans. Nevertheless, just 49 percent of adult Americans voted in the presidential election of 1996 and only 39 percent turned out for the 1994 con-

gressional elections. At the local level the situation is even worse, with elections for city council often drawing less than a quarter of the voters and school board elections sometimes less than 10 percent.

CONVENTIONAL PARTICIPATION

4   Although the line is hard to draw, political scientists generally distinguish between two broad types of participation: conventional and unconventional. Conventional participation includes many widely accepted modes of influencing government: voting, trying to persuade others, ringing doorbells, running for office, and so on. In contrast, unconventional participation includes activities that are often dramatic, such as protesting, civil disobedience, and even violence.

5   The number of Americans for whom political activity is an important part of their everyday life is minuscule, totaling at most in the tens of thousands. Yet, millions do take part in political activities beyond simply voting. In two comprehensive studies of American political participation conducted by Sidney Verba and his colleagues, samples of Americans were asked in 1967 and 1987 about their role in various kinds of political activities.

Unconventional protest techniques are the trademark of ACT-UP, an AIDS protest group. Here, members of the group are lying down near the White House, defying police orders to disperse. Members of ACT-UP believe that such dramatic protests are necessary to keep the issue of AIDS in the public eye.

Included were voting, working in campaigns, contacting government officials, and working on local community issues. As you can see in Figure 2, voting is the only aspect of political participation that a majority of the population reported engaging in. At the same time, voting is also the only political activity for which there is evidence of a decline in participation in recent years. Substantial increases in participation can be found on the dimensions of giving money to candidates and contacting public officials, and small increases are evident for all the other activities. Thus, while the decline of turnout is a development Americans should rightly be concerned about (see Chapter 8), a broader look

Figure 2   Interpreting a Linear Graph

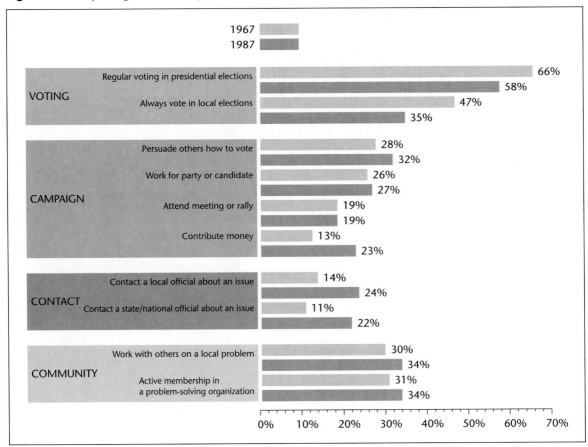

Source: Adapted from data presented in Sidney Verba, Kay Lehman Schlozman, and Henry E. Brady, *Voice and Equality* (Cambridge, MA: Harvard University Press, 1995), 72.

at political participation points to some positive developments for participatory democracy.

PROTEST AS PARTICIPATION

6   Unconventional forms of political participation are missing from the list of activities shown in Figure 2. From the Boston Tea Party to burning draft cards, Americans have engaged in countless political protests. Protest is a form of political participation designed to achieve policy change through dramatic and unconventional tactics. The media's willingness to cover the unusual can make protest worthwhile, drawing attention to a point of view that many Americans

might never encounter. Indeed, protests today are often orchestrated to provide television cameras with vivid images. Demonstration coordinators steer participants to prearranged staging areas and provide facilities for press coverage.

7   Throughout American history, individuals and groups have sometimes used **civil disobedience,** that is, they have consciously broken a law that they thought was unjust. The Reverend Martin Luther King, Jr., won a Nobel Peace Prize for his civil disobedience against segregationist law in the 1950s and 1960s. His "Letter from a Birmingham Jail" is a classic defense of civil disobedience. Sometimes political participation can be violent. The history of violence in American politics is a long one—not surprising, perhaps, for a nation born in rebellion. The turbulent 1960s included many outbreaks of violence. African-American neighborhoods in American cities were torn by riots. College campuses were sometimes turned into battle zones as protesters against the Vietnam War fought police and national guard units. At Kent State, Jackson State, Cornell, Columbia, and elsewhere, peaceful demonstrations turned violent, and many were hurt (or, at Kent State and Jackson State, killed). Although supported by few people, throughout American history violence has been a means of pressuring the government to change its policies.

—Edwards et al., *Government in America,* pp. 90–92

VOCABULARY REVIEW

1. For each of the words listed below, use context; prefixes, roots, and suffixes; and/or a dictionary to write a brief definition or synonym of the word as it is used in the reading.

    a. humanism (para. 1) _____

    b. encompasses (para. 2) _____

    c. subtle (para. 2) _____

    d. modes (para. 4) _____

    e. miniscule (para. 5) _____

    f. substantial (para. 5) _____

    g. orchestrated (para. 6) _____

    h. turbulent (para. 7)_____

2. Underline new specialized terms introduced in the reading.

COMPREHENSION QUESTIONS

1. What are the primary conventional ways Americans participate in politics? Which is the most popular?
2. Define and give an example of nonconventional participation.
3. For what form of political participation was there greatest change between 1967 and 1987?
4. In the campaigns section of Figure 2, which one area has shown a significant increase in the 20 year period studied? Which area has shown the largest decrease?
5. What forms of political participation have increased between 1967 and 1987? Which have decreased?

THINKING CRITICALLY

1. Why do you think more Americans contributed to campaigns in 1987 than they did in 1967? What are some factors that could account for this increase?
2. Although fewer Americans voted in 1987 than 1967, more Americans contributed to political campaigns. To what can you attribute this apparent discrepancy?
3. Brainstorm possible reasons for relatively low voting percentages in the U.S. What can be done to improve it?
4. If the research described in Figure 2 were being conducted today, would you expect to find a significantly higher percentage of participation in community involvement? Why or why not?
5. The photograph in the reading depicts people holding a protest. Which do you think is more effective: describing this event in words or illustrating it in this photograph? Why? What are the advantages and disadvantages of each?
6. What forms of political participation have you been involved in over the past year? Which was most rewarding? Why?

LEARNING/STUDY STRATEGIES

1. Predict an essay question that might be based on this reading.
2. Draw a map or diagram that visually displays the key points presented in this reading.

AMERICAN GOVERNMENT

PREREADING QUESTIONS

1. In what countries might you expect to find low voter turnout?
2. Do you think that low voter turnout in the U.S. is a symptom of apathy or of other factors?

THE VANISHING ELECTORATE

Edward S. Greenberg and Benjamin I. Page

1   Early increases in voting participation have given way, in the twentieth century, to serious declines. The disturbing fact is that today a much smaller proportion of people participate in politics than did during most of the nineteenth century. Since 1912, only about 55 to 65 percent of eligible Americans have voted in presidential elections and still fewer in other elections: 40 to 50 percent in off-year (non-presidential-year) congressional elections and as few as 10 to 20 percent in primaries and minor local elections. In recent years, the **turnout** rate has dropped to the low end of those ranges. It was only 36 percent in the 1986 congressional elections, 37 percent in 1990, and 39 percent in 1994; in those off years, little more than *one-third* of eligible Americans participated in electing congressional representatives. Hence the talk about a vanishing electorate (see Figure 3).

2   Despite the early development of broad suffrage rights in the United States, our voting turnout rate is exceptionally low compared with other modern industrialized countries, where 80 percent rates are common (see Figure 4). Most observers consider this a serious problem for democracy in America, particularly since (as we will see) those who vote tend to be different from those who do not. Nonvoters do not get an equal voice in political choices. Political equality, one of the key elements of democracy, is violated.

Causes of Low Turnout

3   Why do so few Americans participate in elections? Scholars have identified several possible factors.

4   **Barriers to Voting**   In the United States, only citizens who take the initiative to register before an election are permitted to vote. Sometimes registration is made difficult by limited locations, limited office hours, and requirements to register long before the election. This is especially hard on people who move from one community to another. In one presidential election, about 35 percent

Figure 3 The Rise and Fall of Turnout in Presidential Elections, 1789–1996
Turnout in presidential elections rose sharply during the nineteenth century but has declined in the twentieth century.

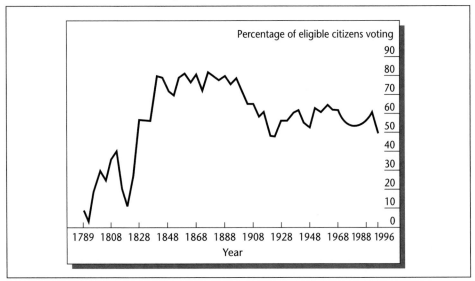

Sources: Walter Dean Burnham, "The Turnout Problem," in A. James Reichley, ed., *Elections, American Style* (Washington, DC: Brooking Institution, 1987), pp. 113–114; U.S. Bureau of the Census.

of the nonvoters, and only 16 percent of voters, said that they had moved in the past two years. In most European countries with high turnout rates, the government, rather than individual citizens, is responsible for deciding who is listed as eligible to vote (see Figure 4).

5   The United States could certainly increase political equality and popular sovereignty by making voting easier. The federal "motor voter" law passed in 1993, providing for registration in motor vehicle bureaus and other government offices, was a step in this direction. Another way would be to ease voting itself, by making every election day a holiday, by allowing an extended voting period like the two and a half weeks tried in Texas, by broadening the right of absentee voting as in California, or by allowing voting by mail over an extended period as in Oregon.

6   **Lack of Attractive Choices**   Some scholars believe that the nature of the political parties and the choices they offer also affect turnout. Many American citizens may not like the candidates of either of the major parties well enough to bother voting for them and see no reason to vote for a third party that has no chance of winning.

7   **Changes in Eligibility Rules**   Changes in eligibility rules have also affected turnout rates, at least temporarily. As Figure 3 indicates, turnout as a propor-

Figure 4   Voting Turnout in Various Countries

Turnout tends to be substantially lower in the United States than in other advanced industrial countries.

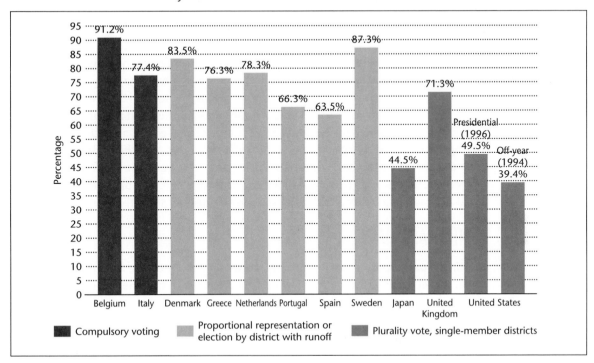

Sources: Federal Election Commission; Keele University.

tion of eligible voters dropped just after women were enfranchised in 1920 because at first, women were less likely to vote than men. But that difference gradually disappeared. In fact, in some recent elections (1988, 1992, and 1996, though not 1990 or 1994), women voted at rates slightly higher than men. Similarly, turnout percentages dropped a bit after 18-year-olds won the vote in 1971 because young people do not participate as much; they are less firmly established in their local communities.

8   **Alienation**   The apathy toward and alienation from politics that many Americans feel have undoubtedly contributed to declines in turnout. Some of this alienation results from well-publicized attacks on government and from recent economic problems, including recessions and job insecurity. But much of it can be traced back as far as the 1960s, to the assassination of popular leaders (e.g., John F. Kennedy, Robert Kennedy, and Martin Luther King, Jr.) and to the Vietnam War, urban unrest, and the Watergate and Iran-Contra scandals.

9   **Lack of Voter Mobilization by Parties**   A related factor may be the failure of the political parties to register low-income citizens, especially African-Americans and Hispanics. In recent years, neither major party has seemed very

eager to increase the number of voters among the poor, possibly because of worries that they would support candidates like Jesse Jackson who are more liberal than most party officials.

Campaigning Involvement and Contacting Public Officials

10   Despite the low voter turnout levels in the United States, however, Americans are actually more likely than people in other countries to participate actively in campaigns. During the 1992 presidential campaign, some 18 percent of adults said they gave money, a remarkable 29 percent said they had attended a political rally, and 5 percent had worked actively in a campaign organization. Much the same thing is true of contacting public officials; about one-third (34 percent) or Americans say they have done so during the past year, most often with local elected officials. Exactly why Americans vote less but campaign for candidates and contact officials more than citizens elsewhere is something of a puzzle.

WHO PARTICIPATES?

11   Political participation varies greatly according to people's income, education, age, and ethnicity as shown in Figure 5. This means that some people have more representation and influence with elected officials than others and thus are

Figure 5   Presidential Election Turnout in 1996, by Social Group
Age, education, race, ethnicity, and gender all affect voting habits. Members of certain social groups are more likely to vote in elections than others.

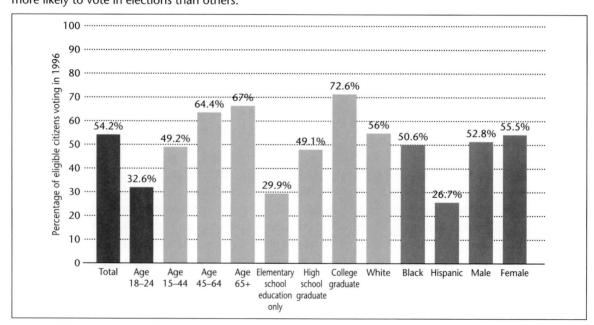

Source: U.S. Bureau of the Census.

more likely, other things being equal, to get their preferences and interests reflected in what government does. This unequal representation, which violates the fundamental democratic norm of political equality, suggests that American politics is not as democratic as it might be.

—Greenberg and Page, *The Struggle for Democracy*, pp. 185–88

VOCABULARY REVIEW

1. For each of the words listed below, use context, prefixes, roots, and suffixes; and/or a dictionary to write a brief definition or synonym of the word as it is used in the reading.

   a. declines (para. 1) _____

   b. suffrage (para. 2) _____

   c. sovereignty (para. 5)_____

   d. enfranchised (para. 7) _____

   e. alienation (para. 8) _____

   f. recessions (para. 8) _____

   g. urban (para. 8) _____

2. Underline new specialized terms introduced in the reading.

COMPREHENSION QUESTIONS

1. Give five reasons why there has been a decline in turnout for U.S. elections.
2. Compared to other countries, the U.S. has the lowest voter turnout rate. Why is this considered a major problem?
3. According to Figure 3, what year in U.S. history saw the lowest percentage of voter turnout?
4. According to Figure 4, which country is second to the U.S. in terms of low voter turnout?
5. According to Figure 5, which age group has the lowest voter turnout? Which has the highest? What is the overall trend?

THINKING CRITICALLY

1. Aside from the suggestions given in the article for increasing voter registration, give at least one other way to increase voter registration.

2. What kind of conclusions might you draw about gender and voter turnout based on Figure 5?
3. Figure 3 indicates that there was a rapid decline in voter turnout for Presidential elections between 1808 and 1818. Can you think of reasons why that was the case?
4. What type of a graph is depicted in Figure 3? Do you think another type would be more effective? Why or why not?

LEARNING/STUDY STRATEGIES

1. Predict an essay question that might be based on this reading?
2. Write a statement that summarizes a trend shown in at least two of the graphs included in these readings.

THINKING ABOUT THE PAIRED READINGS

INTEGRATING IDEAS

1. Between the two readings, there were a total of four graphs. Which graph was the most useful and why?
2. Identify the thought patterns used to organize each reading.
3. What information would you use from each reading to make a speech to a group of high school students about their responsibility to participate in the political process?
4. Write a letter to the editor of your local newspaper. Your purpose is to urge members of your community to become more involved in the political process. Use information or statistics from one or both readings to support your ideas.

GENERATING NEW IDEAS

1. Write a list of suggestions that could be used in a brochure designed to encourage college students to increase their political participation.
2. Assuming that apathy may be a major reason for eligible voters in the U.S. not voting, write an essay on the steps you would take to increase voting if you were in office.
3. Write a brief paper stating whether or not you would ever participate in a demonstration on the White House lawn. Choose a specific issue, and explain why you think it is or is not important enough to participate in a protest.

9 | READING ONLINE

LEARNING OBJECTIVES

- **To learn to locate electronic sources more effectively**
- **To evaluate Internet sources**
- **To develop new reading and thinking strategies for reading electronic sources**
- **To use electronic study aids**

Increasingly, college students are finding the Internet to be a valuable and useful resource. The Internet is a worldwide network of computers through which you can access a wide variety of information and services. Through the Internet, you can access the **World Wide Web** (WWW), a system of Internet servers that allow exchange of information of specially formatted documents. It connects a vast array of resources (documents, graphics, and audio and video files) and allows users to move between and among them easily and rapidly. Many instructors use the Internet and have begun requiring their students to do so. In this chapter, you will learn to read and study electronic sources differently than you do print sources.

Although in most courses, your textbook is still your primary source of information, more and more instructors are expecting their students to use the Internet to supplement their textbook or obtain additional, more current information by visiting Web sites on the Internet. (Textbooks, no matter how up to date they may be, often do not contain information within the past year.)

Other instructors encourage or require their students to use CD-ROMs that accompany their textbooks or use CD-ROMs available in computer labs. Still other instructors expect their students to consult Internet sources in researching a topic for a research paper. Many students, too, are finding valuable information on personal or special interests on the Internet.

For example, Maria Valquez, a student majoring in liberal arts, over the course of a week conducted the following activities using electronic sources.

- Ordered a music CD from Amazon.com, an online book and music store.
- Visited an online writing center, www.purdue.edu, for help with an English paper.
- Searched for Web sites on the topic of tattooing for a sociology research paper.
- Used a CD-ROM tutorial to help her solve problems for her math class.
- Sent and received e-mail from friends.
- Checked the weather in her hometown in anticipation of a weekend trip.
- Visited a Latino student Web site for ideas for organizing a Latino student group on her campus.

Electronic sources are becoming increasingly important in many students' academic and personal lives. Therefore, it is important to know how Web sites are structured, how to locate useful sources, how to evaluate the sources you locate, how to understand differences from print sources, and how to navigate through them in an efficient way.

Although this chapter focuses on using electronic sources, you should realize that the Internet is not always the best source of information. Sometimes, it is easier and quicker to find a piece of information in a book or other traditional sources.

FEATURES OF A WEB SITE

A **Web site** is a location on the World Wide Web where you can obtain information on a particular subject. It is a collection of related pages linked together. Each page is called a **Web page** and stands for a set of information. (It can be any length and is not restricted to a single screen or printed page.) The first page you see when you access a Web site is called its **homepage.**

Major corporations such as Hertz, Burger King, and General Motors have Web sites, as do many universities, government agencies, nonprofit organizations, and local businesses. Web sites are created for a variety of purposes: to sell products, present information, promote a particular viewpoint, share creative work, and so forth.

Web sites have recently been established by textbook publishers and authors to provide information and activities that supplement the textbook. A Web site for a biology text, for example, may contain reviews of recent research and discoveries not included in the text. A Web site for an English composition textbook may contain additional current readings or up-to-date information on documenting electronic sources or exercises that relate to specific portions of the textbook.

EXERCISE 9–1

Visit two of the following Web sites by typing in the Internet addresses listed below. Then answer the following questions.

a.   www.si.edu
b.   www.cnn.com
c.   www.nypl.org
d.   www.irs.ustreas.gov

If any of the above sites is unavailable, substitute a Web site of your own choice.

1.   What is the purpose of each site?
2.   In what ways are they similar, and in what ways do they differ?

Parts of a Web Site

A Web site begins with a home page which is the first screen (and possibly more) of the site; it serves as the site's introduction. You can also think of it as a master directory. A sample home page for the Interamerican University Studies Institute is shown in Figure 9–1 on page 262. You can move to other pages on the site by using either navigational buttons or links. **Navigational buttons** are graphic icons such as symbols, arrows, pictures, or buttons. They usually appear at the top, bottom, or on one side of each page. Clicking on these buttons allows you to move to different pages within the site. On the sample homepage in Figure 9–1, the icon "IUSI Presents 1999 Scholarship" is a button, as is the list of items at the left side of the screen. **Links** are highlighted words or phrases within a document that take you to other pages within the site (related links) or to other Web sites (remote links). In Figure 9–1 "Need a Passport?" and "Check the Weather" are external links; they take you to another Web site.

Because it is easy to get lost when navigating through a site, many sites include buttons on all secondary pages that take the reader back to the homepage.

Well-designed Web sites tend to cluster chunks of related information together. The more important information often appears in the top left or right of the screen, since readers of English use a left-to-right eye movement pattern.

Figure 9–1   A Sample Homepage

Interamerican University Studies Institute

Dedicated to fostering cultural and educational exchange between the U.S. and Latin America

Home Page

Programs:

Program Overview

High School

Undergraduate

Workshops

For Teachers

Independent

Group Tours

Host Countries:

Mexico

Costa Rica

Order Books

Contact Us:

About IUSI

Info Request

Send Us E-mail

Participants in our "Experience Costa Rica" program surrounded by children during a visit to the school of Tilarán, Costa Rica.

Welcome to the Interamerican University Studies Institute web site, offering information on IUSI's programs as well as links to Internet resources regarding Mexico and Latin America.

Click here to view the snapshots we've been collecting from our trips to Mexico and Costa Rica.

Great Programs For Teens In Mexico and Costa Rica

A Special Offer

Need a Passport?

Travel with Children

Suggested Reading

Check the Weather in Mexico or Costa Rica

IUSI Presents 1999 Scholarship

Interamerican University Studies Institute
P.O. Box 10958, Eugene, OR 97440
Phone (541) 687-6968 / Fax (541) 686-5947
Outside area code 541, call 1-800-345-IUSI (4874)
email: office@iusi.org

World To World Literary Translation
Creative Writing in Mexico
Professional Development

Copyright © 2000 Interamerican University Studies Institute.
All rights reserved. Maintained by webmaster@iusi.org.

Source: The Interamerican University Studies Institute (http://iusi.org/index.shtml)

Web Site Addresses

Each Web site has its own address, known as its **URL** (Uniform Resource Locator). Here's how to read a URL for the *San Francisco Chronicle.*

transfer format   host computer directory path file name

http: // www.sfgate.com / chronicle / index.shtml

The transfer format identifies the type of server the document is located on and indicates the type of transfer format to be used. The second names the host computer. The directory path is the "address" part of the Web site. The last is the document name.

Many sites can be contacted using only the transfer format and the host computer address. Once you have contacted the site, you can move to different locations and files within the Web site. For example, suppose you are looking for information on an author, and all you know is that she teaches at Tufts University. You could search for the URL of Tufts University and then get to the University homepage. Once there, you could look under Faculty and you might find information about the author.

Anyone can place a Web site on the Internet. Consequently, you must be cautious and verify that the sources are reliable. A Web page may contain a heading, called a header, that serves as a title for the information on that page. It often appears in bigger, bolder type than the rest of the text on the page. These headers can sometimes serve as valuable, concise descriptions of the contents of the page. If they are descriptive, use them to decide whether the page contains the information you need and if it is worth reading.

LOCATING ELECTRONIC SOURCES ON THE WEB

Begin by gaining access to the Internet. In addition to a computer, you will need a modem and a browser, such as Microsoft Explorer or Netscape Navigator. You will also need an Internet service provider (ISP) to connect your computer to the Internet. Your college's computer center, your telephone or cable company, or a commercial service provider such as America Online can connect you. You will need a name you use online, called a username, and a password. If you need help getting started, check with the staff in your college's computer lab.

Identifying Keywords

To search for information on a topic, you need to come up with a group of specific words that describe your topic; these are known as **keywords.** It is often necessary to narrow your topic in order to identify specific keywords.

For example, if you searched the topic home-schooling, you would find thousands of sources. However, if you narrowed your topic to home-schooling of primary grade children in California, you would identify far fewer sources.

There are three basic groups of search tools you can use to locate information: subject directories, search engines, and meta-search engines.

Using Subject Directories

Subject directories classify Web resources by categories and subcategories. Some offer reviews or evaluations of sites. Use a subject directory when you want to browse the Web using general topics or when you are conducting a broad search. A subject directory would be helpful if you are looking for sites about parenting issues or want to find a list of organizations for animal welfare. Here are several useful directories:

INFOMINE http://infomine.ucr.edu

Lycos top 5% http://www.lycos.com

Yahoo http://www.yahoo.com

Using a Search Engine

A **search engine** is a computer program that helps you locate information on a topic. Search engines search for keywords and provide connections to documents that contain the key words you instruct it to search for. Depending on your topic, some search engines are more useful than others. In addition, each search engine may require a different way of entering the keywords. For example, some may require you to place quotation marks around a phrase ("capital punishment"). Other times, you may need to use plus signs (+) between keywords ("home schooling" + "primary grades" + "California"). The quotes around "home schooling" will create a search for those words as a phrase, rather than as single terms. Be sure to use the "help" feature when you use a new search engine to discover the best way to enter keywords.

Useful search engines include

Alta Vista http://altavista.com

Excite http://www.excite.com

HotBot http://www.hotbot.dom

Go Network http://www.go.com

NetSearch http://home.netscape.com/home/internet-search.html

WebCrawler http://webcrawler.com

Most search engines have help sections that include instructions about how to use them.

Using Meta-Search Engines

You can search a number of search engines at the same time and combine all the results in a single listing using a **meta-search engine.** Use these types of engines when you are searching for a very specific or obscure topic or one for which you are having trouble finding information. Here a few common ones:

MetaFind http://metafind.com

DogPile http://dogpile.com

PROFUsion http://profusion.com

EXERCISE 9–2	*Use one of the search tools listed above to locate three sources on one of the following topics. Then use a different tool or different search engine to search the same topic again. Compare your results. Which engine was easier to use? Which produced more sources?*

1. The Baseball Hall of Fame
2. Telecommuting
3. Your favorite musical group
4. Parenting issues

EVALUATING INTERNET SOURCES

Although the Internet contains a great deal of valuable information and resources, it also contains rumor, gossip, hoaxes, and misinformation. In other words, not all Internet sources are trustworthy. You must evaluate a source before accepting it. Here are some guidelines to follow when evaluating Internet sources.

1. *Check the publisher or sponsor of the site.* If a site is sponsored or provided by a well-known organization, a reputable newspaper such as *The New York Times,* the information is apt to be reliable. One way to discover the sponsoring organization is to check the URL. The last part of a URL,

called the domain, reveals something about the nature of a Web site's sponsor. Here is a list of common domains and their abbreviation as used in a URL.

Commercial	-.com	(Internet providers, AOL, for example; companies, or anyone trying to sell something)
Education	-.edu	(public schools, colleges, universities, students' homepages, term papers)*
Government	-.gov	(State, National agencies)
Network	-.net	
Non Profit Organization	-.org	(non profit groups)
Military	-.mil	
Other countries	-.ca (Canada), -.uk (United Kingdom)	

2. *Check the author.* For Web sites, look for professional credentials or affiliations. Often, the author's professional affiliation will be included at the end of an article he or she has written. Usually, you can trust a reputable sponsor to feature only credible authors. To find out about an author through an Internet search, use a search engine. Type the author's full name in the search box. Place the full name in quotation marks, or choose phrase searching, if it is available.

   For newsgroups or discussion groups (see p. 278), check to see if the author has given his or her name and a signature (a short biographical description included at the end of messages).

3. *Check the date of the posting.* Be sure you are obtaining current information. A credible Web site usually includes the date on which it was last updated.

4. *Discover the purpose of the posting.* Many Web sites are written with an agenda, such as to sell a product, promote a cause, advocate a position, and so forth. Look for bias in the reporting of information.

5. *Check links (addresses of other sources suggested by the Web site).* If these links are no longer working, the Web site you are visiting may be outdated or not reputable.

---

* The .edu abbreviation used to be a good indicator of a higher education academic site, but that is no longer the case. Be sure to check the source.

6. *Cross-check your information.* If you doubt the accuracy of information you have found, try to find the same information in another source.

EXERCISE 9–3	*Evaluate each of the sites you located for Exercise 9–2. Assign a rating of 1–5 (1 = low reliability; 5 = high reliability). Be prepared to discuss your ratings.*

EXERCISE 9–4	*Visit a Web site and become familiar with its organization and content. Evaluate it using the suggested criteria. Then write a brief paragraph explaining why the Web site is or is not a reliable source.*

READING ELECTRONIC TEXT

Reading electronic text (also called hypertext) is very different from reading traditional printed text such as textbooks or magazines or newspaper articles. The term electronic text, as used in this chapter, refers to information presented on a Web site. It does not refer to articles and essays that can be downloaded from Searchbank or from an e-journal, for example. Because Web sites are unique, they require a different mind set and different reading strategies. If electronic text is new or unfamiliar to you, you need to change the way you read and the way you think when approaching Web sites. If you attempt to read Web sites the same way you read traditional text, you may lose focus or perspective, miss important information, or become generally disoriented. Text used on Web sites is different in the following ways from traditional print text.

- *Reading Web sites involves paying attention to sound, graphics, and movement, as well as words.* Your senses, then, may pull you in several different directions simultaneously. Recorded or artificial sounds may compete with animated sequences, flashing graphics, and colorful drawings or photos for your attention. Some Web sites are available in two formats—graphical and text-only. This is most common for academic sites. If you are distracted by the sound and graphics, check to see if a text-only version of the site is available.

- *Text on Web sites comes in brief, independent screenfuls, sometimes called nodes.* These screenfuls tend to be brief, condensed pieces of information. Unlike traditional text, they are not set within a context, and background information is often not supplied. They do not depend on other pages for meaning either. In traditional print text, paragraphs and pages are dependent—you often must have read and understood a previous one in order to comprehend the one that follows it. Electronic pages are often intended to stand alone.

- *Text on Web sites may not follow the traditional main idea–supporting details organization of traditional paragraphs.* Instead, the screen may appear as a group of topic sentences without detail.

- *Web sites are multidirectional and unique; traditional text progresses in a single direction.* When reading traditional text, a reader usually follows a single direction, working through the text from beginning to end as the author has written. Web site text is multidirectional; each electronic reader creates his or her own unique text, by following or ignoring different paths. Two readers of the same Web site may read entirely different material, or the same material in a different orders. For example, one user of the Interamerican University Studies Institute site in Figure 9–1 might begin by reading about the "Experience Costa Rica" program; another user might start by checking the information about IUSI; a third might begin by clicking on the group tours link.

- *Web site text requires readers to make decisions.* Because screens have menus and links, electronic readers must always make choices. They can focus on one aspect of the topic and ignore all others, for example, by following a path of links. Readers of print text, however, have far fewer choices to make.

- *Web sites allow readers the flexibility to choose the order in which to receive the information.* Partly due to learning style, people prefer to acquire information in different sequences. Some may prefer to begin with details and then come to understand underlying rules or principles. Others may prefer to begin in the opposite way. Electronic sources allow readers to approach the text in any manner compatible with their learning style. A pragmatic learner may prefer to move through a site systematically, either clicking or ignoring links as they appear on the screen from top to bottom, for example.

- *Web sites use new symbol systems.* Electronic texts introduce new and sometimes unfamiliar symbols. A flashing or blinking light may suggest a new feature on the site, or an underlined word or a word in a different color may suggest a link. Sound effects, too, may have meanings. For example, on children's Web sites where a child can have books read aloud, and auditory signal may tell the child when to turn the page. Icons and drawings may be used in place of words. (A drawing of a book, for example, may indicate that print sources are available.)

EXERCISE 9–5	*Locate a Web site on a topic related to one of the end-of-chapter readings in this text. Write a list of characteristics that distinguish it from the print readings.*

Changing Your Reading Strategies for Reading Electronic Text

Reading electronic text is relatively new to the current generation of college students. (This will no doubt change with the upcoming generations who, as children, will learn to read both print and electronic text.) Most current college students and teachers first learned to read using print text. We have read print text for many more years than electronic text; consequently, our brains have developed numerous strategies or "work orders" for reading traditional texts. Our work orders, however, are less fully developed for electronic text. Electronic texts have a wider variety of formats and more variables to cope with than traditional texts. A textbook page is usually made up of headings, paragraphs, and an occasional photo or graphic. Web sites have vibrant color, animation, sound, and music as well as words.

Reading is not only different, but it also tends to be slower on the computer screen than on print sources. One expert estimates reading a screen is 25 percent slower than reading on paper. Your eyes can see the layout of two full pages on a book. From the two pages, you can see headings, division of ideas, and subtopics. By glancing at a print page, you get an initial assessment of what it contains. You can tell, for example, if a page is heavily statistical (your eye will see numbers, dates, symbols) or is anecdotal (your eye will see capitalized proper names, quotation marks and numerous indented paragraphs for dialogue, for example). Because you have a sense of what the page contains and how it is organized, you can read somewhat faster. Because a screen holds fewer words, you get far less feedback before you begin to read.

DEVELOPING NEW WAYS OF THINKING AND READING

Reading on electronic sources demands a different type of thinking than print sources. A print source is linear—it goes in a straight line from idea to idea. Electronic sources, due to the presence of links, tend to be multidirectional and let you follow numerous paths (see illustration on next page).

Reading electronic text also requires new strategies. The first steps to reading electronic text easily and effectively are to understand how it is different (see previous section) and realize that you must change and adapt how you read. Some specific suggestions follow.

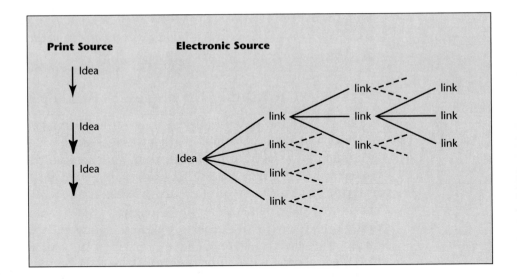

Focus on Your Purpose

Focus clearly on your purpose for visiting the site. What information do you need? Because you must create your own path through the site, unless you fix in mind what you are looking for, you may wander aimlessly, wasting valuable time, or even become lost, following numerous links that lead you farther and farther away from the site at which you began.

Get Used to the Site's Design and Layout

Each Web site has unique features and arranges information differently.

1. *When you reach a new site, spend a few minutes getting used to it and discovering how it is organized.* Scroll through it quickly to determine how it is organized and what information is available. Ask yourself the following questions.
    *   What information is available?
    *   How is it arranged on the screen?

2. *Expect the first screen to grab your attention and make a main point.* (Web site authors know that many people [up to 90 percent] who read a Web page do not scroll down to see the next page.)

3. *Get used to the colors, flashing images, and sounds before you attempt to obtain information from the site.* Your eye may have a tendency to focus

on color or movement, rather than on print. Because Web sites are highly visual, they require visual as well as verbal thinking. The author intends for you to respond to photos, graphics, and animation.

4. *Consider both the focus and limitations of your learning style.* Are you a spatial learner? If so, you may have a tendency to focus too heavily on the graphic elements of the screen. If, on the other hand, you are a verbal learner, you may ignore important visual elements or signals. If you focus *only* on the words and ignore color and graphics on a particular screen, you will probably miss information or may not move through the site in the most efficient way. Review your learning style (p. 8), and consider both your strengths and limitations as they apply to electronic text.

EXERCISE 9–6

In groups of two or three students, consider at least two aspects of learning style. For each, discuss the tendencies, limitations, and implications these particular learning styles may have for reading electronic text. For example, consider how a pragmatic learner would approach a Web site with numerous links and buttons. Then consider how a pragmatic learner's approach might differ.

EXERCISE 9–7

Locate two Web sites that you think are interesting and appealing. Then answer the following questions.

1. How does each use color?
2. How does each use graphics?
3. Is sound or motion used? If so, how?

Pay Attention to how Information Is Organized

Because you can navigate through a Web site in many different ways, it is important to have the right expectations and to make several decisions before you begin.

Some Web sites are much better organized than others. Some have clear headings and labels that make it easy to discover how to proceed; others do not and will require more thought before beginning. For example, if you are reading an article with 10–15 underlined words (links), there is no prescribed order to follow and these links are not categorized in any way. Figure 9–2 (p. 272) shows an excerpt from a Web site titled "Gender and Society" sponsored by Trinity University. Notice that is has numerous links built into paragraphs.

Figure 9–2

GENDER AND SOCIETY

The desire of a man for a woman is not directed at her because she is a human being, but because she is a woman. That she is a human being is of no concern to him.

--Immanuel Kant

In addition to age, gender is one of the universal dimensions on which status differences are based. Unlike sex, which is a biological concept, gender is a <u>social construct</u> specifying the socially and culturally prescribed roles that men and women are to follow. According to Gerda Lerner in *The Creation of Patriarchy*, gender is the "costume, a mask, a straitjacket in which men and women dance their unequal dance" (p.238). As Alan Wolfe observed in "The Gender Question" (*The New Republic,* June 6:27–34), "of all the ways that one group has systematically mistreated another, none is more deeply rooted than the way men have subordinated women. All other discriminations pale by contrast." Lerner argues that the subordination of women preceded all other subordinations and that to rid ourselves of all of those other "isms" -racism, classism, ageism, etc. -it is sexism that must first be eradicated.

Women have always had lower status than men, but the extent of the gap between the sexes varies across cultures and time (some arguing that it is inversely related to social evolution). In 1980, the United Nations summed up the burden of this inequality: Women, who comprise half the world's population, do two thirds of the world's work, earn one tenth of the world's income and own one hundredth of the world's property. In Leviticus, God told Moses that a man is worth 50 sheikels and a woman worth 30 -<u>approximately the contemporary salary differentials of the sexes in the United States.</u> What might be the socio-cultural implications if men were to also be the child bearers? Follow the first human male pregnancy at <u>www.malepregnancy.com.</u>

And the significance of the stamps above? A recent U.S. Postal Service publication, "<u>Women on Stamps,</u>" holds some interesting methodological possibilities. Putting a deceased individual's likeness on a stamp is one way by which <u>political immortality</u> is conferred. Of the hundreds of Americans so immortalized only a handful are women: 16, to be precise, through 1960; 19 through 1970; and 29 through 1980 (any connection between this 50% increase with the ERA movement of the seventies?). An enterprising student may wish to investigate and compare how this female proportion of immortalized citizens varies across countries and time.

Matters of gender are scattered throughout these pages, including <u>gender differences in household duties,</u> in <u>in voting during the 1996 Presidential election,</u> and in <u>suicide rates cross-nationally.</u> Take advantage of <u>this site's search engine</u> by first entering "gender" and next "sex" as the search words.

Source: Michael C. Kearl, "Gender and Society" *A Sociological Tour Through Cyberspace* (http://www.trinity.edu/~mkearl/gender.html)

Use the following suggestions to grasp a site's organization.

1. *Use the site map, if provided, to discover what information is available and how it is organized.* A sample site map, a Web site sponsored by the U.S. Department of Energy and the National Institutes of Health, is shown in Figure 9–3 (p. 274). The site presents information about the Human Genome Project that collects information on genetic research. Notice that the links are categorized by subject: resources, education, research, meetings, and so forth.

2. *Consider the order in which you want to take in information.* Choose an order in which to explore links; avoid randomly clicking on link buttons. Doing so is somewhat like randomly choosing pages to read out of a reference book. Do you need definitions first? Do you want historical background first? Your decision will be partly influenced by your learning style.

3. *Consider writing brief notes to yourself as you explore a complicated Web site.* Alternatively, you could print the homepage and jot notes on it.

4. *Expect shorter, less detailed sentences and paragraphs.* Much online communication tends to be briefer and more concise than in traditional sources. As a result, you may have to mentally fill in transitions and make inferences about relationships among ideas. For example, you may have to infer similarities and differences or recognize cause and effect connections.

EXERCISE 9–8	*Visit two Web sites on the same topic. Write a few sentences comparing and contrasting the sites' organization and design.*

Use Links to Find the Information You Need

Links are unique to electronic text. Here's how to use them.

1. *Plan on exploring links to find complete and detailed information.* Links—both remote links (those that take you to another site) and related links within a site—are intended to provide more detailed information on topics introduced on the homepage.

2. *As you follow links, be sure to bookmark your original site and other useful sites you come across so you can find them again.* **Bookmarking** is a feature on your Internet browser that allows you to record Web site addresses and access them later by simply clicking on the site name.

Figure 9–3 A Website Map

Project Information

- What's New?
- FAQs
- What is the HGP?
- Goals
- Progress
- History
- Timeline
- Budget
- Benefits
- Ethical, Legal, & Social Issues
- Genome Science
- Links

Contact Information

- DOE HGP Administration
- Project Contacts
- About Us
- Site Stats and Credits

Resources

- Glossary
- Acronyms
- Images
- Videos
- Audio Files

Education

- Teachers
- Students
- Careers

Research

- Research in Progress
- Funding
- Research Sites
- Sequencing
- Sequencing Technologies
- Mapping
- Bioinformatics
- Functional and Comparative Genomics
- Ethical, Legal, & Social Issues
- Recent Abstracts
- Chromosome Launchpad
- BACs
- Virtual Library Genetics
- Microbial Genome Program

Publications

- List of all Publications
- Human Genome News
- To Know Ourselves
- Primer on Molecular Genetics
- Your Genes, Your Choices
- 1997 Program Report
- 1999 DOE HGP Abstracts
- ELSI Retrospective
- **NEW** Judicature Genes and Justice issue
- Judges' Journal special genetics issue
- A Vital Legacy
- 1997 DOE BER Exceptional Service Awards
- Miscellaneous

Meetings

- Meetings Calendar
- Workshop Calendar
- Meetings and Reports

Search Human Genome Project Information

Search Web pages:

[   ]

[Search] [Reset]

Search Web pages plus publications:

[   ]

[Search] [Reset]

Survey: After searching this web site, have you found what you wanted?

◯ Yes ◯ No If not, tell us what you were searching for:

[   ] [Submit]

Please do not submit questions here. Send questions via this form: caseydk@ornl.gov .

Medical Applications

- Medicine and the New Genetics
- Disease Diagnosis and Prediction
- Disease Intervention
- Genetic Counseling
- CME
- Genetic Disease Information --pronto!

Topical Fact Sheets

- Cloning
- DOE and the HGP
- Functional Genomics
- Gene Testing
- Sequencing
- SNPs

Source: Oak Ridge National Laboratory Web site wysiwyg://158http://www.ornl.gov/TechResources/Human_Genome/home.html

Different search engines use different terms for this function. Netscape uses the term *Bookmarks;* Microsoft Explorer calls it *Favorites.* In addition, Netscape has a *GO* feature that allows a user to retrace the steps of the current search.

3. *If you use a site or a link that provides many pages of continuous paragraphs, print the material and read it offline.*

4. *If you find you are lacking background on a topic, use links to help fill in the gap or search for a different Web site on the same topic that is less technical.*

5. *If you get lost, most Internet browsers have a history feature.* It allows you to backtrack or retrace the links your followed in a search. On Netscape, for example, click on "Back," it will take you back one link at a time; "History" keeps track of all searches over a given period of time and allows you to go directly to a chosen site, rather than backtracking step by step.

**EXERCISE
9–9**

For one of the Web sites you visited earlier in the chapter or a new site of your choice, follow at least three links and then answer the following questions.

1. What type of information did each contain?
2. Was each source reliable? How do you know?
3. Which was the easiest to read and follow? Why?

ELECTRONIC LEARNING AIDS

In addition to the Web sites on the Internet, you may use many other electronic sources and services as well: CD-ROMs, computer tutorial software, e-mail, listservs, and news groups. Each of the following are described below, along with suggestions for how to use them.

CD-ROMs That Accompany Textbooks

A CD-ROM may be included with the textbook when you purchase it or it may be available in your college's academic computer labs. (Not all textbooks have CD-ROM accompaniments.) CD-ROMs contain a wealth of information, activities, and learning resources. Here is an example of what a CD-ROM that accompanies a psychology text contains.

- review of key topics
- a "click here" function for more information on terms, concepts, etc.

- demonstrations and experiments
- matching games and other learning activities
- review quizzes
- glossary of key terms
- student notepad (for recording your own ideas)
- reference sources

The best part of CD-ROMs is that they are interactive and engaging. The sound, dialogue, and visuals hold your interest and are well-suited if you tend to be an auditory, spatial, or pragmatic learner. They also allow you to choose what and how you want to learn. If you need to review a topic such as learning theory, you click on an icon and are guided through a learning sequence. You can access more information if you need it. When you have finished, you can choose whether or not to take a review quiz to assess what you have learned. Additionally, many of the activities are inter-active—you get involved with the material by responding, rather than merely reading it.

Here are a few guidelines for using CD-ROMs that accompany textbooks.

1. *Try whatever is available.* Even if you have never used a computer before, if software is available, try it out. College computer labs are usually staffed with friendly, helpful people (sometimes other students) who can show you how to get started.

2. *Use them with, but not in place of, your text.* CD-ROMs are supplements. Although they are fun to use, you still must read your textbook.

3. *Use the CD-ROM as a chapter preview.* View the CD-ROM on a particular topic to get an overview of it before reading the corresponding text material.

4. *Use the CD-ROM for review and practice.* After you have read the text, use the CD-ROM to help you learn the material.

5. *Use the quiz or self-test modules when studying for an exam.* Use the quizzes to discover which topics you need to study further. Keep a record of your progress. Many programs will do this for you and allow you to print a progress report. This record will enable you to see your strengths and weaknesses, plan further study, and review troublesome topics.

6. *If the CD-ROM has a notepad (a place where you can write your own notes), use it.* You will learn more efficiently if you express what you have learned in your own words.

7. *Space out your practice.* Because many software programs are fun and engaging, some students work on them for hours at a time. To get maximum benefit from the time you are spending, limit your work to an hour or so. Beyond that, many activities become routine; your mind switches to "automatic pilot," and learning ceases.

8. *Consolidate your learning.* When you finish a module or program segment, do not just exit and shut off the machine. Stop and reflect on what you have learned. If you worked on an algebra module about the multiplication of polynomials, stop and recall the techniques you learned. Write notes or summarize the process in a separate section of your course notebook reserved for this purpose.

E-mail

E-mail (electronic mail) enables you to send messages to another person or place using your computer. A variety of computer programs are available that allow you to send and receive messages electronically, as well as to print them for future reference. There are many academic uses for e-mail. Students in a class may collaborate on a project or critique each others' papers using e-mail. Other times, instructors and students communicate through e-mail. In completing a research paper, it is possible to contact professors or other students doing research on the topic you are studying. You can also transmit word processing files by attaching them to an e-mail message.

Most e-mail follows a consistent format and, consequently, is easy to read. Messages begin with a memo format in which the topic of the message, date the message was sent, sender, and receiver are identified as "Subject" or "Re," "Date," "From," and "To." The message follows this introductory identifying information. Transmittal information that tracks the electronic path through which the message was sent may accompany the message. This information, if it appears, can be ignored unless you wish to verify the source of the sender.

The style of e-mail messages tends to be more casual and conversational than the traditional print forms of communication (letters and memos) but more formal than phone or in-person conversations. Because e-mail is intended to be a rapid, expedient means of communication, some formalities of written communication are relaxed. Expect to find a briefer introduction, more concise sentences, and few or no concluding remarks. Consequently, e-mail requires close attention; unlike print forms of communication, there is little repetition and fewer cues as to what is important.

Figure 9–4 A Sample E-mail Message

```
Subj:        Research on learning styles

Date:        98-02-23 11:49:34 EST

From:        Maryrod@daemon.edu (Mary Rodriguez)

Reply to:    Maryrod@daemon.edu

To:          KateApp@daemon.edu

-------------------------------------------------------

Dear Kate,

In response to your request for recent research

on the learning styles of university versus

community college students, I do know of one

article that may be useful as a starting point:

Henson, Mark and Schemeck, R.R. "Learning Styles

of Community College Versus University Students."

Perceptual Motor Skills, 76(1), 118.

Good luck on your research project.

Mary
```

Reading lengthy e-mail messages may be easier if you print them first. Figure 9–4 shows a sample e-mail message. Notice that the message is a concise yet effective form of communication.

Newsgroups

Newsgroups are collections of people interested in a particular topic or issue who correspond to discuss it. Participants post messages on a given topic; other participants read and respond. Read postings with a critical mind set. Most postings are written by average people expressing their opinions; their ideas may be informative, but they may also contain incorrect information, bias, and unsubstantiated opinion. At times, you also may find postings that are mindless ranting and raving. Here are some tips for reading newsgroup postings.

- Separate fact from opinion (see Chapter 4, p. 100). Take into account the bias, motivation, and prejudices of the author.
- Verify any information you get from a newsgroup with a second source.
- Use newsgroups to explore the range of opinion on a topic or issue.

Usually, newsgroups are open forums; anyone can lurk or "listen in" to the discussion. Newsgroups can yield additional sources of information, as well as a variety of interesting perspectives on a topic. A specialized form of newsgroup is known as a **listserv.** Participation is limited to those who have subscribed. Academic discussion groups are considered listservs. Directories are available to help you locate useful newsgroups and listservs. These include

Directory of professional and Scholarly e-conferences

http://www.n2h2.com/KOVACS/

E-mail Discussion Lists

http://alabanza.com/kabacoff/Inter-Links/listserv.html

Usenet News Groups http://www.liszt.com/news/

EXERCISE 9–10

Visit a newsgroup and either lurk or participate in the discussion. Then answer the following questions.

1. What was the topic of discussion?
2. Were the postings largely fact or opinion?
3. Did you detect bias or prejudice?
4. How useful is the newsgroup as a source of information?

EXERCISE 9–11

Working with another student, select a topic of mutual interest. Discuss it, narrow it down, and write two or three specific research questions. Working independently, use the Internet to locate answers to your research questions. When you have finished, compare your answers and the sources from which you obtained them.

Using a Computer as a Study and Learning Aid

A computer's word processing capability makes it a useful study and learning aid. The following are suggestions for using the computer to organize your study. To make the most of the suggestions, you will need access to a computer on a daily basis.

1. *Use a computer to organize notes from textbook reading.* As you take notes from reading, your notes tend to follow the organization of the text. At times it is useful to reorganize and rearrange your notes. For example, you may want to pull together information on a certain topic that is spread throughout one or more chapters. Once your notes are entered into a computer file, you can use the cut and paste function to rearrange and reorganize your notes or outlines easily without rewriting.

2. *Use a computer to organize lecture notes.* Lecture notes are, of course, recorded by hand as you listen to the lecture, unless you are using a laptop. Typing your notes into a computer file is a means of editing and reviewing, as well as reorganizing.

3. *Use a computer to integrate text and lecture notes.* The computer offers an ideal solution to the problem of how to integrate notes you have taken from your textbook and those you have taken in class. The cut and paste function allows you to move sections of your lecture notes to corresponding sections in your notes from your text.

4. *Use a computer to create lists of new terminology for each of your courses.* The computer's word processing capabilities allow you to group similar terms, organize them by chapter, or sort them into "know" and "don't know" files. A biology student, for example, grouped terms together into the following categories: energy and life, cells, biological processes, reproduction, biological systems, brain and behavior, and environmental issues.

SUMMARY

Reading electronic sources requires unique reading and thinking skills.

A Web site contains unique features:

- homepage
- links to other sites

Locating sources on the World Wide Web (WWW) involves identifying key words and using a search engine.

To evaluate a Web site, consider the following:

- the publisher or sponsor
- author

- date of posting
- links
- purpose of site

Web sites differ from print text in the following ways:

- Web sites involve graphics, sound, color, and animation.
- Language on Web sites tends to be brief.
- Screens are often independent of one another.
- Web sites are multidirectional, require decision-making, and allow flexibility.

Electronic text should be read differently than print text. Be sure to

- Identify the purpose of the site.
- Familiarize yourself with the site's design and layout.
- Pay attention to how the information is organized.
- Use links to find additional information.

Other electronic aids can also help you learn more effectively. These include

- CD-ROMs, which often accompany textbooks, facilitate learning and review.
- E-mail, which is useful to communicate with classmates and professors.
- Newsgroups can yield additional sources of information on a topic and can provide a variety of interesting perspectives on a topic.

ARCHAEOLOGY

PREREADING QUESTIONS

1. How do archaeologists know there might be an important artifact buried under the earth?
2. What can artifacts reveal about the past?

SLICES OF THE PAST

Alan Hall

1   When archaeologists suspect than an important find lies buried beneath the earth, they reach for their shovels, hoping to hit some clue of a buried city or important burial site; sometimes they even call in backhoes and trenching machines. But now, a University of Denver anthropology professor has come up with a groundbreaking alternative that may turn traditional archaeology upside down.

2   <u>Lawerence B. Conyers</u> and his colleague, Dean Goodman, have adapted a technology known as "ground penetrating radar" to pioneer a new era of "noninvasive" archaeology. By pumping radar pulses into the ground and creating images of the radar reflections on a computer, they can obtain detailed pictures of a potentially important site before the first shovel of dirt is lifted. Then, the researchers can decide whether to dig—and where to dig—while doing the least damage to important artifacts.

Field Work. *Conyers and his team have set up their radar base station at a site near Bluff, Utah believed to conceal an ancient ceremonial room, or <u>kiva</u>, of the ancient Anasazi people.*

3   "Archaeologists tend to be very low-tech people," Conyers says. "They have a tendency to be more comfortable digging in the dirt than working with computers. But this radar can help to locate sites and objects that you can't see on the surface. It can help us save sites that could be destroyed with traditional escavation techniques."

4   Gound-penetrating radar has been used for decades for everything from locating buried family treasures hidden from the Nazis to

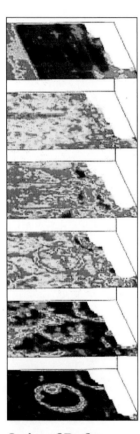

Series of Radar Images *probe beneath an alfalfa field* (top) *in Japan to reveal the long-buried circular moat of an ancient <u>burial mound</u>* (bottom).

finding the engines of the ValuJet crashed in the Everglades. Conyers has used the technology, and the software written by Goodman, to: map a Mayan village buried under 15 feet of volcanic ash in Ceren, El Salvador; create images of a Mayan ceremonial center buried in a sugar cane field in Coatzalmaguapa, Guatemala; located 1,700 year old kiln sites and a large village buried in wind-blown sand between two ceremonial pyraminds in Peru; and disclose details of ancient burial sites in Japan.

5   Closer to his home base in Denver, Conyers has employed the new technique to reveal the history of the ancient Anasazi people of the American West. Because of their sacred nature, the issue of whether to disturb these sites is crucial to their descendants. Near Bluff, Utah, Conyers and his colleagues pinpointed a subterranean kiva, used in ceremonial rites by the Anasazi people. "Even though the people that constructed this kiva have been dead for more than 900 years, these sites are still very sacred," says Conyers. "So radar was a method that we could use to first image what was there and then adjust out excavation procedures to dig only in certain spots to test our scientific ideas."

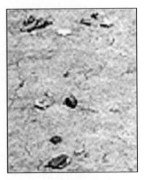

Fragments of Pottery *litter the ground at a site near Bluff, Utah where Conyers and his colleagues located a village of Anasazi "pit houses". The broken ceramics were dated about AD 1100.*

6   Nearby, Conyers and his colleagues also found a field littered with sherds of pottery that dated to 1100 A.D. By searching the area with radar, they located a village of Anasazi "pit houses." Archaeologists usually use this type of evidence to locate sites, but of course have no idea where they are under the gound, says Conyers. "The typical way of finding the buried houses of this sort is to randomly dig test pits or drill auger holes—or even worse use backhoe trenchers that really destroy the site.

7   Mapping these sites using traditional excavation methods would have cost millions of dollars and taken many years. Conyers, using ground-penetrating radar and 3-D imaging software developed by Goodman, can map a site for a fraction of the cost in as little as three weeks. Many buried sites would not have been discovered without the ground-penetrating radar technology and would be potentially at risk from construction and erosion.

8   The next step for Conyers is the creation of moving 3-D images that will allow people to take video "tours" of archaeological sites that have not been unearthed. Maybe those people who Conyers refers to as "dirt archaeologists" will soon retire their shovels.

Related Reading

"Gound-penetrating Radar: An Introduction for Archaeologists," by Lawrence B. Conyers and Dean Goodman, Altamira Press, Walnut Creek, California, 1997.

—Hall, "Slices of the Past," *Scientific American—Exhibit: Radar Archaeology*, June 22, 1998 (http://www.sciam.com)

[By clicking on the "burial mound" link, the following site was located.]

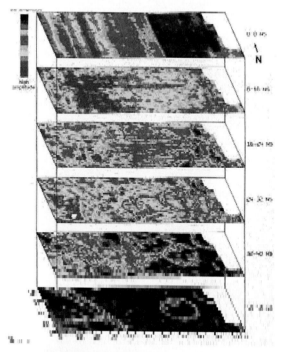

BURIAL MOUND

9   RADAR SURVEY, conducted by Dean Goodman, in Japan revealed a circular burial mound with a burial inside it, which shows up clearly in the bottom slice. The straight line at the left is probably an old fence line when the area was used for horse corrals about 500-600 years ago (Edo Period). The burial moat is much older, probably at least 1100 years old (Kofun Period). The surface is an alfalfa field. "As is usual in these surveys, there were no surface indicators of what was below the ground," says Conyers.

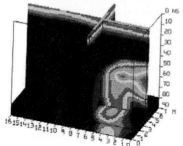

10   IMAGE is a 3-dimensional cutaway of a burial chamber that was found by Dean Goodman on a mound on the Island of Kyushu in Japan. It contained the remains of a warrior with a variety of artifacts, including bronze swords. This is a 3-D cutaway image of this chamber. It reveals a main chamber and a vertical shaft that leads to an offering below the burial.

Images: Lawrence B. Conyers and Dean Goodman, from "Ground-penetrating Radar: An Introduction for Archaeologists," Altamira Press, Walnut Creek, California, 1997.

Back to <u>Slices of the Past</u>

—"Burial Mound," *Scientific American—Exhibit: Radar Archaeology,* June 22, 1998 (http://www.sciam.com)

VOCABULARY REVIEW

1. For each of the words listed below, use context, prefixes, roots, and suffixes; and/or a dictionary to write a brief definition or synonym of the word as it is used in the reading.

a. alternative (para. 1) _____

b. potentially (para. 2) _____

c. artifacts (para. 2) _____

d. excavation (para. 3) _____

e. disclose (para. 4) _____

f. subterranean (para. 5) _____

g. sherds (para. 6) _____

2. Underline new specialized terms introduced in the reading.

COMPREHENSION QUESTIONS

1. Why is the radar procedure referred to as noninvasive?
2. Name two important advantages of using the ground penetrating radar.
3. What is the usual way of finding buried artifacts?
4. Why do archaeologists not like to use backhoe trenchers?
5. Why was it important to use radar to examine the subterranean kivas used by the Anasazi people?
6. How long does it take to map a site using this new radar technique compared to traditional excavation?
7. What did the radar survey conducted by Dean Goodman reveal?

THINKING CRITICALLY

1. What would you do if you wanted to know more about Lawrence B. Conyers?
2. What does Conyers mean by the term *dirt archaeologists*?
3. For what other nonarchaeological situation can you imagine using ground penetrating radar?
4. Do you think archaeologists should be permitted to dig up sacred sites? Explain.
5. How did this Web site differ from a textbook?
6. How useful did you find the link to "burial mound"?

LEARNING/STUDY STRATEGY

Design a study sheet explaining the different types of remote sensing.

ARCHAEOLOGY

PREREADING QUESTIONS

1. Why is the study of archaeology important?
2. What is remote sensing?

Remote Sensing

Arenal, Costa Rica

Chaco Canyon, NM

The Peten, Guatemala

GHCC Home

Other Links

Archeology links

Archeology Journals

Archeology FAQ

* Excerpt of an interview with NASA's only archeologist which appeared in Omni Magazine

The Scout Report for
Social Sciences
Selection
Internet Scout Project

ARCHAEOLOGY

Tom Sever

1   Much of human history can be traced through the impacts of human actions upon the environment. The use of remote sensing technology offers the archeologist the opportunity to detect these impacts which are often invisible to the naked eye. This information can be used to address issues in human settlement, environmental interaction, and climate change. Archaeologists want to know how ancient people successfully adapted to their environment and what factors may have led to their collapse or disappearance. Did they overextend the capacity of their landscape, causing destructive environmental effects which led to their demise? Can this information be applied to modern day societies so that the mistakes of the past are not repeated?

2   Remote sensing can be used as a methodological procedure for detecting, inventorying, and prioritizing surface and shallow-depth archeological information in a rapid, accurate, and quantified manner. Man is a tropical creature who has invaded every environment on earth successfully; now we are ready to explore, and eventually colonize, the delicate environments of Space. Understanding how ancient man successfully managed Earth is important for the success of current and future societies.

3   "The stereotype has archaeologists just digging up spearheads and pottery and anthropologists just writing down the words of primitive tribes. But we're examining how people adapted to their environment throughout time, how they experienced environmental shift, why cultures come and go. Soils associated with artifacts are as important as the artifacts themselves—probably more relevant to us than the actual objects. Now more than ever, archaeological research is interdisciplinary: botany, forestry, soil science, hydrology—all of which contribute to a more complete understanding of the earth, climatic shifts, and how people adapt to large regions. This understanding is critical to future decision making affecting the planet.

4   In Costa Rica, the culture survived repeated volcanic explosions that repeatedly destroyed the environment, explosions equal to the force of a nuclear blast. Other cultures, like the advanced Maya societies, did not survive or recover from similar eruptions. Did it have to do with the size and violence of the eruption, the way they farmed their land over time, or territorial and political struggle?"

> We have not inherited the earth from our fathers, we are borrowing it from our children
> Amish Farmer

Comments regarding our web service may be e-mailed to:

   webmaster@wwwghcc.msfc.nasa.gov

Responsible Official: Dr. Timothy L. Miller (tim.miller@msfc.nasa.gov)
Page Author: Tom Sever
Page Curator: Diane Samuelson (diane.samuelson@msfc.nasa.gov)

Last Updated: May 12, 1998

[By clicking on the "Remote Sensing" link, the following site was located.]

—Sever, "Archaeology," Global Hyrology and Climate Center, NASA/Marshall Space Flight Center Web site (http://www.msfc.nasa.gov)

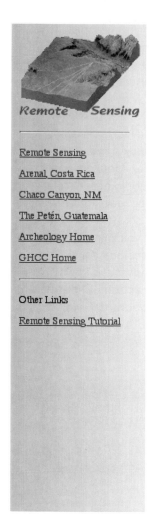

ARCHAEOLOGICAL REMOTE SENSING

5   Now more than ever, archaeological research is interdisciplinary: botany, forestry, soil science, hydrology—all of which contribute to a more complete understanding of the earth, climate shifts, and how people adapt to large regions.

6   As a species, we've been literally blind to the universe around us. If the known <u>electromagnetic spectrum</u> were scaled up to stretch around the Earth's circumference, the human eye would see a portion equal to the diameter of a pencil. Our ability to build detectors that see for us where we can't see, and computers that bring the invisible information back to our eyesight, will ultimately contribute to our survival on Earth and in space.

7   The spectrum of sunlight reflected by the Earth's surface contains information about the composition of the surface, and it may reveal traces of past human activities, such as agriculture. Since sand, cultivated soil, vegetation, and all kinds of rocks each have distinctive temperatures and emit heat at different rates, sensors can "see" things beyond ordinary vision or cameras. Differences in soil texture are revealed by fractional temperature variations. So it is possible to identify loose soil that had been prehistoric agricultural fields, or was covering buried remains. The Maya causeway was detected through emissions of infrared radiation at a different wavelength from surrounding vegetation. More advanced versions of such multi-spectral scanner (Visible & IR) can detect irrigation ditches filled with sediment because they hold more moisture and thus have a temperature different from other soil. The ground above a buried stone wall, for instance, may be a touch hotter than the surrounding terrain because the stone absorbs more heat. Radar can penetrate darkness, cloud cover, thick jungle canopies, and even the ground.

8   Remote sensing can be a discovery technique, since the computer can be programmed to look for distinctive "signatures" of energy emitted by a known site or feature in areas where surveys have not been conducted. Such "signatures" serve as recognition features or fingerprints. Such characteristics as elevation, distance from water, distance between sites or cities, corridors, and transportation routes can help to predict the location of potential archaeological sites.

9   Computational techniques used to analyze data.

1.   sun-angle correction
2.   density slicing
3.   band ratioing

4. edge enhancement
5. synthetic color assignment
6. filtering
7. multichannel analysis

Remote Sensing Instruments

10   Aerial Photography:

Many features which are difficult or impossible to see standing on the ground become very clear when seen from the air. But, black and white photography only records about twenty-two perceptible shades of gray in the visible spectrum. Also, optical sources have certain liabilities; they must operate in daylight, during clear weather, on days with minimal atmospheric haze.

11   Color Infrared Film (CIR):

Detects longer wavelengths somewhat beyond the red end of the light spectrum. CIR film was initially employed during World War II to differentiate objects that had been artificially camouflaged. Infrared photography has the same problems that conventional photography has, you need light and clear skies. Even so, CIR is sensitive to very slight differences in vegetation. Because buried archaeological features can affect how plants grow above them, such features become visible in color infrared photography.

12   Thermal Infrared Multispectral Scanner (TIMS):

A six channel scanner that measures the thermal radiation given off by the ground, with accuracy to 0.1 degree centigrade. The pixel (picture element) is the square area being sensed, and the size of the pixel is directly proportional to sensor height. For example, pixels from Landsat satellites are about 100 feet (30 m) on a side, and thus have limited archaeological applications. However, pixels in TIMS data measure only a few feet on a side and as such can be used for archeological research. TIMS data were used to detect ancient Anasazi roads in Chaco Canyon, NM.

13   Airborne Oceanographic Lidar (ADI):

A laser device that makes "profiles" of the earth's surface. The laser beam pulses to the ground 400 times per second, striking the surface every three and a half inches, and bounces back to its source. In most cases, the beam bounces off the top of the vegetation cover and off the ground surface; the difference between the two give information on forest height, or even the height of grass in pastures. As the lidar passes over an eroded footpath that still affects the topography, the pathway's indentation is recorded by the laser beam. The lidar data can be processed to reveal tree height as well as elevation, slope, aspect, and slope length of ground features. Lidar can also be used to penetrate water to measure the morphology of coastal water, detect oil forms, fluorescent dye traces, water clarity, and organic pigments including chlorophyll. In this case, part of the pulse is reflected off the water surface, while the rest travels to the water bottom and is reflected. The time elapsed between the received impulses allows for a determination of water depth and subsurface topography.

14   Synthetic Aperture Radar (SAR):
SAR beams energy waves to the ground and records the energy reflected. Radar is sensitive to linear and geometric features on the ground, particularly when different radar wavelengths and different combinations of the horizontal and vertical data are employed. Different wavelengths are sensitive to vegetation or to ground surface phenomena. In dry, porous soils, radar can penetrate the surface. In 1982, radar from the space shuttle penetrated the sand of the Sudanese desert and revealed ancient watercourses. Using airborne radar in Costa Rica, prehistoric footpaths have been found.

15   Microwave Radar:
Beaming radar pulses into the ground and measuring the echo is a good way of finding buried artifacts in arid regions (water absorbs microwaves). Man-made objects tend to reflect the microwaves, giving one a "picture" of what is underground without disturbing the site.

Selected Papers

"Remote Sensing Methods," In *Advances in Science and Technology for Historic Preservation,* edited by Ray Williamson, Plenum Press. (In Press).

"Remote Sensing," In *American Journal of Archaeology,* 99:83–84, 1995.

"Applications of Ecological Concepts and Remote Sensing Technologies in Archaeological Site Reconnaissance," with F. Miller
and D. Lee. (In *Applications of Space-Age Technology in Anthropology,* edited by Clifford Behrens and Thomas Sever. NASA, Stennis Space Center, MS, 1991.)

"Remote Sensing," Chapter 14 of *Benchmarks In Time and Culture: Introductory Essays in the Methodology of Syro-Palestinian Archaeology.* Scholars Press. March, 1988.

"Cultural and Ecological Applications of Remote Sensing." Final Report of a Conference Sponsored by the National Science Foundation. With Daniel Gross and Paul Shankman. University of Boulder Colorado, Boulder. April, 1988.

"Conference on Remote Sensing: Potential for the Future." NASA, Stennis Space Center, Science and Technology Laboratory, SSC, MS., January, 1985.

webmaster@wwwghcc.msfc.nasa.gov

Responsible Official: Dr. Timothy L. Miller (tim.miller@msfc.nasa.gov)
Page Author: Tom Sever
Page Curator: Diane Samuelson (diane.samuelson@msfc.nasa.gov)

Last Updated: May 12, 1998

—Global Hyrology and Climate Center, NASA/Marshall Space Flight Center Web site (http://www.msfc.nasa.gov)

VOCABULARY REVIEW

1. For each of the words listed below, use context, prefixes, roots, and suffixes; and/or a dictionary to write a brief definition or synonym of the word as it is used in the reading.

   a. impacts (para. 1) _____

   b. demise (para. 1) _____

   c. methodical (para. 2) _____

   d. prioritizing (para. 2) _____

   e. quantified (para. 2) _____

   f. emit (para. 7) _____

   g. infrared (para. 7) _____

   h. perceptible (para. 10) _____

   i. optical (para. 10) _____

   j. camouflaged (para. 11) _____

   k. eroded (para. 13) _____

   l. morphology (para. 13) _____

   m. porous (para. 14) _____

2. Underline new specialized terms introduced in the reading.

COMPREHENSION QUESTIONS

1. Why do archaeologists need remote sensing?
2. What is the value of research that allows archaeologists to uncover previously invisible information?
3. Describe one archaeological discovery that was made using remote sensing.
4. What characteristics can predict the potential of an archaeological site?
5. Why might the ground above a buried stone wall be a little warmer than the ground surrounding it?
6. Name and briefly describe one remote sensing instrument.

THINKING CRITICALLY

1. If you did not understand the term *remote sensing,* what would you do?
2. What is the purpose of the quotation given in paragraphs 2–4?
3. Which of the remote sensing instruments might be useful in environmental preservation and conservation of wetland and coastal areas?
4. Name two advantages of reading material electronically (as opposed to a print source) that this electronic reading provided?
5. If you wanted additional information on synthetic aperture radar, how would you go about finding it?
6. Evaluate this Web site using the criteria suggested in the chapter

LEARNING/STUDY STRATEGIES

1. Locate at least three additional electronic articles on ground penetrating radar.
2. Evaluate each source you identify.

THINKING ABOUT THE PAIRED READINGS

INTEGRATING IDEAS

1. Which of the two readings do you think offers the most informaton?
2. Compare the author's purpose in both readings?
3. How do the readings differ?
4. Which of the two readings offers a more scientifically based definition of radar as used in the study of archaeology? Explain your answer.
5. If you came across these two readings online, which one would you find more "user friendly" and why?

GENERATING NEW IDEAS

1. Visit one or both of the Web sites from which these readings were taken. Search for updated information on research tools in archaeology. Write a brief summary of your findings.
2. Write a cause-effect essay explaining how technology has affected and changed the field of archaeology.

10 | USING WRITING TO LEARN

LEARNING OBJECTIVES

- **To use writing to monitor your comprehension**
- **To use highlighting to improve textbook reading**
- **To use note taking to organize, synthesize, and retain ideas**
- **To use mapping to show relationships**
- **To use summaries to condense information**
- **To use writing as a discovery process**

Most students think of writing in college as something they do for others—writing essay exams and term papers, for example. Writing is a vehicle of expression, of course, but it is also a very effective way to learn. You can use it, for example, to organize your ideas, pull information together, discover what you think about an issue, or make a difficult reading assignment understandable.

Research studies indicate that you learn information more easily if you elaborate upon it. *Elaboration,* which means "building upon," is a process of expanding your thinking. It involves the multilevel thinking skills discussed in Chapter 1: building connections, developing associations, seeing relationships, and considering applications. Elaboration makes information meaningful and, therefore, easier to recall. Writing is one way to help you elaborate. It forces you to think about the material, to make connections, and to consider applications. This chapter discusses ways to use writing to strengthen comprehension and offers numerous writing strategies that facilitate learning. Not all strategies work equally well for everyone. Experiment to discover which work well for you.

WRITING TO ASSESS AND STRENGTHEN COMPREHENSION

Writing is an excellent means of assessing your comprehension. Let's suppose you are reading a difficult assignment in your political science text. You realize you are not understanding much of it, so you need to try a new approach. One effective technique is to test yourself as you read. After each paragraph, write the main point of the paragraph in your own words. Your writing could take any number of different forms: a summary sentence, an outline, or a list. If you cannot do this, then you know you have not fully understood the paragraph and that you need to reread it.

Try the same kind of self-test when you finish a section. Finally, when you've completed the assignment, write a review of key points. Any time you can't state or recall key points, you need to do more work.

Not only is writing a good way to test whether you are understanding what you read, but it also will improve your comprehension of difficult or complicated material. When you are reading a complex argument for a logic course, you can improve your understanding by writing a list of the argument's main points. Writing each point forces you to think about each one, so connections and relationships become more apparent. Writing also forces you to spend enough time with the material to understand it fully.

Similarly, when you are solving math problems, writing will increase your understanding of the process. Listing the steps used to solve the problem makes the process "real" and more manageable. Writing makes problem solving practical rather than theoretical. There are many other situations in which writing strengthens comprehension. You can use writing to summarize case studies, explain how a process works, or describe similarities and differences among readings.

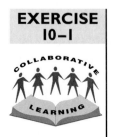

EXERCISE 10–1

Suppose you have been assigned three chapters to read in your psychology textbook. The next exam in psychology will emphasize these three chapters. Because of time limitations, your instructor will not discuss the chapters in class. Form groups of three or four students, and discuss the following issues.

1. How you would learn the chapters' content.
2. What writing strategies you would use.
3. How you would know when you were adequately prepared for the exam.

HIGHLIGHTING AND ANNOTATING TEXTBOOKS

Highlighting and annotating are excellent means of improving your comprehension and recall of textbook assignments. Highlighting forces you to decide what is important and to sort the key information from less important material. Sorting ideas this way improves both comprehension and recall. To decide what to highlight, you must think about and evaluate the relative importance of each idea. Highlighting has the following added benefits.

- Highlighting keeps you physically active as you read.
- The physical activity focuses your attention and improves your concentration.
- Highlighting helps you discover how ideas are related.
- Highlighting is a good test of whether you understand what you are reading. If you have difficulty deciding what to highlight, it indicates that you are not comprehending the material.

How to Highlight

To highlight textbook material most effectively, apply these guidelines.

1. *Analyze the assignment.* Preview the assignment, and define what type of learning is required. This will help you determine how much and what type of information you need to highlight.

2. *Assess your familiarity with the subject.* Depending on your background knowledge, you may need to highlight only a little or a great deal. Do not waste time highlighting what you already know. In chemistry, for example, if you already have learned the definition of a mole, then do not highlight it.

3. *Read first, then highlight.* Finish a paragraph or self-contained section before you highlight. As you read, look for signals to academic thought patterns. Each idea may seem important as you first encounter it, but you must see how it fits in with the others before you can judge its relative importance.

4. *Use the boldface headings.* Headings are labels that indicate the overall topic of a section. These headings serve as indicators of what is important to highlight. For example, under the heading "Objectives of Economic Growth," you should be certain to highlight each objective.

5. *Highlight main ideas and only key supporting details.* Try to keep academic thought patterns in mind.

6. *Avoid highlighting complete sentences.* Highlight only enough so that your highlighting makes sense when you reread it. In the following selection, note that only key words and phrases are highlighted. Now read only the highlighted words. Can you grasp the key idea of each paragraph?

BIOMES

By using imagination, we can divide the earth's land into several kinds of regions called biomes, areas of the earth that support specific assemblages of plants. As would be expected, certain kinds of animals occupy each type of biome, since different species of animals are dependent on different sorts of plant communities for food, shelter, building materials, and hiding places. . . .

Tropical rain forests are found mainly in the Amazon and Congo Basins and in Southeast Asia. The temperature in this biome doesn't vary much throughout the year. Instead, the seasons are marked by variation in the amount of rainfall throughout the year. In some areas, there may be pronounced rainy seasons. These forests support many species of plants. Trees grow throughout the year and reach tremendous heights, with their branches forming a massive canopy overhead. The forest floor, which can be quite open and easy to travel over, may be dark and steamy. Forests literally swarm with insects and birds. Animals may breed throughout the year as a result of the continual availability of food. Competition is generally considered to be very keen in such areas because of the abundance of species.

—Wallace, *Biology: The World of Life*, pp. 708, 710

7. *Move quickly through the document as you highlight.* If you have understood a paragraph or section, then your highlighting should be fast and efficient.

8. *Develop a consistent system of highlighting.* Decide, for example, how you will mark main ideas, how you will distinguish main ideas from details, and how you will highlight new terminology. Some students use a system of symbols such as brackets, asterisks, and circles to distinguish various types of information; others use different colors of highlighters to make distinctions. The specific coding system you devise is unimportant; what is important is that you devise some consistent approach to highlighting. At first, you will need to experiment, testing various systems. However, once you have settled on an effective system, use it regularly.

9. *Use the 15–25 percent rule of thumb.* Although the amount you will highlight will vary from course to course, try to highlight no more than 15 to 25 percent of any given page. If you exceed this figure, it often means that you are not sorting ideas as efficiently as possible. Other times, it may mean that you should choose a different strategy for reviewing the material. Remember, the more you highlight, the smaller your time-saving dividends will be as you review. The first paragraph of the following excerpt provides an example of effective highlighting.

Biomes (cont'd)

Temperate deciduous forests once covered most of the eastern United States and all of Central Europe. The dominant trees in these forests are hardwoods. The areas characterized by such plants are subject to harsh winters, times when the trees shed their leaves, and warm summers that mark periods of rapid growth and rejuvenation. Before the new leaves begin to shade the forest floor in the spring, a variety of herbaceous (nonwoody) flowering plants may appear. These wildflowers are usually perennials, plants that live and produce flowers year after year. In the early spring, they don't have time to manufacture the food needed to grow and bloom suddenly. Instead, they draw on food produced and stored in underground parts during the previous year. Rainfall may average 75 to 130 centimeters or more each year in these forests and is rather evenly distributed throughout the year.

People who live in temperate deciduous biomes often consider the seasonal changes as both moving and fascinating. They describe a certain joy that swells within them each spring and a secret pensiveness that overcomes them in the fall as the days darken and the forests become more silent. (Perhaps we are exceeding technical descriptions here, but these are my favorite places.)

Taiga (pronounced "tie-gah") is quite unmistakable; there is nothing else like it. It is confined almost exclusively to the Northern Hemisphere and is identified by the great coniferous forests of pine, spruce, fir, and hemlock that extend across North America, Europe, and Asia. Some of these trees are the largest living things on earth.

Taiga is marked by long, cold, wet winters and short summer growing seasons. The forest is interrupted here and there by extensive bogs, or muskegs, which are the remains of large ponds. The forest floor is usually covered by a carpet of needles. In the dim light at ground level, there may be mosses, ferns, and a few flowering plants. One may move silently on the muffling needles through the Canadian taiga observing a host of mammals, including porcupines, moose, bear, rodents, hares, and wolverines.

Tundra is the northernmost land biome. It is covered throughout most of the year by ice and snow. This biome is most prevalent in the far north (arctic tundra), but it may also appear at high elevations in other parts of the world (alpine tundra). For example, in the United States, it may be seen in the high Rocky Mountains. Tundra appears in places where summer usually lasts two to four months, just long enough to thaw a few feet of the soil above the permafrost, or permanently frozen soil. Thaw brings soggy ground, and ponds and bogs appear in the depressions. The plant life consists mostly of lichens, herbs, mosses, and low-lying shrubs and grasses, as well as a few kinds of trees, such as dwarf willows and birches. Such plants obviously must be hardy, but their hardiness disguises their fragility. Once disturbed, these areas take very long periods to restore themselves.

—Wallace, *Biology: The World of Life*, pp. 712–13

EXERCISE 10–2

Finish highlighting the above passage.

Evaluating Your Highlighting

As with any learning strategy, you must ask the question "Is it working?". Your final answer, of course, will come when you take your first major examination. If you were able to review the material within a reasonable time and you earn an acceptable grade, you will know your system was effective.

There are two common mistakes you can make when you are highlighting.

Highlighting too much. Using the tired, worn-out "rather safe than sorry" rule, you may tend to highlight almost every idea on the page. Highlighting nearly everything is about as effective as highlighting nothing because no sorting occurs: key ideas are not distinguished from other, less important, ones. Highlighting too much can become a way of escaping or postponing the real issue: deciding what to learn.

Highlighting too little. If you find you are highlighting less than 10 percent per page, this often is a signal that you are having difficulty understanding the material. If you cannot explain the content of a given section in your own words, then you have not understood it. If, however, you understand what you read but are highlighting very little, then you may need to redefine your purpose for reading.

Evaluate your own highlighting by

- Selecting a sample page, highlighting it, and rereading only your highlighting. Then ask yourself the following questions: "Does my highlighting convey the key ideas of the passage?" "Can I follow the author's train of thought and his or her progression of ideas by reading only my highlighting?" "Is the highlighting appropriate for my purposes?"
- Comparing your highlighting with that of another student. Although there will be individual differences, both sets of highlighting should emphasize the same key ideas.

EXERCISE 10–3

Evaluate your highlighting in Exercise 10–2 by using one of the preceding suggestions.

Marginal Annotation

In many situations, highlighting alone is not a sufficient means of identifying what to learn. It does not separate the main ideas from the examples, and each of these from new terminology. Nor does it give you any opportunity to comment on or react to the material. Therefore, it is often necessary to make marginal annotations as well as to highlight.

Using Writing to Learn

Annotating is an active reading process. It forces you to monitor your comprehension as well as react to ideas. Table 10–1 suggests various types of annotation used in marking a political science textbook chapter.

Annotation as a means of analysis and evaluation is discussed on page 107 in Chapter 4. Review this section now for additional suggestions on how to annotate effectively.

TABLE 10–1   MARGINAL ANNOTATION

TYPES OF ANNOTATION	EXAMPLE
Circling unknown words	. . . redressing the apparent (asymmetry) of their relationship
Marking definitions	*def* To say that the balance of power favors one party over another is to introduce a disequilibrium.
Marking examples	*ex* . . . concessions may include negative sanctions, trade agreements . . .
Numbering lists of ideas, causes, reasons, or events	components of power include ① self-image, ② population, ③ natural resources, and geography ④
Placing asterisks next to important passages	* Power comes from three primary sources . .
Putting question marks next to confusing passages	? → war prevention occurs through institutionalization of mediation . . .
Making notes to yourself	Check def in soc text — power is the ability of an actor on the international stage to . . .
Marking possible test items	T There are several key features in the relationship . . .
Drawing arrows to show relationships	. . . natural resources . . . , . . . control of industrial manufacture capacity
Writing comments, noting disagreements and similarities	Can terrorism be prevented through similar balance? war prevention through balance of power is . . .
Marking summary statements	*sum* the greater the degree of conflict, the more intricate will be . . .

EXERCISE 10–4 | *Add annotations to the excerpt that you highlighted in Exercise 10–2 and compare them with those of another student.*

EXERCISE 10–5 | *Select a two- to three-page excerpt from one of your textbooks. Read, highlight, and annotate the selection. Do you feel the combination of processes is more effective than highlighting alone? Why or why not?*

EXERCISE 10–6 | *Working with another student in the class, choose one of the end-of-chapter readings in this text. Assume it is a reading assignment for one of your courses. Each of you should read, highlight, and annotate the selection. Then discuss similarities and differences in your work and evaluate each other's annotations.*

EXERCISE 10–7 | *Choose a two- or three-page section from one of your textbooks and highlight it, using the guidelines suggested in this chapter. Then evaluate the effectiveness of your highlighting in preparation for an objective exam on the material.*

NOTE TAKING TO ORGANIZE IDEAS

Note taking is a writing strategy that can assist you in organizing information and pulling ideas together. It is also an effective way to pull together information from two or more sources—your textbook and class lectures, for example. Finally, note taking is a way to assess your comprehension and strengthen your recall. Use the following tips to take good notes.

1. *Read an entire section and then jot down notes.* Do not try to write notes while you are reading the material for the first time.

2. *As you read, be alert for academic thought patterns.* These patterns will help you organize your notes.

3. *Record all of the most important ideas in the briefest possible form.*

4. Think of your notes as a list of the main ideas and supporting details of a selection. Organize them to show how the ideas are related or to reflect the organization of the material.

5. Use words and short phrases to summarize ideas. Do not write in complete sentences.

6. Write in your own words; do not copy sentences or parts of sentences from the selection.

7. Be highly selective. Unless you are sure that a fact or idea is important to remember, don't include it. If you are not selective, you will find that your notes are nearly as long as the selection itself and you will save little time as you review the material.

8. Use an outline system of indentation to separate main ideas and details. As a general rule, the greater the importance of an idea, the closer it is placed to the left margin. Ideas of lesser importance are indented and appear closer to the center of the page. Your notes might follow a format such as this:

> TOPIC
>> Main Idea
>>> Supporting detail
>>>> fact
>>>> fact
>>> Supporting detail
>> Main Idea
>>> Supporting detail
>>> Supporting detail
>>>> fact
>>>> fact

To further illustrate the techniques of note taking, study the notes shown in Figure 10–1 (p. 302). They are based on a portion of the excerpt on biomes that appears earlier in this chapter.

EXERCISE 10–8

Write a brief set of notes for the reading selection "Body Adornment: The Use of Cosmetics" at the end of this chapter. Working with a classmate, compare, discuss, and revise your notes.

Figure 10–1   Sample Notes

Biomes
- Regions of earth's land
- Each has own plants and animals

Tropical Rain Forests

- Amazon & Congo Basins and SouthEast Asia
- Seasons vary according to rainfall amount
- Trees grow throughout year
    - branches form canopy, forest floor dark, steamy
- Animals breed throughout year
    - keen competition

EXERCISE 10–9

Select a three- to four-page section from one of your textbooks. Write a brief set of notes, including the key ideas.

Academic Application

MAPPING TO SHOW RELATIONSHIPS

Mapping is a way of drawing a diagram to describe how a topic and its related ideas are connected. It organizes and consolidates information, often emphasizing a particular thought pattern. Mapping is a visual means of learning by writing.

This section discusses four types of maps: conceptual maps, process diagrams, part and function diagrams, and time lines. Each utilizes one of the thought patterns discussed in Chapter 6.

Conceptual Maps

A conceptual map is a form of outline that presents ideas spatially rather than in list form. It is a "picture" of how ideas are related. Use the following steps to construct a conceptual map.

Figure 10–2   Sample Conceptual Map

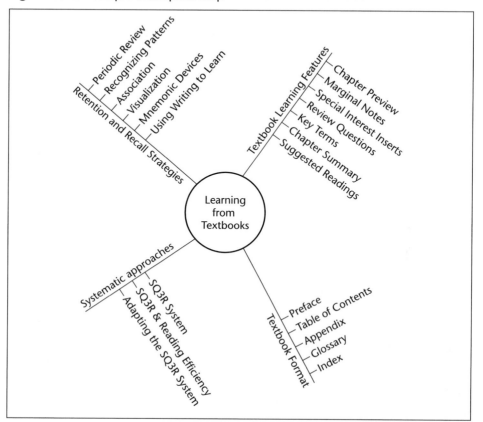

1. Identify the topic and write it in the center of the page.

2. Identify ideas, aspects, parts, and definitions that are related to the topic. Draw each one on a line radiating from the topic.

3. As you discover details that further explain an idea already recorded, draw new lines branching from the idea that the details explain.

A map of Chapter 7 is shown in Figure 10–2. Take a moment now to refer to Chapter 7 before studying the map.

Process Diagrams

In the technologies and the natural sciences, as well as in many other courses, *processes* are an important part of the course content. A diagram that visually describes the steps, variables, or parts of a process will simplify learning. For example, the diagram in Figure 10–3 (p. 304) visually describes the steps in the search process for using library sources.

Figure 10–3   Sample Process Diagram

The Search Process				
Encyclopedia →	Bibliographies →	Books →	Periodicals →	Specialized Sources
overview of topic	identify outstanding sources	basic information	detailed information; current information	specialized & specific information

---

EXERCISE 10–10

Draw a conceptual map of Chapter 3 of this book.

EXERCISE 10–11

Draw a conceptual map of the reading titled "Body Adornment: The Use of Cosmetics" at the end of this chapter.

EXERCISE 10–12

The following paragraph describes the sequential effects of taking the psychedelic drug LSD. Read the paragraph and then draw a process diagram that describes this response sequence. Compare your diagram with those of several other students.

Psychedelics are ... a group of drugs that produce hallucinations and various other phenomena that very closely mimic certain mental disorders. These drugs include lysergic acid diethylamide (LSD), mescaline, peyote, psilocybin, and various commercial preparations such as Sernyl and Ditran.

Of these, LSD is probably the best known, although its use has apparently diminished since its heyday in the late 1960s. LSD is synthesized from lysergic acid produced by a fungus (ergot) that is parasitic on cereal grains such as rye. It usually produces responses in a particular sequence. The initial reactions may include weakness, dizziness and nausea. These symptoms are followed by a distortion of time and space. The senses may become intensified and strangely intertwined— that is, sounds can be "seen" and colors "heard." Finally, there may be changes in mood, a feeling of separation of the self from the framework of time and space, and changes in the perception of the self. The sensations experienced under the influence of psychedelics are unlike anything encountered within the normal range of experiences. The descriptions of users therefore can only be puzzling to nonusers. Some users experience bad trips or "bummers," which have been known to produce long-term effects. Bad trips can be terrifying experiences and can occur in experienced users for no apparent reason.

—Wallace, *Biology: The World of Life,* pp. 632–33

Part and Function Diagrams: Classification

In courses that deal with the use and description or classification of physical objects, labeled drawings are an important learning tool. In a human anatomy and physiology course, for example, the easiest way to learn the parts and functions of the brain is to draw it. To study, sketch the brain and test your recall of each part and its function. A sample part and function diagram of the brain appears at the end of Chapter 6 on page 181.

EXERCISE 10–13

The following paragraph describes the outer layers of the earth. Read the paragraph, and then draw a diagram that will help you to visualize how the earth is structured.

OUTER LAYERS OF THE EARTH

The Earth's crust and the uppermost part of the mantle are known as the *lithosphere*. This is a fairly rigid zone that extends about 100 km below the Earth's surface. The crust extends some 60 km or so under continents, but only about 10 km below the ocean floor. The continental crust has a lower density than the oceanic crust. It is primarily a light granitic rock rich in the silicates of aluminum, iron, and magnesium. In a simplified view, the continental crust can be thought of as layered: On top of a layer of igneous rock (molten rock that has hardened, such as granite) lies a thin layer of sedimentary rocks (rocks formed by sediment and fragments that water deposited, such as limestone and sandstone); there is also a soil layer deposited during past ages in the parts of continents that have had no recent volcanic activity or mountain building.

Sandwiched between the lithosphere and the lower mantle is the partially molten material known as the *asthenosphere*, about 150 km thick. It consists primarily of iron and magnesium silicates that readily deform and flow under pressure.

—Berman and Evans, *Exploring the Cosmos*, p. 145

Time Lines

When you are studying a topic in which the sequence or order of events is a central focus, a time line is a helpful way to organize the information. Time lines are especially useful in history courses. To map a sequence of events, draw a single line and mark it off in year intervals, just as a ruler is marked off in inches. Then write events next to the correct year. For example, the time line in Figure 10–4 (p. 306) displays major events during the presidency of Franklin D. Roosevelt. The time line shows the sequence of events and helps you to visualize them more clearly.

Figure 10–4 Sample Time Line

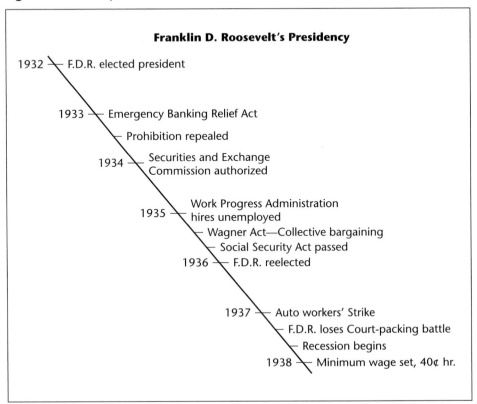

**EXERCISE
10–14**

The following passage reviews the chronology of events in public school desegregation. Read the selection, and then draw a time line that will help you to visualize these historical events.

DESEGREGATING THE SCHOOLS

The nation's schools soon become the primary target of civil-rights advocates. The NAACP concentrated first on universities, successfully waging an intensive legal battle to win admission for qualified blacks to graduate and professional schools. Led by Thurgood Marshall, NAACP lawyers then took on the broader issue of segregation in the country's public schools. Challenging the 1896 Supreme Court decision *(Plessy v. Ferguson)* which upheld the constitutionality of separate but equal public facilities, Marshall argued that even substantially equal but separate schools did profound psychological damage to black children and thus violated the Fourteenth Amendment.

A unanimous Supreme Court agreed in its 1954 decision in the case of *Brown v. Board of Education of Topeka.* Chief Justice Earl Warren, recently appointed by President Eisenhower, wrote the landmark opinion which flatly declared that "separate educational facilities are inherently unequal." To divide grade-school children "solely because of their race," Warren argued, "generates a feeling of inferiority as to their status in the community that may affect their hearts and minds in a way unlikely ever to be undone." Despite this sweeping language, Warren realized that it would be difficult to change historic patterns of segregation quickly. Accordingly, in 1955 the Court ruled that implementation should proceed "with all deliberate speed" and left the details to the lower federal courts.

The process of desegregating the schools proved to be agonizingly slow. Officials in the border states quickly complied with the Court's ruling, but states deeper in the South responded with a policy of massive resistance. Local White Citizen's Councils organized to fight for retention of racial separation; 101 congressmen and senators signed a Southern Manifesto in 1956 which denounced the *Brown* decision as "a clear abuse of judicial power." School boards, encouraged by this show of defiance, found a variety of ways to evade the Court's ruling. The most successful was the passage of pupil-placement laws . . . .

Southern leaders mistook Ike's silence for tacit support of segregation. In 1957, Governor Orville Faubus of Arkansas called out the national guard to prevent the integration of Little Rock's Central High School on grounds of a threat to public order . . . .

Despite the snail's pace of school desegregation, the *Brown* decision led to other advances. In 1957, the Eisenhower administration proposed the first general civil-rights legislation since Reconstruction. Strong southern resistance and compromise by both the administration and Senate Democratic leader Lyndon B. Johnson of Texas weakened the bill considerably. The final act, however, did create a permanent Commission for Civil Rights, one of Truman's original goals. It also provided for federal efforts aimed at "securing and protecting the right to vote." A second civil-rights act in 1960 slightly strengthened the voting-rights section.

—Divine et al., *America Past and Present,* pp. 890–91

SUMMARIZING TO CONDENSE IDEAS

Like note taking, summarizing is an excellent way to learn from your reading and to increase recall. A summary is a brief statement that reviews the key points of what you have read. It condenses an author's ideas or arguments into sentences written in your own words. A summary contains only the gist of the text, with limited explanation, background information, or supporting detail. Writing a summary is a step beyond recording the author's ideas; a summary must pull together the writer's ideas by condensing and grouping them. Writing a summary is a useful strategy when an overview of the material is needed, as in the following situations:

- Answering an essay question
- Reviewing a film or videotape
- Writing a term paper
- Recording results of a laboratory experiment or demonstration
- Summarizing the plot of a short story
- Quickly reviewing large amounts of information

Before writing a summary, be sure you understand the material and that you have identified the writer's major points. Then use the following suggestions.

1. *As a first step, highlight or write brief notes for the material.*

2. *Write one sentence that states the writer's overall concern or most important idea.* To do this, ask yourself what one topic the material is about. Then ask what point the writer is trying to make about that topic. This sentence will be the topic sentence of your summary.

3. *Be sure to paraphrase, using your own words rather than those of the author.*

4. *Next, review the major supporting information that the author gives to explain the major idea.*

5. *The amount of detail you include, if any, depends on your purpose for writing the summary.* For example, if you are writing a summary of a television documentary for a research paper, it might be more detailed than if you were writing it to jog your memory for a class discussion.

6. *Normally, present ideas in the summary in the same order in which they appeared in the original material.*

7. *If the writer presents a clear opinion or expresses an attitude toward the subject matter, include it in your summary.*

8. *If the summary is for your own use only and is not to be submitted as an assignment, do not worry about sentence structure.* Some students prefer to write summaries using words and phrases rather than complete sentences.

A sample summary of the article on biomes which appears earlier in this chapter is shown in Figure 10–5.

Figure 10–5 Sample Summary

> The earth is divided into regions called biomes. Each biome has its own species of plants and animals. Tropical rain forests have consistent temperatures but seasonal variation in rainfall. Trees grow throughout the year and animals breed year round. Both plants and animals are abundant in forests. Temperate deciduous forests have seasonal change in temperature; rainfall is evenly distributed. Tiaga, areas of coniferous pine forests, has long wet winters and short summers. Tundra refers to land covered by ice and snow most of the year. Plant life is limited to hardy lichens, herbs, mosses, low-lying shrubs, and dwarf trees.

EXERCISE 10–15

Write a summary of one of the end-of-chapter readings that you have already read. Working with a classmate, compare, discuss, and revise your summary.

EXERCISE 10–16

Select a five- to six-page section from one of your textbooks. Write a brief summary of the section, using the guidelines suggested above.

BRAINSTORMING TO DISCOVER IDEAS

Brainstorming is a writing and thinking exercise that is particularly effective for generating ideas. It works like this: Suppose you are trying to think of a topic for a three-minute informative speech for your speech class.

Begin by making a list of any topics that come into your mind. Write continuously. Do not be concerned about whether you are writing in complete sentences or whether the topics are practical or connected to one another. Write continuously for a set period—two or three minutes. When you have finished, reread what you have written. You will be surprised at the number of different topics you have discovered. Highlight those topics that are worth further exploration.

Brainstorming is also a way to get interested in a topic before beginning to read about it. Suppose you must read several lengthy research articles on the psychological effects of color. Before you start, brainstorm. List every possible effect of color and ways to measure its effects. Then read to confirm what you knew and to find out what you didn't know.

EXERCISE 10–17

Assume you will be reading several journal articles on drug testing in schools for a sociology class. Brainstorm for three minutes to discover what you already know about the issue.

EXERCISE 10–18

For each of the following statements, suggest one or more writing strategies that would enhance learning.

1. Some math students are having difficulty because they confuse several similar types of problems and choose incorrect solutions.

    _____

2. A political science class does not have a standard textbook. Instead, the instructor assigns weekly library readings on which she bases class discussions and lectures.

    _____

3. An anthropology student is preparing for an essay exam. She plans to predict possible questions and answer them.

    _____

4. A student in a computer literacy course must learn procedures for merging files using the word processing software.

    _____

5. For an English literature class, a student must write a paper comparing two poems by the same poet.

    _____

Preparing for Essay Exams

Essay exams demand complete recall. Starting with a blank sheet of paper, you are required to retrieve from your memory all the information that answers the question.

1. *Identify possible topics.* There are several sources from which you can identify topics: boldface textbook headings, chapter objectives and summaries, end-of-chapter discussion questions, and the course outline distributed by your instructor at the beginning of the course.

2. *Predict essay questions.* Perhaps the best source of information is your instructor, who probably has been consciously or unconsciously giving clues all semester about what questions will be asked. Specifically, look for your instructor's approach, focus, and emphasis with respect to the subject matter. For example: Does your history instructor emphasize the causes

and dates of events? Or is he or she more concerned with the historical importance and lasting effects of events? Is your ecology instructor concerned with specific changes that a pollutant produces or with its more general environmental effects?

3. *Prepare study sheets.* Include all the information you would want to remember if you were going to write an essay on each topic. As you prepare these study sheets, organize the information so that you could write a clear, concise essay on every topic.

4. *Use a key-word outline.* Summarize each idea on your study sheet with a single word or phrase. You can memorize these key words or phrases in a particular order. Together, they form a mini-outline of the ideas or topics you want to include in your essay.

SUMMARY

Writing is a process that can strengthen your comprehension and facilitate learning. Through self-testing, you can use writing to monitor your comprehension. Writing can strengthen your understanding of difficult or complex material by forcing you to analyze it step by step.

This chapter discusses five writing strategies.

- Highlighting and annotating are useful in textbook reading, because they enable you to distinguish what is important to learn and remember.
- Note taking is a writing strategy for organizing information and pulling ideas together.

- Mapping—drawing a diagram that describes how a topic and its related ideas are connected—is an effective way to organize and consolidate information. The four types of maps are
  - conceptual maps
  - process diagrams
  - diagrams of part functions
  - time lines
- Summaries condense ideas and provide a review of key points.
- Brainstorming enables you to discover and clarify ideas, as well as to generate interest in your reading assignments.

CULTURAL ANTHROPOLOGY

PREREADING QUESTIONS

1. How could you define the term *cosmetics?*
2. Does the manner in which cosmetics are used vary from society to society?

BODY ADORNMENT: THE USE OF COSMETICS

David Hicks and Margaret A. Gwynne

1 One way in which people adorn their bodies is by temporarily decorating their skin with cosmetics, the general term for preparations designed to improve the appearance of the body, or part of it, by directly but temporarily applying them to the skin. In Western society, cosmetics take the form of various mass-produced, petroleum-based, colored creams, oils, or powders. These are usually applied to the face, and are much more frequently used by females than by males. In other societies, the term *cosmetics* may refer to body as well as face paints, usually made by combining animal or vegetable oils with colored powders made from naturally occurring minerals.

2 The extent to which cosmetics are used in human societies, from the remote jungles of South America to the high-fashion capitals of western Europe, suggests that the notion of adorning or enhancing the surface of the body, like the idea of covering it with clothing, comes close to

Cosmetics are universally used to beautify people, protect them from harm, express their social status, or identify them as members of particular groups. In Liberia, a Bassa girl being initiated into the Sande, an all-female secret society, is covered with a chalky white clay.

being a human universal. There are differences of placement, emphasis, and extent among various traditions of cosmetic use, but the reasons for wearing cosmetics are similar.

3   In every society with a cosmetic tradition, including Western society, one reason bodies are decorated is to enhance them—to make them appear more perfectly in accord with society's ideals of beauty (although what is considered attractive varies widely from society to society). But in some societies, the use of cosmetics quite consciously provides other benefits as well. Cosmetics may protect people from harm, express their social status, or identify them as members of particular classes or families. Benefits of this kind are probably part of the reason behind Western cosmetic use also, although Western cosmetics users may not be aware of it.

4   If Westerners differ little from members of other societies in their primary motivations for applying cosmetics, they do differ from some in the relatively modest extent to which they decorate themselves. Cosmetic use in some societies is so extensive it would make the heavy-handed application of cosmetics to a female American screen star by a Hollywood makeup artist seem moderate.

5   A well-turned-out Nuba male from Kordofan Province in the Sudan of northern Africa is literally painted from head to foot. Among the Nuba, body painting begins in infancy, when a baby's scalp is decorated with either red or yellow paint, depending on its family membership (Faris 1972:30). Thereafter, body painting is used to suggest one's social and physical status as well as to beautify, and it becomes more and more complex with advancing age. A young Nuba boy, for example, wears simple, inconspicuous, red and greyish white decorations on his scalp, gradually earning the right to use increasingly elaborate, colorful, and extensive designs as he matures. Each change of age and status means a new kind of decoration for the boy, as with advancing years he earns the right to use more products in a wider range of colors and designs. (Westerners, too, sometimes use cosmetics as an age marker, as when an American girl is forbidden by her parents to wear lipstick until she has reached a certain age.)

6   The scalp, face, chest, back, arms, and legs of a young adult Nuba male may literally be covered with colorful designs (Faris 1972:18–19, 62), both purely decorative (straight and curved lines, dots, triangles, crosshatching) and representational (animals, airplanes, lightning, stars—even English words, which may or may not be intelligible to the Nuba). Often these designs are asymmetrically placed on the face or body and are strikingly modern looking. They may take up to an hour to apply and may be redone daily.

7   Decorating the body as well as the face with cosmetics is by no means limited to rural or small-scale societies. Some modern, urban girls and women in North Africa, the Middle East, and South Asia, decorate their skin with henna, an

orange-red dye made from leaves. Urban Moroccan women, for example, may be decorated on suitable occasions with fine lines and dots forming intricate designs. These are typically applied to the hands and feet, which then look as if they are clad in lace gloves or stockings. Henna is applied at a "henna party," to which the girl or woman to be decorated invites her friends, a professional henna artist, and sometimes professional musicians or other entertainers. During the long and careful process of decorating, the guests eat, sing songs, tell jokes, and dance around the woman being decorated (Messina 1988).

8   Moroccan women who use henna say they apply it for a variety of reasons. A girl or woman may be decorated in preparation for a religious festival or her wedding, to cheer her up in late pregnancy, to soften her skin, to prevent spirits called *jinni* from causing illness or misfortune, or to calm her nerves. Whatever the reason, applying henna is cause for celebration; a henna party provides a "lively departure" from formal Islamic expectations of proper female behavior (Messina 1988:46). People from different regions admire different designs, and styles of decoration change constantly, but the designs themselves have no explicit meanings.

—Hicks and Gwynne, *Cultural Anthropology*, pp. 378–80

VOCABULARY REVIEW

1. For each of the words listed below, use context; prefixes, roots, and suffixes; and/or a dictionary to write a brief definition or synonym of the word as it is used in the reading.

    a. status (para. 3) _____

    b. inconspicuous (para. 5) _____

    c. elaborate (para. 5) _____

    d. representational (para. 6) _____

    e. asymmetrically (para. 6) _____

    f. explicit (para. 8) _____

2. Highlight new specialized terms introduced in the reading.

COMPREHENSION QUESTIONS

1. What main point about the use of cosmetics does this reading make?
2. How does the use of cosmetics differ between Western and other societies?

3. For what single purpose do all societies use cosmetics?
4. Explain how cosmetics are used by males in the Nuba society.
5. How do Moroccan women use henna?

THINKING CRITICALLY

1. What is the author's purpose for writing?
2. What generalizations do the authors make about the use of cosmetics? What types of evidence do the authors give to support their generalizations?
3. Discuss the use of cosmetics in Western society. For what purposes are they used? How does their use vary from subgroup to subgroup?

LEARNING/STUDY STRATEGIES

1. Draw a map that shows the key ideas of this reading.
2. Assume you have to write a short paper for a sociology class explaining why Western women use cosmetics. Review the reading, and make annotations that would help you develop ideas for your paper.

CULTURAL ANTHROPOLOGY

PREREADING QUESTIONS

1. In what ways do people decorate their bodies?
2. Do you think most people are comfortable with their bodies? Why?

THE DECORATED BODY

France Borel

1   Human nakedness, according to social custom, is unacceptable, unbearable, and dangerous. From the moment of birth, society takes charge, managing, dressing, forming, and deforming the child—sometimes even with a certain degree of violence. Aside from the most elementary caretaking concerns—the very diversity of which shows how subjective the motivation is—an unfathomably deep and universal tendency pushes families, clans, and tribes to rapidly modify a person's physical appearance.

2   One's genuine physical makeup, one's given anatomy, is always felt to be unacceptable. Flesh, in its raw state, seems both intolerable and threatening. In its naked state, body and skin have no possible existence. The organism is acceptable only when it is transformed, covered with signs. The body only speaks if it is dressed in artifice.

3   For millennia, in the four quarters of the globe, mothers have molded the shape of their newborn babies' skulls to give them silhouettes conforming to prevalent criteria of beauty. In the nineteenth century, western children were tightly swaddled to keep their limbs straight. In the so-called primitive world, children were scarred or tattooed at a very early age in rituals which were repeated at all the most important steps of their lives. At a very young age, children were fitted with belts, necklaces, or bracelets; their lips, ears, or noses were pierced or stretched.

4   Some cultures have designed sophisticated appliances to alter physical structure and appearance. American Indian cradleboards crushed the skull to flatten it; the Mangbetus of Africa wrapped knotted rope made of bark around the child's head to elongate it into a sugarloaf shape, which was considered to be aesthetically pleasing. The feet of very young Chinese girls were bound and spliced, intentionally and irreversibly deforming them, because this was seen to guarantee the girls' eventually amorous and matrimonial success.[1]

5   Claude Levi-Strauss said about the Caduveo of Brazil: "In order to be a man, one had to be painted; whoever remained in a natural state was no

different from the beasts."[2] In Polynesia, unless a girl was tattooed, she would not find a husband. An unornamented hand could not cook, nor dip into the communal food bowl. Pink lips were despicable and ugly. Anyone who refused the test of the tattoo was seen to be marginal and suspect.

6   Among the Tivs of Nigeria, women called attention to their legs by means of elaborate scarification and the use of pearl leg bands; the best decorated calves were known for miles around. Tribal incisions behind the ears of Chad men rendered the skin "as smooth and stretched as that of a drum." The women would laugh at any man lacking these incisions, and they would never accept him as a husband. Men would subject themselves willingly to this custom, hoping for scars deep enough to leave marks on their skulls after death.

7   At the beginning of the eighteenth century, Father Laurent de Lucques noted that any young girl of the Congo who was not able to bear the pain of scarification and who cried so loudly that the operation had to be stopped was considered "good for nothing."[3] That is why, before marriage, men would check to see if the pattern traced on the belly of their intended bride was beautiful and well-detailed.

8   The fact that such motivations and pretexts depend on aesthetic, erotic, hygienic, or even medical considerations has no influence on the result, which is always in the direction of transforming the appearance of the body. Such a transformation is wished for, whether or not it is effective.

9   The body is a supple, malleable, and transformable prime material, a kind of modelling clay, easily molded by social will and wish. Human skin is an ideal subject for inscription, a surface for all sorts of marks which make it possible to differentiate the human from the animal. The physical body offers itself willingly for tattooing or scarring so that, visibly and recognizably, it becomes a social entity.

10   The absolutely naked body is considered as brutish, reduced to the level of nature where no distinction is made between man and beast. The decorated body, on the other hand, dressed (if even only in a belt), tattooed, or mutilated, publicly exhibits humanity and membership in an established group. As Theophile Gautier said, "The ideal disturbs even the roughest nature, and the taste for ornamentation distinguishes the intelligent being from the beast more exactly than anything else. Indeed, dogs have never dreamed of putting on earrings."

11   So, it is by their categorical refusal of nakedness that human beings are distinguished from nature. The "mark makes unremarkable"—it creates an interval between what is biologically and brutally given in the animal realm and what is won in the cultural realm. The body is tamed continuously; social custom demands, at any price—including pain, constraint, or discomfort—that wildness be abandoned. Each civilization chooses—through a network of elective relationships which are difficult to determine—which areas of the body deserve

transformation. These areas are as difficult to define and as shifting as those of eroticism or modesty. An individual alone eludes bodily modifications; they are the expression of a homogeneous collectivity which, at a chosen moment, comes to a tacit agreement to attack one or another part of the anatomy.

12   Whatever the choices, options, or differences may be, that which remains constant is the transformation of appearance. In spite of our contemporary western belief that the body is perfect as it is, we are constantly changing it: clothing it in musculature, suntan, or makeup; dying its head hair or pulling out its bodily hair. The seemingly most innocent gestures for taking care of the body very often hide a persistent and disguised tendency to make it adhere to the strictest of norms, reclothing it in a veil of civilization. The total nudity offered at birth does not exist in any region of the world. Man puts his stamp on man. The body is not a product of nature, but of culture.

—Borel, "The Decorated Body," *Parabola,* Fall 1994, Vol. 19, No. 3, p. 74

VOCABULARY REVIEW

1. For each of the words listed below, use context; prefixes, roots, and suffixes; and/or a dictionary to write a brief definition or synonym of the word as it is used in the reading.

   a. diversity (para. 1) _____

   b. subjective (para. 1) _____

   c. prevalent (para. 3)_____

   d. swaddled (para. 3)_____

   e. aesthetically (para. 4) _____

   f. spliced (para. 4) _____

   g. marginal (para. 5) _____

   h. scarification (para. 6) _____

   i. pretexts (para. 8) _____

   j. erotic (para. 8) _____

   k. inscription (para. 9) _____

   l. interval (para. 11) _____

   m. tacit (para. 11) _____

2. Highlight new specialized terms introduced in the reading.

COMPREHENSION QUESTIONS

1. What is the author's view of human nakedness?
2. How did the Mangbetus of Africa change the heads of children?
3. What was done to Chinese girls to alter their appearance? Why was this done?
4. Why did the men of the Congo check the stomachs of their brides before marrying them?
5. Describe how the Tiv women of Nigeria treated their legs.

THINKING CRITICALLY

1. What is the author's purpose in writing this article?
2. What can you conclude about human beauty from this reading?
3. In Polynesia, a girl without a tattoo would not be considered for marriage. Why do you think that was?
4. How do young men and women in the American culture decorate their bodies today?
5. The author states that humans decorate their bodies to designate their membership in an established group. In what other ways do humans signal group membership?

LEARNING/STUDY STRATEGY

Create a chart which lists the cultures referred to in this reading and describes the type of body decoration each used.

THINKING ABOUT THE PAIRED READINGS

INTEGRATING IDEAS

1. In what ways do the authors agree on the purposes for body decoration, and in what ways do they differ?
2. How do the two readings differ in content?
3. What do you think would be the best way to learn the information in these readings in light of what you have learned in this chapter?
4. If you were writing a 10-page research paper on the purposes and types of body decoration, what further information would you need?
5. What aspects of both readings apply to people in the U.S. today?
6. Of the two readings, which do you think was the most difficult to read and remember? Why?

GENERATING NEW IDEAS

1. Take 10 minutes to brainstorm ideas about body adornment in order to narrow a topic for a two-page paper.
2. Suppose you have a friend or relative who lives in a foreign country and is unfamiliar with western forms of body decoration. Your friend is planning to visit the U.S. soon. Write a letter to that person describing what unusual decorations he or she might expect to see.

11 | READING RESEARCH, REFERENCE, AND COLLATERAL ASSIGNMENTS

LEARNING OBJECTIVES

- **To learn a systematic approach for reading research materials**
- **To develop alternative reading strategies**
- **To learn note taking**
- **To develop skills for reading collateral reading assignments**
- **To learn to evaluate sources**

Your political science professor assigns a 20-page research paper. Your psychology professor assigns a text and 30 related readings—research articles from *Science Digest*. Your marketing professor requires that you read and abstract two articles per week on topics related to her weekly lectures. You probably have discovered that your reading assignments are not limited to textbooks; many of your professors require that you locate sources, read research articles, and report their findings. Some professors distribute reading lists and direct you to read or write a specified number of abstracts. Others place materials to be read on reserve in the library. Still others assign a research paper on a related topic of your choice.

Many students make the mistake of reading research and supplementary material in the same way they read their textbook assignments. Consequently, they become frustrated with the assignments, claiming, "I'll never finish the research for this paper" or "These reading assignments are impossible!" This chapter describes new approaches to dealing with research, reference, and collateral reading assignments that are distinct from textbook reading techniques.

READING RESEARCH MATERIALS

Reading research and reference materials is very different from reading textbooks. When reading textbooks, your goal is usually a high level of retention and recall. In reading research papers, however, complete retention is not always necessary. You may be searching for evidence to support an argument, reading widely to gain overall familiarity with a subject, or locating a particular statistic. Also, whereas textbooks have a consistent format and organization, research and reference sources differ widely in these characteristics. Consequently, you must adapt your reading strategy to suit the nature of the material. The following sections present a systematic approach to reading research and reference material when you must prepare a written report or research paper.

Define and Focus Your Topic

The first critical step in doing research for a written assignment is to define and focus your topic. It is a waste of time to begin a full search for information and to read numerous sources until you know exactly what you are looking for. Suppose you begin with a topic, such as "Hypnotism." This subject is much too broad. You couldn't possibly cover everything about hypnotism in one paper in any meaningful way. It may take two or three attempts at narrowing to arrive at a topic you can reasonably handle. For example, "Hypnotism" could be narrowed to "Uses of Hypnotism," then to "Modern Uses of Hypnotism," and finally to "Modern Medical Uses of Hypnotism."

To help narrow your topic, especially if it is one with which you are not familiar, some preliminary research or reading may be helpful. Here are some suggestions.

1. *Consult with your reference librarian to find out whether computerized searches are available.* Many libraries have access to data banks that identify all possible sources on a given topic. (Some libraries charge a fee for this service.)

2. *Read an encyclopedia entry to get an overview of the subject.*

3. *Check the* Reader's Guide to Periodical Literature *for listings on your topic.* Look through the list of articles for ideas on how to narrow your topic.

4. *Check the card catalogue or on-line computer system to see how your topic is subdivided.*

5. Consult your instructor if you're not sure whether your topic is sufficiently narrow.

Once you have narrowed your topic, try to establish a focus or direction for your research. Your paper should focus on, explore, and answer a question; it should take a position. For example, your paper on "Modern Medical Uses of Hypnotism" might discuss the ways hypnotism is useful in modern medicine, or it might take the position that hypnotism is of limited use in modern medical practice, or even that hypnotism is dangerous and that its use should be restricted.

EXERCISE 11–1

Assume that one of your professors has assigned a research paper on one of the following subjects. Choose one subject, and narrow it to a topic that is manageable in a 10-page paper.

1. Environmental problems
2. Pornography
3. Test-tube babies
4. Professional sports

Devise a Search Strategy

In researching a topic, some students begin by gathering all the sources on the topic and then working through them randomly. This approach is time-consuming and often repetitious. Instead, devise and follow a search strategy—an orderly way of sifting through available sources on your topic. A search strategy enables you to select the most suitable materials and to approach the topic in a logical fashion. A search strategy proceeds from general to specific. You begin by reading general materials that provide an overview of your topic. You then move gradually to more detailed sources that address a particular aspect of your topic. Of course, your search strategy depends on your topic, your familiarity with it, and the requirements of your assignments, but a common search strategy is shown in Table 11–1.

As you proceed through the search strategy, you will find additional references. Each source will list its own references; eventually, the sources will converge. That is, you will come on the same sources several times and will begin to recognize authorities in the field. For example, as you research quality control in business and industry, you keep coming across the name of W. Edwards Deming, so you realize you need to know more about him and his ideas. If you have difficulty locating bibliographies or working through the search strategy, reference librarians are ready to offer valuable, time-saving assistance.

TABLE 11–1   A SEARCH STRATEGY

SOURCE	PURPOSE
1. Encyclopedia	Obtain an overview; learn the language of the subject; discover subdivisions.
2. Bibliographies and Indexes (list of sources on a topic)	Locate a list of sources on the subject.
3. Books	Obtain basic information on the topic (or aspects of the topic).
4. Periodicals	Investigate particular aspects of the topic; obtain current or recent information.
5. Special sources (documents, directories, review of the literature, pamphlet files, media resources)	Zero in on specialized information.

Previewing Sources

As you proceed through your search strategy, it is useful to preview sources before delving into them. Previewing is an excellent research strategy; it enables you to select the most useful sources and to select sources of appropriate difficulty and complexity.

Let's assume you have located 15 books for a term paper on the psychological effects of terrorism on its victims. Your next step is to preview those sources to determine which are useful to your paper. If your paper requires current information, check the copyright date and eliminate any sources that are outdated. Next, glance through the table of contents to get an overall idea of the material covered by each source. Check the index to determine how extensively the source treats your specific topic. Select only those sources that provide a comprehensive treatment of your topic. Once you have identified these sources, randomly select a sample page in each and skim it to get a "feel" for the source. Pay particular attention to the level of difficulty. Is the source too basic, containing little more information than is in your course textbook? Or is the source too complicated? Does it assume extensive background knowledge of the subject, such as an extensive knowledge of psychoanalysis, for example? Previewing will enable you to select sources that contain sufficient information and that are of an appropriate degree of difficulty.

Defining Your Purpose

Be sure to have a specific purpose for reading each reference source. Your purpose determines *how* you will read the material, as well as what type of note taking, if any, is necessary. To define your purpose, determine what level of comprehension and retention is expected. Is complete recall necessary, or is familiarity with key concepts sufficient? Your choice will hinge in part on the type of follow-up activity, if any, that will be involved. Will you be expected to write a summary or abstract, discuss the material in class, or use the information to write a term paper? (Refer to "Documentation and Note Taking" later in this chapter for suggestions.)

Comprehension is not an either/or situation. Rather, comprehension is a continuum, and many levels of understanding are possible. In this respect, you might think of comprehension as similar to temperature: There is a wide range of conditions between freezing and boiling. And just as snowball fights go with freezing temperatures and cool drinks in the shade go with high temperatures, so are various levels of comprehension appropriate for various materials and types of assignments. An extremely high level of comprehension is necessary if you are reading a critical interpretation of a poem for an English literature paper. Each detail is important. However, a lower level of comprehension is appropriate for reading excerpts from a biography assigned for an American history course. Here, you would not be expected to recall each descriptive detail or bit of conversation.

The reading strategy you select is also shaped by the tasks that will follow your reading. If, for example, you are reading an encyclopedia article to get an overview of a subject so that you can narrow a topic for a term paper, then complete comprehension is not needed. You require only an understanding of the major aspects or divisions of the subject in order to begin topic selection. Therefore, moderate to low comprehension is appropriate. Suppose, however, you are required to write a critical evaluation of a magazine article arguing against capital punishment. A high or complete level of comprehension is required, because you need to follow the argument carefully, search for points of inconsistency, and so forth.

TABLE 11–2   LEVELS OF COMPREHENSION

LEVEL OF COMPREHENSION	PERCENTAGE OF RECALL	WHEN USED
Complete	100%	Reading critical analysis; reading directions or procedures.
High	90–100%	Reading a primary reference source.
Moderate	70–90%	Reading for an overview of a subject.
Low	50–70%	Reading to obtain background information; reading only for key ideas.
Selective	50% or below	Looking up a statistic in an almanac; checking a date in a biographical dictionary.

Comprehension can, somewhat arbitrarily, be divided into five levels: complete, high, moderate, low, and selective, as described in Table 1–3 on page 15. Study Table 11–2 before continuing to read.

EXERCISE 11–2

Working with a classmate, select a level of comprehension that seems appropriate for each of the following research situations.

1. Reading a biographical entry on Ella Fitzgerald in *The Encyclopedia of Jazz* for a term paper on the history of jazz.
2. Locating names of leaders of Third World countries in the *International Yearbook* and *Statesman's Who's Who.*
3. Reading the directions for using a computerized card catalogue.
4. Reading a source to verify that you have not missed any key information in sources you have already used.
5. Reading a newspaper review of a performance of *Cats* in preparation for a drama class discussion on audience responsiveness.

ALTERNATIVE READING STRATEGIES

Now that you have learned to gauge the level of comprehension appropriate for various reading assignments, the next step is to learn alternative reading strategies to meet these varied comprehension demands.

Most students are accustomed to reading everything completely. They read each word successively, from beginning to end. Few students realize there are other options available. Two alternative reading strategies are presented here: skimming and scanning.

When and How to Skim

Most textbook assignments must be read completely; complete or high comprehension is required. However, for some reading assignments that demand lower levels of comprehension, you can afford to read some parts and skip others. This strategy is known as **skimming.** Skimming is a technique in which you selectively read and skip in order to find only the most important ideas. Here are a few situations in which skimming is appropriate.

1. *Reading a section of a textbook chapter that reviews the metric system.* If you have already learned and used the metric system, you can afford to skip over much of the material.

2. *Reading a section of a reference book that you are using to complete a research paper.* If you have already collected most of your basic

information, you might skim through additional references, looking only for new information not discussed in sources you have used before.

3. *Sampling a two-page, 30-item supplementary reading list for a sociology class.* Your instructor has encouraged you to review as many of the items as possible. You anticipate that the final exam will include one essay question that is related to these readings. Clearly, you cannot read every entry, but you can skim a reasonable number.

4. *Reviewing a textbook chapter you have already read.* To review the chapter for a class discussion, you could skim it.

In skimming, your goal is to identify those parts of any reading material that contain the main ideas. The type of material you are reading will, in part, determine how you should adapt your reading techniques. Authors use different patterns of organization and various formats, and skimming is a highly flexible technique that can be adapted to these varying structures and formats. To acquaint you with the process of skimming, here is the procedure. Generally, read the following items.

1. *The title.* The title announces the subject of the material and provides clues about the author's approach or attitude toward it.

2. *The subtitle or introductory byline.* Some material includes, underneath the title, a statement that further explains the title or is written to catch the reader's interest.

3. *The introductory paragraph.* The first paragraph often provides important background information and introduces the subject. It also may provide a brief overview of the treatment of the subject.

4. *The headings.* A heading announces the topic that will be discussed in the paragraphs that follow it. When read successively, the headings form an outline or a list of topics covered in the material.

5. *The first sentence of each paragraph.* Most paragraphs are built around a topic sentence that states the main idea of the paragraph. The most common position for the main idea is in the first sentence of the paragraph. If you read a first sentence that clearly is not the topic sentence, then you might jump to the end of the paragraph and read the last sentence. Your goal as you skim each paragraph should be to get an overview of its structure and content. The first sentence, if it functions as a topic sentence, usually states the main idea and provides clues about how the rest of the paragraph is organized.

6. *The remainder of the paragraph.* Quickly glance through the remainder of the paragraph. Let your eyes quickly sweep through the paragraph. Try

to pick out words that answer questions such as "who," "what," "when," "where," or "how much" about the main idea of the paragraph. Also, note any words that indicate a continuation or a change in thought pattern as you glance through the paragraph. Try to pick up names, numbers, dates, places, and capitalized or italicized words and phrases. Note any numbered sequences too. This quick glance will add to your overall impression of the paragraph and will confirm that you have identified the main idea of the paragraph.

7. *The title or legend of any maps, graphs, charts, or diagrams.* The title or legend will state what is depicted and suggest what important event, idea, or relationship is emphasized.

8. *The last paragraph.* The last paragraph often provides a conclusion or summary for the article. It might concisely state the main points of the article, or it might suggest new ways to consider the topic.

Now that you are familiar with the procedure for skimming, you are probably wondering how fast to skim, how much to skip, and what level of comprehension to expect. Generally, your reading rate should be about three or four times as fast as you normally read. You should skip more than you read. Although the amount to skip varies according to the type of material, a safe estimate is that you should skip about 70 to 80 percent of the material. Because you are skipping large portions of the material, your comprehension will be limited.

To give you a better idea of what the technique of skimming is like, the following article has been highlighted to indicate the portions of the article that you might read when skimming. Of course, this is not the only effective way to skim this article. Depending on your purpose for reading it, you could identify different parts of the article as important. You also might select different key words and phrases while glancing through each paragraph.

AN OVERVIEW OF LEGAL GAMBLING: THE ISSUE AT A GLANCE

Not so long ago—1977—casino gambling was a crime in 49 states and a Mafia founded enterprise in Nevada. Now gambling (or "gaming," as supporters prefer to call it) is a national pastime, a pastime that many Americans consider simply another form of entertainment. While the expansion of legal gambling seems to have leveled off in recent years, it has become a fact of life in communities around the nation.

Competition for the gambling dollar is so cut-throat that a casino industry group in Nevada distributes anti-gambling literature to discourage other states from legalizing casinos. Many state lotteries are evolving into state casinos as they install video gambling machines in bars, restaurants, gas stations, and convenience stores. And couch potatoes need not leave home, as the Internet provides 24-hour-a-day access to Aruba Palms, Sportz Casino, and 20 other international casinos that provide high-stakes gambling via the family computer. Federal law prohibits the use of telephones for gambling, and American casinos have not yet gone online. If they do, experts say the Internet would revolutionize the gambling industry and present new challenges to families.

Gambling has evolved with dizzying speed. Polling suggests most Americans haven't had time to adjust and still have mixed views about the practice.

Waves of History

Illegal gambling, of course, has always been with us, but even legal gambling is nothing new in American history. Historians say legal gambling has been through several cycles of boom and ban, dating back to the very beginning of the colonial era. The first American settlement in Jamestown, for example, was funded by an English lottery. Then again, the Pilgrims limited gambling to the well-to-do in 1621, just a year after they arrived—they thought it wouldn't be right to entice poor people to gamble in a "shining city on a hill."

In each of the earlier cycles, legal gambling spread because states and communities needed the money; and contracted because somebody stole the money. The early 19th Century saw widespread use of lotteries, till a series of scandals over corruption and mismanagement led to restrictions in the 1840s. After the Civil War, gambling was widely used as a economic-development tool for war-ravaged states, then died out by 1910 as a byproduct of Progressive Era anti-corruption campaigns. Nevada legalized casinos again in 1931 to fight the Great Depression, but the taint of Mafia involvement kept other states from following suit for more than 40 years.

So far, the latest wave of gambling has been driven by the same need for revenue—New Jersey legalized casinos as a tool for urban redevelopment in Atlantic City; Native American tribes have used their status as sovereign nations to open casinos on disadvantaged reservations; and 37 state governments now run lotteries as a relatively painless way to raise tax revenue. The growth of legal gambling has slowed in recent years after the explosion of the 1980s and early 1990s, with voters in seven states rejecting various gambling proposals in 1996.

A new twist on an old concern has come up during the latest expansion; compulsive gambling, formerly considered a character flaw, is now labeled as a mental health problem. Gamblers Anonymous, founded in 1957, now has 2,000 chapters worldwide, and the American Psychiatric Association has added compulsive gambling to its official Diagnostic and Statistical Manual of Mental Disorders. A Harvard Medical School study sponsored by a casino trade group found compulsive gambling among adults increased from 0.84 percent to 1.29 percent over the past 20 years, and among people being treated for some other mental illness or substance abuse the rate was 14.3 percent. Compulsive gambling among adolescents, however, has held relatively steady at 4 percent, the study found.

The Public View

The public is still coming to terms with legal gambling and its financial and moral implications. A substantial number of Americans (44 percent) view gambling as harmless recreation, while 26 percent said it is fundamentally immoral and 25 percent consider it "somewhere in-between." When it comes to the social and economic impact of gambling, 46 percent of Americans said casino gambling is more likely to aid economic growth, while 39 percent said it would more likely cause crime and social problems.

In a 1996 Gallup Organization poll, most Americans cited three major concerns with legalized gambling: it would make compulsive gamblers out of people who would never participate in illegal gambling; it encourages people who can least afford it to squander their money; and it would not deter organized crime. Yet a significant minority of Americans didn't see these problems.

Gallop found that most Americans opposed the legalization of casino gambling in 1993. But three years later, in response to a differently worded question, most Americans said they were resigned to gambling's growth: people will gamble whether it's legal or not, most Americans told Gallup, so the state might as well make it legal to get some of the revenue.

Three Perspectives

The Perspectives section offers three public approaches to legalized gambling:

- Cut the red tape on gaming and treat the industry as a beneficial generator of jobs and entertainment;
- Regulate gambling to make it safer, by treating games of chance like alcohol—a pleasant but potentially dangerous activity that can be abused without government oversight.
- Stop gambling to the extent possible, treating the industry as a predatory business that should be phased out.

—*Public Agenda Online*, October 1999

EXERCISE 11–3

After you have skimmed "An Overview of Legal Gambling: The Issue at a Glance," *p. 329, answer the following questions.*

1. What is the purpose of the article?
2. Name one recent problem created by gambling.
3. Why has legal gambling spread?
4. Name at least one future action that might be taken regarding legalized gambling.

EXERCISE 11–4

Skim "Giving Viruses a Cold Reception," *and answer the following questions.*

1. What is the main point of the article?
2. How are cold viruses transmitted?

3. What should you do to prevent colds?
4. List several symptoms that suggest that an infection may be more serious than a cold.
5. List several things to do to relieve cold symptoms.

GIVING VIRUSES A COLD RECEPTION

The immune system learns to recognize specific disease agents through exposure to them. Antigen exposure can occur through vaccination or by natural means. We acquire immunity to chickenpox, measles, mumps, tetanus, cholera, smallpox, and many other life-threatening diseases. So, one might wonder, if the immune system can do such amazing things, why can't it defend us from the common cold?

We are susceptible to at least 200 different cold-causing viruses. The most common type, rhinoviruses (literally "nose viruses"), cause about 30 to 50 percent of all colds in adults. As soon as the immune system learns to recognize and defend us from one, another comes along, and then another. This antigenic diversity creates quite a challenge for the immune system, so much so that most people succumb to one to six colds per year.

Nonspecific Resistance

Cold symptoms are not produced directly by the cold virus, but by the body's nonspecific immune response as it fights the virus. When viruses invade the cells lining the nasal passages, your body responds with inflammation and the production of extra mucus. This causes nasal congestion, a "stuffy nose." As mucous membranes in the nose accelerate their secretion of antibody-containing mucus, you get a runny nose. Congestion in the middle ear or sinuses can cause dizziness or a headache.

The "swollen glands" sometimes felt during a cold are actually swollen lymph nodes. The nodes swell as immune cells, including macrophages, T-cells, and B cells, work overtime to fight pathogens. A sore throat can result from "postnasal drip" as the sinuses drain mucus into the throat. Throat tissue can also become dry and irritated from breathing through your mouth or coughing.

Like the nasal passages, the trachea and bronchial tubes become inflamed and produce extra secretions if invaded by the cold virus. A wheezing sound indicates airway congestion as mucus accumulates and restricts the flow of air. A "productive" cough assists the respiratory passages in getting rid of the mucus and the virus. A "nonproductive" or dry cough is usually caused by throat irritation. Your body may produce a fever to create an inhospitable climate for the virus. Most cold viruses prefer temperatures of 86 to 96° F (30 to 35.5° C). Since fever is a helpful part of your nonspecific resistance, medication should only be used if the fever exceeds 101.5° F (38.6° C) or is needed to treat accompanying aches and pains.

Cold Prevention

Despite its name, a cold is not caused by cold weather, wet feet, or getting cold, at least according to laboratory studies. Colds do occur more frequently in the winter than in the summer, but no one knows why. The incidence of colds usually rises sharply in the early fall and spring. Some believe that when children go back to school and are exposed to each other's viruses, they bring them home to their families.

Research indicates that most of the time cold viruses are transmitted from the hands of an infected person to the hands of a susceptible person. The virus can survive on the skin for only a few hours and must reach the nose in order to invade the body. On the face near the nose is no good, since the skin provides an effective barrier. The mucous membranes of the mouth are also an inhospitable environment; kissing seldom spreads colds.

If all goes well for the virus, eventually the hand delivers the virus to its new home, the person's respiratory system, by touching the mucous membranes of the nose or the eyes (the virus can travel down the tear duct to the upper nose). One study found that 40 to 90 percent of people with colds had rhinoviruses on their hands. The viruses were also found on about 15 percent of nearby objects, such as door knobs, telephones, and coffee cups.

It is not known what makes some people more susceptible to colds. Small children are the most susceptible, because their immune systems are still immature and haven't learned to recognize as many pathogens. People who are around children a lot also get colds more frequently. Smokers are more likely to catch colds than nonsmokers, partly because smoking inhibits the airway cilia that help move mucus. Some studies have shown that stress can decrease the effectiveness of the immune system, and many people believe that stress and fatigue increase their susceptibility to colds.

Given what we know about the transmission of colds, the single best way to prevent colds is frequent handwashing, especially when you're around people who have colds. Avoid sharing telephones, glasses, towels, and other objects with a person who has a cold. And try not to touch your nose or eyes.

Getting enough rest, eating well, exercising moderately, and managing stress certainly won't hurt and may help keep your resistance up. If you're a smoker, cold prevention is yet another good reason to quit.

What about vitamin C? Studies have failed to show that vitamin C prevents colds, although some research has found that it may lessen the severity of cold symptoms. Vitamin C also increases the intactness of cell membranes, so it may make them harder for viruses to penetrate.

Cold Self-Care

Since a cure for colds continues to elude medical researchers, the best we can do is to treat the symptoms. It's been said that with aggressive medical treatment a cold will disappear in seven days, while if left alone a cold will last a week. Nevertheless, symptom treatment can at least make us feel better until the cold has run its course.

The first step in cold self-care is to decide whether your symptoms are those of a cold or something more serious requiring medical attention. People who have heart disease, emphysema, diabetes, or another health condition should get professional advice before initiating self-care, especially before taking over-the-counter medication. Pregnant and lactating women should also check with their doctors before taking any medication.

Symptoms that indicate your infection may be more than a cold include:

1. Oral temperature over 103° F (39.5° C).
2. Sore throat with temperature above 101° F (38.5° C) for over 24 hours.
3. Temperature over 100° F (37.5° C) for three days.
4. Severe pain in ears, head, chest, or stomach.
5. Symptoms that persist more than a week.
6. Enlarged lymph nodes.
7. In a child, difficulty breathing or greater than normal irritability or lethargy.

Once you decide you have a cold, there are several things you can do to help yourself feel better. They include the following.

1. Chicken soup, broth, or other hot drinks. Your mother was right: hot fluids help relieve congestion by increasing the flow of nasal secretions. They also soothe irritated throats.
2. Gargle with salt water (1/4 teaspoon salt in 8 oz. water) to soothe a sore throat.
3. Use a vaporizer or humidifier to increase humidity, especially if the air is very dry. Humid air is gentler on nose and throat.
4. Breathing steam gives your nose a temporary fever, creating an inhospitable environment for the virus. It also helps to thin the mucus causing a stuffy nose, and thus temporarily relieve congestion. The steam may also feel soothing to irritated throats and nasal passages.
5. While rest may not hasten your recovery, it may help you feel better. It's good to stay out of circulation for the first few days of a cold to keep others from getting it.
6. Many over-the-counter cold medications are available. If you decide you need something, avoid combination drugs that contain several active ingredients to treat several symptoms. If, instead, you buy single drugs for the symptoms you wish to treat, you will avoid taking unnecessary drugs and decrease unpleasant side effects.

Should You Exercise When You Have a Cold?

Many people wonder whether they should continue their exercise programs when they have a cold. Some hope that the exertion will create a fever and "burn out the cold," while others believe that the added stress of exercise will only exhaust an already overwhelmed immune system. At this point, there is nothing but anecdotal evidence for these two beliefs. As long as symptoms are mild, exercising doesn't appear to either prolong the cold or hasten recovery.

It is important to recognize, however, that colds can sometimes lead to more serious complications, such as secondary bacterial infection in the middle ear, sinuses, or respiratory system. Medical authorities generally advise rest during the initial days of infection, just to be sure that what you are catching (or that what is catching you) is really just a cold. People who insist on exercising should start slowly. If they begin to feel better after five or ten minutes, then the exercise is probably not harmful.

—Tortora, *Introduction to the Human Body: The Essentials of Anatomy and Physiology,* pp. 407–08

EXERCISE 11–5

Working with another student, select and skim one of the end-of-chapter readings in this text. Then question each other on the main points of the reading by using the comprehension questions as guidelines.

EXERCISE 11–6

Look ahead to the chapter you will study next in one of your textbooks. Skim one or two sections of this chapter and write a brief summary including the main point and most important information. Then check the accuracy of your summary by reading those sections more closely.

When and How to Scan

Have you ever become frustrated when trying to locate a statistic in an almanac or find a reference to a particular research study in a lengthy research review? Have you ever had to read an article completely in order to find a particular fact? These frustrations probably occurred because you were not scanning in the most effective, systematic manner. *Scanning* is a technique for quickly looking through reading material to locate a particular piece of information—a fact, a date, a name, a statistic.

Every time you use a dictionary to find a particular word, you are scanning. When you locate a call number in a card catalogue or find a book on a library shelf, you are scanning. In each case, you are looking for a particular piece of information, and your only purpose in looking through the material is to locate that information. In fact, when you scan you are not at all interested in anything else on the page, and you have no reason to notice or remember any other information.

Many people do not scan as efficiently as possible because they randomly search through the material, hoping to stumble on the information they are seeking. Scanning in this way is time-consuming, is frustrating, and often forces the reader to "give up" and read the entire selection. The key to effective scanning is to approach the material in a systematic manner, as outlined in the following steps.

Know Your Purpose   Fix in your mind what you are looking for. Scanning is effective only if you have a very specific purpose. Before you begin to scan, try to form very specific questions that you need to answer. For example, instead of scanning for information on the topic of abortions in New York state, it would be more effective to develop questions such as:

How many abortions were performed in 1999?

What rules and limitations restrict abortions?

Where are the majority of abortions performed?

The more specific your purposes and questions are, the more effectively you will be able to scan.

Check the Organization   Before you begin to scan, check to see how the article or material is organized.

For graphics (maps, tables, graphs, charts, and diagrams), this step is especially important. The title of the item you are scanning and other labels, keys, and legends are important. They state what the graphics are intended to describe and tell you how they are presented.

For prose selections, assessing the organization is similar to previewing. Your purpose should be to notice the overall structure of the article so that you will be able to predict where in the article you can expect to find the information you are looking for. Headings are especially important, because they clearly show how a selection is divided into subtopics.

Anticipate Clue Words   The next step is to anticipate clues that may help you locate the answer. For example, if you were trying to locate the population of New York City in an article on the populations of cities, you might expect the answer to appear in digits, such as 4,304,710, or in an estimate form using words such as "four million." If you were looking for the name of the researcher in a journal article, you would expect to find the name capitalized. In looking for the definition of a particular term, you might look for italics and you might scan for the word itself or for words or phrases such as "means," "can be defined as," or "refers to." As accurately as possible, then, try to fix the image of your clue words or phrases in your mind before you begin to scan.

Identify Probable Answer Locations   Using what you have learned from checking the organization of the material, try to identify places where you are likely to find the information you are looking for. You might be able to identify a column or section that could contain the needed information, you might be able to eliminate certain sections, or you might be able to predict that the information will probably appear in a certain portion of the article.

Use a Systematic Pattern Once you know what you are looking for and can anticipate the location and form of your answer, you are ready to scan. Scanning should be organized and systematic. Do not randomly skip around, searching for clues. Instead, rhythmically sweep your eyes through the material. The pattern or approach you use will depend on the material. For material printed in narrow six- or seven-word columns (newspaper articles, for example), you might move your eyes straight down the middle, catching the phrases on each half of the line. For wider lines of print, a zigzag or Z pattern might be more effective. Each of these patterns is shown in Figure 11–1. Using this pattern, you move your eyes back and forth, catching several lines in each movement. When you do come to the information you are looking for, it may almost seem as though the clue words "pop out" at you.

Confirm Your Answer Once you think you have located the answer you have been looking for, read the sentence or two that contain the answer to confirm that it is the information you need. Often, you can be misled by headings and key words that seem to indicate that you have found your answer when in fact you have located related information, opposite information, or information for another year, a different country, or a merely similar situation.

Now try out this procedure. Assume that you are writing a term paper on applications of genetic engineering and need to find out how it is regulated in agricultural production. You have located a reference book on

Figure 11–1 Scanning patterns

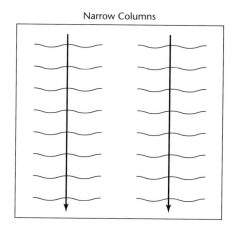
Narrow Columns

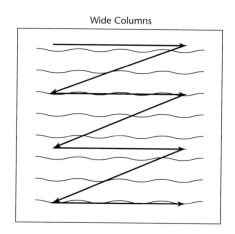
Wide Columns

animal science that contains the following section. Scan to find the answer to one of your research questions: What government agency determines the guidelines for genetically engineered foods coming from plants?

REGULATION OF GENETICALLY ENGINEERED PRODUCTS

Three federal agencies currently regulate genetically engineered products: the Environmental Protection Agency (EPA), the Food and Drug Administration (FDA), and the United States Department of Agriculture (USDA). In addition, most states monitor development and testing of genetically monitored products within their borders.

Animal and Plant Health Inspection Service (APHIS), a division of the United States Department of Agriculture, regulates genetically engineered products under several statutes. Genetically engineered crops are regulated under the Federal Plant Pest Act. This legislation enables APHIS to regulate interstate movement, importation into the United States, and field testing of altered crops.

The Food and Drug Administration has broad authority and primary responsibility for regulating the introduction of all new foods, including genetically engineered foods, under the Federal Food, Drug, and Cosmetic Act (FFDCA). Two different sets of provisions in the FFDCA pertain to genetically engineered foods. The first are the "adulteration" provisions, which give the FDA authority to remove unsafe foods from the market. The other pertinent section of the act requires premarket approval of food additives. In 1992, the FDA released guidelines for genetically engineered foods coming from plant sources. These guidelines can be found in the Federal Register, and vol. 57, pages 22984 and 22986–88. Because the FDA has authority over drug approval, it also has authority over drugs produced through biotechnological means. In this case, the fact that a drug is produced through biotechnology is not the issue. The FDA already had authority over drugs.

The Environmental Protection Agency oversees genetically engineered microbial pesticides and certain crops that are genetically engineered to produce their own pesticides under the Federal Insecticide, Fungicide, and Rodenticide Act (FIFRA). The FFDCA authorized the FDA to set tolerances and establish exemptions for pesticide residues on and in food crops. Nonpesticidal, nonfood microbial products are regulated under the Toxic Substances Control Act (TSCA). The regulation under which the TSCA Biotechnology Program functions is titled "Microbial Products of Biotechnology; Final Regulation Under the Toxic Substances Control Act," which can be found in the Federal Register, vol. 62, No. 70, pages 17909–58. This rule was developed under TSCA because intergeneric microorganisms are considered new chemicals under the act.

Animal vaccines are regulated under the Virus, Serum, and Toxin Act; and engineered poultry and livestock fall under various meat inspection statutes. Transgenic animals other than poultry and livestock are not regulated for environmental risks.

—Damron, *Introduction to Animal Science*, pp. 202–03

Scanning Lists and Tables

In scanning information in list form, the most important step is to become familiar with how the writer has arranged the information. Check the overall organization, and then see whether it is divided in any particular way. For instance, a TV program schedule is organized by day of the week, but it is also arranged by time. In scanning a table of metric equivalents, you would see that it is arranged alphabetically but that it is subdivided into measures of volume, length, and so on. Column titles, headings, and any other clues are important to show the organization of the material.

Many reference books that are arranged alphabetically have guide words at the top of each page to indicate the words or entries that are included on each page. For instance, in the upper-right or upper-left corner of a page of a dictionary, you might find the two words *cinder-circle*. These guide words indicate that the first entry on the page is *cinder* and that the last entry on the page is *circle*. Guide words are valuable shortcuts to help you quickly locate the appropriate page to scan. For lengthy alphabetical material that does not include guide words, you should check the first entry and the last entry on a page to determine whether that page contains the item you are looking for.

In scanning columnar material, often you will be able to scan for a specific word, phrase, name, date, or place name, and it may not be necessary to guess at the form of your answer. For example, in scanning an almanac to find the length of Lake Ontario, you are looking for one very specific statistic. Similarly, you can check *Taber's Cyclopedic Medical Dictionary* just for a description of brittle diabetes.

When scanning material that is arranged alphabetically, focus on the first letter of each line until you reach the letter that begins the word you are looking for. Then focus on the first two letters until you reach the two-letter combination you seek. Successively widen your focus until you are looking for whole words.

EXERCISE 11–7

Scan Figure 11–2 (p. 340) from the Reader's Guide to Periodical Literature *to locate the answers to the following questions.*

1. Under what heading can you locate information on voice communications on the Internet?
2. In what periodical did L. Dormen publish an article on the social uses of the Internet?
3. What is the title of the article by N. Weinberg on TV and the Internet?
4. In what periodical was an article published on blocking out pornography on the Internet?
5. Locate an article about using the Internet to learn about taking cruises.

Figure 11–2 Reader's Guide to Periodical Literature

INTERNET— *cont.*

Real estate use

Using a mouse to hunt for a house. T. Gutner. il *Business Week* p162 Je 24, '96

Religious use

See also

Partenia (World Wide Web site)

Free speech or piracy? Copyright ruling favors Scientologists. C. Reid. *Publishers Weekly* v243 p14 Ap 15 '96

The Word and the Web [comparison of biblical cross-references to hyperlinks] E. Mendelson. il *The New York Times Book Review* v101 p35 Je 2 '96

Scientific use

See also

Science on-line (Periodical)

Science journals go wired. G. Taubes. il *Science* v271 p764–6 F 9 '96

Securities

The next Microsoft. M. K. Evans. i. *Gentlemen's Quarterly* v66 p101+ Mr '96

Security measures

Inoculating against invaders. L. Wiener. il *U.S. News & World Report* v120 p78 Ap 29 '96

Privacy and data collection on the Net. A. Eisenberg. il *Scientific American* v274 p120 Mr '96

Stop, thief! J. C. McCune. il *Success* v43 p54 Mr '96

Surveillance in cyberspace [journalists may be ensnared by Usenet spies] W. Andrews. il *American Journalism Review* v18 p13 Mr '96

Self help use

Can going on-line make you healthier? P. Hise. il *Glamour* v94 p46+ F '96

Hope for nail biters [online support groups for nail biters and hair pullers] W. Block. il *American Health* v15 p41 Ap '96

Sexual aspects

See also

Communications Decency Act

Internet dangers. C. Rubenstein. il *Parents* v71 p145–6+ Mr '96

Policing cyberspace [programs to block out pornography] S. Curtis. il *Maclean's* v109 p56–7 F 19 '96

Port central [Microsystems Software] D. Steinberg. il *Gentlemen's Quarterly* v66 p88+ Ap '96

Sex and the single modem. A. Billen. *World Press Review* v43 p15 Je '96

When kids prowl the Net, parents need to be on guard. R. M. Bennefield. il *U.S. News & World Report* v120 p75 Ap 29 '96

Shopping services

See also

Firefly (World Wide Web site)

On-line shoppers: "just looking, thanks". S. J. Vaughan-Nichols. il *Byte* v21 p34 Mr '96

Shopping for electronics [on the Internet] D. Karagiannis. il *Popular Electronics* v13 p28---30 Mr '96

Social use

E-mail romance: can the Internet help your love life? L. Dormen. il *Glamour* v94 p108 F '96

He typed, she typed. M. Greaves ad J. Valentine. il pors *Essence* v26 p77+ F '96

It's a jungle out there. M. Mannix. il *U.S. News & World Report* v120 p73–5 Ap 29 '96

Sports use

Olympic torch burns online. M. Cahlin. il *PC Novice* v7 p78–9 Ap '96

Taxation

Shaking down the Net. J. Simons. il *U.S. News & World Report* v120 p60 Je 10 '96

Television broadcasting

Destination family room: PC-TV [Destination from Gateway 2000] C. O'Malley. il *Popular Science* v248 p74–5 Ap '96

Getting granny to surf the Net. N. Weinberg. il *Forbes* v157 p119+ My 6 '96

I want my Web TV! il *PC Computing* v9 p297 My '96

Television arrives on the Internet. J. Browning. il *Scientific American* v274 p28 My '96

Traffic

Bandwidth blues. M. Hawn. il *Macworld* v13 p145–7 F '96

Circumventing traffic jams on the Internet. I. Peterson. il *Science News* v149 p181 Mr 23 '96

It's the end of the Net as we know it. W. Gurley. il por *Fortune* v133 p181–2+ Ap 29 '96

Stress, strain and growing pains. J. Simons. il *U.S. News & World Report* v120 p59 My 6 '96

Terminal congestion? D. Kelly. il *World Press Review* v43 p37–8 My '96

Travel use

Adventures on-line . . . D. Ruben. il *Working Woman* v21 p60–4+ Ap '96

California dreamin'. B. Foster. il *Home Office Computing* v14 p46–7 Mr '96

Internet address book. P. J. Bell. il *Gourmet* v56 p100 Ap '96

A little plane talk on the Web. K. T. Beddingfield. il *U.S. News & World Report* v120 p64 Je 3 '96

Surfing for safaris—or cruises, beaches, b&bs . . . E. C. Baig. il *Business Week* p106–7 My 20 '96

Traveling by Net and by phone. *Time* v147 p70 Ap 22 '96

Unauthorized use

Free speech or piracy? Copyright, ruling favors Scientologists. C. Reid. *Publishers Weekly* v243 p14 Ap 15 '96

Voice communications

See Internet telephony

Canada

Plugging into the future [cover story; special section] i. *Maclean's* v109 p28–35 Ja 29 '96

INTERNET AND BLACKS

See also

BET Networks (World Wide Web site)

Getting connected: an African-American guide to surfing the Internet. M. C. Brown. *American Visions* v11 p34–5 Ap/My '96

INTERNET AND THE BLIND

A word is worth a thousand pictures. B. Logue. il *Byte* v21 p236 Ap '96

INTERNET AND WOMEN

An insider's guide to the Internet. J. Schwartz. i. *Working Woman* v21 p49–53 Mr '96

INTERNET AND YOUTH

See also

Communications Decency Act

Internet dangers. C. Rubenstein. il *Parents* v71 p145–6+ Mr '96

Media mongrels [sales pitches to children on the Internet] M. Frankel. il *The New York Times Magazine* p20+ Je 2 '96

When kids prowl the Net, parents need to be on guard. R. M. Bennefield. il *U.S. News & World Report* v120 p75 Ap 29 '96

INTERNET APPLIANCES

The $500 PC: dumber is dumb. S. Manes. il *PC World* v14 p39 F '96

Cadillac or Model T? A. J. Kessler. por *Forbes* v157 p286 My 20 '96

First Web Pcs arrive. D. L. Andrews. il *Byte* v21 p24–5 Ap '96

Inside the Web PC [cover story] T. R. Halfhill. il *Byte* v21 p44–8+ Mr '96

Internet appliances. il *PC Computing* v9 p291 Mr '96

The next home computer. G. Smith. il *Popular Science* v248 p32 Ap '96

Rethinking the PC [L. Ellison's network computer] R. Laver. il *Maclean's* v109 p48 Mr 18 '96

The spinal column of civilization. J. Holtzman. *Electronics Now* v67 p79–81 Ap '96

Total recall. J. C. Dvorak. il *PC Computing* v9 p47 Ap '96

Will Oracle's 'fantasy' come to pass? [network computers] R. D. Hof. il. *Business Week* p38 My 27 '96

INTERNET EXPLORER (COMPUTER PROGRAM) *See* Microsoft Internet Explorer (Computer program)

INTERNET MANIA (CD-ROM)

Cut your surf time on the Net. R. Schwerin. il *PC Computing* v9 p106 Mr '96

INTERNET PCS *See* Internet appliances

INTERNET PHONE (COMPUTER PROGRAM)

Free phone calls on the Net. R. C. Kennedy. il *PC Computing* v9 p66 My '96

Hey baby, call me at my IP address. P. Wayner. il *Byte* v21 p142–4 Ap '96

INTERNET PROTOCOLS

File transfer for business. M. L. Corbett. il *Black Enterprise* v26 p46+ My '96

INTERNET SEARCH ENGINES

See also

Alta Vista (Internet search engine)

Infoseek (Internet search engine)

Yahoo (Internet search engine)

Bye, Netscape. P. Somerson. il *PC Computing* v9 p45 Ap '96

Find it on the Net [cover story] R. Scoville. il *PC World* v14 p124–30 Ja '96

Source: H. W. Wilson Company, *Reader's Guide to Periodical Literature,* August 1996, Vol. 96, No. 6, p. 358

EXERCISE 11–8	*Scan Figure 11–3 (p. 342) from* Book Review Digest *to locate the answers to the following questions.*

1. Who is the author of a book of biographies of various artists?
2. Is Krupinski's book fiction or nonfiction?
3. What does Janice Voltzow think of Krupinski's writing in "Bluewater Journal; the Voyage of the Sea Tiger"?
4. What is the subject of the book written by Virginia L. Kroll?
5. Which book concerns itself with foreign economic relations?

Scanning Prose Materials

Prose materials are more difficult to scan than columnar material. Their organization is less apparent, and the information is not so concisely or obviously stated. And unless the headings are numerous and concise, you may have to scan large amounts of material with fewer locational clues. To scan prose materials, you must rely heavily on identifying clue words and predicting the form of your answer.

It is useful to think of scanning prose materials as a floating process in which your eyes drift quickly through a passage searching for clue words and phrases. Your eyes should move across sentences and entire paragraphs, noticing only clue words that indicate you may be close to locating the answer. As you become skilled at scanning prose material, your clue words will "pop out" at you as though they were in boldface print.

EXERCISE 11–9	*Scan the article titled "Giving Viruses a Cold Reception" on pp. 332–335 and answer the following questions.*

1. How many cold-related viruses are humans susceptible to?

   _____

2. What is the difference between a "productive" and a "nonproductive" cough?

   _____

3. Why are small children most susceptible to colds?

   _____

4. What effects might vitamin C have on cold viruses?

   _____

5. How does breathing steam relieve cold symptoms?

   _____

Figure 11–3 Book Review Digest

KROLL, VIRGINIA L.—*Continued*
REVIEW: *SLJ* v41 p102 Je '95. Barbara Osborne Williams (104w)

"A unique offering. Kroll creatively captures the visual essence and diversity of the African continent and the poetic gaiety of Mother Goose. . . . Full-color illustrations depict topography, urban centers, forest, jungle, desert, plain, and marketplace. Colors are rich and vibrant, reflecting the warmth of the African continent. A welcome, interesting addition."

REVIEW: *Small Press* v13 p78 Summ '95. Karima A. Haynes (150w)

"Virginia Kroll brings an African sensibility to the time-honored [Mother Goose] rhymes by setting them against a backdrop of modern African culture. 'Hickory, Dickory Dock' becomes 'Chicory Pickory Pock.' Likewise, 'The Old Woman Who Lived in the Shoe' is now 'The Old Woman Who Lived by the Nile.' Artist Katherine Roundtree brings the continent to life in a resplendent rainbow of illustrations that showcase diversity. Each page is bordered in beautiful patterns with the country of origin from which the rhymes are derived. The book also includes a map of Africa to help children identify the location of each country."

KRUEGER, ANNE O. American trade policy; a tragedy in the making. 141p $29.95; pa $12.95 1995 AEI Press
   382 1. United States—Commercial policy 2. United States—Foreign economic relations
   ISBN 0-8447-3888-3; 0-8447-3889-1 (pa)   LC 95-9946

SUMMARY: "Krueger analyzes the apparent shift in US trade policy from leadership of the General Agreement on Tariffs and Trade (GATT) to administered protection where the US negotiates trade policies on a country-by-country, bilateral basis." (Choice) Bibliography. Index.

REVIEW: *Choice* v33 p662 D '95. R.L. Lucier (230w)

"The shift toward bilateralism and administered protection puts the US government in a 'good cop, bad cop' game where the administration convinces US trading partners that a bilateral resolution of a trading conflict will be preferable to the protectionist legislation which the US Congress would impose. Examples [Krueger] offers include the 'voluntary' export restraints the US negotiated in auto and steel trade. Following a discussion of bilateral trade negotiations—particularly between the US and Japan—she turns to the question of regional trading blocs. . . . In the Uruguay Round of GATT and the newly developed World Trade Organization (WTO). The monograph is well documented and displays a familiarity with recent research on world trade policies and disputes. Graduate; faculty; professional."

REVIEW: *Libr J* v120 p94 Jl '95. Lisa K. Miller (150w)

"This work is an examination of our country's trade policy and its repercussions. Over the past several years, we have been moving away from multilateralism toward bilateralism, a trend Krueger sees as dangerous. She encourages our participation in and support of the newly formed World Trade Organization, which promotes an open multilateral trading system. In fact, the book seems to be a treatise to promulgate her opinions, based on study, about the direction of world trade. She discusses the impact of NAFTA and GATT on our trade policy and devotes considerable space to the various regional trade associations, such as EFTA, ASEAN, EC, and EACM. Extensive footnotes supplement the text. Recommended for all international business collections."

KRULL, KATHLEEN, 1952—. Lives of the artists; masterpieces, messes (and what the neighbors thought); written by Kathleen Krull; illustrated by Kathryn Hewitt. 96p col il $19 1995 Harcourt Brace & Col.
   709.2 1. Artists—Biography—Juvenile literature
   ISBN 0-15-200103-4 LC 94-35357

SUMMARY: This book presents biographies for such artists as "Leonardo, Bruegel, Cassatt, Van Gogh, Picasso, O'Keeffe, Dali, Noguchi, Rivera, Kahlo, and Warhol." (Booklist) Index. "Grade six and up." (SLJ)

REVIEW: *Booklist* v92 p468 N 1 '95. Carolyn Phelan (140w)

"The subject seems well suited to Kroll's format: informative short biographies that focus on the subjects' personal lives and eccentricities rather than chronologies of their masterpieces. A few notes on major artworks follow each biography. . . . Each chapter begins with one of Hewitt's distinctive portrait paintings, handsome caricatures of the artists and a few significant or distinctive objects indicating their interests and individual traits. A lively, entertaining presentation. . . . Grades four to six."

REVIEW: *SLJ* v41 p164 O '95. Kenneth Marantz (190w)

"Tidbits flood the brief biographies: Leonardo's and Michelangelo's homosexuality, Van Gogh's 'ear episode,' Bruegel's fondness for practical jokes, Cassatt's support of women's suffrage, etc. These morsels are integrated into chapters with an easy-flowing sequence of short paragraphs, and supplemented with an 'Artworks' section that adds a few pithy comments about several specific pieces, such as O'Keeffe's bone paintings. . . . Hewitt supplies a full-page watercolor and colored-pencil portrait and vignette for each artist. These are friendly representations that also include personal objects like Matisse's fiddle, Chagall's village, Duchamp's snow shovel, etc. They add pleasant visual attractions to the lighthearted approach in this inviting introduction to a few of the Big Names in our artworld. A page of artistic terms is also included."

KRUPINSKI, LORETTA, 1940—. Bluewater journal; the voyage of the Sea Tiger. col il $14.95/Can$19.95; lib bdg $14.89 1995 HarperCollins Pubs.
   ISBN 0-06-023436-9; 0-06-023437-7 (lib bdg)   LC 94-13241

SUMMARY: Based on "logbooks, journals and letters found at the Mystic Seaport Museum in Connecticut, this fictional account in diary form relates the story of young Benjamin Slocum's 1860 voyage with his family from Boston to the Sandwich Islands (present-day Hawaii). . . . The Sea Tiger, captained by Benjamin's father, races to reach Honolulu before its rival clipper ship Morning Star. . . . Grades two to five." (SLJ)

REVIEW: *Bull Cent Child Books* v48 p351 Je '95. Elizabeth Bush (200w)

"As Benjamin describes the . . . fictional 1860 voyage, readers form a vivid picture of four months at sea--the genteel but cramped nest of a stateroom, livestock for fresh milk, eggs, and meat, polite society that entertains them in Rio Janeiro and Honolulu, the treacherous waters off Cape Horn, and a race for port against the rival Morning Star. The text will entice independent readers, and the single-page journal entries will work well as a classroom read aloud; although the figures in Krupinski's ouache paintings are as still as a mainmast, . . . the audience will be fascinated by the precision of nautical details, and viewers in the back of the room will appreciate the illustrations' size and clarity. Budding navigators can use Krupinski's map to trace Sea Tiger's route."

REVIEW: *Sci Books Films* v31 p215 O '95. Janice Voltzow (120w)

"Although the [book's] premise is good, the writing is sometimes awkward and not very convincing. The text gives some insights as to what life on board the ship might have been like. Whales, seasickness, domestic animals, storms, and a race with another clipper ship add a small touch of drama, but not enough to make the story very interesting. It is never clear why the boy, his mother, and his sister are accompanying their father, the sea captain, or why, once they finally arrive in Honolulu, they leave again for Hong Kong."

REVIEW: *SLJ* v41 p65 Jl '95. Marie Orlando (180w)

"Text on lefthand pages is adorned with small watercolor pictures, while full-page or page-and-a-third paintings on the right, in gouache and colored pencil, illustrate the events of the trip which include a powerful lightning storm, a stop in Brazil, and a dramatic whale sighting. . . . An author's note, afterword, and glossary augment the information incorporated into the text and pictures. . . . Krupinski has made a fine contribution to that group of picture books that provide an accurate sense of time and place for older children."

Source: H. W. Wilson Company, *Book Review Digest,* October 1996, Vol. 92, No. 7, p. 254

DOCUMENTATION AND NOTE TAKING

As you read reference sources for a research paper, documentation and note taking are important. You must record carefully the sources you use and take clear and concise notes to use when writing your paper.

Documentation Format and Systems

Documentation—recording the sources you use—is necessary for preparing the footnotes and bibliography of any paper you write. As you use sources, you will need to keep a record of the complete title, author, publisher, place, date, and pages referred to. Before you begin, select the format you will use for the paper's bibliography, and use this format to record sources as you use them. Several documentation styles are available; often a particular style is preferred in a specific academic discipline. The two most common styles are those of the MLA and the APA, which are explained in the following manuals. Instructors usually require one style or the other.

> Gibaldi, Joseph. *MLA Handbook for Writers of Research Papers,* 5th ed. New York: MLA, 1999.

> American Psychological Association. *Publication Manual of the American Psychological Association,* 4th ed. Washington, DC: APA, 1994.

Documentation rules are complex and may seem picky and annoying, especially if you have to learn different styles for different courses, but there is good reason for them. If your source is fully documented, your reader can follow up, explore further, or research a topic in more depth. Documentation also may be useful to you. As you complete your paper, for example, you may need to return to a source to get an important date you missed or to check a name spelled two different ways in your notes.

Many researchers list their sources on 3 x 5 inch index cards, which make it possible to alphabetize rapidly when preparing the bibliography. For each source, record the library call number in addition to bibliographic information. (This will save you time should you need to locate the source again.) A sample source card is shown in Figure 11–4 (p. 344).

Note-Taking Cards

For taking notes, 5 x 8 inch or 4 x 6 inch index cards are best. Use a separate card for each subtopic or aspect of your topic. In the upper-left corner, record the author's last name and the pages you used. In the upper-right corner, record the subtopic. Be sure to write only on one side of the card. A sample note-taking card is also shown in Figure 11–4. Here are a few suggestions for taking good research notes.

Figure 11–4   Sample Source and Note-Taking Cards

Source Card

Critchlow, Arthur J.

Introduction to Robotics

New York : Macmillan, 1995,

pp. 39-51

- TJ
  211
- C69
  1995

Note Card

Critchlow, P. 42   Payback on
                                          investment

formula for   =   capital cost of system
payback   yearly   _   operations
                    savings   cost

$$\left(P = \frac{c}{s-o} \right)$$

Capital includes robot, auxiliary, safety
equipment, installation and training
Operations include overhead and maintenance,
wages and salaries of operators

Record the information in your own words instead of copying the author's words. By recording the author's wording, you run the risk of using it in your paper, perhaps without realizing that you have done so. Whenever you use an author's words or ideas instead of your own, you are required to use quotation marks and/or give proper credit by indicating the author and source from which the material was taken. Failure to give credit is known as **plagiarism.** Plagiarism is a form of theft and therefore a serious error; many institutions penalize students who either knowingly or unknowingly plagiarize.

Try to summarize and condense information. You will find that it is impossible to record all the information that appears in your sources. If you have already made a note once, do not spend time writing it again. (You might, however, want to note the fact that there is common agreement in a number of sources about the information.) Occasionally, you may need to check back through your notes to see what you already have recorded.

Record useful quotes. If you find a statement that strongly supports your thesis, you may want to include it as a quotation in your paper. Copy it down exactly and place it in quotation marks in your notes, along with its page reference. Photocopy important articles so you can refer to them while you work.

READING COLLATERAL ASSIGNMENTS

In addition to the course textbook, many professors assign collateral readings. These assignments are drawn from a variety of sources: other textbooks, paperbacks, newspapers, periodicals, scholarly journals, and reference books. Often, your professor will place the required book or periodical on reserve in the library. This means the book is held at the reserve desk, where its use is restricted to a specified period of time. Collateral assignments may present

- new topics not covered in your text
- updated information
- alternative points of view
- applications or related issues
- realistic examples, case studies, or personal experiences

Reading collateral assignments requires different skills and strategies than reading textbooks. Unless the assignment is from another textbook, you may find that the material is not as well or as tightly organized as it would be in a textbook. It may also be less concise and factual.

Analyzing the Assignment

First, determine the purpose of the assignment: How is it related to the course content? Listen carefully as your professor announces the assignment; he or she often provides important clues. Next, determine what type and level of recall are necessary. If the purpose of an assignment is to present new and important topics not covered in your text, then a high level of recall is required. If, on the other hand, an assignment's purpose is to expose you to alternative points of view on a controversial issue, then key ideas are needed but highly factual recall is not.

Choosing Reading and Study Strategies

Depending on the purpose of the assignment and the necessary level and type of recall, your reading choices range from a careful, thorough reading to skimming to obtain an overview of the key ideas presented. Before you begin, you need to select a strategy to enable you to retain and recall the information. Table 11–3 lists examples of supplementary assignments and their purposes and suggests possible reading and retention strategies for each. The table shows how strategies vary widely to suit the material and the purpose for which it was assigned.

TABLE 11-3   STRATEGIES FOR COLLATERAL READINGS

ASSIGNMENT	PURPOSE	READING STRATEGIES	RETENTION STRATEGIES
Historical novel for American history course.	To acquaint you with living conditions of the period being studied.	Read rapidly, noting trends, patterns, characteristics; skip highly detailed descriptive portions.	Write a brief synopsis of the basic plot; make notes (including some examples) of lifestyles, living conditions (social, religious, political, as well as economic).
Essay on exchange in Moroccan bazaars (street markets) for economics course.	To describe system of barter.	Read for main points, noting process, procedures, and principles.	Underline key points
Article titled "What Teens Know about Birth Control" assigned in a maternal care nursing course.	To reveal attitudes toward, and lack of information about, birth control.	Read to locate topics of information, misinformation, and lack of information; skip details and examples.	Prepare a three-column list: information, misinformation, and lack of information.

Working on Nonprint Collateral Assignments

Occasionally, a professor may ask you to view videotapes, films, lectures, or television documentaries. Approach these assignments as you would approach a reading assignment. It is particularly important to determine your purpose and to take adequate notes at the time because it is usually difficult, or impossible, to review the material later. Making notes on nonprint materials is, in some ways, similar to taking notes on class lectures. In the case of films, dramatic recreations, or performances, your notes should reflect your impressions as well as a brief review of the content.

EXERCISE 11–10	*Summarize how you would approach each of the following collateral assignments. What would be your purpose? What reading and study strategies would you use?*

1. Reading a *Time* magazine article about a recent incident of terrorism for a discussion in your political science class.
2. Reading two articles that present opposing opinions and evidence about the rate of the spread of AIDS throughout the United States.
3. Reading a recent journal article on asbestos control to obtain current information for a term paper on the topic.
4. Reading a case study of an autistic child for a child psychology course.
5. Reading IBM's end-of-the-year statement for stockholders for a business class studying public relations strategies.

EVALUATING SOURCES

Through your research and supplementary reading, you will encounter a variety of sources ranging from newspaper editorials to professional journal research reports. Not all sources are equal in accuracy, scholarship, or completeness. In fact, some sources may be inaccurate, and some may be purposely misleading. Other sources that were once respected are now outdated and have been discredited by more recent research. Part of your task as a researcher is to evaluate available sources and select those that seem the most reliable and appropriate. Use the following suggestions in evaluating sources.

1. *Assess the authority of the author.* In standard reference books such as encyclopedias and biographical dictionaries, you can assume the publisher has chosen competent authors. However, when using individual source materials, it is important to find out whether the author is qualified to write on the subject. Does he or she have a degree or experience in the field? What is the author's present position or university

affiliation? This information may appear in the preface or on the title page of a book. In journal articles, a brief paragraph at the end of the article or on a separate page in the journal may summarize the author's credentials. If the author's credentials are not provided, then it may be necessary to consult reference sources to establish or verify the author's qualifications. Sources such as *Who's Who, Directory of American Scholars* and numerous biographical dictionaries are available in the library reference section. By appraising the sources the author cites (footnotes and bibliography), you also can judge the competence of the author.

2. *Check the copyright date.* The date the source was published or revised is indicated on the back of the title page. Especially in rapidly changing fields such as computer science, the timeliness of your sources is important. Using outdated sources can make a research paper incomplete or incorrect. Consult at least several current sources, if possible, to discover recent findings and new interpretations. Suppose that in doing research on regulations for day care centers, you have located several articles. One was written in 1993, another in 1996, another in 2000. The 1993 and 1997 articles may be outdated because regulations change frequently.

3. *Evaluate the fulfillment of the work's purpose.* Does the work accomplish what it promises? Purposes are often stated or implied in the title, subtitle, preface, and introduction. Does the author recognize appropriate limitations, or does he or she claim the source is a complete study of a topic?

4. *Assess the intended audience.* For whom is the work intended? Some sources are written for children, others for young adults, and others for a general-interest audience. The work should suit the audience in format, style, complexity of ideas, and amount of detail. Some sources may be too technical and detailed for your purposes. For example, if a book on control of water pollution control is written for engineers, then it may be too complicated.

5. *Verify one source against another.* If you find information that seems questionable, unbelievable, or disputable, verify it by locating the same information in several other reputable sources. Ask your reference librarian for assistance, if necessary. If you do verify the information in other sources, then you can be reasonably confident that the information is acceptable. You cannot, however, assume that it is correct—only that it is one standard or acceptable approach or interpretation. For instance, in researching global warming, you might encounter several theories of its cause and many projections of its long-range effects.

Eventually, you'll recognize the more standard theories and the more widely accepted projections.

6. *Look for a consensus of opinion.* As you read differing approaches to or interpretations of a topic, sometimes it is difficult to decide what source(s) to accept. When you encounter differing opinions or approaches, the first thing to do is locate additional sources; in other words, do more reading. Eventually, you will discover the consensus.

7. *Evaluate statistics carefully.* Many students regard statistical figures as correct and indisputable and assume that no interpretation or evaluation of statistics is required. Actually, statistics must be carefully evaluated, along with the conclusions the authors draw from them. Suppose you read a statement that "at present, a recent survey indicated that 52 percent of single-parent household heads lack a high school diploma, compared to 22 percent in 1965." To evaluate this statistic, you might ask questions such as, "What year is the 'present'? How were these data obtained? How many single-parent households were surveyed? How were they surveyed? What was the survey response rate? How is a high school diploma defined? Does it include high school equivalency diplomas? How were the 1965 data obtained?" You can see that the answers to these questions can influence how the statistics should be interpreted. In general, ask questions about

sample size (the size of the group studied)

sample composition (who was included)

method of obtaining the data

definition of terms

Approach statistics as critically, then, as you would any other type of information.

8. *Consider whether the article is fact or opinion.* Question the author's purpose, the use of generalizations, any basic assumptions, and the type of evidence presented. For a review of these criteria, refer to the sections in Chapter 4 entitled "Assess the Author's Ideas."

**EXERCISE
11–11**

What questions would you ask when evaluating each of the following sources?

1. An article in *Newsweek* reporting a dramatic increase in domestic violence in the United States.

2. An article written by the president of Chrysler Corporation describing effective and ineffective business management strategies.

_____

3. An essay in a right-to-life pamphlet reporting a high incidence of injury and maternal death resulting from abortion. Other articles, using other sources, report a much lower incidence.

_____

4. An article, published in an advertising trade journal, titled "Teenage Drinking: Does Advertising Make a Difference?"

_____

5. An article in *TV Guide* titled "Should TV Stop Projecting Election Winners?"

_____

 STUDY Tips   Controlling Test Anxiety

Do you get nervous and anxious just before an exam begins? If so, your response is normal; most students feel some level of anxiety before an exam. However, some students become highly nervous and emotional and lose their concentration. Their minds seem to go blank, and they are unable to recall material they have learned. The following suggestions are intended to help you ease test anxiety.

1. *Be sure test anxiety is not an excuse.* Many students say they have test anxiety when actually they have not studied and reviewed carefully or thoroughly.

2. *Become familiar with the building and room in which the test is given.* Visit the room when it is empty and take a seat. Visualize yourself taking a test there.

3. *Develop practice or review tests.* Treat them as real tests, and do them in situations as similar as possible to real test conditions.

4. *Practice working with time limits.* Set an alarm clock and work only until it rings.

5. *Take as many tests as possible,* even though you dislike them. Always take advantage of practice tests and makeup exams. Buy a review book for the course you are taking or a workbook that accompanies your text. Treat each section as an exam, and have someone else correct your work.

6. *Think positively.* Send yourself positive messages. Say to yourself, "I have studied hard and I deserve to pass," "I know that I know the material," or "I know I can do it!" Remember, being well-prepared is one of the best ways to reduce test anxiety.

7. *Answer easy questions first.* To give yourself an initial boost of confidence, begin with a section of the test that seems easy. This will help you to work calmly and you will prove to yourself that you can handle the test.

SUMMARY

This chapter discusses reading strategies for nontextbook materials and presents a systematic approach for reading research sources. The steps include

- defining and focusing your topic
- devising a search strategy
- previewing sources
- defining your purpose for reading

Two alternative reading strategies will help you get the most from research materials.

- Skimming is a rapid reading technique that enables you quickly to obtain main ideas only.
- Scanning is a process of searching for a specific piece of information.

As you read reference sources, a note card system can help you with documentation and note taking. Collateral reading assignments require that you analyze the assignment and select the appropriate reading and study strategies. Finally, evaluating sources is an important step in reading research.

ENGLISH

INTEGRATING

PAIRED **READINGS**

IDEAS

PREREADING QUESTIONS

1. What does documenting sources mean?
2. On what three topics does this reading focus?

DOCUMENTING SOURCES

John M. Lannon

1   Documenting research means acknowledging one's debt to each information source. Proper documentation satisfies professional requirements for ethics, efficiency, and authority.

Why You Should Document

2   Documentation is a matter of ethics in that the originator of borrowed materials deserves full credit and recognition. Moreover, all published material is protected by copyright law. Failure to credit a source could make you liable to legal action, even if your omission was unintentional.

3   Documentation is also a matter of *efficiency*. It provides a network for organizing and locating the world's printed knowledge. If you cite a particular source correctly, your reference will enable interested readers to locate that source themselves.

4   Finally, documentation is a matter of *authority*. In making any claim (say, "A Mercedes-Benz is more reliable than a Ford Taurus"), you invite challenge: "Says who?" Data on road tests, frequency of repairs, resale value, workmanship, and owner comments can help validate your claim by showing its basis in *fact*. A claim's credibility increases in relation to the expert references supporting it. For a controversial topic, you may need to cite several authorities who hold various views, as in this next example, instead of forcing a simplistic conclusion on your material.

> Opinion is mixed as to whether a marketable quantity of oil rests under Georges Bank. Cape Cod geologist John Blocke feels that extensive reserves are improbable ("Geologist Dampens Hopes" 3). Oil geologist Donald Marshall is uncertain about the existence of any oil in quantity under Georges Bank ("Offshore Oil Drilling" 2). But the U.S. Interior Department reports that the Atlantic continental shelf may contain 5.5 billion barrels of oil (Kemprecos 8).

Readers of your research report expect the *complete* picture.

What You Should Document

5   Document any insight, assertion, fact, finding, interpretation, judgment or other "appropriated material that readers might otherwise mistake for your own" (Gibaldi and Achtert 155). Specifically, you must document

- any source from which you use exact wording, or
- any source from which you adapt material in your own words, or
- any visual illustration: charts, graphs, drawings, or the like.

6   You don't need to document anything considered *common knowledge:* material that appears repeatedly in general sources. In medicine, for instance, it is common knowledge that foods high in fat cause some types of cancer. Thus, in a research report on fatty diets and cancer, you probably would not need to document that well-known fact. But you would document information about how the fat/cancer connection was discovered, subsequent studies (say, of the role of saturated versus unsaturated fats), and any information for which some other person could claim specific credit. If the borrowed material can be found in only one specific source, and not in multiple sources, document it. When in doubt, document the source.

How You Should Document

7   Borrowed material has to be cited twice: at the exact place you use that material, and at the end of your document. Documentation practices vary widely, but all systems work almost identically: a brief reference in the text names the source and refers readers to the complete citation, which enables the source to be retrieved.

8   Many disciplines, institutions, and organizations publish their own documentation manuals. Here are a few:

> *Style Guide for Chemists*
>
> *Geographical Research and Writing*
>
> *Style Manual for Engineering Authors and Editors*
>
> *IBM Style Manual*
>
> *NASA Publications Manual*

When no specific format is stipulated, consult one of the following three general manuals: *The MLA Handbook for Writers and Research Papers,* the *Publication Manual of the American Psychological Association,* or the *Chicago Manual of Style.* (The formats in any of these three manuals can be adapted to most research writing.)

—Lannon, *Technical Writing,* pp. 188–89

VOCABULARY REVIEW

1. For each of the words listed below, use context, prefixes, roots, and suffixes, and/or a dictionary to write a brief definition or synonym of the word as it is used in the reading.

    a. ethics (para. 2) _____

    b. originator (para. 2) _____

    c. unintentional (para. 2) _____

    d. network (para. 3)_____

    e. cite (para. 3) _____

    f. claim (para. 4) _____

    g. credibility (para. 4) _____

    h. stipulated (para. 8) _____

2. Underline new specialized terms introduced in the reading.

COMPREHENSION QUESTIONS

1. Give three reasons for documenting sources.
2. What types of material should be documented?
3. In what two places should borrowed materials be cited in a paper?

THINKING CRITICALLY

1. Suppose you are doing a research paper on in-line skating. Give three examples of types of information that should be documented.
2. Explain why documentation is a matter of ethics.
3. In what types of research would authority be particularly important?
4. Describe the author's purpose for writing.
5. If you had to explain to a child in fifth grade why she should not copy information from an encyclopedia without acknowledging that she had done so, what would you say?

LEARNING/STUDY STRATEGIES

1. Write a brief outline of this reading.
2. Draw a map of this reading.

SPEECH COMMUNICATION

PREREADING QUESTIONS

1. What is plagiarism?
2. How can it be avoided?

USING SOURCE MATERIAL ETHICALLY

Bruce E. Gronbeck et al.

1   Now that we've discussed locating and generating material for your speeches, we come to a major ethical issue—plagiarism. **Plagiarism** has been defined as "the unacknowledged inclusion of someone else's words, ideas, or data as one's own." (Louisiana State University, "Academic Honesty and Dishonesty," adapted from *LSU's Code of Student Conduct,* 1981.) One of the saddest things an instructor has to do is cite a student for plagiarism. In speech classes, students occasionally quote material from *Reader's Digest, Newsweek, Time, Senior Scholastic,* or other easy-to-obtain sources, not realizing how many speech teachers habitually scan the library periodicals section. Even if the teacher has not read the article, it soon becomes apparent that something is wrong—the wording differs from the way the person usually talks, the speech does not have a well-formulated introduction or conclusion, and the organizational pattern is not one normally used by speakers. Often, too, the person who plagiarizes an article reads it aloud badly, another sign that something is wrong.

2   Plagiarism is not, however, simply undocumented verbatim quotation. It also includes (a) undocumented paraphrases of others' ideas and (b) undocumented use of others' main ideas. For example, if you paraphrase a movie review from *Newsweek* without acknowledging that staff critic David Ansen had those insights, or if you use the motivated sequence as a model for analyzing speeches without giving credit to Alan Monroe for developing it, you are guilty of plagiarism.

3   Suppose you ran across the following excerpt from Kenneth Clark's *Civilisation: A Personal View:*

> It was the age of great country houses. In 1722 the most splendid of all had just been completed for Marlborough, the general who had been victorious over Voltaire's country: not the sort of idea that would have worried Voltaire in the least, as he thought of all war as a ridiculous waste of human life and effort. When Voltaire saw Blenheim Palace he said, "What a great heap of stone, without charm or taste," and I can see what he means. To anyone brought up on Mansart and

Perrault, Blenheim must have seemed painfully lacking in order and propriety . . . Perhaps this is because the architect, Sir John Vanbrugh, although a man of genius, was really an amateur. Moreover, he was a natural romantic, a castle-builder who didn't care a fig for good taste and decorum.

Imagine that you decided to use the excerpt in a speech. The following examples illustrate what would constitute plagiarism and suggest ways that you could avoid it:

1. *Verbatim quotation of a passage* (read it aloud word for word). To avoid plagiarism: say, "Kenneth Clark, in his 1969 book *Civilisation: A Personal View,* said the following about the architecture of great country estates in eighteenth-century England: [then quote the paragraph]."

2. *Undocumented use of the main ideas:* "In eighteenth-century England there was a great flurry of building. Country estates were built essentially by amateurs, such as Sir John Vanbrugh, who built the splendid Blenheim Palace for General Marlborough. Voltaire didn't like war and he didn't like Blenheim, which he called a great heap of stone without charm or taste. He preferred the order and variety of houses designed by French architects Mansart and Perrault." To avoid plagiarism: say, "In his book *Civilisation: A Personal View,* Kenneth Clark makes the point that eighteenth-century English country houses were built essentially by amateurs. He uses as an example Sir John Vanbrugh, who designed Blenheim Palace for the Duke of Marlborough. Clark notes that, when Voltaire saw the house, he said, 'What a great heap of stone, without charm or taste.' Clark can understand that reaction from a Frenchman who was raised on the neoclassical designs of Mansart and Perrault. Clark explains English style arose from what he calls 'natural romanticism.'"

3. *Undocumented paraphrasing:* "The eighteenth century was the age of wonderful country houses. In 1722 the most beautiful one in England was built for Marlborough, the general who had won over France. When Voltaire saw the Marlborough house called Blenheim Palace, he said it was a great heap of stones." To avoid plagiarism: use the same kind of language noted under Example 2, giving Clark credit for his impressions.

4. Plagiarism is easy to avoid if you take reasonable care. Moreover, by citing such authorities as Clark, who are well educated and experienced, you add their credibility to yours. Avoid plagiarism to keep from being expelled from the class or even your school, and avoid it for positive reasons as well: improve your ethos by associating your thinking with that of experts.

—Gronbeck et al., *Principles of Speech Communication,* pp. 27–29

VOCABULARY REVIEW

1. For each of the words listed below, use context, prefixes; roots, and suffixes; and/or a dictionary to write a brief definition or synonym of the word as it is used in the reading.

    a. verbatim (para. 2, 3) _____

    b. paraphrase (ing) (para. 2, 3) _____

    c. constitute (para. 3) _____

    d. expelled (para. 4) _____

    e. ethos (para. 4) _____

2. Underline new specialized terms introduced in the reading.

COMPREHENSION QUESTIONS

1. Define plagiarism.
2. Why does plagiarism carry a severe penalty?
3. Summarize three ways to avoid plagiarism.

THINKING CRITICALLY

1. What are possible penalties for plagiarism? Do you think they are fair, too severe, or not severe enough?
2. The reading suggests how to avoid plagiarism when making speeches. How useful are these suggestions for avoiding plagiarism when writing a paper?
3. Can plagiarism be unintentional? If so, should the penalties be the same?
4. What implications does this reading have for your research note-taking techniques?
5. Suppose you needed further information about plagiarism. What sources would you consult, and how would you locate them?

LEARNING/STUDY STRATEGIES

1. Write a paraphrase of paragraph 2 of this reading.
2. Identify the overall thought pattern(s) used in this reading.
3. Draw a conceptual map (p. 302) or write a summary (p. 307) of one of these readings.

THINKING ABOUT THE PAIRED READINGS

INTEGRATING IDEAS

1. In what ways are the two readings similar?
2. In what ways are they different?
3. In what ways do the authors' purposes differ?

GENERATING NEW IDEAS

Using both readings as sources, write a tip sheet for beginning college students who are about to begin their first research paper. Include advice and information that would be helpful to them.

PART 3

STRATEGIES FOR SPECIFIC DISCIPLINES

12 | **READING IN THE SOCIAL SCIENCES**

LEARNING OBJECTIVES

- **To learn why social sciences are "sciences"**
- **To discover specialized reading techniques for the social sciences**
- **To learn what common thought patterns to anticipate**
- **To adapt your study techniques for social science courses**

The social sciences are concerned with the study of people, their development, and how they function together and interact. These disciplines deal with the political, economic, social, cultural, and behavioral aspects of human beings. The social sciences include psychology, anthropology, sociology, political science, and economics. History, which is sometimes considered one of the humanities, and geography, which is sometimes treated as a physical science, are included among the social sciences for the purposes of this book. During your college career, you probably will take at least two or three social science courses; many students take more.

As you select these courses, it is helpful to understand the basic focus and approach of each discipline. Each one of the social sciences focuses on selected aspects of human behavior, social relationships, or social systems and the laws or principles that govern them. Table 12–1 provides an overview of each discipline and shows how they differ by giving examples of the questions each discipline would ask about a particular topic—in this case, an accident on an oil tanker in the Gulf of Mexico resulting in a major oil spill.

WHY STUDY THE SOCIAL SCIENCES?

On many campuses, courses in the social sciences are among the most popular. Because social science courses focus on how people develop, behave, and interact, students find they learn a great deal about themselves and

TABLE 12–1	THE SOCIAL SCIENCE DISCIPLINES TOPIC: OIL SPILL	
DISCIPLINE	**OVERVIEW**	**QUESTIONS**
Anthropology	Examines concepts, customs, and rules in different societies and cultures.	Does each country involved view the spill the same way? What rules and customs must be followed?
Economics	Studies how goods, services, and wealth are produced, consumed, and distributed within societies.	How will environmental damage affect the economy of each country?
Geography	Focuses on the surface of the earth, its divisions, climate, inhabitants, and resources.	What environmental damage has occurred? How will the spill affect the ecology of each area involved?
History	Provides a chronological record of past events; tells story of people's usable past.	What other oil spills have occurred? How is this spill similar to and different from others?
Political science	Studies political power, governments, processes.	How will each country be compensated for environmental damage? Who will decide the amount of compensation?
Psychology	Focuses on human mental processes and behavior.	How will the pilot and crew of the tanker cope with the accident and its effects?
Sociology	Deals with human relationships, social systems, and societies.	What leadership patterns emerged on the tanker after the accident? How were the cleanup efforts organized? What groups were most active?

those around them. They also learn answers to many questions they have always wondered about: Why do some people commit violent crimes? Why and how do people fall in love? What can we learn from events of the past? Why is religion important in our lives, and how did it evolve? What factors determine how many jobs are available in a given city?

Social science courses are required courses for many college degrees because social science links to many other fields. If you plan to become a nurse, interacting with patients is important. If you plan to work in business, your success often depends on understanding people and the economy in which you are working. If you plan to work as a commercial Web site designer, you have to understand what motivates people to purchase goods and services. You can see, then, that social science courses are valuable in the workplace because all jobs require you to interact with people to some degree.

THE SOCIAL SCIENCES: A SCIENTIFIC APPROACH

Although each social science focuses on a different aspect of human life, they have much in common. Each is interested in general laws, principles, and generalizations that describe how events, facts, and observations are related. The author of your social science textbook and your course instructor are both social scientists, and their approach to problems and the way they organize ideas are similar and predictable. Once you are familiar with this approach, you'll find social science courses much easier to handle.

All social sciences use the scientific method. This is a systematic way of drawing conclusions about events and observations. Social scientists insist on evidence and proof and are careful to avoid subjectivity, judgments, and bias. The scientific method is a means of discovering the rules and principles that govern human behavior.

Five steps are commonly included in the scientific approach. You might think of them as a logical process that scientists follow in investigating problems.

1. *Problem or Research Question.* A researcher poses a problem or research question.

2. *Observations.* Researchers record what they can observe about a given problem or behavior. They emphasize facts and measurable, observable behaviors.

3. *Formulation of Hypothesis.* On the basis of observations, researchers form a preliminary hypothesis. A hypothesis is a statement about a relationship or occurrence that can be tested or evaluated.

4. *Research Design.* Researchers design a plan to gather the data necessary to test the hypothesis. This plan may include survey research, the use of secondary data, or an experiment with control and experimental groups.

5. *Data Analysis.* Data from the experiment are analyzed, and the hypothesis is supported or rejected. These findings often are published or shared with other researchers.

An overview of the method and an example of its use are shown in Table 12–2. In this case, the problem is "What are the effects of portraying violence on television?"

The scientific method is the standard operating procedure for all social sciences. Consequently, textbooks in the social sciences share several characteristics.

1. *The emphasis is on facts.* Especially in introductory courses, an instructor's first task often is to acquaint you with what has already been

TABLE 12–2	THE SCIENTIFIC METHOD

STEP	EXAMPLE
Problem or question	Does the portrayal of violence on television produce aggressive behavior in viewers?
Observations	A great deal of violence is shown on television. Crime rates are increasing.
Hypothesis	Children who watch highly violent TV programs exhibit more aggressive behavior than children who watch nonviolent programs.
Research design	Two groups established; TV watching habits of each group controlled. Aggression measured by hidden observers during play periods following viewing. An aggression score is assigned for each group.
Data analysis	Viewers of violent programs received aggression scores three times higher than viewers of nonviolent programs. The research result supports the hypothesis that viewing violence produces aggressive behavior.

discovered—known principles, rules, and facts—so that you can use this information to approach new problems and situations. Consequently, you must comprehend and retain large amounts of factual information. Refer to "Locating Main Ideas and Supporting Details" in Chapter 2 and "Retention and Recall Strategies" in Chapter 7 for specific suggestions.

2. *Many new terms are introduced.* Each social science has developed an extensive terminology to make its broad topics as objective and as quantifiable as possible.

3. *Graphics are important.* Refer to Chapter 8, "Reading Graphics," for specific suggestions on reading and interpreting charts, tables, and graphs.

4. *Research references are stressed.* Many texts present research studies as supporting evidence. In introductory courses, the outcome of the research and what it proves or suggests usually are most important.

5. *Theories and their creators are emphasized.* Often, the social scientists who have developed important theories are discussed at length.

Now that you are familiar with the scientific method, you will understand how social scientists approach their subject matter and how you will be expected to think and analyze information in social science courses. You will have a competitive advantage over other students who mistakenly regard social science courses as subjective or unscientific.

SPECIALIZED READING TECHNIQUES

Especially in introductory-level social science courses, you will need to learn a large volume of information. Use the following suggestions to read social science materials and retain as much information as possible.

Identify Key Terms

The key to mastering any new discipline is to learn its language: specialized and technical terms unique to the discipline. The social sciences use precise terminology to describe observations as well as processes. Terminology in the social sciences includes everyday words with specialized meanings as well as new words not used elsewhere. Instructors recognize the importance of learning terminology; consequently, often they include items on their exams to test your knowledge of key terms. Refer to Chapter 3 for specific suggestions for learning specialized terminology.

In social science courses, it is particularly important to learn

- Terms that describe general behavior and organizational patterns
  Examples: denial, power, aggression, primary/secondary groups, free trade
- Names of stages and processes
  Examples: Piaget's stages of cognitive development, Maslow's hierarchy of needs
- Laws, principles, theories, and models
  Examples: figure-ground principles, income/expenditures model, models of attention, Keynesian theory
- Names of important researchers and theorists
  Examples: Marx, Freud, Skinner, Durkheim, Leakey

Understand Theories

An important part of most social science courses is the study of theories that explain various behaviors. A theory is a set of propositions that explains a certain phenomenon or occurrence. You might, for example, develop a theory to explain why your roommate cannot fall asleep without music or why your history professor always opens class with the same comment. A theory is a reasoned explanation of an observable occurrence. Theories are often tested using the scientific method. In sociology, you may study exchange theory, which explains social behavior as a series of exchanges or trade-offs involving rewards (benefits) and costs. In economics, you may study the natural rate hypothesis that states that workers do not immediately react to changes in wages.

When studying theories, read to find the following information:

- What is the theory?
- Who proposed the theory?
- When was it proposed? (Is it recent or historical?)
- What behavior or occurrence does it explain?
- What evidence or rationale is offered that the theory is correct?
- What use or application does the theory have?

Read the following excerpt from a sociology text. Note how the text has been marked to indicate the answers to each of the questions listed above.

Conflict Theory

behavior —— Conflict theory also had its origins in early sociology, especially in the work of
origin — Marx. Among its more recent proponents are such people as Mills, Coser, and
recent proponents — Dahrendorf. They share the view that society is best understood and analyzed in
statement of theory terms of conflict and power.

rationale Karl Marx began with a very simple assumption: the structure of society is determined by economic organization, particularly the ownership of property. Religious dogmas, cultural values, personal beliefs, institutional arrangements, class structures—all are basically reflections of the economic organization of a society. Inherent in any economic system that supports inequality are forces that generate revolutionary class conflict, according to Marx. The exploited classes eventually recognize their submissive and inferior status and revolt against the dominant class of property owners and employers. The story of history, then, is the story of class struggle between the owners and workers, the dominators and the dominated, the powerful and the powerless.

applications Contemporary conflict theorists assume that conflict is a permanent feature of social life and that as a result societies are in a state of constant change. Unlike Marx, however, these theorists rarely assume that conflict is always based on class or that it always reflects economic organization and ownership. Conflicts are assumed to involve a broad range of groups or interests: young against old, male against female, or one racial group against another, as well as workers against employers. These conflicts result because things like power, wealth, and prestige are not available to everyone—they are limited commodities, and the demand exceeds the supply. Conflict theory also assumes that those who have or control desirable goods and services will defend and protect their own interests at the expense of others.

—Eshleman et al., *Sociology: An Introduction*, p. 46

In some texts, you may find several theories presented to explain a single phenomenon. Often, these theories are not compatible, and they may even be contradictory. In this case, first make certain that you understand each theory; then examine how they differ and consider the evidence offered in support of each.

EXERCISE 12–1

Write a summary of the conflict theory described above. Refer to page 307 for suggestions on writing summaries. Compare your summary to those of several classmates.

EXERCISE 12–2

Read this excerpt from a psychology textbook, and answer the questions that follow.

KOHLBERG'S THEORY OF MORAL DEVELOPMENT

How children learn to reason about and make judgments about what is right and wrong is an aspect of cognitive development that has received considerable attention (Darley & Schultz, 1990; Vitz, 1990). Piaget included the study of moral development in his theory, arguing that morality is related to cognitive awareness, and that children are unable to make moral judgments until they are at least 3 or 4 years old (Piaget, 1932/1948).

Lawrence Kohlberg (1963, 1969, 1981, 1985) has offered a theory that focuses on moral development. Like Piaget's approach, Kohlberg's is a theory of stages, of moving from one stage to another in an orderly fashion. Kohlberg's database comes from the responses made by young boys who were asked questions about stories that involve a moral dilemma. A commonly cited example concerns whether a man should steal a drug in order to save his wife's life after the pharmacist who invented the drug refuses to sell it to him. Should the man steal the drug; why or why not?

On the basis of responses to such dilemmas, Kohlberg proposed three levels of moral development, with two stages (or "orientations") at each level. The result is the six stages of moral development. . . . For example, a child who says that the man should not steal the drug because "he'll get caught and be put in jail" is at the first, *preconventional*, level of reasoning because the prime interest of the child is simply with the punishment that comes from breaking a rule. A child who says that the man should steal the drug because "it will make his wife happy, and probably most people would do it anyway" is reflecting a type of reasoning at the second, *conventional*, level because the judgment is based on an accepted social convention, and social approval matters as much as or more than anything else. The argument that "no, he shouldn't steal the drug for a basically selfish reason, which in the long run would just promote more stealing in the society in general" is an example of moral reasoning at the third, *postconventional*, level because it reflects complex, internalized standards. Notice that what matters most is not the choice the child makes, but the reasoning behind the choice.

—Gerow, *Psychology: An Introduction*, p. 290

1. Who proposed the theory?
2. What is it intended to explain?
3. Explain the three levels in your own words.
4. How did Kohlberg arrive at the theory?
5. What practical uses can you see for the theory?
6. Underline terminology in the passage that is important to learn.
7. Construct a story about a moral dilemma, and indicate responses at each of the three levels.

Read Research Reports

Because the social sciences rely heavily on observation, research, and experimentation based on the scientific method, textbooks often include brief descriptions of, or references to, research studies. When such references are made to other works, the source of the reference is indicated in parentheses as shown in the excerpt below. Footnotes or endnotes sometimes are used to provide more detailed information.

When reading reports about research, keep these guidelines in mind:

- Determine who conducted the research.
- Identify its purpose.
- Find out how the research was done.
- Understand the results of the research.
- Find out what theory the results support or what conclusion was drawn.
- Discover the implications and applications of the research. Ask "Why is it important?".

The following excerpt from a sociology textbook describes research on masculine and feminine behavior. See how the marked passages reflect the guidelines given above.

Although biologically men are men and women are women, roles—that is, definitions of masculine and feminine behavior—differ widely from one culture to another. The discovery of cross-cultural variation in gender was one of the earliest kinds of evidence against the idea that each sex has a "natural" temperament and set of interests. In American culture, for example, it is considered "feminine" to be artistic and emotional, but in other cultures men are supposed to be more emotionally expressive and artistic than women. Margaret Mead's (1935) classic study of sex and temperament in three cultures was the earliest <u>study of the variability of gender patterning</u>. In one of the New Guinea tribes, the Arapesh, both men and

Purpose

Results

women were found to be cooperative, unaggressive, and gentle. In contrast, the Mundugumor prescribed what would be a masculine temperament in our culture for both sexes—ruthlessness, aggressiveness, and severity. Neither the Arapesh nor the Mundugumor emphasized a contrast between the sexes. In a third New Guinea tribe, the Tchambuli, however, there was such a contrast, but it was the reverse of sex-role temperament in our culture. Tchambuli women tended to be aggressive, domineering, and managerial, whereas the men tended to be

Conclusion

dependent, artistic, and sensitive. In short, the study concludes that sex differences are arbitrary and do not reflect any underlying predisposition.

—Skolnick, *The Intimate Environment: Exploring Marriage and the Family*, pp. 193–94

EXERCISE 12–3

Read the following excerpt from a psychology textbook and answer the questions that follow.

Researchers have looked at the relationship between adolescent drug use and psychological health (Shedler & Block, 1990). Participants in this investigation were 18-year-olds who had been under study since they were 3 years old. Based on their level of drug use, they were divided into one of three groups: (1) *abstainers* (N = 29), who had never tried any drug; (2) *experimenters* (N = 36), who had used marijuana "once or twice, or a few times" and who tried no more than one other drug; and (3) *frequent users* (N = 20), who used marijuana frequently and tried at least one other drug. There were no socioeconomic or IQ differences among the groups.

The researchers found that *frequent users* were generally maladjusted, alienated, deficient in impulse control, and "manifestly" distressed. The *abstainers* were overly anxious, "emotionally constricted," and lacking in social skills. These same results were apparent when the researchers examined records from when the same subjects were 7 and 11 years old. Generally, the *experimenters* were better adjusted and psychologically "healthier" than either of the other two groups. The authors of this study are concerned that their data may be misinterpreted—that their data might be taken to indicate "that drug use might somehow improve an adolescent's psychological health." Clearly, this interpretation would be in error. You recognize these as correlational data from which no conclusion regarding cause and effect is justified.

While drug use among adolescents is a matter of great concern, there is evidence that we need not get hysterical about infrequent drug use among teenagers.

—Gerow, *Psychology: An Introduction*, pp. 305–06

1. Who conducted the research?
2. What was its purpose?
3. What methods were used?
4. What were the results?
5. What did the results demonstrate?

6.   What is the practical value of the research?
7.   Why did the author feel compelled to caution against misinterpretation?

Read to Make Comparisons and Connections

In the social sciences, the ability to see relationships among different ideas and concepts is a necessary skill. Often neither your instructor nor your textbook will make explicit, direct comparisons, yet you will be expected to compare or contrast ideas and concepts. Suppose you are reading about three forms of imperfect economic competition: monopoly, oligopoly, and monopolistic competition. You would, of course, be expected to under-stand each form. However, you must also know how they are similar, how they are different, and in what economic situation each is found.

When making comparisons, keep the following question in mind: "What does what I am reading have to do with other topics in the chapter?" Then spend a few minutes thinking about how the topics and ideas in the chapter are connected to one another. Begin by doing a review of the chapter using the steps you used to preview it (see Chapter 1). Then study your text's detailed table of contents and review the lecture notes that correspond to the chapter. For example, one student connected the forms of imperfect competition to other market variables she had learned in economics: number of sellers, ease of entry, product type, price influ-ence, and price level. Then she drew the chart shown in Table 12–3 to com-pare the three forms according to the market variables that she identified.

TABLE 12–3   SAMPLE COMPARISON CHART

	FORMS OF IMPERFECT COMPETITION		
	MONOPOLY	**OLIGOPOLY**	**MONOPOLISTIC COMPETITION**
Number of sellers	One	Several.	Many.
Entry	Difficult	Less difficult.	Easy.
Product	Unique	Homogeneous or differentiated.	Differentiated.
Price influence	Price makers	Price makers.	Limited price makers.
Price level	Higher price, lower quantity than competition	Somewhat higher price and lower quantity than competition.	Slightly higher price than competition and frequently higher production costs.

In addition to charts, you can organize comparisons by making outlines or lists or by drawing maps that summarize similarities and differences (refer to Chapter 10).

EXERCISE 12–4

COLLABORATIVE LEARNING

Read the following excerpt from a sociology textbook chapter titled "Religious Groups and Systems," and make comparisons between Hinduism and Buddhism by listing, charting, or mapping. Compare your work with the work of other students, discussing its relative effectiveness.

Hinduism

The great majority of Hindus in the world live in India and Pakistan. In India, approximately 85 percent of the population is Hindu. Hinduism has evolved over about 4000 years and comprises an enormous variety of beliefs and practices. It hardly corresponds to most Western conceptions of religion because organization is minimal, and there is no religious hierarchy.

Hinduism is so closely intertwined with other aspects of the society that it is difficult to describe it clearly, especially in regard to castes . . . . Hindus sometimes refer to the ideal way of life as fulfilling the duties of one's class and station, which means obeying the rules of the four great castes of India: the Brahmins, or priests; the Kshatriyas, warriors and rulers; the Vaisyas, merchants and farmers; and the Sudras, peasants and laborers. A fifth class, the Untouchables, includes those whose occupations require them to handle "unclean objects."

These classes encompass males only. The position of women is ambiguous. In some respects, they are treated as symbols of the divine, yet in other ways, they are considered inferior beings. Traditionally, women have been expected to serve their husbands and to have no independent interests, but this is rapidly changing.

Although caste is a powerful influence in Hindu religious behavior, a person's village community and family are important as well. Every village has gods and goddesses who ward off epidemics and drought. Hindu belief holds that the universe is populated by a multitude of gods (polytheism) who behave much as humans do, and worship of these gods takes many forms. Some are thought to require sacrifices, others are worshipped at shrines or temples, and shrines devoted to several gods associated with a family deity are often erected in private homes.

To Hindus, the word *dharma* means the cosmos, or the social order. Hindus practice rituals that uphold the great cosmic order. They believe that to be righteous, a person must strive to behave in accordance with the way things are. In a sense, the Hindu sees life as a ritual. The world is regarded as a great dance determined by one's karma, or personal destiny, and the final goal of the believer is liberation from this cosmic dance. Hindus also believe in *transmigration of souls*: After an individual dies, that individual's soul is born again in another form, as either a higher or lower being, depending on whether the person was righteous or evil in the previous life. If an individual becomes righteous enough, the soul will be liberated and will cease to be reborn into an earthly form and will exist only as spirit.

A fundamental principle of Hinduism is that our perceptions of the external world are limitations. When we think about one thing, we are cut off from the infinite number of things we are not thinking about but could be. If we think of nothing, we become in tune with the universe and freed of these limitations. One means of doing this is through meditation.

The actual belief systems of India are extremely confusing to Westerners, because so many different tribal religions have been assimilated into Hinduism, but the basic nature of polytheism in general and of Hinduism in particular permits new gods to be admitted.

Buddhism

It is impossible to precisely determine the number of Buddhists because many people accept Buddhist beliefs and engage in Buddhist rites while practicing other religions such as Shintoism, Confucianism, Taoism, or Hinduism.

Buddhism is thought to have originated as a reaction against the Brahminic tradition of Hinduism in the fifth century B.C. At this time, a prince named Siddhartha Gautama was born in northern India to a prosperous ruling family. As he grew older, he was distressed by the suffering he witnessed among the people. At the age of 29, he left his wife and family to go on a religious quest. One day, sitting under a giant fig tree, he passed through several stages of awareness and became the Buddha, the enlightened one. He decided to share his experience with others and became a wandering teacher, preaching his doctrine of the "Four Noble Truths": (1) this life is suffering and pain; (2) the source of suffering is desire and craving; (3) suffering can cease; and (4) the practice of an "eightfold path" can end suffering. The eightfold path consisted of right views, right intentions, right speech, right conduct, right livelihood, right effort, right mindfulness, and right concentration. It combined ethical and disciplinary practices, training in concentration and meditation, and the development of enlightened wisdom. This doctrine was Buddha's message until the age of 80, when he passed into final nirvana, a state of transcendence forever free from the cycle of suffering and rebirth.

After Buddha's death, legends of his great deeds and supernatural powers emerged. Stories were told of his heroism in past lives, and speculations arose about his true nature. Some groups viewed him as a historical figure, whereas others placed him in a succession of several Buddhas of the past and a Buddha yet to come. Differing views eventually led to a diversity of Buddhist sects in different countries. Some remained householders who set up Buddha images and established many holy sites that became centers of pilgrimage. Others became monks, living in monastic communities and depending on the laity for food and material support. Many monks became beggars, and in several Southeast Asian countries, they still go on daily alms rounds. They spend their days in rituals, devotions, meditation, study, and preaching. Flowers, incense, and praise are offered to the image of the Buddha. These acts are thought to ensure that the monks will be reborn in one of the heavens or in a better place in life, from which they may be able to attain the goal of enlightenment.

In every society where Buddhism is widespread, people combine Buddhist thought with a native religion, supporting the monks and paying for rituals in the temples. These societies are also organized around other religions, however.

Today, the integration of Buddhism into many cultures has resulted in different interpretations of the way to Buddhahood. Yet we can supposedly reach Nirvana by seeing with complete detachment, by seeing things as they really are without being attached to any theoretical concept or doctrine.

—Eshleman et al., *Sociology: An Introduction*, pp. 356–58

Read to Make Practical Applications

In many courses, instructors want students to apply what they learn to everyday, practical situations. Consequently, instructors expect and encourage students to use their reasoning skills to go beyond what is stated in the text and consider practical applications of textbook information. For example, your psychology instructor may ask this question on a midterm exam.

> Five-year-old Sammy tells his grandmother that three dinosaurs are hiding in his closet. Knowing this is not true, his grandmother spanks Sammy. Grandmother should be
>
> a. encouraged to be consistent, spanking Sammy whenever he talks about dinosaurs.
> b. reminded that children of this age often confuse fantasy and reality.
> c. thanked for acting as a good role model for Sammy.
> d. told that her authoritarian response will improve his ability to relate to adults.

Or, in your American government class, the following question might appear on an essay exam.

> Project the key political issues that will be involved in the next presidential election.

To be prepared for questions such as these, consider the practical applications of what you read. Try to relate each idea to a real-life situation, and, if possible, connect the material to your own experience.

Focus on Large Ideas

Because many social science courses present a great deal of factual information, it is easy to become convinced that the facts are all you need to learn. Actually, factual information is only a starting point, a base from which to approach the real content of a course. Most social science instructors expect you to go beyond facts to analysis—to consider the meaning of facts and details. Many students fail to understand the overriding concepts of their courses because they are too concerned with memorizing information. They fail to ask, "Why do I need to know this? Why is this important? What principle or trend does this illustrate?" Table 12–4 gives examples of details from a course in American history and the more important trends, concepts, or principles they represent.

Be certain you stay focused on major ideas; after you preview a chapter, write a list of key topics and concepts you expect to read about. After you have read about each one, check it off on your list. Before you continue, mentally review what you have learned. After completing an assignment, return again to your list to reestablish what is important and recheck your recall. Restate each idea in your own words; if you can do so, you can be confident that you understand the ideas, rather than just recall the author's words.

TABLE 12–4   IDENTIFYING KEY CONCEPTS

TOPICS	FACTS	IMPORTANCE
The slavery controversy	On May 22, 1856, Representative Brooks from South Carolina approached Senator Sumner of Massachusetts (who had recently given a speech condemning the South for trying to extend slavery) on the floor of the Senate and beat him with a cane until he was near death.	The antagonism between the North and South had become bitter and violent by 1856.
Annexation of territories to the U.S.	Texas was annexed in 1845. In 1845 and 1846 a great controversy arose over the Oregon territory. The Democrats wanted to make all of the Oregon territory (stretching north above today's border into British Columbia) part of the U.S. The British also claimed this land. A war over the territory was barely avoided.	In the late 1840s a belief called *Manifest Destiny* was widespread. People felt it was the fate of the U.S. to spread from the Atlantic Ocean to the Pacific Ocean and eventually take over the entire continent.
Industry	Henry Ford perfected the Model T for manufacture in 1914, and by 1924 more than 40,000 workers were working in the first mass-production assembly line factory.	This began the trend toward mass production, which led the second Industrial Revolution.

THOUGHT PATTERNS IN THE SOCIAL SCIENCES

Four thought patterns that predominate in the social sciences are comparison and contrast, cause and effect, listing, and definition. Table 12–5 describes the uses of each pattern and includes several examples from a specific discipline.

TABLE 12–5	THOUGHT PATTERNS IN THE SOCIAL SCIENCES	
PATTERN	**USES**	**TOPICAL EXAMPLES**
Comparison and contrast	To evaluate two sides of an issue; to compare and contrast theories, groups, behaviors, events.	*Anthropology* Limbic and nonlimbic communication Theories of aggression Anatomical comparison: archaic and modern People Relative versus chronometric dating methods
Cause and effect	To study behavior and motivation; to examine connections between events, actions, behaviors.	*Economics* Price determination Factors affecting individual's demand curve Aggregate effects of taxes Factors influencing consumption and saving
Listing	To present facts, illustrations, or examples; to list research findings.	*Sociology* Types of adult socialization Three sociological research methods Myths about old age Agencies of socialization
Definition	To label and describe behaviors, social systems, laws, cycles, etc.	*Political Science* Coercive power Utilitarian power Capitalism Conservatism

EXERCISE 12–5

Figure 12–1 is a chapter outline from a sociology textbook. Read the headings and subheadings and identify the thought pattern of each shaded section. For some headings, more than one pattern may be identified. Refer to Chapter 6 for a review of thought patterns.

Figure 12–1   Chapter Outline

Socialization

Nature Versus Nurture	Religion
Becoming Human	Peers
The Effects of Social Isolation	The Workplace
Personality Development: A Psychological View	The Mass Media
Developing a Concept of Self: A Sociological Approach	**Socialization: Future Directions**
Socialization and the Life Course	*Box 4.1 Sociological Focus:*
Childhood Socialization	*Nature Versus Nurture:*
Adult Socialization	*The Case of Willie Bosket Jr.*
Resocialization	*Box 4.2 Applied Sociology:*
Major Agents of Socialization	*Resocialization in a Marine Corps Boot Camp*
The Family	
Schools	

Source: Thompson and Hickey, *Society in Focus: An Introduction to Sociology,* p. 81.

EXERCISE 12–6

Form groups of three students, and have each student bring a social science text-book to class. Each group should select one text and, using the table of contents, work together to agree on a list of patterns likely to appear in the first five chapters.

ADAPTING YOUR STUDY TECHNIQUES

Use the following suggestions in adapting your study methods to the social science field.

1. *Schedule several 2- to 3-hour blocks of time per week for reading, review, and study.* Avoid last-minute cramming. Study that is distributed over several periods is more effective than one marathon session.

2. *Recognize that understanding is not the same as learning and recall.* Do not assume that because you have read an assignment, you have learned it. To ensure learning, use writing to organize the information. Refer to Chapter 10 for specific strategies.

3. *Use the SQ3R system, or your own adaptation of it, to learn the material.* Review this system in Chapter 7. Writing is useful in the recitation step because it allows for greater retention of information through multiple sensory stimulation.

4. *Review frequently.* Review each assignment immediately after you have read it and again the next day. Add periodic reviews to your regular study sessions.

5. *Make connections between topics and chapters.* Each topic is an essential part of the discipline, as is every chapter. Information gained in one chapter should be used and applied in subsequent chapters.

6. *Use the study guide.* Many social science textbooks have a study guide that may be purchased separately. These guides contain useful reviews, sample test questions, and additional practice materials.

7. *Keep a log of total hours studied per week.* The log will help maintain your motivation and enable you to see how the grades you are earning are related to the amount of time you spend studying.

 STUDY Tips   ## Preparing for Exams in the Social Sciences

Many exams you will take in social science courses will be objective: multiple choice, true-false, matching, or fill-in-the-blank. Your task in these types of questions is to recognize correct answers. To prepare for objective exams, use the following suggestions:

1. *Attend review classes if your instructor conducts them.*

2. *Prepare study sheets.* Organize and summarize important information from your notes and your text on topics you expect the exam to cover.

3. *Use index cards to record factual information that you must learn* (names, dates, definitions, theories, research findings). Record the name, date, name of theory, and so forth on the front of the card, and record what the person is noted for, the event, or the theory itself on the back. Test yourself by reading the front of the card and trying to recall what is on the back. Shuffle the pack of cards so that you do not learn the material in a fixed order.

4. *Review previous exams and quizzes.* Look for patterns of errors, and identify kinds of questions you missed (knowledge or critical thinking), as well as topics that you need to review.

SUMMARY

This chapter describes reading strategies for the social sciences. All social sciences use the scientific method, which is a systematic way of drawing conclusions about events or observations.

The specialized reading techniques necessary for the social sciences are

- identifying key terminology
- understanding theories
- reading reports of research
- making comparisons
- making applications
- focusing on large ideas

Four thought patterns predominate in the social sciences:

- comparison and contrast
- cause and effect
- listing
- definition

SOCIOLOGY

PREREADING QUESTIONS

1. What is a crowd?
2. How is one crowd different from another?

CROWD BEHAVIOR

J. Ross Eshleman, Barbara J. Cashion, and Laurence A. Basirico

CHARACTERISTICS OF CROWDS

1   A **spatially proximate collective** exists when people are geographically close and physically visible to one another. The most common type of spatially proximate collective is the **crowd,** a temporary group of people in face-to-face contact who share a common interest or focus of attention. This common interest may be unexpected and unusual, but it is not necessarily so. Although people in a crowd interact a good deal, the crowd as a whole is organized poorly if at all. According to Turner (1985), crowds have four features that make them a unique area for study: anonymity, suggestibility, contagion, and emotional arousability.

2   Most types of collective behavior involve *anonymity*. People who do not know those around them may behave in ways that they would consider unacceptable if they were alone or with their family or neighbors. During a riot, the anonymity of crowd members makes it easier for people to loot and steal. In a lynch mob, brutal acts can be committed without feelings of shame or responsibility. Whatever the type of crowd, the anonymity of the individuals involved shifts the responsibility to the crowd as a whole.

Crowds exist when many people are in face-to-face contact and share a common interest. Some crowds, such as at a sporting event or outdoor concert, may behave collectively by shouting, clapping, jumping, or waving when the performers engage in a particular activity: a home run or touchdown, a hit song, an emotionally charged speech, and so forth.

3   Because crowds are relatively unstructured and often unpredictable, crowd members are often highly *suggestible*. People who are seeking direction in an uncertain situation are highly responsive to the suggestions of others and become very willing to do what a leader or group of individuals suggests, especially given the crowd's anonymity.

4   The characteristic of *contagion* is closely linked to anonymity and suggestibility. Turner (1985) defines this aspect of crowd behavior as "interactional amplification." As people interact, the crowd's response to the common event or situation increases in intensity. If they are clapping or screaming, their behavior is likely to move others to clap or scream, and contagion increases when people are packed close together. An alert evangelist, comedian, or rock singer will try to get the audience to move close to one another to increase the likelihood of contagion and to encourage the listeners to get caught up in the mood, spirit, and activity of the crowd.

5   A fourth characteristic is *emotional arousal*. Anonymity, suggestibility, and contagion tend to arouse emotions. Inhibitions are forgotten, and people become emotionally charged to act. In some cases, their emotional involvement encourages them to act in uncharacteristic ways. During the Beatles concerts in the early 1960s, for example, teenage girls who were presumably quite conventional most of the time tried to rush on stage and had to be carried away by police. The combination of the four characteristics of crowds makes their behavior extremely volatile and frightening.

6   Although these four aspects of crowds behavior may be seen in almost any crowd, their intensity varies. Some crowds permit greater anonymity than others, and some have higher levels of suggestibility and contagion, yet one or more of these characteristics may not appear at all. The presence or absence of certain crowd features can be used to organize crowds into different categories.

TYPES OF CROWDS

7   All crowds are spatially proximate and temporary, and every crowd shares a common focus. However, some crowds are very low in emotional arousal and are highly unstructured, whereas others are quite emotional, aggressive, and even dangerous to one's safety.

8   The literature on collective behavior, following the lead of Herbert Blumer (1939), tends to label the nonemotional, unstructured crowd as a **casual crowd.** People who stop to look at an animated holiday display or who gather to watch a street musician would be of this type. Another type of crowd, sometimes called a **conventional crowd,** is more highly structured and occurs, for example, when spectators gather at a baseball game, attend a concert, or ride on an airplane. Although the participants are generally unknown to one another (anonymous), they have a specific goal or common purpose and are expected

to follow established norms and procedures. At symphony concerts, for example, people applaud at the end of the music (an established procedure). When the music is being played, however, they do not run up and down the aisles or call out to a friend at the opposite side of the concert hall (not an established procedure).

9   The ... crowds that attract the most public attention are called **acting crowds,** the behavior of which is centered around and typifies aroused impulses. The two most dramatic forms of acting crowds are mobs and riots.

10   **Mobs** are groups that are emotionally aroused and ready to engage in violent behavior. They are generally short-lived and highly unstable. Their violent actions often stem from strong dissatisfaction with existing government policies or social circumstances; extreme discontentment with prevailing conditions is used to justify immediate and direct action. Disdainful of regular institutional channels and legal approaches, mobs take matters into their own hands.

11   Most mobs are predisposed to violence before their actions are triggered by a specific event. When feelings of frustration and hostility are widespread, leaders can easily recruit and command members. With aggressive leadership, an angry, frustrated mob in an atmosphere of hostility can be readily motivated to riot, commit lynchings, throw firebombs, hang people in effigy, or engage in destructive orgies.

12   Mob violence has erupted in many different circumstances. During the French Revolution of the 1780s and 1790s, angry mobs stormed through Paris, breaking into the Bastille prison for arms and calling for the execution of Louis XVI. In nineteenth-century England, enraged workers burned the factories in which they worked. Lynchings of blacks in the United States for real or imagined offenses continued into the twentieth century, often with little or no opposition from the formal agencies of control—police, courts, and public officials. Although lynch mobs are uncommon today, occasional instances of mob behavior take place over civil rights issues such as busing or housing, during political conventions and rallies, and among student or labor groups angry about perceived injustices. In 1987, for example, mob violence erupted in all-white Forsyth County, Georgia, when a white mob disrupted a march by whites and blacks protesting discriminatory antiblack housing policy.

13   **Riots** are collective actions involving mass violence and mob actions. The targets of their hostility and violence are less specific than those of mobs, and the groups involved are more diffuse. Most riots result from an intense hatred of a particular group with no specific person or property in mind. Destruction, burning, or looting may be indiscriminate, and unfocused anger can lead to violent acts against any object or person who happens to be in the wrong area at the wrong time. Like mobs, rioters take actions into their own hands when they feel that institutional reaction to their concerns about war, poverty, racial injustices, or other problems are inadequate.

—Eshleman et al., *Sociology: An Introduction*, pp. 487–90

VOCABULARY REVIEW

1. For each of the words listed below, use context; prefixes, roots, and suffixes; and/or a dictionary to write a brief definition or synonym of the word as it is used in the reading.

   a. anonymity (para. 1, 2) _____

   b. contagion (para. 1, 4)_____

   c. suggestible (para. 1, 3) _____

   d. arousal (para. 1, 5) _____

   e. evangelist (para. 4) _____

   f. uncharacteristic (para. 5)_____

   g. volatile (para. 5)_____

   h. typifies (para. 9)_____

   i. disdainful (para. 10) _____

   j. channels (para. 10) _____

   k. predisposed (para. 11) _____

   l. effigy (para. 11) _____

   m. orgies (para. 11) _____

   n. indiscriminate (para. 12) _____

   o. diffuse (para. 13) _____

2. Underline new specialized terms introduced in the reading.

COMPREHENSION QUESTIONS

1. Identify and explain the four features of a crowd.
2. Name two characteristics that all crowds have in common.
3. Describe the difference between a "casual" crowd and a "conventional" crowd.
4. What are two forms of acting crowds?
5. Describe a mob and give an example of one.
6. How do mobs and riots differ from one another?

THINKING CRITICALLY

1. Explain how school pep rallies make use of the four features of a crowd to engage the spectators.
2. How can we use our knowledge of crowds to prevent crowd violence?

3. Give a specific example of a persuasive leader inciting a crowd to violence.
4. Explain why the right of people to assemble is often the first right restricted by leaders who gain governmental control forcibly.

LEARNING/STUDY STRATEGIES

1. Review the section on "Characteristics of Crowds" by completing the following study chart on features of crowds and how they support unacceptable behaviors by individuals within the crowd.

FEATURE	SUPPORTS UNACCEPTABLE BEHAVIOR BY:
1.	
2.	
3.	
4.	
5.	

2. What is the overall thought pattern used in this reading?

ON-LINE RESEARCH: CROWD BEHAVIOR*

Sociology, like the other social sciences, has many practical applications. For example, examine these sites on the World Wide Web (WWW) that describe two different types of crowd management and answer the questions that follow.

1. Go to http://crowdsafe.com/taskrpt/chpt1.html to access "Crowd Management," part of a report on managing crowd behavior at public events such as concerts. In the second section, "Crowd Behavior," sociologist Dr. Irving Goldaber is quoted as saying that various "sociological signals" received by people attending an event can influence their behavior. What specific examples does the report give of these signals?
2. Access the article "Crowd Control Measures" from the Naval Support Activity's training for law enforcement officers at http://web.nps.navy.mil/~police/123.htm. Read the section titled "The Crowd." How is the classification of different types of crowds similar to and different from the the four types of crowds noted in the textbook reading?

*If any of these sites is unavailable, use a search engine to locate a new Web site on the same topic.

13 | READING IN BUSINESS

LEARNING OBJECTIVES

- ■ To understand the focus of business courses
- ■ To develop specialized reading techniques for business
- ■ To discover thought patterns commonly used in business
- ■ To adapt study techniques for business courses

Business is a diverse field that includes business management, information systems, accounting, finance, statistics, retailing, organizational behavior, and corporate strategy. In general, business is concerned with the production and sale of economic goods or services that satisfy people's needs and yield a profit. Because business is a broad field, course work for a degree in business often includes requirements in such related fields as computer science, economics, and communications.

BUSINESS: A FOCUS ON ORGANIZATION AND MANAGEMENT

Suppose you decided to start a new business that would produce and sell six varieties of gourmet desserts throughout the country. Now suppose you hired 200 employees and that all you told your workers was that their job was to make and sell these desserts. Your business would probably be a dismal failure; none of your employees would know what to do or how to do it. Your business lacked two essential ingredients: organization and management. These ingredients also are a key to your success in getting the most from your business courses.

Organization is a system or structure, and management is a process by which all parts of the system—employees, technology, job responsibilities, and resources—are combined and coordinated. In business courses, you study how businesses are set up and how they are made to operate effectively. These two key aspects, however, encompass numerous other areas: product development, communication, marketing, labor relations, retailing, advertising, financing, banking, accounting, computer systems, legal aspects, and international trade.

Business courses are practical, then. They deal with aspects of creating or operating a business. Business courses are inter-related. Business economics courses use concepts from accounting; marketing courses use concepts from management courses, and so on. Math is also an important part of some business courses. For advice on reading mathematics, see Chapter 15.

Why Study Business?

All of us are in contact with businesses on a daily basis. When you stop for gas, buy a sandwich, or pick up the telephone, you are involved in a business transaction. The world of business surrounds us. Business courses have a number of advantages, as follows:

- Business courses can make you a savvy, better-informed consumer. You discover how to make better informed buying decisions and to spend your money wisely.
- Business courses will help you make career decisions. You'll discover a wide range of employment opportunities.
- Business courses will help you become a successful employee. Getting a job is only the first step to a successful career; you must be successful at it. By learning how businesses operate, you will be able to contribute effectively to your company.
- Business courses will help you start your own business. If you plan to start your own business, business courses will give you the knowledge and skills to make your business a success.

Current Hot Topics in Business

Whenever you take a course, you should always try to discover the trends, issues, and themes that are emphasized. Identifying these "hot topics" will help you predict essay exam questions, choose worthwhile topics for papers and assignments, and make valuable contributions to class discussions.

In business courses, there are at least five current topics:

- **Globalization of Business.** Growing numbers of U.S. companies are doing business with firms in other countries. U.S. businesses compete in foreign markets, and the number of international trade agreements continue to grow. Consequently, it is important to recognize business as an international venture and understand the role of the U.S. in the world market.

- **Role of Technology.** As technology continues to develop and change, so must businesses change and adapt to keep pace. The Internet, telecommunications, computers, robotics, all have an impact on business. For example, growing numbers of businesses have Web sites; increasing numbers of employees are telecommuting (working at home), and small robots are used increasingly in manufacturing. Awareness of technology will keep you on the cutting edge of business growth and change.

- **Importance of Diversity.** Today's workforce consists of individuals from a variety of cultural and ethnic groups. A wider range of interests, social customs, and value systems are represented. Diversity can be a strong advantage for a company by offering a variety of resources and perspectives.

- **Growth and Role of Small Businesses.** Increasing numbers of small businesses are also a major source of employment. A report to the president on the state of small businesses estimates that nearly 71 percent of future employment is likely to come from small businesses. Besides providing employment, small businesses provide competition and are responsible for change and innovation. Many people mistakenly think of businesses as only large corporations. By recognizing the role and importance of small businesses, you'll approach business courses with a broadened perspective.

- **Importance of Ethical Decisions and Social Responsibility.** There is an increasing emphasis in business on making ethical decisions and demonstrating social responsibility. Business ethics is the application of moral standards to business situations. Ethical issues include fairness and honesty, conflict of interest (between personal and business interests), and communication. Using misleading advertising, falsifying information, taking bribes, and endangering a consumer's health are examples of ethical problems that companies strive to avoid.

SPECIALIZED READING TECHNIQUES

Business courses often require you to read and work with models, case studies, specialized graphics, and supplemental readings. The following sections describe these features and offer strategies for reading each one.

Reading Models

Because business courses focus on organization and management, many texts include models to describe these structures and processes. A model is an overall plan or representation that describes how something is designed, how it functions, or why it occurs.

Models contain general features or characteristics that pertain to many situations. For example, you could construct a model that describes the enrollment/advisement/registration process at your college. It would describe the procedures most students follow from the time they apply for college admission to the time they first attend classes.

Models also may function as explanations of complex processes. For example, you may study models of decision making, information processing, or leadership. These models contain all the pertinent variables, factors, and characteristics that control how something works or explain why it occurs. Diagrams often accompany text descriptions of the model.

The following excerpt shows a model and accompanying introductory explanation taken from a business text. It describes how a company develops short-term financial plans. The remainder of the chapter from which this introduction was taken provides detailed information about the process. The excerpt has been annotated to indicate the types of information to look for as you read models.

Short-Term (Operating) Financial Plans

purpose/function — Short-term (operating) financial plans specify short-term financial actions and the anticipated impact of those actions. These plans most often cover a 1- to

time frame — 2-year period. Key inputs include the sales forecast and various forms of operating and financial data. Key outputs include a number of operating budgets, the cash

key parts — budget, and pro forma [document prepared in advance] financial statements. The entire short-term financial planning process is outlined in the flow diagram of

reference to diagram — Figure 1 (p. 387).

Short-term financial planning begins with the sales forecast. From it production plans are developed that take into account lead (preparation) times and include estimates of the required types and quantities of raw materials. Using the production plans, the firm can estimate direct labor requirements, factory overhead out-

Summary of Model — lays, and operating expenses. Once these estimates have been made, the firm's pro forma income statement and cash budget can be prepared. With the basic inputs— pro forma income statement, cash budget, fixed asset outlay plan, long-term financing plan, and current-period balance sheet—the pro forma balance sheet can finally be developed. Throughout the remainder of this chapter, we will concentrate on the key outputs of the short-term financial planning process: the cash budget, the pro forma income statement, and the pro forma balance sheet.

—Gitman, *Principles of Managerial Finance*, pp. 581–82

Figure 1   The short-term (operating) financial planning process

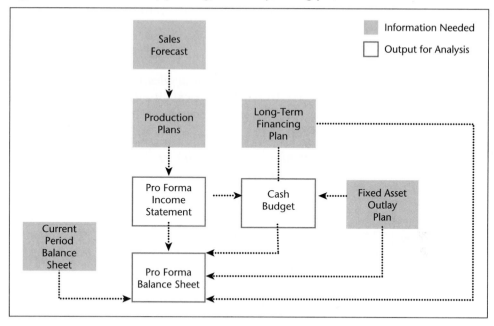

When reading and studying models, be sure to:

1. *Find out what the model represents and why it is considered a model.* In the example above, the model explains the communication process and factors that affect it. You should also know who developed the model and when it was developed. Models often are named after the person who proposed them.

2. *Determine how the model was derived.* Was it developed through study and research (theory), or by observing and working with the actual process (practice)? (In the previous excerpt, the text author does not include information on the development of the model under discussion.)

3. *Discover what, if any, basic assumption the model makes about the subject.* For example, the model in the previous excerpt assumes that all communication is intentional; that is, no information passes between people unless it is intended. Often, the textbook author points out the key assumption.

4. *Analyze the model closely.* Identify each stage or step, and understand the relationship between each part or step. In the previous excerpt, the steps are numbered and the numbering corresponds to text descriptions, making the model easy to follow. If a diagram such as the one shown there is not included, try to draw one.

5. *Summarize the model in your own words, including its key features.* This will test your understanding and strengthen your recall.

6. *Examine the model critically.* Does it account for all aspects or variations of the process? What are its limitations?

7. *Determine the usefulness or application of the model.* How and when can you use it? To what practical situations will it apply? The author may suggest applications, as was done in the previous excerpt, or this task may be left to the reader.

8. *If more than one model is presented for a given process, focus on their similarities and differences.*

<table>
<tr><td>

EXERCISE 13–1

</td><td>

The following excerpt presents a model of group collaboration—the process whereby members of a group work together toward a common goal. Study the model and answer the accompanying questions.

</td></tr>
</table>

CHARACTERISTICS OF GROUP COLLABORATION

Group collaboration has several characteristics. One characteristic is *when* the collaboration takes place and another is *where* it takes place. This section examines these characteristics to provide a basis for understanding workgroup information systems.

Time and Place of Collaboration

Two of the basic characteristics of group collaboration are *time* and *place*—the "when" and "where" of collaboration. Figure 1 (page 389) shows these characteristics in two dimensions. If two or more people collaborate, they may do so at the same time or at different times. To work together at the same time, they could be in a room together or talk by telephone. To collaborate at different times, they could leave voice messages, send faxes, use overnight delivery, or send regular mail.

People may also work together at the same place or at different places. They may be in the same room or building, making it possible for them to have direct contact. Alternatively, they may be at widely separated locations, in which case they cannot have direct contact without extensive travel.

Figure 1 shows four possible combinations of these characteristics. People working at the same time and place can collaborate directly. A face-to-face meeting is an example of this type of collaboration. People working at the same time but in different places often use the telephone for collaboration. Conference calls also are common in this situation. When people work at different times but at the same place, they collaborate by leaving messages, either on the telephone or by paper notes. Putting written messages in mailboxes in staff mail rooms is a common way

Figure 1 Time and place of group collaboration

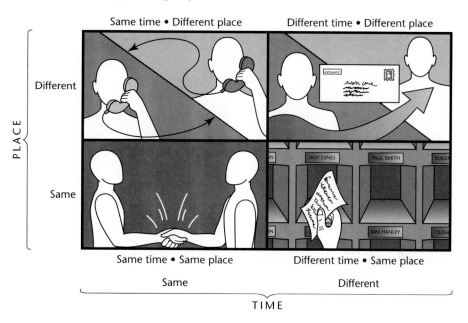

of communicating in this situation. The most complex situation is when people working at different times and places need to collaborate. Voice messages, faxes, overnight deliveries, and regular mail are used in this situation.

Form of Communication

Another way of characterizing group collaboration is by the *form* that the communication between people takes—the "what" of collaboration. Figure 2 (page 390) summarizes some of the forms taken. Perhaps the most often used form of communication in business is *audio communication;* people talk to each other, either in person or on the telephone. Audio communication is not only what is said, but also how it is said. Tone, inflection, and other characteristics of speech often express information. In addition to live, verbal communication, recorded sound is used in group collaboration. Voice mail, taped sound, and other recorded sound are part of audio communication.

A second form of communication in group collaboration is *visual communication,* specifically sights of people or other real things. When groups meet in person, the members of the group can see each other. Their facial expressions and body language give visual clues that provide information about what they are saying and thinking. Recorded sights also are used in some collaborative situations. Still pictures or moving images on video tape may be shown to groups for discussion.

A final form of communication used in group collaboration is *document* (or *data*) *communication.* Documents may contain text, numbers, table, diagrams, graphs, and

Figure 2 Forms of communication in group collaboration

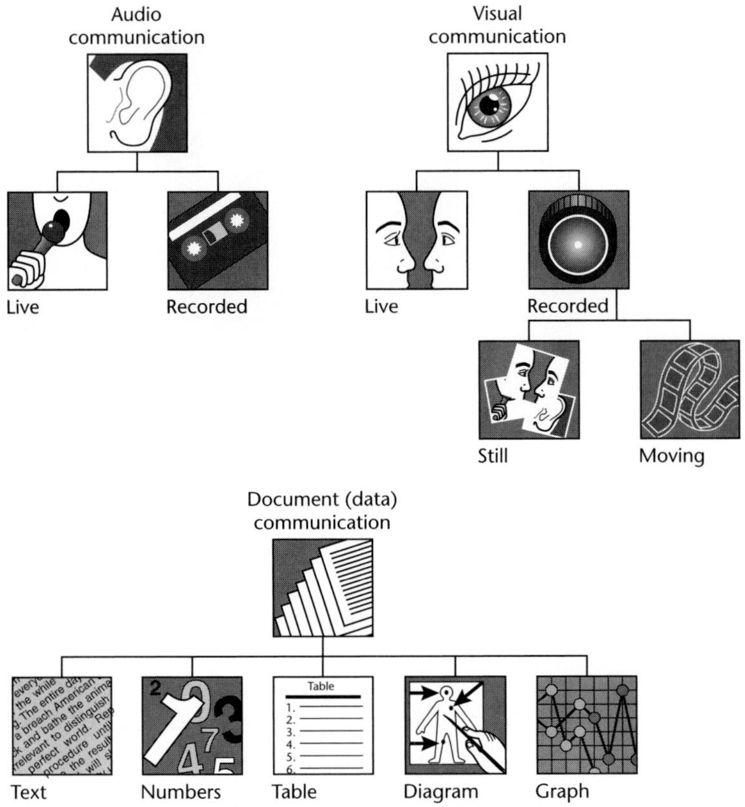

other written representations of information. Examples are a report sent to members of a team, a table of data examined by committee members, a diagram of a design examined by several people, and a graph of data discussed by a group.

—Nickerson, *Business and Information Systems*, pp. 263–65

1. What is the model intended to show?
2. Summarize the process described in the model.
3. Evaluate the model. Does the model account for all possibilities? What are its limitations?
4. Of what practical use is the model? When might you use it?

Reading Case Studies

Case studies often are included in business texts. Case studies are reports of single incidents or evaluations of a particular individual, firm, or transaction. They describe how a particular business is organized or how it manages a particular problem or process. They may be intended to introduce a concept, illustrate a principle, describe a situation, or provoke discussion and evaluation. Case studies also give you insights into and experience with actual problems or situations you may face on the job. In some texts, case studies are referred to as "business profiles" or simply as "cases." Other texts include a short case study, known as a "vignette," that provides a brief insight into a particular problem or issue.

The brief case study that follows appears in a marketing text. As you read it, try to discover why it was included in a chapter titled "Basic Product Concepts." The excerpt has been annotated to indicate the kinds of information presented.

This case study describes how Rollerblade developed a market for in-line skates. The case was included to provide an example of how marketing strategies can increase sales.

When reading a case study, keep the following questions in mind.

1. What is the subject of the case study?

2. What key points does it make about the subject of the chapter?

3. What is the case study intended to demonstrate? For example, does it illustrate practical problems? Discuss limitations? Point out advantages or disadvantages? Demonstrate a process? Describe a management strategy? Demonstrate a particular philosophy or approach?

SKATING TO SUCCESS

background

In-line skates appear to have left traditional roller skates in the dust. Introduced in 1980 by Rollerblade, Incorporated, in-line skates sport wheels lined up in a row rather than two in front and two in back. The product class represents the fastest growing segment of the sporting goods industry according to American Sports Data, Incorporated.

At last count there were 33 direct competitors, in addition to Rollerblade, also producing in-line skates.

subject

Rollerblade faced a far different competitive situation when it introduced the first in-line skates in 1980. In effect, there was no direct competition. In the early 1980s, sales for Rollerblade grew very slowly and were made primarily to ice hockey players and skiers who used the skates for training. In 1986 Rollerblade decided it needed to raise general consumer awareness and build primary demand if sales were to take off. Mary Horwath, the firm's former Director of Promotion, describes the strategies that were implemented to grab attention and create a sport around the skate. The goal, as Horwath describes it, was to get the skate noticed.

marketing strategies

1)

To accomplish the goal, Rollerblade began by plotting ways to get people talking about in-line skates. Skates were given away to anyone deemed high-profile and consistent with the product's desired image of youthful sportiness. Cyclists, skiers,

2)

football players, and even pizza-delivery services fit the bill. <u>Rollerblade also gave skates to rental shops</u> located along <u>trendy</u> Venice Beach in California. Horwath estimates that the resulting publicity was worth the equivalent of $250,000 in advertising.

3)

The firm also worked to <u>establish promotional tie-ins with other companies whose target markets were</u> consistent with <u>Rollerblade's desired customers.</u> Deals were cut with the likes of General Mills (for Golden Grahams cereal), Swatch watches and Pepsi.

4)

The company went on to <u>demonstrate the product any place it felt the target market</u> might congregate. The firm created Team Rollerblade, a group of the world's best professional in-line skate athletes. The team put on demonstrations around the world. Specially equipped vans also took to the streets offering "free trials"—a welcome feature when consumers are being asked to part with as much as $300 for a product they understood little about.

results growth

sales

The results of Rollerblade's efforts were <u>astounding.</u> From 1987 to 1991 the firm experienced a compounded annual growth rate of 135 percent. From an annual sales level of $3 million in 1987 the firm's sales had grown to more than $100 million by 1990 and more than $150 million by 1993. Not surprisingly, Rollerblade had trouble keeping up with demand through these years of growth.

competition

This opened the door for the competition. Despite the influx into the market, Rollerblade continues to prosper. Industry sales are growing at a rate that seems to accommodate all comers.

current status

John Hetterick, President and CEO of Rollerblade, believes that the market is far from saturated. A recent study of U.S. households found that only 7 percent participated in the sport of in-line skating (versus 48 percent for bicycling). Hetterick, however, recognizes that "the business will not support 33 competitors in the long run." In fact, Hetterick was hired by Rollerblade in 1992 to lead the company through what he refers to as the "maturation process" of the industry.

—Kinnear et al., *Principles of Marketing*, p. 278

EXERCISE 13–2

Read the following brief case study taken from a business textbook chapter titled "An Overview of Marketing" and answer the questions that follow.

CAMPBELL SOUP SERVES UP VARIETY

Over 120 years ago, the Campbell Soup Company introduced canned condensed soup and gave the world its first convenience food. Since then, those well-known red and white labels and the sigh "Mmmm, mmmm, good" have become symbols of American culture. However, today's increasingly health-conscious consumers often spurn canned soup in favor of those made with fresh ingredients.

Although sales of the popular brand total $1.1 billion, earning the line 48.9 percent of the canned soup market, Campbell faces declining domestic sales. Turning to global markets, the company's executives hope that by the year 2000, more than half of the firm's profits will come from sales outside the United States.

Experts caution that strong cultural and regional tastes and preferences make food more difficult to translate to foreign markets than soda or laundry detergent. The editor of *Food and Drink Daily* recently stressed the importance of recognizing the unique characteristics of individual global market segments. Just because Americans love to ladle out clam chowder and tomato soup by the bowl full doesn't mean those same flavors appeal to customers around the world. Marketers at Campbell know that demographics, lifestyle, and geography influence customer choices, with diet especially sensitive to local fancies. To avoid potential pitfalls that differences often create, Campbell conducts extensive research in specific consumer segments before generating and marketing brands.

All over the globe, Campbell's research and taste tests are resulting in new, locally pleasing recipes. In Argentina, consumers don't take to the enduring American favorite, chicken noodle soup, but they do like split pea with ham. Emphasizing *Sopa de Campbell's* fresh ingredients, regional ads proclaim it "the real soup." Polish soup lovers, who eat an average of five bowls each week, can choose from eight varieties of Campbell's *zupa,* including *flaki*—tripe soup spiced with lots of pepper. To please Mexican palates, Campbell came up with hot and spicy Cream of Chile Poblano.

To become a major player in the global market. Campbell will face stiff competition. British consumers, for example, have known and preferred Heinz canned soup for many years. To attract more British shoppers, Campbell is creating new products developed specifically to meet English tastes. To expand its Japanese distribution from Tokyo and Osaka to include all of Japan, the soupmaker recently entered a joint venture with Nakano Vinegar Company of Japan.

Is the world ready for Campbell's soup? The company's CEO believes the answer is a resounding yes. His considerable international experience—as a former marketing executive with Colgate-Palmolive in South Africa and with Parke-Davis in Hong Kong—tells him that responding to consumer preferences leads to increased sales.

—Pride et al., *Business,* pp. 386–87

1. What is the purpose of the case study?
2. What is this case study intended to demonstrate about global marketing?
3. What does this study tell you about the problems of global marketing?
4. What motivated the Campbell Soup Company to explore global marketing?
5. What factors influence consumer choice of soups?

Graphics: Reading Organization Charts

Because the focus in the field of business is on organization and process, business texts frequently include graphs, charts, and tables to synthesize and/or summarize text material that describes those structures and processes. Chapter 8 offers general techniques for reading each of these graphic aids.

Particularly common in the field of business is the organization chart. Organization charts often are used to reflect structure or to define relationships; they may, for example, show levels of responsibility, roles, or functions. The chart shown in Figure 13–1 describes the organization of a corporation, emphasizing its financial structure.

Organization charts also may be used to describe group behaviors or define employee responsibilities. The impact of decisions or marketing strategies, and the classification of markets, also may be shown on an organization chart.

When reading organization charts, keep in mind the following tips.

1. *Read the text that accompanies the chart.* It should establish the context and provide details about the chart.

2. *Read the caption or title of the chart.* Note the key, abbreviations, or coding.

3. *Study the chart carefully.* Determine how the chart is organized. Charts often use a vertical or horizontal structure, moving from top to bottom or left to right in diminishing degrees of authority, importance, or responsibility. In Figure 13–1, the chart is organized vertically, with the positions of highest authority at the top.

4. *Decide how the items are related.* In Figure 13–1, each position on the same horizontal line is of equal importance.

5. *Determine what pattern, principle, or concept the chart describes.* Figure 13–1 describes the financial functions within a corporation.

EXERCISE 13–3

Study the organization chart shown in Figure 13–2, and answer the questions that follow.

1. What is the chart intended to show?
2. Describe how the chart is organized and how the items are related.

EXERCISE 13–4

Construct an organization chart that describes the structure of an organization (college, church, club, or business) with which you are familiar.

Figure 13–1   Organization Chart

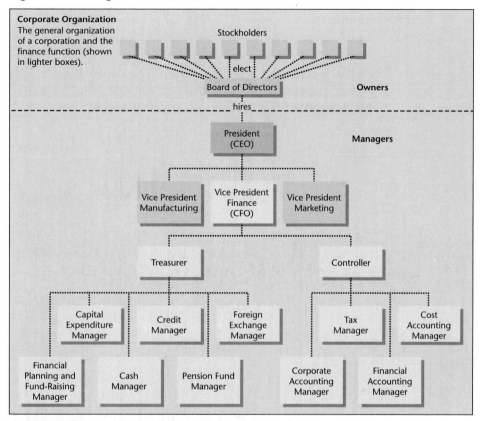

Source: Gitman, *Principles of Managerial Finance,* p. 8

Figure 13–2   Organization Chart

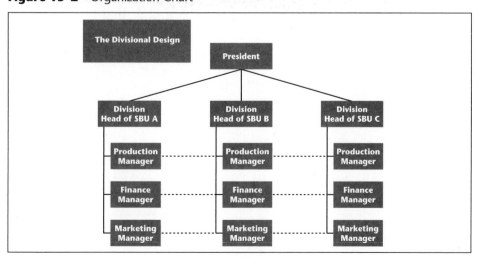

Source: Van Fleet, *Contemporary Management,* p. 251

Graphics: Reading Flowcharts

A flowchart is a specialized diagram that shows how a process or procedure works. Lines or arrows are used to show the direction (route or routes) through the procedure. Various shapes (boxes, circles, rectangles) enclose what is done at each stage or step. You could draw, for example, a flowchart to describe how to apply for and obtain a student loan or how to locate a malfunction in your car's electrical system.

Figure 13–3   Sample Flowchart

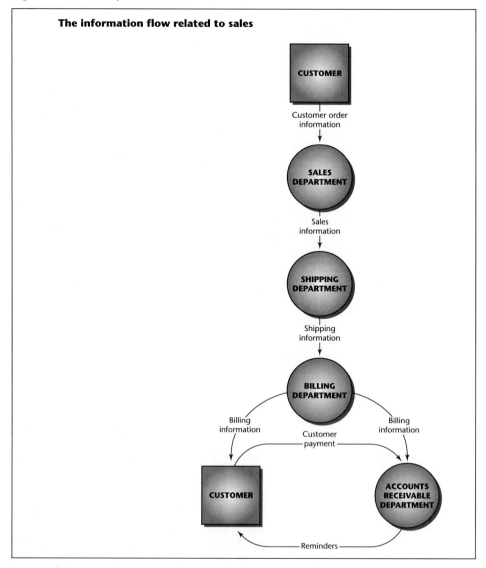

Source: Nickerson, *Business and Information Systems,* p. 40

A sample flowchart, taken from a business law text, is shown in Figure 13–3; it describes the operation of an inventory floating lien—a financial arrangement in which a business uses its assets as collateral on a loan.

To read flowcharts effectively, use the following suggestions:

1. Decide what process the flowchart illustrates. Figure 13–3 shows the process by which information flows from a sale.

2. Next, follow the arrows, and read each step in the chart.

3. When you've finished, summarize the process in your own words. For example, you might write "When a customer places an order, the order information is transmitted to the sales department. The sales department sends sales information to the shipping department—the shipping department sends shipping information to the billing department who sends billing information to the customer and to accounts receivable department. Customer payment is sent to the accounts receivable department, which also sends reminders to customers." Then try to draw the chart from memory without referring to the text. Compare your drawing with the chart, and note any discrepancies.

**EXERCISE
13–5**

The flowchart shown in Figure 13–4, taken from a business text, describes a process for human resource planning. Study the chart and then, without referring to it, list the steps or sketch your own flowchart.

Figure 13–4   Flowchart

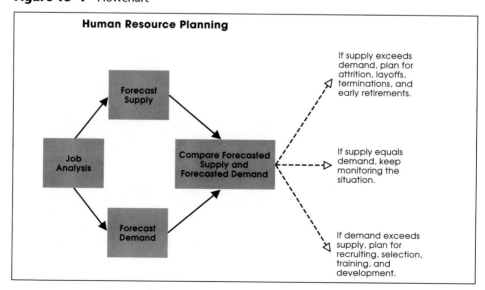

Source: Van Fleet, *Contemporary Management,* p. 270

THOUGHT PATTERNS IN BUSINESS

The three most common thought patterns you will find in business courses are classification, process, and enumeration, although others may be used as well. Refer to Chapter 6 for a complete discussion of these patterns.

Classification—subdividing a topic into its parts—is commonly encountered because it is an effective means of describing the components of management. Process—the study of how events occur—is used frequently because of the focus on *how* a business operates and is managed. Enumeration, or listing, is a commonly used pattern because much information in the business field is descriptive: listings of characteristics, factors, principles, and theories that affect a business's organization and management. A sample page from the table of contents of a business marketing text is shown in Figure 13–5. The figure is marked to indicate the patterns you should anticipate. As you can see, process, enumeration, and classification patterns appear, as well as definition and comparison-contrast.

Figure 13–5 Table of Contents

Chapter 1 Information Systems in Business   3

Basic Information System Concepts   5
    What Is an Information System?   5 ——— *definition*
    Examples of Information Systems   6 — *enumeration*
Bookmark: *Inventory Control at Guess?*   7
    Information System Functions   9
    Data versus Information   10 ——— *comparison—contrast*
Types of Information Systems   12 ——— *classification*
    Individual Information Systems   12
    Workgroup Information Systems   13
    Organizational Information Systems   15
    Interorganizational Information Systems   17
    International Information Systems   18
Bookmark: *International Information System at Timberland*   19
Information System Users   19
    How Users Use Information Systems   20 ——— *process*
    The Ethical Use of Information Systems   20
Connecting Users to Information Technology   21
    Networks   21
    The Internet   21
Benefits of Information Systems   22
    Better Information   22
    Improved Service   23
    Increased Productivity   23
An Approach to the Study of Information Systems   23
Chapter Summary   24

Source: Nickerson, *Business and Information Systems,* p. xvii

ADAPTING YOUR STUDY TECHNIQUES

Because the field of business is diverse and includes courses in a wide range of topics, it is especially important to adapt your study techniques to suit each course you are taking. Here are a few suggestions for handling your course load.

1. *Begin each class by analyzing course content.* Study course objectives, pay close attention to the course syllabus, and analyze your textbook's preface and individual chapter learning objectives for additional clues. Then select reading and study strategies for each course. Decide what types of reading are required and what level of recall is demanded; then identify appropriate reading strategies to use. Refer to Chapter 2 for a discussion of adjusting your reading rate. Also select appropriate learning and review strategies and decide how writing could help you with each course. (Refer to Chapter 6 for a review of various strategies.)

2. *Take time to shift gears.* It is important to "shift gears" as you move from studying one course to studying another. Do this by taking a 10- to 15-minute break between study periods. As you begin working on the next course, spend a minute or two focusing your attention on it. You can do this easily by reviewing a previous assignment, your last set of lecture notes, or the last homework assignment you completed. Finally, preview your current assignment, define your goals, and set a time limit to complete the task. Monitor your comprehension as you work, by using the suggestions in Chapter 1.

3. *Use available text supplements.* Some business texts have accompanying study guides, problem sets, exercise books, or simulations. If they are recommended by your instructor, they will guide you in applying chapter content. These guides also will introduce you to the type of questions you may be asked on exams. Some of these materials are available on computer diskettes as well as in printed form.

4. *Use chapter aids.* Business textbook chapters typically contain numerous features that supplement and enhance basic chapter content. These include learning objectives, lists of key words, chapter outlines, special-interest material, summaries, and review exercises. These features are intended to make the chapter easier to understand, study, and learn. Chapter 7 describes how to use each of these features effectively.

5. *Learn formulas and problem-solving strategies.* Some courses, such as accounting, investment, and finance, rely heavily on learning formulas and solving problems. For reading and study strategies useful in these courses, refer to Chapter 15, "Reading Mathematics."

Test-Taking Tips—Objective Exams

Exams in business are often objective. Refer to the test-taking tips in Chapter 12 for suggestions on preparing for objective exams. When taking exams, keep the following suggestions in mind.

1. *Be sure to arrive at the exam on time.* Sit in the front of the room; you'll avoid distractions and be able to concentrate more easily.

2. *Preread the exam.* Look through the whole exam before beginning. Then plan your time: Decide how much time to spend on each part.

3. *Read the directions carefully.*

4. *Leave nothing blank.* Guess if you are not sure of an answer; circle the question number so you can return to it later if you have time.

5. *Be sure to read all choices before answering a multiple-choice question;* often, the directions require you to select the "best" choice.

6. *If you are uncertain about a multiple-choice item, eliminate obviously wrong choices.* Then analyze those that remain. When two choices seem similar, analyze how they differ.

7. *Express similar or confusing choices in your own words.* Often, this process will help you discover the right answer.

SUMMARY

This chapter describes specialized reading strategies for business. This diverse field focuses on the organization and management of various types of businesses.

Specialized reading techniques involve

- interpreting models
- reading case studies
- understanding graphics (including organization charts and flowcharts) and supplemental readings

Three thought patterns predominate in business texts.

- classification
- process
- enumeration

Strategies for adapting study strategies to suit business courses are offered.

Marketing

PREREADING QUESTIONS

1. What are the functions of modern packages?
2. What must marketers consider when designing and developing packages?

Packaging

Thomas C. Kinnear, Kenneth L. Bernhardt, and Kathleen A. Krentler

1 Marketers have increasingly recognized the importance of packaging. Traditionally a package was perceived as a container, and the emphasis was on the ability of the package to protect the product. Today most marketers recognize that a package is also a presentation and welcome to customers. The promotional aspects of packaging are important because packages can contribute to substantially increased sales.

2 A package has two important functions. First, it must have utility for the consumer and for the intermediaries in the channels of distribution. The package should protect the product, prevent breakage or spoilage, and extend the product's life. It should be convenient for the consumer to use and convenient for intermediaries to ship, store, and stack on a shelf. Resellers prefer packages that help cut shipping costs and reduce shoplifting. The package should also be easily disposable but not contribute to excessive waste.

3 Second, the package should facilitate promotional communication by allowing clear brand identification and promoting a product's features. A good label on the package, together with proper instruction on a product's use, for example, can reduce the amount of personal selling needed to convince the consumer to buy the product. Packaging such as an attractive Christmas box or a distinctive shape can lead to a substantial increase in a product's sales. These features, of course, must be weighed against the negative impact that charges of improper packaging can carry. L'Eggs pantyhose, for example, was successful for years with a distinctive, egg-shaped package. In 1991, however, the firm announced that the plastic L'Eggs egg would be scrapped in favor of a more environmentally friendly cardboard package. A properly designed package can communicate the quality of a product, such as a slip-on box for a high-quality book. Also, there is no question that attractive, innovative packaging can help a marketer obtain additional shelf space for the company's products.

4   Some examples of successful packaging include

- Vitel Mineral Water has distinguished itself from the competition by using a square plastic bottle rather than a round bottle. The company promotes, as a competitive advantage, the fact that its bottle will not roll when laid on its side.
- The success of Procter & Gamble's Pringles Potato Chips is largely attributable to packaging. The round can used for Pringles products protects the chips better than traditional potato chips bags and takes less space on retailers' shelves and in home pantries.
- Numerous producers of motor oil targeted at the do-it-yourself oil changer have switched to packages with convenient build-in spouts for pouring. The spouts make it easier to use the product and have helped increase the number of consumers who change their own oil.
- Many frozen dinner manufacturers have replaced traditional aluminum trays with plastic so the consumer can pop the product, package and all, into the microwave.

Factors in Package Design

5   Several factors must be considered in designing and developing a package. These include environmental and resource considerations, financial and cost factors, governmental regulations, and consumer behavior.

6   **Environmental and resource considerations.** Marketers are under pressure to pay attention to the environmental impact of their packaging. Litter is always an important problem, and there is a growing concern about space for landfills. It has been estimated that packaging materials currently occupy one-third of all landfill space. Environmental and resource considerations have increased the use of recycled paper and recycled beverage containers. Patagonia, Incorporated, has begun producing jackets that contain polyester fiber spun from recycled plastic bottles.

7   **Financial and cost factors.** Out of each dollar a consumer spends, approximately $.10 goes for packaging. In some product categories the figure is much higher. Packaging in the cosmetics industry, for example, accounts for almost 40 percent of the product's cost. A major change in packaging often requires new molds, dyes, and handling equipment, and thus can be very costly. For example, the cylindrical cardboard package used for Pringles potato chips costs almost twice as much as the traditional potato chip package. A marketer must be confident that a more expensive package will increase sales enough to justify the additional cost.

8   **Government regulations.** The U.S. government has been very active in regulating what marketers can and cannot say on packages. As of May 8, 1994, most

food packages sold in the United States must carry a nutritional information label developed by the Food and Drug Administration. Figure 6 (below) illustrates the label and the information it provides. While these new requirements offer a major advancement in information for consumers, in fact the federal government has been regulating packaging for many years. The Federal Fair Packaging and Labeling Act of 1966 contained regulations about information that must be on packages. The Federal Hazardous Substances Act forbids the use of certain types of containers for products dangerous to ingest. The Consumer Products Safety Commission has requirements for packages, the most famous of which is the childproof aspirin bottle. Additionally, in the wake of the incident in the 1980s when Tylenol packages were tampered with, causing consumer deaths, many states have passed tamper-proof requirements for packaging. States have also outlawed certain types of packages such as non-biodegradable packages and no-deposit, no-return beverage containers.

9   **Consumer behavior and marketing strategy factors.** A marketer is always interested in knowing how much a package will help sell the product. This, of course, depends upon consumer behavior. For example, several producers of laundry detergent have introduced highly concentrated products that can be sold in smaller packages. The smaller packages can reduce landfill space occupied by packaging as well as take less space on retailers' shelves and be lighter to carry and easier to use. It remains to be seen, however, how consumers will accept the new, smaller packages. Consumers accustomed to

Figure 6   New U.S. Labeling Requirements

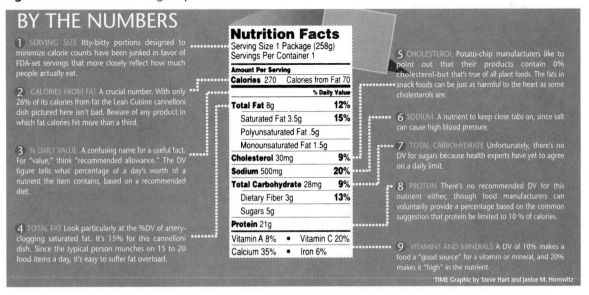

having a certain size package and using a certain amount of detergent per load of laundry may find it difficult to adjust their behavior to the new packaging.

10   Milk producers have encountered difficulties in gaining consumer acceptance of milk packaged in plastic pouches instead of plastic jugs or paper cartons. The pouches are better for the environment, more durable, space-saving, and tamper-evident. Milk in pouches stays fresh longer because of reduced potential for contamination. Despite these advantages, consumers have been slow to accept this new packaging.

11   Consumer response to packaging can differ by country, making it important for global marketers to investigate variations in the markets they serve around the world. For example, more than 90 percent of the tennis balls sold in the United States come three to a can. Japanese consumers, however, prefer a two-pack and Europeans a four pack.

—Kinnear et al., *Principles of Marketing*, pp. 300–03

VOCABULARY REVIEW

1. For each of the words listed below, use context; prefixes, roots, and suffixes; and/or a dictionary to write a brief definition or synonym for the word as it is used in the reading.

    a. aspects (para. 1) _____

    b. utility (para. 2) _____

    c. intermediaries (para. 2) _____

    d. facilitate (para. 3) _____

    e. innovative (para. 3) _____

    f. ingest (para. 8) _____

    g. nonbiodegradable (para. 8)_____

    h. durable (para. 10) _____

    i. global (para. 11)_____

2. Underline new specialized terms introduced in the reading.

COMPREHENSION QUESTIONS

1. The author states that a package must have "utility" for the consumer. Explain what this means.
2. How should a package "facilitate promotional communication"?

3. There are a number of factors in package design. Name and explain one.
4. What does the Federal Hazardous Substances Act forbid?
5. How much of each consumer dollar spent goes for packaging?
6. From a consumer's point of view, what is the advantage of buying milk in pouches as opposed to cartons?
7. Why is it sometimes difficult for manufacturers to sell highly concentrated products in smaller packages?
8. Name two types of packages that have been outlawed in some states.

THINKING CRITICALLY

1. Give an example of a product you feel was packaged with the consumer in mind and tell why.
2. If you were going to package a cosmetic to reduce the cost to the consumer, how would you do it? (That is, what would the package look like?)
3. How do you think packages could be produced in order to be environmentally safe? Give an example of an unsafe package that is already on the market, and explain how you would make it safe.
4. What kinds of products, aside from cosmetics and Pringles, would you expect to have more expensive packaging?
5. If you were the director of the Consumer Products Safety Commission, what one change would you make in product packaging?

LEARNING/STUDY STRATEGY

Draw a chart that summarizes the factors that influence package design. Use the following format.

FACTOR	DESCRIPTION	EXAMPLE
1.		
2.		
3.		
4.		

ON-LINE RESEARCH: PACKAGING*

Marketing is concerned with selling products and services, and how products are packaged is an important aspect of marketing. Visit these sites on the World Wide Web (WWW) that provide more information on packaging and answer the questions that follow.

1. Read the press release "Saga Software Unveils Revolutionary New Packaging for Its Enterprise Integration Product Suite" at http://biz.yahoo.com/bw/991006/va_saga_s0_2.html. Which factors of package design mentioned in the textbook reading does the Saga article refer to? What advantages does the Saga packaging have over more traditional packages?
2. Read the information about "Package Design" at http://www.infousa.com/toolkit/home/text/P03_5100.htm. What products do you use that have a clear, strong graphic identity? What features of the graphic design seem to make the company or its product immediately identifiable?

*If any of these sites is unavailable, use a search engine to locate a new Web site on the same topic.

14 | READING IN THE HUMANITIES AND ARTS

LEARNING OBJECTIVES

■ **To learn specialized reading techniques for literature**
■ **To develop an approach to studying visual arts**
■ **To learn to read and use criticism**
■ **To identify predominant thought patterns**
■ **To adapt your learning skills for the humanities and arts**

The humanities and the arts are areas of knowledge concerned with human thought and ideas and their creative expression in written or visual form. They deal with large, global questions such as, "What is worthwhile in life?" "What is moral?" "What is beautiful?" This chapter will consider two major branches of study: literature and the visual arts.

LITERATURE: A FOCUS ON IDEAS

Literature focuses on the search for reasons, values, and interpretation in all areas of human interest and experience. In literature classes, you will examine numerous literary works and will discuss and write about their value and meaning. Literature courses, then, concentrate on the analysis, subjective evaluation, and interpretation of ideas expressed through literary, philosophical, or artistic works. At first, literature courses may seem easier than other courses because most emphasize interpretation rather than factual recall. However, literature courses are demanding: They require critical reading, analysis, and evaluation.

Why Study Literature?

Literature describes human experience. It is a creative record of the thoughts, feelings, emotions, or experiences of other people. By reading literature, you can learn about yourself and understand both painful and joyful experiences without actually going though them yourself. For example, you can read a poem about the birth of a child and come to understand the range of feelings parents share, even though you may not be a parent. In other words, literature allows you to live vicariously, sharing the lives of others without physical participation.

READING AND ANALYZING LITERATURE

Literature includes poetry, drama, essays, short stories, and novels. Each is a literary form, or *genre,* through which a writer shares his or her view of the world and of humanity. The focus on reading any form of literature is interpretation. Your goal is to discover what the writer means. You are looking for a statement or message the writer is making about an issue, problem, attitude, or feeling. Use the following suggestions to guide your reading of literature.

- *Read slowly and carefully.* Literature uses language in unique ways that require interpretation and reaction. Consequently, you must read carefully and slowly, paying attention to numerous language features that provide clues to meaning. For example, observe word choice, syntax, and the order and arrangement of ideas.
- *Plan on reading the work several times.* Unlike some other types of material, a single reading is *not* sufficient to understand some literary works adequately. During the first reading, try to become familiar with the work and its literal meaning. On the second and subsequent readings, focus on the writer's message, on the significance of the work, and on literary concerns such as the use of language.
- *Ask questions to establish the literal meaning first; then work on interpretation.* In order to interpret and analyze a literary work, first try to understand it on a literal, or factual, level. An effective approach to reading literature is first to establish, "who did what, when, and where." Then ask why the writer wrote the piece and determine the message the writer is conveying.

Who?	Identify the subject or topic.
What is happening?	Describe the basic plot or sequence of events.
When/Where?	Establish the scene, setting, or context (for essays).

Why?	Why did the author write this?
Message?	What is the message the author is conveying and what is its significance?

This approach is shown in the following poem, "Mirror," written by Sylvia Plath.

MIRROR

Sylvia Plath

I am silver and exact. I have no preconceptions.
Whatever I see I swallow immediately
Just as it is, unmisted by love or dislike.
I am not cruel, only truthful—
The eye of a little god, four-cornered.
Most of the time I meditate on the opposite wall.
It is pink, with speckles. I have looked at it so long
I think it is a part of my heart. But it flickers.
Faces and darkness separate us over and over.
Now I am a lake. A woman bends over me,
Searching my reaches for what she really is.
Then she turns to those liars, the candles or the moon.
I see her back, and reflect it faithfully.
She rewards me with tears and an agitation of hands.
I am important to her. She comes and goes.
Each morning it is her face that replaces the darkness.
In me she has drowned a young girl, and in me an old woman
Rises toward her day after day, like a terrible fish.

—*The Collected Poems of Sylvia Plath*, ed. by Ted Hughes

Questions	**Responses**
Who or What?	A mirror
What is happening?	Plath describes what the mirror reflects.
When/Where?	The mirror is hanging on a wall facing another wall.
Why?	Plath is using the mirror to comment on life and peoples' desire to know how they appear to others or to see their true selves.
Message?	The mirror is exact, accurate, and truthful. Life, in contrast, is affected, untruthful, and cruel.

- *Annotate as you read.* To understand the message, jot down your reactions, hunches, insights, feelings, and questions. Mark or underline words, sentences, or sections you feel are important statements, and words and phrases that provide clues to meaning. A sample annotation follows.

MIRROR

Sylvia Plath

I am silver and exact. I have no preconceptions. ——open—clear view
consumes — Whatever I see I swallow immediately
reality — Just as it is, unmisted by love or dislike. —— *unemotional, untainted*
I am not cruel, only truthful—all
The eye of a little god, four-cornered. ——*mirror is godlike—all knowing*
reflecting shows truth whatever it is — Most of the time I meditate on the opposite wall.
It is pink, with speckles. I have looked at it so long
I think it is a part of my heart. But it flickers.
Faces and darkness separate us over and over. *obstacles of life*
deep, reflective — Now I am a lake. A woman bends over me,
Searching my reaches for what she really is. *searching for truth about herself*
Then she turns to those liars, the candles or the moon. ——*deceptive, not faithful*
I see her back, and reflect it faithfully.
not usually thought of as rewards — She rewards me with tears and an agitation of hands.
I am important to her. She comes and goes. *she comes and goes through reality*
Each morning it is her face that replaces the darkness.
inescapable reality of aging — In me she has drowned a young girl, and in me an old woman *mirror holds the past*
Rises toward her day after day, like a terrible fish.

- *Identify themes and patterns.* After you have read and annotated, the next step is to study your annotations, looking for themes and patterns. Try to discover how ideas work together to suggest themes. Themes are large or universal topics or subjects that are important to nearly everyone. A study of the Plath poem and annotations indicates that her theme is the realities of life. Possible themes in literature are

  - Questions, issues, problems raised by the story: moral, political, philosophical, religious
  - Abstract ideas: love, death, heroism, escapism, honor
  - Conflicts: appearance versus reality, freedom versus restraint, poverty versus wealth, men against women, humans against society, humans versus nature
  - Common literary topics: self-realization, inescapability of death, fall from innocence, search for the meaning of life

EXERCISE 14–1

Refer to the multilevel thinking skills discussed in Chapter 1 and predict exam questions that might be asked about the Plath poem. Compare your questions with those of another student.

Understanding the Language of Literature

Literature is unique in its extensive use of descriptive, connotative, and figurative language to express images, attitudes, and feelings. In order to succeed in your literature courses, you need to be able to use and understand the specialized vocabulary of literary works.

Descriptive Language Writers often use words that create sensory impressions or responses. They are intended to help the reader re-create mentally what the author is describing. For example, in describing a stormy night, a poet may write, "Under the thunder-dark clouds, the storm mounts, flashes, and resounds." These terms give you a feeling about the storm and help you imagine its strength. Instead of saying two characters looked at each other, a novelist may write, "their eyes locked momentarily in a gaze, reflecting the strength of their opposing wills." Now, read the following paragraph. Note, in particular, the underlined words.

> Old men, old women, almost 20 million of them. They constitute 10 percent of the total population, and the percentage is steadily growing. Some of them, like <u>conspirators,</u> walk all <u>bent over, as if hiding some precious secret, filled with self-protection.</u> The body seems to gather itself around those vital parts, <u>folding shoulders,</u> arms, <u>pelvis like a fading rose.</u> Watch and you see how <u>fragile</u> old people come to think they are.
>
> —Curtin, "Aging in the Land of the Young," *Nobody Ever Died of Old Age*

Connotative Language The connotations of a word are the meanings it commonly suggests or implies beyond its primary, denotative meaning. Thus the word *dinner* denotes an evening meal but connotes a time of conversation, friendship, and interaction. The word *father* means "male parent" but often connotes a person who guides and directs. A connotative meaning may carry either a positive or a negative impression. For example, all of the following words mean an assembled group of people, but they have very different connotations.

crowd, congregation, mob, gang, audience, class

Read the following paragraph, which is taken from Martin Luther King, Jr.'s "Letter from Birmingham Jail." He wrote it after being jailed for leading a civil rights demonstration.

We have waited for more than 340 years for our constitutional and God-given rights. The nations of Asia and Africa are moving with <u>jetlike</u> speed toward gaining political independence, but we still <u>creep</u> at <u>horse-and-buggy pace</u> toward gaining a cup of coffee at a lunch counter. I guess it is easy for those who have never felt the <u>stinging darts of segregation</u> to say, "Wait." But when you have seen <u>vicious mobs lynch</u> your mothers and fathers at will and drown your sisters and brothers at whim; when you have seen <u>hate-filled</u> policemen <u>curse, kick,</u> and even kill your black brothers and sisters; when you see the vast majority of your 20 million Negro brothers <u>smothering</u> in an airtight <u>cage of poverty</u> in the midst of an affluent society; when you suddenly find your tongue twisted and your speech <u>stammering</u> as you seek to explain to your six-year-old daughter why she can't go to the public amusement park that has just been advertised on television, and see tears <u>welling up</u> in her eyes when she is told that Funtown is closed to colored children, and see <u>ominous clouds of inferiority</u> beginning to form in her little mental sky, and see her beginning to distort her personality by developing an unconscious bitterness toward white people.... then you will understand why we find it difficult to wait.

—King, "Letter from Birmingham Jail," *Why We Can't Wait*, p. 363

The underlined words reveal King's feeling toward segregation and discrimination. For example, notice that King uses the phrase "vicious mobs lynch" rather than "groups of people kill" and "hate-filled policemen curse, kick," instead of "policemen shout and strike." These choices of words are deliberate. King hopes to create an emotional response among his readers.

Figurative Language Figurative language is a way of describing something that makes sense on an imaginative level but not on a literal or factual level. Many common expressions are figurative:

The exam was a piece of cake.

Sam eats like a horse.

He walks like a gazelle.

In each of these expressions, two unlike objects are compared on the basis of some quality they have in common. Take, for example, Hamlet's statement "I will speak daggers to her, but use none." Here the poet is comparing the features of daggers (sharp, pointed, dangerous, harmful) with something that can be used like daggers—words.

Figurative language is striking, often surprising, even shocking. This reaction is created by the unlikeness of the two objects being compared. To find the similarity and understand the figurative expression, focus on connotative meanings rather than literal meanings. For example, in reading the lines:

> A sea
> Harsher than granite

from an Ezra Pound poem, you must think not only of rock or stone but also of the characteristics of granite: hardness, toughness, impermeability. Then you can see that the lines mean that the sea is rough and resistant. Figurative words, which are also called figures of speech, are used to communicate and emphasize relationships that cannot be communicated through literal meaning. For example, the statement by Jonathan Swift, "She wears her clothes as if they were thrown on by a pitchfork," creates a stronger image and conveys a more meaningful description than saying "She dresses sloppily."

The three most common types of figurative expressions are similes, metaphors, and symbols. Similes make the comparison explicit by using the word *like* or *as*. Metaphors, on the other hand, directly equate the two objects. Here are several examples of each.

SIMILES

We lie back to back.
Curtains lift and fall,
like the chest of someone sleeping.

—Kenyon

Life, like a dome of many-colored glass,
stains the white radiance of Eternity.

—Shelley

METAPHORS

My Life has stood—a Loaded Gun—
In Corners—till a Day
The Owner passed—identified—
And carried Me away—

—Emily Dickinson

. . . his hair lengthened into sunbeams . . .

—Gustave Flaubert

EXERCISE 14–2

Working with a group of classmates, make a list of figurative expressions you use in everyday speech.

EXERCISE 14–3

Explain the meaning of each of the following figures of speech. Several interpretations are possible.

Shall I compare thee to a summer's day?
Thou art more lovely and more temperate.

—Shakespeare

In plucking the fruit of memory,
one runs the risk of spoiling its bloom.

—Joseph Conrad

The scarlet of the maples can shake me like a cry
Of bugles going by.

—Carman

THE EAGLE

He clasps the crag with crooked hands;
Close to the sun in lonely lands,
Ringed with the azure world, he stands.

The wrinkled sea beneath him crawls;
He watches from his mountain walls,
And like a thunderbolt he falls.

—Tennyson

Symbols also make a comparison, but only one term of the comparison is stated. A symbol suggests more than its literal meaning. In fact, sometimes more than one meaning is suggested. In your everyday life, a flag is a symbol of patriotism; a four-leaf clover stands for good luck. A writer may describe a character dressed in white to symbolize her innocence and purity, but the words *innocence* and *purity* will not be mentioned. It is left to the reader to recognize the symbol and to make the comparison.

Symbols often are crucial to the writer's theme or essential meaning. For example, Hemingway's short story "A Clean, Well-lighted Place" describes an aging man who visits a café. In this story, the café symbolizes an escape from loneliness, old age, and death. Hemingway's theme is the inevitability and inescapability of aging and death; the café closes, and the man's escape is short-lived. Melville's novel *Moby Dick* is the story of a white whale given the name Moby Dick. But the novel is about much more than an aquatic mammal; the whale takes on numerous meanings. The novel's characters imply he is the devil. Later, the whale seems to represent the forces of nature or the created universe.

Symbols, then, are usually objects—concrete items, not abstract feelings such as pity or hate. To recognize symbols, look for objects given a particular or unusual emphasis. The object may be mentioned often, or it may even be suggested in the title. The story or poem may open and/or close with reference to the object. Objects that suggest more than one meaning are possible symbols. Perhaps the best way to identify symbols is to look for objects that point to the author's theme.

EXERCISE 14–4	*Reread Sylvia Plath's poem "Mirror" on page 409. Is the mirror a symbol? If so, what does it symbolize?*

EXERCISE 14–5	*Read the following poem by Langston Hughes and answer the questions that follow.*

THE NEGRO SPEAKS OF RIVERS
Langston Hughes

I've known rivers:
I've known rivers ancient as the world and older than the flow of human blood in human veins.

My soul has grown deep like the rivers.

I bathed in the Euphrates when dawns were young.
I built my hut near the Congo and it lulled me to sleep.
I looked upon the Nile and raised the pyramids above it.
I heard the singing of the Mississippi when Abe Lincoln went down to New Orleans, and I've seen its muddy bosom turn all golden in the sunset.

I've known rivers:
Ancient, dusky rivers.

My soul has grown deep like the rivers.

—Hughes, *Selected Poems*

1. What does the river symbolize?
2. Explain any metaphors or similes the poem contains.

Reading and Analyzing Poetry

Poetry is a form of expression in which ideas are presented in a unique format. Poems are written in verse-lines and stanzas rather than paragraphs. Often, poetry requires more reading time and greater concentration than other types of material. In reading prose, you could skip a word in a paragraph and your comprehension of the whole paragraph would not suffer; poetry, however, is very compact and precise. Each word is important and carries a special meaning. You have to pay attention to each word—its sound, its meaning, and its meaning when combined with other words. Here are a few guidelines to help you approach poetry more effectively.

1. *Read the poem once straight through, without any defined purpose.* Be open-minded, experiencing the poem as it is written. If you meet an unknown word or confusing reference, keep reading.

2. *Use punctuation to guide your comprehension.* Although poetry is written in lines, do not expect each line to make sense by itself. Meaning often flows on from line to line, eventually forming a sentence. Use the punctuation to guide you, as you do in reading paragraphs. If there is no punctuation at the end of the line, consider it as a slight pause, with an emphasis on the last word.

3. *Read the poem a second time.* Identify and correct any difficulties, such as an unknown word.

4. *Notice the action. Who* is doing *what, when,* and *where?*

5. *Analyze the poem's intent.* Decide what it was written to accomplish. Does it describe a feeling or a person, express a memory, present an argument?

6. *Determine who is speaking.* Poems often refer to an unidentified "I" or "we." Try to describe the speaker's viewpoint or feelings.

7. *Establish the speaker's tone.* Is the author serious, challenging, saddened, frustrated? Read aloud; your intonation, your emphasis on certain words, and the rise and fall of your voice may provide clues. You may "hear" a poet's anger, despondency, or elation.

8. *Identify to whom the poem is addressed.* Is it written to a person, to the reader, to an object? Consider the possibility that the poet may be writing to work out a problem or as an emotional outlet.

9. *Reread difficult or confusing sections.* Read them aloud several times. Copying these sections word for word may be helpful. Look up unfamiliar words.

10. *Check unfamiliar references.* A poet may refer to people, objects, or events outside of the poem. These are known as *allusions.* Often, the allusion is important to the overall meaning of the poem. When you see Oedipus mentioned in a poem, you'll need to find out who he was. Paperback books on mythology and literary figures are a good investment.

11. *Analyze the language of the poem.* Consider connotative meanings and study figures of speech.

12. *Look for the poet's meaning or the poem's theme.* Paraphrase the poem; express it in your own words and connect it to your own experience. Then put all the ideas together to discover its overall meaning. Ask yourself, "What is the poet trying to tell me?" "What is the message?"

Now read the poem "Dream Deferred," by Langston Hughes, applying the preceding guidelines.

DREAM DEFERRED
Langston Hughes

What happens to a dream deferred?

Does it dry up
like a raisin in the sun?
Or fester like a sore—
And then run?
Does it stink like rotten meat?
Or crust and sugar over—
like a syrupy sweet?
Maybe it just sags.
like a heavy load.

Or does it explode?

—Hughes, *The Panther and the Lash: Poems for Our Times*

One key to understanding the poem is the meaning of the word *deferred*. Here, it means put off or postponed. A dream deferred, then, refers to unfulfilled or postponed hopes. A poet questions what happens to a dream that is deferred and offers six alternatives. Note the connotative meanings of the first four choices: "dry up," "fester, "stink," "crust and sugar over." Each of these suggests some type of decay. The term sags suggests heaviness and inaction. The last alternative, "explode," is active: posing a threat and implying danger. The poet's purpose is to explore the negative consequences of unfulfilled hopes and to suggest that violent outcomes may result.

EXERCISE 14–6

Read the following poem by Emily Dickinson, and use the guidelines for analyzing poetry to help you answer the questions below.

BECAUSE I COULD NOT STOP FOR DEATH
Emily Dickinson

Because I could not stop for Death—
He kindly stopped for me—

The Carriage held but just Ourselves—
And Immortality.

We slowly drove—He knew no haste
And I had put away
My labor and my leisure too,
For His Civility—

We passed the School, where Children strove
At Recess—in the Ring—
We passed the Fields of Gazing Grain—
We passed the Setting Sun—

Or rather—He passed Us—
The Dews drew quivering and chill—
For only Gossamer,[1] my Gown—
My Tippet[2]—only Tulle—

We paused before a House that seemed
A Swelling of the Ground—
The Roof was Scarcely visible—
The Cornice[3]—in the Ground

Since then—'tis Centuries—and yet
Feels shorter than the Day
I first surmised the Horses' Heads
Were toward Eternity—

—The Poems of Emily Dickinson, ed. by Thomas H. Johnson

[1] A light, thin cloth
[2] Cape
[3] Section beneath roof

1. Summarize the literal action in the poem. Your summary should include answers to the questions given earlier in this chapter (who, what, where, when, and why).
2. Annotate the poem by marking words and phrases that describe death or the poet's attitude toward it.
3. What message is the author communicating about death?

Reading and Analyzing Short Stories and Novels

A short story is a brief work of prose narrative with an organized plot. It differs from the novel not only in length but also in magnitude: the size and proportion of the story, its scope, its impact, and its effects. A short story may discuss one event that shaped a person's life, whereas a novel describes the numerous actions that contribute to a character's development. However, both the short story and the novel share basic features.

Plot   The plot is the basic storyline—the sequence of events as they occur in the work. The plot, however, also consists of the actions through which the work's meaning is expressed. The plot is a story of conflict and often follows a predictable structure. Frequently, the plot begins by setting the scene, introducing the main characters, and providing background information needed to follow the story. Often, there is a complication or problem that arises. Suspense is built as the problem or conflict unfolds. Near the end of the story, events come to a climax: the point at which the outcome of the conflict will be decided. A conclusion quickly follows as the story ends.

Characterization   Characters are the actors in a narrative story. The characters reveal themselves by what they say—the dialog—and by their actions, appearance, thoughts, and feelings. The narrator, or person who tells the story, also may comment on or reveal information about the characters. Sometimes, the narrator is not the author, in which case you need to consider his or her characterization as well. As a critical reader, you need to analyze the characters' traits and motives, analyze their personalities, study their interaction, and examine character changes.

Setting   The setting is the time, place, and circumstances in which the action occurs. The setting provides a framework in which the actions occur and establishes an atmosphere in which the characters interact.

Point of View   The point of view is the way the story is presented or from whose perspective or outlook the story is told. Often, the author of a story is not the narrator. The story may be told from the perspective of a narrator who is not one of the characters or by one of the characters themselves. In analyzing the point of view, determine the narrator's role and function. Is the narrator accurate and knowledgeable (even all-knowing), or is his or her view limited or restricted? Sometimes the narrator is able to enter the minds of some or all of the characters, knowing their thoughts and understanding their actions and motivations. Other times, a narrator may be naive or innocent, unable to understand the actions or implications of the story.

Tone   The tone of a story suggests the author's attitude. Like tone of voice, tone in a story suggests feelings. Many ingredients contribute to tone, including the author's choice of details, characters, events, and situations. The tone of a story may be amusing, angry, or contemptuous. The author's feelings are not necessarily those of the characters or of the narrator. Instead, it is through the characters' actions and the narrator's description of them that we infer tone. The style in which a work is written often suggests the tone. Style means the way a writer writes, especially his or her use of language.

Theme The theme of the story is the main point or message it conveys through all of the above elements. It is an insight into life revealed by the story. Themes are often large, universal ideas: life and death, human values, or human existence. To establish the theme, ask yourself, "What is the author trying to say about life by telling the story?" Try to explain it in a single sentence. If you are having difficulty stating the theme, try the following suggestions.

1. *Study the title.* Now that you have read the story, does it take on any new meanings?

2. *Analyze the main character.* Does he or she change? If so, how, and in reaction to what?

3. *Look for broad, general statements that a character or the narrator makes about life or the problems the characters face.*

4. *Look for symbols, figurative expressions, and meaningful names* (for example, Mrs. Goodheart), or objects that hint at bigger ideas.

Read "The Story of an Hour" by Kate Chopin, paying particular attention to each of the above features.

THE STORY OF AN HOUR
Kate Chopin

Knowing that Mrs. Mallard was afflicted with heart trouble, great care was taken to break to her as gently as possible the news of her husband's death.

It was her sister Josephine who told her, in broken sentences; veiled hints that revealed in half concealing. Her husband's friend Richards was there, too, near her. It was he who had been in the newspaper office when intelligence of the railroad disaster was received, with Brently Mallard's name leading the list of "killed." He had only taken the time to assure himself of its truth by a second telegram, and had hastened to forestall any less careful, less tender friend in bearing the sad message.

She did not hear the story as many women have heard the same, with a paralyzed inability to accept its significance. She wept at once, with sudden, wild abandonment, in her sister's arms. When the storm of grief had spent itself she went away to her room alone. She would have no one follow her.

There stood, facing the open window, a comfortable, roomy armchair. Into this she sank, pressed down by a physical exhaustion that haunted her body and seemed to reach into her soul.

She could see in the open square before her house the tops of trees that were all aquiver with the new spring life. The delicious breath of rain was in the air. In the street below a peddler was crying his wares. The notes of a distant song which someone was singing reached her faintly, and countless sparrows were twittering in the eaves.

There were patches of blue sky showing here and there through the clouds that had met and piled one above the other in the west facing her window.

She sat with her head thrown back upon the cushion of the chair, quite motionless, except when a sob came up into her throat and shook her, as a child who has cried itself to sleep continues to sob in its dreams.

She was young, with a fair, calm face, whose lines bespoke repression and even a certain strength. But now there was a dull stare in her eyes, whose gaze was fixed away off yonder on one of those patches of blue sky. It was not a glance of reflection, but rather indicated a suspension of intelligent thought.

There was something coming to her and she was waiting for it, fearfully. What was it? She did not know; it was too subtle and elusive to name. But she felt it, creeping out of the sky, reaching toward her through the sounds, the scents, the color that filled the air.

Now her bosom rose and fell tumultuously. She was beginning to recognize this thing that was approaching to possess her, and she was striving to beat it back with her will—as powerless as her two white slender hands would have been.

When she abandoned herself a little whispered word escaped her slightly parted lips. She said it over and over under her breath: "free, free, free!" The vacant stare and the look of terror that had followed it went from her eyes. They stayed keen and bright. Her pulses beat fast, and the coursing blood warmed and relaxed every inch of her body.

She did not stop to ask if it were or were not a monstrous joy that held her. A clear and exalted perception enabled her to dismiss the suggestion as trivial.

She knew that she would weep again when she saw the kind, tender hands folded in death; the face that had never looked save with love upon her, fixed and gray and dead. But she saw beyond that bitter moment a long procession of years to come that would belong to her absolutely. And she opened and spread her arms out to them in welcome.

There would be no one to live for her during those coming years; she would live for herself. There would be no powerful will bending hers in that blind persistence with which men and women believe they have a right to impose a private will upon a fellow-creature. A kind intention or a cruel intention made the act seem no less a crime as she looked upon it in that brief moment of illumination.

And yet she had loved him—sometimes. Often she had not. What did it matter! What could love, the unresolved mystery, count for in face of this possession of self-assertion which she suddenly recognized as the strongest impulse of her being!

"Free! Body and soul free!" she kept whispering.

Josephine was kneeling before the closed door with her lips to the keyhole, imploring for admission. "Louise, open the door! I beg; open the door—you will make yourself ill. What are you doing, Louise? For heaven's sake open the door."

"Go away. I am not making myself ill." No; she was drinking in a very elixir of life through that open window.

Her fancy was running riot along those days ahead of her. Spring days, and summer days, and all sorts of days that would be her own. She breathed a quick prayer that life might be long. It was only yesterday she had thought with a shudder that life might be long.

She arose at length and opened the door to her sister's importunities. There was a feverish triumph in her eyes, and she carried herself unwittingly like a goddess of Victory. She clasped her sister's waist, and together they descended the stairs. Richards stood waiting for them at the bottom.

Someone was opening the front door with a latchkey. It was Brently Mallard who entered, a little travel-stained, composedly carrying his grip-sack and umbrella. He had been far from the scene of accident, and did not even know there had been one. He stood amazed at Josephine's piercing cry; at Richards' quick motion to screen him from the view of his wife.

But Richards was too late.

When the doctors came they said she had died of heart disease—of joy that kills.

—Chopin, *The Awakening: Selected Stories of Kate Chopin*

The plot of this short story involves a surprise ending: Mrs. Mallard learns that her husband, who she thought had been killed in a railroad disaster, is alive. She ponders his death and relishes the freedom it will bring. Upon discovering that her husband is not dead, Mrs. Mallard suffers a heart attack and dies. The key character is Mrs. Mallard; her thoughts and actions after learning of her husband's supposed death are the crux of the story. The setting is one hour in a time near the present in the Mallards' home. The story is told by a third-person narrator who is knowledgeable and understands the characters' actions and motives. In the story's last line, the narrator tells us that doctors assumed Mrs. Mallard died of "the joy that kills."

EXERCISE 14–7

Answer the following questions about Chopin's "The Story of an Hour."

1. When did you first realize that Mrs. Mallard's reaction to her husband's death would be unusual? Underline words and phrases that led you to suspect her response would be unusual.

2. Explain the meaning of the phrase "the joy that kills."

3. What do Mrs. Mallard's response to the news of her husband's death and the surprise ending suggest about life and death and the nature of true happiness?

THE VISUAL ARTS: EXPRESSION WITHOUT WORDS

A work of art, such as a painting or a sculpture is the visual expression of an idea. The idea is expressed using a medium—a material such as canvas, clay, fiber, stone or paint. In a poem, the medium is words; in a sculpture, the medium may be marble. The medium is the vehicle through which the idea is expressed.

Why Study Art?

Many people study art because it is beautiful and they enjoy it. Art can arouse emotions and feelings, stimulate our imaginations, and help us think in new ways. It can enrich our lives. Besides enjoyment and enrichment, art also can be a form of communication. By studying the stained glass window in a cathedral, for example, you can learn how, during the Middle Ages, religion was taught to an illiterate population. Art may also have a spiritual (religious) value. Cave drawings may have been used by pre-historic humans to depict animals they valued for food or to magically exert control over them. Finally, art may have a functional value. Some works of art were useful in daily life. Intricately dyed or carved rawhide may have been used to transport personal goods, for instance. By studying works of art, we can learn about a society's religious beliefs and daily living habits.

How to Study Art

To study art, you have to think visually. Use the following suggestions to develop your visual thinking skills. As you read through this section, refer to a photograph taken by Dorothea Lange, *Migrant Mother, Nipomo, California,* 1936 shown on page 424.

See As Well As Look   Looking means taking in what is before you in a physical, mechanical way. Your eyes focus on visual images. Seeing is a more active, mental as well as physical process. It may require conscious effort. The distinction between looking and seeing is similar to that between hearing and listening. When you hear, you take in sound. When you listen, you understand meaning and grasp the speaker's message. When you see a work of art, you take away some meaning or under-standing. What do you *see* in Lange's photograph?

Dorothea Lange, Migrant Mother,
Nipomo, California, 1936.
Source: Courtesy of the Dorothea Lange
Collection © 1982. The Oakland Museum,
The City of Oakland, California.

Identify the Subject Matter   Decide who or what the work of art depicts or describes. For example, Michelangelo's "The Creation of Adam" describes, as its title suggests, the biblical creation of the first human. An Inuit stone carving may depict an animal valued by Inuit tribes, such as an eagle or bear. In Lange's photograph, the subject is a mother and her children.

Consider the Title   The title often offers clues that will help you construct an interpretation of the work. You should be aware that not all titles were given to the work by the original artist. The title of Lange's photograph is very revealing. We learn that the woman is a migrant worker and can infer that the children are her children. We also learn that the photograph was taken in California and can infer that the woman was a migrant worker there.

Study the Visual Elements   When you look at a painting the first time, you may notice only a face, or when you study a sculpture, you may notice only its shape. Broaden your study to include the common visual elements. They are line, shape, mass, time, motion, light, color, and texture. Not every element exists within every work of art, but some are important in each.

These elements, sometimes referred to as the form, contribute to the meaning. Small details are important. For example, the grain of marble in a sculpture or the kinds of brush strokes in a painting are meaningful. A painting with deep heavy, sharply angular lines creates a different impression from one with softly flowing lines.

In Lange's photograph, light seems to be shining on the woman's face and hand. You see harsh, strong lines in her face. Her arm is angular, not graceful. The children seem less sharp.

Write Your Reactions   As you study a work of art, jot down your responses. Write questions, initial reactions, your emotions, and so forth. Don't worry about the order of your ideas or about expressing them in grammatically correct sentences. Just record your impressions. Together, these may help you develop an interpretation of the work. While studying Lange's photograph, one student wrote the following:

- The photo is disturbing—not pleasing
- The children's faces are hidden—are they ashamed? or perhaps crying? or afraid?
- The woman seems worried. Her hand is at her mouth
- The children seem highly dependent on her; they seem emotionally close
- The woman seems to be thinking, but there is no action or movement in the photograph
- The family seems poor and disheveled
- The mother seems in control
- Are they homeless?

Analyze the Work   Analyzing means dividing something into parts in order to understand it. If you are looking at a statue, for instance, you might examine the pose, size, facial expression, medium, gestures, clothing, and so forth. In Lange's photograph, you might first analyze the woman and then the children. Or you might analyze how each is holding his or her body and then how each is dressed. In Lange's photograph, the woman's facial expression is particularly striking.

Consider the Meaning of the Work   An interpretation is a description of a meaning of the work. Many art historians believe that a work of art can have more than one meaning. One meaning is the meaning that it had for the artist; another is the meaning it had for the first people who looked at it. Still another is the meaning it offers to us today. Other art historians argue that a work has no meaning in itself; its only meaning is that given to it by those who view it.

Charles White.
PREACHER, *1952.*

Source: Collection of Whitney Museum of American Art, Purchase 52.25. Photograph © 2000. Whitney Museum of American Art, New York.

For Lange's photograph, one meaning that the photograph seems to be depicting is the plight of migrant workers, thus suggesting sympathy. Another meaning may be drawn from the similarity of the pose of the woman and her children to traditional paintings of the Madonna and child, perhaps suggesting that the migrant woman is a universal mother figure. Many women share her worry and concern about their place in life.

EXERCISE 14–8

Study the work of art shown above and answer the questions that follow.

1. Describe the subject.
2. Identify striking visual elements. For example, consider the size and balance of the preacher's body parts. Consider, too, the background.
3. Write your reactions.
4. Describe the meaning of the work.

READING CRITICISM

Criticism discusses, interprets, and evaluates a particular work. Some students erroneously assume that criticism is only negative, or limited to finding fault with a work. Actually, its primary purpose is to analyze and interpret; it may include both positive and negative aspects. Film and book reviews are examples of criticism. Criticism also includes scholarly works that carefully research or closely examine a particular aspect, theme, or approach in literature or art. Often, in order to complete a term paper, you will be required to consult several critical sources. Other times, to understand a work better, you may decide to read several interpretations by critical authorities.

Following is a brief excerpt from a critical work discussing Emily Dickinson's poem "Because I Could Not Stop for Death," which appears on page 417 in this chapter. Read the excerpt, and note that it offers an interpretation of the poem's meaning: The poet fears life and escapes this fear through a journey to death.

> Naive, blank-faced, repelling thought and emotion, the speaker permits herself to be transported to worlds unknown. The first step is easy. The gentleman-caller she calls Death is kindly, civil. The threesome is cozy, he does what she cannot do, the unexamined space of the carriage arouses no anxiety in her, the journey is a leisured one.... She has all the time in the world, and in other worlds besides. Remarking on the presence of a third figure, Immortality, she cannot stop to ask herself what this barely personified abstraction, the shard of a disintegrated religious tradition, signifies. Wholly engrossed as she is by her deceptive double, she cannot afford to question whether beneath the smooth, seductive surface his intentions are equally decorous. What she has done is to yield herself up to the power of a dominant obsession. What this obsession is we do not know absolutely. The poem invokes a reason only to dismiss it: "Because I could not ... He." Thus, although the idea of suicide is implicit in its denial, so too is the idea of controlling this death-wish by displacing it onto another character who is initially capable of masking the deception motif the poem is designed to reveal. In limited terms, perhaps this obsession may be described as the compulsion to repress the anxiety that the circumstances of her life have aroused in her. In its broadest terms, perhaps this obsession may be described as her fear of mortality itself.
>
> —Pollak, *Dickinson: The Anxiety of Gender*, p. 191

In using critical sources, follow these guidelines.

1. *Read the original work carefully and thoroughly before you consult critical sources.*

2. *Make a preliminary interpretation of the work before reading criticism.* Decide what *you* think the work means and why it was produced. Record these ideas in note form. If you consult sources before forming your own impressions, your judgment will be colored by what you read and you will have difficulty separating your ideas from those you encounter as you read.

3. Recognize that not all critics agree; you may encounter three critics who present three different interpretations of Shakespeare's *Hamlet or* Renoir's *The Luncheon of the Boating Party*.

4. Make certain that the interpretations you read are substantiated with references to the original work.

5. Although it is perfectly acceptable to revise your own interpretations on the basis of your reading, do not discard your own interpretation as soon as you encounter one that differs. Look to the original work to develop support for your interpretations.

6. Make notes on your readings, recording only key points.

To locate criticism on a particular literary or artistic work, consult one of several reference sources.

The Reader's Guide to Periodical Literature

Essay and General Literature Index

The MLA Bibliography

In many libraries, computerized versions are available.

EXERCISE 14–9

The following excerpt provides another critical interpretation of Dickinson's poem "Because I Could Not Stop for Death." *Read the excerpt, and answer the questions that follow.*

At first reading, the orthodox reassurance against the fear of death appears to be invoked, though with the novelty of a suitor replacing the traditional angel, by emphasizing his compassionate mission in taking her out of the woes of this world into the bliss of the next. 'Death,' usually rude, sudden, and impersonal, has been transformed into a kindly and leisurely gentleman. Although she was aware this is a last ride, since his 'Carriage' can only be a hearse, its terror is subdued by the 'Civility' of the driver who is merely serving the end of 'Immortality.' The loneliness of the journey, with Death on the driver's seat and her body laid out in the coach behind, is dispelled by the presence of her immortal part that rides with her as a co-passenger, this slight personification being justified by the separable concept of the soul. Too occupied with life herself to stop, like all busy mortals, Death 'kindly stopped' for her. But this figure of a gentleman taking a lady for a carriage ride is carefully underplayed and then dropped after two stanzas.

The balanced parallelism of the first stanza is slightly quickened by the alliterating 'labor' and 'leisure' of the second, which encompass vividly all that must be renounced in order to ride 'toward Eternity.' So the deliberate slow-paced action that lies suspended behind the poem is charged with a forward movement by the sound pattern, taking on a kind of inevitability in the insistent reiteration of the following stanza:

> We passed the School, where Children strove
> At Recess—in the Ring—
> We passed the Fields of Gazing Grain—
> We passed the Setting Sun—

Here her intensely conscious leave-taking of the world is rendered with fine economy, and instead of the sentimental grief of parting there is an objectively presented scene. The seemingly disparate parts of this are fused into a vivid re-enactment of the mortal experience. It includes the three stages of youth, maturity, and age, the cycle of day from morning to evening, and even a suggestion of seasonal progression from the year's upspring through ripening to decline. The labor and leisure of life are made concrete in the joyous activity of children contrasted with the passivity of nature and again, by the optical illusion of the sun's setting, in the image of motion that has come to rest. Also the whole range of the earthly life is symbolized, first human nature, then animate, and finally inanimate nature. But, absorbed 'in the Ring' of childhood's games, the players at life do not even stop to look up at the passing carriage of death. And the indifference of nature is given a kind of cold vitality by transferring the stare in the dead traveler's eyes to the 'Gazing Grain.' This simple maneuver in grammar creates an involute paradox, giving the fixity of death to the living corn while the corpse itself passes by on its journey to immortality. Then with the westering sun, traditional symbol of the soul's passing, comes the obliterating darkness of eternity. Finally, the sequence follows the natural route of a funeral train, past the schoolhouse in the village, then the outlying fields, and on to the remote burying ground.

—Anderson, *Emily Dickinson's Poetry: Stairway to Surprise,* pp. 245–46

1. According to this critic, what is the speaker's attitude toward death?
2. Does the criticism enhance your understanding of the poem? If so, how?
3. How does this critic's interpretation compare with that of the earlier interpretation on page 427? Discuss the similarities and differences.
4. Compare this critic's interpretation with your own interpretation.

THOUGHT PATTERNS IN THE HUMANITIES AND ARTS

Common thought patterns in the humanities and arts include process, chronological order, cause and effect, and comparison and contrast. Table 14–1 on page 430 describes the uses of these patterns and offers examples.

TABLE 14–1   THOUGHT PATTERNS

PATTERNS	USES	EXAMPLES
Process	Examining the process through which the writer achieved his or her effect.	Studying e.e. cummings' use of space and print size.
Chronological order	Sequence of events in fictional works; noting the development of various artists or historical or literary periods.	Noting development of Impressionist style of painting.
Cause-and-effect	Examining character motivation, studying effects of various literary and artistic techniques.	Evaluating the effect of harsh brush strokes in a painting.
Comparison/ contrast	Studying two or more artists, works, writers, or schools of thought.	Comparing the works of Wordsworth and Coleridge.

LEARNING STRATEGIES FOR HUMANITIES AND ART COURSES

Humanities and art courses are unique. Grades are often based on papers or essay exams rather than on objective tests or quizzes. Frequently, the focus is on ideas and your interpretation and evaluation of them. Here are several suggestions to help you get the most from these courses.

1. *Learn appropriate terminology.* Learn the names and meanings of literary devices (stream of consciousness, pathos, persona, intrigue). Consult M. L. Abrams's *A Glossary of Literary Terms.*

2. *Learn classifications.* In literature and art history, works and authors are often grouped or classified, and groupings may be chronological (the Romantic period, 1789–1832; the Victorian period, 1832–1901 in literature, for example). Learn these periods (names, inclusive dates, and characteristics) so that you will understand the historical context of a particular work.

3. *Focus on themes and patterns.* Always analyze and evaluate. Focus on a work's significance and literary merit.

4. *Highlight and annotate as you read.* Mark key figures of speech, global statements by characters, and words and phrases that suggest the theme. Mark confusing sections or unknown references as well.

5. *Write for review.* Write plot summaries of short stories. Make brief outlines of essays. Write a statement of your interpretation of a poem or work or art. These statements will be useful as you prepare for exams or select topics for papers.

6. *Predict exam questions.* Exams are usually in essay form or call for short answers. Prepare for this by predicting the questions and drafting outline answers.

7. *Discuss the work with a classmate.* If you are having difficulty with a particular work, consult with your instructor.

Preparing for Exams in the Humanities and Arts

In many literature classes, you write papers instead of taking exams, although some instructors do give brief objective tests based on the assigned readings. Most final essay assignments require you to analyze and write about a work or works you have read.

You may be given several types of writing assignments. It is important to know what is expected in each.

1. *Explication.* An explication is a full, detailed explanation of the meaning of the work. It proceeds through the work line by line or even word by word, explaining meanings and examining word choices, figures of speech, and so forth. Although it is detailed, it is not limited to a discussion of specifics. Larger concerns such as theme and plot are also discussed.

2. *Analysis.* Analysis involves separating the work into components and then examining and explaining closely one or more of the parts. Usually, analyses are limited to one aspect or element, such as Hawthorne's use of symbolism in *The Scarlet Letter* or an analysis of the point of view in Poe's "The Tell-Tale Heart."

3. *Comparison and Contrast.* Writing assignments may ask you to compare two or more works or two or more authors. To do this, you must examine similarities and differences. If you are given a choice of works or authors, choose two that have much in common; you'll find you have more to say than if the two are widely divergent. For suggestions on how to compare two works, refer to Chapter 4. When writing a comparison paper, you should generally integrate your discussion of the works rather than discuss each separately. Select several points or aspects that you'll discuss for each work, and then organize your paper to proceed from aspect to aspect.

4. *Synopsis.* Some instructors ask students to write a synopsis or summary of a work. This assignment demands a concise description of major features of the work, such as plot, setting, and characterization. Others ask for a card report (a point-by-point description of various elements, usually on an index card). Generally, some form of evaluation of the work is also expected. If you are not certain what aspects to include or what format to use, ask your instructor.

SUMMARY

Literature focuses on the search for reasons, values, and interpretations in all areas of human interest and experience.

Understanding the language of literature involves working with descriptive, connotative, and figurative language. Specific suggestions are given for reading and analyzing each genre.

- Poetry. Reread frequently. Note the poem's action, audience, and tone. Analyze the poem's intent, and search for its theme.
- Short stories and novels. Focus on plot, characterization, setting, point of view, tone, and theme.

The visual arts focus on the expression of an idea through a medium, such as canvas, clay, or fiber. Studying art requires visual thinking and analysis. Interpretation and meaning are important.

Strategies for reading literary criticism are given. Predominant thought patterns include

- process
- chronological order
- cause-and-effect
- comparison and contrast

LITERATURE

PREREADING QUESTIONS

(Answer after reading the entire poem once.)
1. What is the subject of the poem?
2. Summarize the literal action.

LEAVES

Lloyd Schwartz

I.

1   Every October it becomes important, no, *necessary*
    to see the leaves turning, to be surrounded
    by leaves turning: it's not just the symbolism,
    to confront in the death of the year your death,
5   one blazing farewell appearance, though the irony
    isn't lost on you that nature is most seductive
    when it's about to die, flaunting the dazzle of its
    incipient exit, an ending that at least so far
    the effects of human progress (pollution, acid rain)
10 have not yet frightened you enough to make you believe
    is real; that is, you know this ending is a deception
    because of course nature is always renewing itself—
       the trees don't *die,* they just pretend,
       go out in style, and return in style: a new style.

2.

15 It is deliberate how far they make you go
    especially if you live in the city to get far
    enough away from home to see not just trees
    but only trees. The boring highways, roadsigns, high
    speeds, 10-axle trucks passing you as if they were
20 in an even greater hurry than you to look at leaves:
    so you drive in terror for literal hours and it looks
    like rain, or *snow,* but it's probably just clouds
    (too cloudy to see any color?) and you wonder,
    given the poverty of your memory, which road had the

25   most color last year, but it doesn't matter since
      you're probably too late anyway, or too early—
          whichever road you take will be the wrong one
          and you've probably come all this way for nothing.

                                    3.
      You'll be driving along depressed when suddenly
30   a cloud will move and the sun will muscle through
      and ignite the hills. It may not last. Probably
      won't last. But for a moment the whole world
      comes to. Wakes up. Proves it lives. It lives—
      red, yellow, orange, brown, russet, ocher, vermillion,
35   *gold.* Flame and rust. Flame and rust, the permutations
      of burning. You're on fire. Your eyes are on fire.
      It won't last, you don't want it to last. You
      can't stand any more. But you don't want it to stop.
      It's what you've come for. It's what you'll
40   come back for. It won't stay with you, but you'll
          remember that it felt like nothing else you've felt
          or something you've felt that also didn't last.
                          —Schwartz, "Leaves," *Goodnight, Gracie*

VOCABULARY REVIEW

1. For each of the words listed below, use context; prefixes, roots, and
    suffixes; and/or a dictionary to write a brief definition or synonym of
    the word as it is used in the reading.

    a. irony (line 5) _____

    b. seductive (line 6) _____

    c. incipient (line 8) _____

    d. vermillion (line 34)_____

    e. permutations (line 35) _____

COMPREHENSION QUESTIONS

1. In line 3, Schwartz mentions symbolism. To what symbolism is he
    referring?
2. What is the poet's attitude toward human progress (line 9)?
3. To whom does the word *they* refer in line 15?

4. Describe the poem's tone.
5. What is the poem's theme?

THINKING CRITICALLY

Why does the author mention pollution and acid rain in line 9?

LEARNING/STUDY STRATEGY

Annotate the poem using the suggestions on page 410.

ON-LINE RESEARCH: POETRY*

Poetry, like other creative arts, depends on the reader, viewer, or listener for interpretation. How would your interpretation of a poem change if you could hear the poet reading the poem, instead of only reading it on the page? You can hear poets reading their own poems at the following World Wide Web (WWW) sites. Go to one of the sites, and then follow the directions below. (*Note:* You need a program called RealAudio to hear the poems. It can be downloaded from these sites.)

*   *The Atlantic Monthly Unbound* includes an "audible anthology of poetry" at http://www.theatlantic.com/unbound/poetry/antholog/schwartz/airport.htm. Here you can find Lloyd Schwartz reading another one of his poems, "Small Airport in Brazil."
*   The Academy of American Poets web site includes a "Listening Booth" at http://www.poets.org/LIT/findfst.htm. Here you can choose whether to only listen to the poem or to read it yourself while it is being read by the poet.

1. Choose a poem from one of the anthologies. Depending on which site you have chosen, either listen to the poem first and then read it yourself; or read it yourself and then listen to the poet read it.
2. How does the author's rendering of the poem affect your interpretation? Why?

*If any of these sites is unavailable, use a search engine to locate a new Web site on the same topic.

15 READING MATHEMATICS

LEARNING OBJECTIVES

- **To understand the sequential nature of mathematics**
- **To develop a systematic approach for reading mathematics textbooks**
- **To solve word problems in mathematics**
- **To learn common thought patterns used in mathematics**
- **To develop study techniques for mathematics**

Although mathematics uses its own language, it is concerned with ideas, concepts, relationships, and problems—just like other disciplines. Mathematics demands logical and critical thinking and the ability to deal with abstractions, relationships, and theoretical ideas. This subject is extremely rewarding because you *see* yourself learning and making progress; you can solve a problem today that you couldn't solve yesterday.

MATHEMATICS: A SEQUENTIAL THINKING PROCESS

Learning mathematics is a sequential process. You solve problems by estimating answers, trying a variety of special techniques, and verifying the results. In mathematics, much of what you learn is based on skills you have learned earlier; it is cumulative. In algebra, you have to understand radicals before you can solve quadratic equations, whose solutions involve radicals. In business math, to use a compound interest schedule, you must understand simple interest.

Because mathematics is sequential and cumulative, it is most important that you begin with a course at the proper level. For example, a calculus course often is required for accounting majors. However, if you have not studied trigonometry, you lack the necessary background for calculus and should take a trigonometry course first. Check the course description in your college catalog for prerequisites, or consult your academic advisor for information on appropriate course placement. If it has been several years since your last math course, your college learning center may offer a placement test to assess your present level of skill.

Mathematics is a process of solving problems—a process of reasoning about situations and understanding the relationships between variables. Too many students learn steps, memorize procedures, and follow rules to solve problems without understanding why they are performing the operations. In mathematics, understanding the meaning of the various operations is essential. Make your learning practical and useful by understanding *how* and *why* the operations work.

Why Study Mathematics?

Mathematics is a required course in many fields of study. It is essential for majors in nursing, accounting, business and finance, technologies, and the natural sciences, for example. Mathematics provides the tools with which to explore relationships and solve problems. In nursing, mathematics allows you to compute and measure dosages of drugs. In accounting, it is mathematics that enable you to calculate profits and losses, for instance.

Besides fulfilling degree requirements, however, mathematics trains you to think logically, quantitatively, and analytically. Mathematics is fun because it is exact and precise; you are either right or wrong in solving a problem. Mathematics can provide the same satisfying, deep concentration that solving a crossword puzzle or playing a game of chess does.

READING MATHEMATICS TEXTBOOKS

To learn from mathematics texts, you must allow plenty of time and work at peak concentration. Mathematics texts are concise and to the point; nearly everything is important. Use the following suggestions to develop a systematic approach for reading in mathematics.

Preview Before Reading

Previewing before reading is as important in mathematics as it is in every other discipline. For mathematics texts, however, your preview should include a brief review of your previous chapter assignment. Because learning new skills hinges on remembering what you have learned before, a brief review of previously learned material is valuable.

Understand Mathematical Language

One of the first steps to success with mathematics is learning to understand its language. Mathematics uses a symbolic language in which notations, symbols, numbers, and formulas are used to express ideas and relationships. Working with mathematics requires that you be able to convert mathematical language to everyday language. To understand a formula, for example, $I = prt$, you must translate mathematical language into everyday language: "Interest equals principal times rate times time." To solve a word problem expressed in everyday language, first you must convert it into mathematical language. You might think of equations as mathematical sentences. Just as an everyday sentence expresses a complete idea, an equation describes a mathematical relationship. Here are a few examples.

Sentence	Equation
The speed of train A is four times the speed of train B.	$A = 4B$
When I am as old as my mother (m), I shall be five times as old as my daughter (d) is now.	$5d = m$
In a sewing box, there are three times as many pins as needles, and one-third as many needles as buttons; the total number of pins, needles, and buttons is 1872.	$3n + n + \frac{1}{3}n = 1872$

Figure 15–1   Aspect of Mathematical Language

Type	Function	Example
Punctuation marks	Make clear what parts of a statement are or are not separable; distinguish groups within groups	$(0, 1, 2, \ldots)$ $[3 - (a + b)^2]$
Models (graphs, charts, drawings)	Present a pictorial representation of a relationship or situation	
Numbers	Indicate size, order	3, 7, 9, 11
Variables	Represent a number that is unknown or may vary	x, y
Signs for relations	Indicate relationships	$a = b$ (a equals b) $c > d$ (c is greater than b)
Signs for operations	Give instructions	$15 \div 3$ (divide 15 by 3) $a - b$ (subtract b from a)

When you learn a foreign language, it is not sufficient only to learn the new vocabulary; you also must learn the rules of word order, grammar, punctuation, and so forth. To read and understand mathematics, then, you must know not only the signs and symbols (the vocabulary) but also the basic rules for expressing relationships in mathematical form. Figure 15–1 shows five important types of symbols and mathematical language and gives examples of each, taken from introductory algebra.

Figure 15–2 shows a sample page from an introductory algebra textbook. It has been marked to indicate the types of mathematical language used.

Figure 15–2   Sample Textbook Page

OBJECTIVE ▶ Inequalities can be used to solve applied problems involving phrases that suggest inequality. The chart below gives some of the more common such phrases, along with examples and translations.

Phrase	*Example*	*Inequality*
Is more than	A number *is more than* 4	$x > 4$
Is less than	A number *is less than* –12	$x < -12$
Is at least	A number *is at least* 6	$x \geq 6$
Is at most	A number *is at most* 8	$x \leq 8$

Caution
Do not confuse phrases like "5 more than a number" and statements like "5 *is* more than a number." The first of these is expressed as "$x + 5$" while the second is expressed as "$5 > x$."

E X A M P L E   8   Finding an Average Test Score
Brent has test grades of 86, 88, and 78 on his first three tests in geometry. If he wants an average of at least 80 after his fourth test, what score must he make on his fourth test?

Let x represent Brent's score on his fourth test. To find the average of the four scores, add them and find $\frac{1}{4}$ of the sum.

Variable ⸺

Average ↓

is at least 80. ↓ ↓

Sign for relation

$$\frac{1}{4}(86 + 88 + 78 + x) \geq 80$$

Signs for operation

$$4 \cdot \frac{1}{4}(252 + x) \geq 4 \cdot 80 \qquad \text{Multiply by 4.}$$

$$252 + x \geq 320 \qquad \text{Multiply.}$$

$$252 - 252 + x \geq 320 - 252 \qquad \text{Subtract 252.}$$

$$x \geq 68 \qquad \text{Combine terms.}$$

He must also score 68 or more on the fourth test to have an average of *at least* 80.

Source: Lial et al., *Introductory Algebra,* pp. 163–64

Much information is packed into small units of mathematical language. Some students find it helpful to translate formulas into words as they read, as is shown in the following equation for a right triangle:

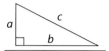

$c^2 = a^2 + b^2$ means the square of the hypotenuse of a right triangle is equal to the sum of the squares of the two remaining sides.

In mathematics, you must know the *exact* meaning of both words and symbols. There are several places to find the definition of a new term. If it is from the current chapter, look at the end-of-chapter material, which often includes key vocabulary. You might also check the index to find page numbers or use the glossary to read a brief definition, if one is included. Use the index card system described in Chapter 3 to help you learn the language of mathematics. Record the term or symbol, its meaning, an example, and a diagram, if possible. Also include a page reference to where the term is used in your textbook. Two sample index cards are shown in Figure 15–3.

EXERCISE 15–1

Read the excerpt from an algebra text shown in Figure 15–4, and underline five examples of mathematical language that the author assumes you know.

1. Write a definition of each term you have underlined.
2. Write your own definition of the phrase, "evaluating an expression." Include an example to illustrate your definition.

Figure 15–3   Sample Index Cards

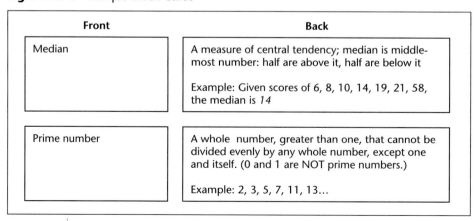

Figure 15–4   Excerpt from an Algebra Text

Evaluating an Expression   If you like to fish, you can use an expression (rule) like the one below to find the approximate weight (in pounds) of a fish you catch. Measure the length (in inches) of the fish and then use the correct expression for that type of fish. For a northern pike, the weight expression is shown.

Variable (length of fish) $\dfrac{l^3}{3600}$

where l is the length of the fish in inches.

To evaluate this expression for a fish that is 43 inches long, follow the rule by calculating

$$\frac{43^3}{3600}$$ Replace l with 43, the length of the fish in inches.

In the numerator, you can multiply $43 \cdot 43 \cdot 43$ or use the $\boxed{y^x}$ key on your calculator. Then divide by 3600.

Enter 43 $\boxed{y^x}$ 3 $\boxed{\div}$ 3600 $\boxed{=}$ **Calculator shows 22.08527778**

        Base   Exponent

The fish weighs about 22 pounds.

Now evaluate the expression to find the approximate weight of a northern pike that is 37 inches long. (Answer: about 14 pounds.)

Notice that variables are used on your calculator keys. On the $\boxed{y^x}$ key, y represents the base and x represents the exponent. You evaluated y^x by entering 43 as the base and 3 as the exponent for the first fish. Then you evaluated y^x by entering 37 as the base and 3 as the exponent for the second fish.

Source: Lial and Hestwood, *Prealgebra*, p. 87

Follow the Chapter Organization

Chapters in most mathematics textbooks contain four essential elements: the presentation or explanation, sample problems, graphs and diagrams, and exercises. Mathematics textbook chapters often use a decimal system for dividing the chapter into sections. For example, Chapter 3 might be numbered 3.1, 3.2, 3.3, and so on. Each number with a decimal is a new section of the chapter.

Reading Chapter Explanations   Each new operation, process, or term is explained in the text. As you read this explanation, focus on *how* and *why* the process works. Discover the reasoning behind the process. If the author refers to a sample problem in the explanation, it is necessary to move back and forth between the explanation and the sample problem. Read a sentence or two and then refer to the sample problem to see how the information is

Figure 15–5 Problem Solving Step by Step

Since the enactment of the **Federal Truth-in-Lending Act** (Regulation Z) in 1969, lenders must report their **finance charge** (the charge for credit) and their **annual percentage rate.** The truth-in-lending law does not regulate interest rates or credit charges but merely requires a standardized and truthful report of what they are. The individual states set the allowable interest rates and charges. } background

Find the annual percentage rate by first finding the **total installment cost** (or the **deferred payment price**) and the finance charge on the loan. Do this with the following steps. } overview of process

Finding total in-stallment cost and finance charge

Step 1. Find the total installment cost.

Total installment cost = Down payment
+ (Amount of each payment x Number of payments)

Step 2. Find the finance charge.

Finance charge = Total installment cost – Cash price

Step 3. Finally, find the amount financed.

Amount financed = Cash price – Down payment

} step-by-step procedure

Example Diane Phillips bought a motorcycle for $980. She paid $200 down and then made 24 payments of $39.60 each. Find the (a) total installment cost, (b) finance charge, and (c) amount financed. } Sample problem

Solution (a) Find the total installment cost by multiplying the amount of each payment by the number of payments, and adding the down payment.

Total installment cost = $200 + ($39.60 x 24)
= $200 + $950.40
= $1150.40

(b) The finance charge is the difference between the total installment cost and the cash price.

Finance charge = $1150.40 – $980
= $170.40

Phillips pays an additional $170.40 for the motorcycle because it is bought on credit.

(c) The amount financed is
$980 – $200 = $780

} Solution

Source: Miller and Salzman, *Business Mathematics,* p. 373.

applied. Your purpose is to see how the sample problem illustrates the process being described. The steps to follow in computing the total install-ment cost and finance charge on a credit card are given in Figure 15–5 above. Then the authors give a sample problem and show how it is solved using the steps they have listed.

As you read, refer to previous chapters if an operation is unclear or if unfamiliar terms are used. In mathematics, you should expect to look back frequently because much of the material is sequential.

Reading Sample Problems Sample problems demonstrate how an operation or process works. It may be tempting to skip over sample prob-lems because they require time to work through or because they lack an accompanying verbal explanation. However, careful study of the sample problems is an essential part of learning in mathematics. Follow these steps in reading sample problems.

1. *Before you read the solution, think of how you would solve the problem, choose a method, and solve the problem.* More than one approach may be possible.

2. *Read the solution and compare your answer with the textbook's.*

3. *Be sure you understand each step; you should know exactly what calculations were performed and why they were done.*

4. *When you have finished reading the sample problem, explain the steps in your own words. This will help you remember the method later.* The best way to verbalize is to write the process down; this forces you to be clear and precise. Figure 15–6 presents two sample problems and shows how a student verbalized each process.

5. *Test your understanding by covering up the text's solution and solving the problem yourself.* Finally, look over the solution, verifying its reasonableness and reviewing the process once again.

Figure 15–6   Verbalizing a Process

Problem 1: Find the principal of a loan that gives an interest of $30 at 10% per year for 91 days.

Solution	Verbalization
1. $P = \dfrac{I}{RT}$	1. The formula for computing principal is interest divided by the product of the rate multiplied by the time.
2. $P = \dfrac{30}{.10 \times \dfrac{91}{365}}$	2. The interest is $30. The rate, 10% per year, is converted to a decimal, .10, and the time is expressed as a fraction of a year.
3. $P = \dfrac{30}{.025}$	3. The denominator is simplified.
4. $P = \$1200$	4. The principal is $1200.

Problem 2: $\sqrt{3x+1} - \sqrt{x+9} = 2$

Solution	Verbalization
1. $\sqrt{3x+1} = 2 + \sqrt{x+9}$	Isolate one radical on one side of the equation.
2. $(-\sqrt{3x+1})^2 = (2 + \sqrt{x+9})^2$	Square both sides.
3. $3x + 1 = 4 + 4\sqrt{x+9} + x + 9$	Use formula $(a+b)^2 = a^2 + 2ab + b^2$.
4. $2x - 12 = 4\sqrt{x+9}$	Isolate the radical.
5. $x - 6 = 2\sqrt{x+9}$	Factor out 2 on the left side. Divide the equation by 2.
6. $(x-6)^2 = (2\sqrt{x+9})^2$ $x^2 - 12x + 36 = 4(x+9)$	Square both sides.
7. $x^2 - 12x + 36 = 4x + 36$ $x^2 - 16x = 0$ $x(x-16) = 0$ $x = 16$	Solve for x.

Ignore the solution $x = 0$ because it will not check in the original equation. Extraneous roots can occur when you square both sides of an equation.

Source: Johnson and Steffensen, *Elementary Algebra*, p. 178.

EXERCISE 15–2

For each of the following problems and solutions, verbalize the process and write each step in your own words. Compare your verbalization with that of another student.

1. Problem: The sum of two number is 21 and their difference is 9. Find the numbers.

    Solution: Let x, y be the two numbers.
    $$x + y = 21$$
    $$x - y = 9$$
    $$2x = 30$$
    $$x = 15$$
    $$\text{Then, } 15 + y = 21$$
    $$\text{so, } y = 21 - 15$$
    $$y = 6$$

2. Problem: Solve $x^2 - 6x + 8 = 0$ using the quadratic formula.

    Solution: $a = 1$, $b = -6$, $c = 8$

    $$x = \frac{-b \pm \sqrt{b^2 - 4ac}}{2a}$$

    $$= \frac{-(-6) \pm \sqrt{(-6)^2 - 4(1)\,(8)}}{2(1)}$$

    $$= \frac{6 \pm \sqrt{36 - 32}}{2}$$

    $$= \frac{6 \pm \sqrt{4}}{2} = \frac{6 \pm 2}{2}$$

    $$x = \frac{6 + 2}{2} = \frac{8}{2} = 4$$

    or

    $$x = \frac{6 - 2}{2} = \frac{4}{2} = 2$$

    $$x = 4, 2$$

Reading and Drawing Graphs, Tables, and Diagrams   Graphs, diagrams, and drawings are often included in textbook chapters. These are intended to help you understand processes and concepts by providing a visual representation. Treat these drawings as essential parts of the chapter. Here are a few suggestions on how to use them:

1. *Study each drawing closely, frequently referring to the text that accompanies it.* Test your understanding of the drawing by reconstructing and labeling it without reference to the text drawing; then compare drawings.

2. *Use the drawings in the text as models on which to base your own drawings.* As you solve end-of-chapter problems, create drawings similar to those included in the text. These may be useful as you decide how to solve the problem.

3. *Draw your own diagrams to clarify or explore relationships.* For example, an algebra student drew the following diagram of the trinomial equation.

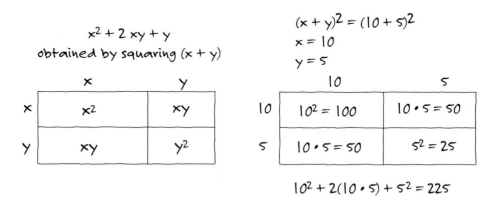

Another student drew the following diagram to explain why the formula for finding the area of a parallelogram is $A = bh$.

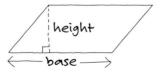

Cut off the triangle on left side of parallelogram.

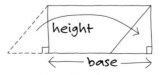

Move the triangle to create a rectangle.
Area of rectangle = base • height
so Area of parallelogram also = base • height
$A = bh$

4. *Use tables to organize and categorize large amounts of complicated data.* For example, a student made the following table to solve a frequency distribution problem in statistics, in which she was asked to identify the frequency of female Democrats and male Republicans. She was provided with the following information: Of a sample of 150 people, 62 males and 31 females are Democrats. Thirty eight males and 19 females are Republicans.

	Democrat	**Republican**	**Totals**
Male	62	38	100
Female	31	19	50
Totals	93	57	150

Solving Word Problems   Most textbook chapters have numerous problem-solving exercises; quizzes and exams also consist primarily of problems. Often, the problems are expressed in words and are not conveniently set up for you in formulas or equations. Solving word problems is a seven-step process. In your textbook, be sure to work through exercises as they occur in the chapter. Do not wait until the end and try to work them all at once. Read the problem once to get an overview of the situation; then use the following steps:

1. *Identify what is asked for.* What are you supposed to find?

2. *Locate the information that is provided to solve the problem.* (Some math problems may include irrelevant information; if so, underline or circle pertinent data.)

3. *Draw a diagram, if possible. Label the diagram.*

4. *Estimate your answer.* If possible, make a reasonable guess about what the answer should be.

Using End-of-Chapter Material   Many mathematics texts include useful review material at the end of the chapter. Typically, there is a summary of key ideas from the chapter, often with sample worked examples; key terms, review exercises, and a chapter test. Use these materials to test yourself.

1. *Decide on a procedure to solve the problem.* Recall formulas you have learned that are related to the problem, and look for clue words that indicate a particular process. For example, the phrase "how fast" means *rate;* you may be able to use the formula $r = d/t$. If you do not know how to solve a problem, look for similarities between it and sample problems you have studied.

2. *Solve the problem.* Begin by choosing variables to represent the unknown quantities. Then set up an equation.

3. *Verify your answer.* Compare your answer with your estimate. If there is a large discrepancy, this is a signal that you have made an error. Be sure to check your arithmetic.

Figure 15–7 gives an example of how this problem-solving process works.

Figure 15–7   Sample Word Problem

Problem: A four-ton passenger paddleboat goes 210 miles down the Mississippi River in the same time it can go 140 miles upriver. The speed of the current is five miles per hour. Find the speed of the boat in still water.

Steps	*Solution*
1. Identify what is asked for.	speed in still water
2. Locate given quantities.	210 miles down 140 miles up
3. Draw a diagram.	

down → 5 mph → 210 miles ⎫
up → -5 mph → 140 miles ⎬ equal time ⎭

4. Estimate the answer.	Estimate: 20 mph
5. Decide on a procedure; recall formulas.	$d = rt$ (distance = rate x time)
6. Solve the problem.	x = speed in still water time up = time down $d = r \times t$ downstream $210 = (x + 5)t$ upstream $140 = (x - 5)t$
(a) Solve for t.	$d = rt$ $t = d/r$
(b) Determine t values.	$t \text{ (downstream)} = \dfrac{210}{(x + 5)}$ $t \text{ (upstream)} = \dfrac{140}{(x - 5)}$
(c) $t = t$	$\dfrac{210}{(x + 5)} = \dfrac{140}{(x - 5)}$
(d) Multiply both sides by $(x + 5)$ $(x - 5)$.	$(x + 5)(x - 5)\dfrac{210}{(x + 5)} = (x + 5)(x - 5)\dfrac{140}{(x - 5)}$
(e) Solve the equation.	$210 (x - 5) = 140 (x + 5)$ $210x - 1050 = 140x + 700$ $70x = 1750$ $x = 25$
7. Compare with estimate and check arithmetic.	answer 25 mph (estimate was 20 mph)

EXERCISE 15–3

Complete each of the following problems using the procedure outlined above. Label each step.

1. Samantha receives an 11% commission on her sales of cosmetics. During one week, her daily sales were $482.10, $379.80, $729.62, $524.24, and $310.40. Find her gross earnings for the week.

2. If a microwave oven costs the retailer $325 and the markup is 35% on the selling price, find the selling price.

3. Two joggers start jogging from the same point on a highway. One is running north, and the other is running south. One jogs 2 miles per hour faster than the other. They are 24 miles apart after 3 hours. At what rate is each jogging?

4. A collection of nickels and dimes is worth $2.85. If there are 34 coins in the collection, how many of each type of coin are there?

5. One number is 6 larger than another. The square of the larger is 96 more than the square of the smaller. Find the numbers.

**EXERCISE
15–4**

Write three sample word problems. Exchange your problems with another student, and solve each other's problems.

Use Writing to Learn

As in most disciplines, reading is not sufficient for learning mathematics. Highlighting and marking are the strategies students generally use to enhance learning; however, these techniques do not work well in mathematics. Mathematics texts are concise; everything is important. Writing, instead of highlighting, is a useful reading and learning strategy in mathematics. Writing in your own words will force you to convert mathematical language to everyday language. It will also demonstrate what you understand and what you do not. The following list suggests a few ways to use writing to increase your understanding and learning in mathematics.

1. *Definitions.* Read the textbook definition; then close the book and write your own. Compare it to the textbook definition, noticing and correcting discrepancies. Rewrite your definition until it is correct and complete.

2. *Class notes.* Rewrite your notes, including more detail and explanation. Focus on process; include reasons and explanations. Include information from the corresponding textbook section.

3. *Questions.* Write lists of questions based on chapter assignments, homework assignments, and your class notes. Seek answers from classmates, your instructor, a review book, or the learning lab or tutorial services.

4. *Problems.* Once you think you understand a particular problem or process, write down what you understand. To test your recall, write several questions based on your written explanation. Put aside both your

explanation and your questions for several days. Then take out the question sheet and, without reference to your explanation, try to answer your questions. Compare your answers with your original explanation.

5. *Tests.* When preparing for an exam, construct and answer sample questions and problems. It is also effective to exchange self-constructed problems with a classmate and solve them.

6. *Diagrams.* Draw diagrams of sample problems as you read, and diagram actual problems before you attempt a solution. Describing the situation in visual terms often makes it more understandable.

7. *Review.* Review your course weekly. Write a description of what you have learned in the past week. You might compare your description with those of your classmates. Keep your weekly descriptions; they will be useful as you review for tests and final exams.

EXERCISE 15–5

Read Figure 15-8 (p. 450), an excerpt from a basic college mathematics textbook on the Pythagorean Theorem. Then complete each of the following steps.

1. List the terminology that is essential to understand when reading this excerpt.
2. Without referring to the text, write a definition of *hypotenuse.* Make a diagram to illustrate your definition. Compare your definition and diagram with the text excerpt. Revise your definition and diagram, if necessary.
3. Without referring to the text, describe how to use the Pythagorean Theorem to find the unknown length of the hypotenuse in a right triangle. Compare your description with the text excerpt. Revise your description if necessary.
4. Find the unknown length in the following right triangles.

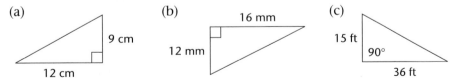

(a)   9 cm   12 cm

(b)   16 mm   12 mm

(c)   15 ft   90°   36 ft

Expect Gradual Understanding

Mathematics is a reasoning process: a process of understanding relationships and seeing similarities and differences. Consequently, mathematics is not an "either you understand it or you don't" discipline. Your understanding will develop by degrees; it grows as you work or "play with"

Figure 15–8 Pythagorean Theorem

Objective ◆ One place you will use square roots is when working with the *Pythagorean Theorem*. This theorem applies only to *right* triangles (triangles with a 90° angle). The longest side of a right triangle is called the **hypotenuse** (hy-POT-en-oos). It is opposite the right angle. The other two sides are called *legs*. The legs form the right angle.

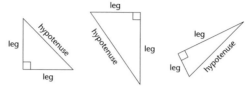

Examples of right triangles

Pythagorean Theorem

$$(hypotenuse)2 = (leg)2 + (leg)2$$

In other words, square the length of each side. After you have squared all the sides, the sum of the squares of the two legs will equal the square of the hypotenuse.

$$(hypotenuse)^2 = (leg)^2 + (leg)^2$$
$$5^2 = 4^2 + 3^2$$
$$25 = 16 + 9$$
$$25 = 25$$

If you know the lengths of any two sides in a right triangle, you can use the Pythagorean Theorem to find the length of the third side.

Pythagorean Theorem

To find the hypotenuse, use this formula:

$$hypotenuse = \sqrt{(leg)^2 + (leg)^2}$$

EXAMPLE 2 Finding the Unknown Length in a Right Triangle
Find the unknown length in this right triangle.

The length of the side opposite the right angle is unknown. That side is the hypotenuse, so use this formula.

$hypotenuse = \sqrt{(leg)^2 + (leg)^2}$	Find the hypotenuse.
$hypotenuse = \sqrt{(3)^2 + (4)^2}$	Legs are 3 and 4.
$= \sqrt{9 + 16}$	$3 \cdot 3$ is 9 and $4 \cdot 4$ is 16
$= \sqrt{25}$	
$= 5$	

The hypotenuse is 5 ft. long.

Note: You use the Pythagorean Theorem to find the *length* of one side, *not* the area of the triangle. Your answer will be in linear units, such as ft, yd, cm, m, and so on (*not* ft², cm², m²).

Source: Lial et al., *Basic College Mathematics*, pp. 548–49

problems. Here's how you can work toward developing your understanding as you read.

1. *Plan on reading, and then reading and solving, and finally re-solving, problems.* As you reread and re-solve problems, you often will come to a new understanding of the process involved. (This is similar to seeing a film or reading a novel a second time; you will notice and discover things you didn't see the first time.)

2. *Experiment with the chapter's content.* The style of most textbooks is concise, but this does not mean that there is no room for creativity or experimentation. Try various solutions to problems. As you experiment, you will come to a new understanding of the problems and solutions.

3. *Take risks.* Attempt a solution to a problem even if you do not fully understand it. As you work, you may discover more about how to arrive at the correct answer.

4. *Be active.* Active reading (see Chapter 1) is essential in mathematics. Get involved with the ideas, ask questions, and search for applications.

THOUGHT PATTERNS IN MATHEMATICS

Many students think that memorizing formulas, entire problems, and complete theories is the key to success in mathematics. This does not usually work because one predominant thought pattern in mathematics is *process.* Your goal in many situations is to see *how* a problem is solved or *how* a theory applies. As you make notes on chapters and as you rewrite class notes, explain, in your own words, how and why things work. Include reasons, explain relationships, and state why a particular operation was selected or why one problem-solving strategy was chosen over another.

Problem solving is also a primary pattern in most mathematics courses. Class activities, homework, and exams all require problem solving. Problem solving in mathematics involves creativity and even playfulness. It is not, as many students think, a matter of merely plugging numbers into a preselected formula and completing the necessary computations. Instead, problem solving is the process of assessing a situation (problem) and assembling and applying what you have learned that fits the problem. As you attempt to solve problems, don't immediately reach for a formula. Instead, analyze, think, and experiment while you work. Try several approaches and decide which one works best.

A third common thought pattern evident in many mathematics courses is comparison and contrast. Understanding and solving problems often requires you to see the similarities and differences among problem types and to study variations of sample problems. Often, you must look at a series of examples and detect a pattern (similarities) and then find a way to state this pattern as an equation or formula or rule. As you read and study, then, make notes about similarities and differences as they occur to you. Write, in your own words, how one problem differs from, or is a variation of, a type of problem you have previously learned about.

STUDYING MATHEMATICS

Be certain to attend all classes. Because mathematics is sequential, if you miss one specific skill, that gap in your understanding may cause you trouble all term. Expect regular homework assignments and complete them on time, even if your instructor does not require you to turn them in. Practice is an essential element in all mathematics courses. Never let yourself get behind or skip assignments. Try to study mathematics at least three times a week—more often, if possible. Use the following suggestions to learn mathematics more effectively.

Preparing for Class

1. *Emphasize accuracy and precision.* In mathematics, knowing how to solve the problem is not enough; you must produce the right answer. A small error in arithmetic can produce a wrong answer, even when you know how to solve the problem. Use a calculator if your instructor allows it.

2. *Read the chapter carefully before working on exercises.* Don't worry if you don't understand everything right away. Then, as you work on the problems, refer to the chapter frequently.

3. *Before you begin a new chapter or assignment, always review the previous one.* If you take a break while working on an assignment, do a brief one-minute review when you resume study.

4. *Read the portion of your textbook that covers the next day's lecture before attending class.* The lecture will be more meaningful if you have some idea of what it is about beforehand.

5. *In your class notes, be sure to record sample problems that your instructor solves in class.* If you get behind in taking notes, leave some blank space; then fill in what is missing later by working with a classmate or asking your instructor. After class, review and organize your notes, rewriting them if necessary. Add your own observations and ideas from your textbook as well.

6. *Rework sample problems solved in class.* This is an excellent means of review.

7. *Find a study group and work together to solve problems immediately after class.* Get the phone numbers of a few people in class whom you can call if you've missed an assignment or are stuck on a problem.

8. *Keep your homework in a special notebook.* Star the problems you have trouble with. Bring this notebook with you when you ask your instructor for help so that you can go immediately to those problems. When you review for a test, study the starred problems.

Preparing Sample Tests

One of the best ways to learn mathematics is to create your own sample tests. Use index cards to write your questions. Try to create three or four test question cards for each section of the chapter as you go along. Write the problem, including the directions, on the front of the card; write the solution and a page number reference to your text on the back. When preparing for a test, shuffle the cards so you are forced to work the problems out of order. Try to simulate test conditions; give yourself a time limit, allow yourself the same equipment (such as a calculator), and so forth.

Building Your Confidence

1. Approach mathematics confidently. Both men and women can suffer what has come to be known as "math anxiety." Math anxiety often reflects a negative self-concept: "I'm not good at math." Some students think, incorrectly, that one either has or does not have a mathematical mind. This is a myth. Some people may find the subject easier than others, but any average student can learn mathematics.

2. If you feel uncomfortable about taking your first math course, consider taking a basic refresher course in which you are likely to be successful. You may not earn college credit, but you will build your confidence and prove to yourself that you can handle math. Other students find working with computerized review programs helpful when catching up on fundamentals. The machine is nonthreatening, offers no time pressures, and allows you to review a lesson as many times as you want. Many campuses offer workshops on overcoming math anxiety. To find out what help is available, check with your instructor, the learning lab, or the counseling center. A particularly useful book is *Conquering Math Anxiety,* by Cynthia Arem.

Preparing for Exams in Mathematics

Exams in mathematics are usually problems to solve. Use the following tips to prepare for exams in mathematics.

1. *When studying for exams, pay attention to what your instructor has emphasized.* Predict what will be on the exam, and make a sample test that includes all the important topics and practice answering it.

2. *When studying for an exam, review as many sample problems as possible.* Don't just read the problems; practice solving them. Try to anticipate the variations that may appear. For example, a variation of the distance problem shown in Figure 15–7 may give you the rate but ask you to compute the distance.

3. *Identify problems that are most characteristic of the techniques presented in the chapter you are studying.* Record these on a study sheet, and summarize in your own words how you worked them. Compare your study sheet with that of a friend.

4. *As you solve homework problems and review returned exams and quizzes, search for a pat-* tern of errors. Is there one type of problem you frequently have trouble with? Do you make mistakes when setting up the equation, in factoring, or in computation? If you identify such a pattern, pay special attention to correcting these errors.

5. *If you are having trouble with your course, get help immediately;* once you get behind, it is difficult to catch up. Consult with your instructor during his or her office hours. Check with the learning lab for tutoring or computer-assisted review programs.

6. *If you find you are weak in a particular fundamental such as fractions, correct the problem as soon as possible.* If you do not, it will interfere with your performance.

7. *Obtain additional study aids.* Schaum's *College Outline Series* offers excellent study guides. Check with your instructor for additional references.

8. *When a test is returned, rework the problems on which you lost points to find out exactly what you did wrong.*

SUMMARY

This chapter discusses reading strategies for mathematics. Mathematics is largely sequential and cumulative; each skill builds on—and hinges on—previously learned skills.

Techniques for reading mathematics are

- learning mathematical language
- following chapter organization (including explanations, sample problems, diagrams, and graphs)

- dealing with word problems
- using writing to learn

Thought patterns that are among the most common in mathematics are

- process
- problem/solution
- comparison and contrast

Suggestions are offered for adapting study techniques to mathematics.

MATHEMATICS

PREREADING QUESTIONS

1. On the basis of your preview, write a sentence describing the contents of this selection.
2. How difficult do you predict it will be to complete the exercises at the end of this selection?

INTRODUCTION TO STATISTICS: MEAN, MEDIAN, AND MODE

Margaret L. Lial and Diana L. Hestwood

1   The word *statistics* originally came from words that mean *state numbers*. State numbers refer to numerical information, or *data,* gathered by the government such as the number of births, deaths, or marriages in a population. Today the word *statistics* has a much broader meaning; data from the fields of economics, social science, science, and business can all be organized and studied under the branch of mathematics called *statistics.*

2   **Objective ▶** Making sense of a long list of numbers can be hard. So when you analyze data, one of the first things to look for is a *measure of central tendency*— a single number that you can use to represent the entire list of numbers. One such measure is the *average* or **mean.** The mean can be found with the following formula.

Finding the Mean (Average)

3
$$\text{mean} = \frac{\text{sum of all values}}{\text{number of values}}$$

EXAMPLE 1   Finding the Mean

4   David had test scores of 84, 90, 95, 98, and 88. Find his average or mean score. Use the formula for finding mean. Add up all the test scores and then divide by the number of tests.

$$\text{mean} = \frac{84 + 90 + 95 + 98 + 88}{5} \quad \begin{array}{l} \leftarrow \text{Sum of test scores} \\ \leftarrow \text{Number of tests} \end{array}$$

$$= \frac{455}{5} \quad \text{Divide.}$$

$$= 91$$

David has a mean score of 91.

---

5   **Objective** ▶ Some items in a list of data might appear more than once. In this case, we find a **weighted mean,** in which each value is "weighted" by multiplying it by the number of times it occurs.

EXAMPLE 2   Understanding the Weighted Mean

6   The following table shows the amount of contribution and the number of times the amount was given (frequency) to a food pantry. Find the weighted mean.

	Contribution	
Value	**Frequency**
$ 3	4
$ 5	2
$ 7	1
$ 8	5
$ 9	3
$10	2
$12	1
$13	2

7   The same amount was given by more than one person: for example, $5 was given twice and $8 was given five times. Other amounts, such as $12, were given once. To find the mean, multiply each contribution value by its frequency. Then add the products. Next, add the numbers in the *frequency* column to find the total number of values.

Value	**Frequency**	**Product**
$ 3	4	$(3 \cdot 4) = \$12$
$ 5	2	$(5 \cdot 2) = \$10$
$ 7	1	$(7 \cdot 1) = \$ 7$
$ 8	5	$(8 \cdot 5) = \$40$
$ 9	3	$(9 \cdot 3) = \$27$
$10	2	$(10 \cdot 2) = \$20$
$12	1	$(12 \cdot 1) = \$12$
$13	2	$(13 \cdot 2) = \$26$
Totals	**20**	**$154**

Finally, divide the totals.

$$\text{mean} = \frac{\$154}{20} = \$7.70.$$

The mean contribution to the food pantry was **$7.70**.

8   A common use of the weighted mean is to find a student's *grade point average,* as shown by the next example.

EXAMPLE 3   Applying the Weighted Mean

9   Find the grade point average for a student earning the following grades. Assume A = 4, B = 3, C = 2, D = 1, and F = 0. The number of credits determines how many times the grade is counted (the frequency).

Course	Credits	Grade	Credits • Grade
Mathematics	3	A (= 4)	$3 \cdot 4 = 12$
Speech	3	C (= 2)	$3 \cdot 2 = 6$
English	3	B (= 3)	$3 \cdot 3 = 9$
Computer Science	3	A (= 4)	$3 \cdot 4 = 12$
Lab for Computer Science	2	D (= 1)	$2 \cdot 1 = 2$
Totals	14		41

It is common to round grade point averages to the nearest hundredth. So the grade point average for this student is shown below.

$$\frac{41}{14} \approx 2.93$$

10   **Objective** ▶ Because it can be affected by extremely high or low numbers, the mean is often a poor indicator of central tendency for a list of numbers. In cases like this, another measure of central tendency, called the **median** (MEE-dee-un), can be used. The *median* divides a group of numbers in half; half the numbers lie above the median, and half lie below the median.

11   Find the median by listing the numbers *in order* from *smallest* to *largest.* If the list contains an *odd* number of items, the median is the *middle number.*

EXAMPLE 4   Using the Median

12   Find the median for the following list of prices.

$7, $23, $15, $6, $18, $12, $24

First arrange the numbers in numerical order from smallest to largest.

Smallest $\rightarrow$ 6, 7, 12, 15, 18, 23, 24 $\leftarrow$ Largest

Next, find the middle number in the list.

$$\underbrace{6, 7, 12,}_{\text{Three are below}} 15, \underbrace{18, 23, 24}_{\text{Three are above}}$$

Middle number

The median price is $15.

13   If a list contains an *even* number of items, there is no single middle number. In this case, the median is defined as the mean (average) of the *middle two* numbers.

EXAMPLE 5   Finding the Median

14   Find the median for the following list of ages.

74, 7, 15, 13, 25, 28, 47, 59, 32, 68

First arrange the numbers in numerical order. Then find the middle two numbers.

Smallest $\rightarrow$ 7, 13, 15, 25, $\underbrace{28, 32,}$ 47, 59, 68, 74 $\leftarrow$ Largest

Middle two numbers

The median age is the mean of these two numbers.

$$\text{median} = \frac{28 + 32}{2} = \frac{60}{2} = 30 \text{ years}$$

15   **Objective** ▶ The last important statistical measure is the **mode,** the number that occurs most often in a list of numbers. For example, if the test scores for 10 students were

$$\downarrow \qquad\quad \downarrow \qquad\qquad\qquad \downarrow$$

74, 81, 39, 74, 82, 80, 100, 92, 74, and 85

then the mode is 74. Three students earned a score of 74, so 74 appears more times on the list than any other score.

16   A list can have two modes; such a list is sometimes called *bimodal*. If no number occurs more frequently than any other number in a list, the list has *no mode*.

Measures of Central Tendency

17   The **mean** is the sum of all the values divided by the number of values. It is the mathematical average.

The **median** is the middle number in a group of values that are listed from smallest to largest. It divides a group of numbers in half.

The **mode** is the value that occurs most often in a group of values.

—Lial and Hestwood, *Prealgebra*, pp. 347–50

VOCABULARY REVIEW

1. For each of the words listed below, use context; prefixes, roots, and suffixes; and/or a dictionary to write a brief definition of the word as it used in the reading.

    a. state numbers (para. 1) _____

    b. data (para. 2) _____

    c. values (para. 3)_____

    d. frequency(para. 6); _____

2. Underline new specialized terms introduced in the reading.

COMPREHENSION QUESTIONS

1. To assess your comprehension, define each of the following terms in your own words without reference to the reading: *statistics, measure of central tendency, mean, median, mode.* Verify your definitions by comparing them with the definitions in the reading.
2. What is the difference between a mean and a mode?
3. What is the difference between a mean and a median?

THINKING CRITICALLY

1. List the names and ages of 15 friends or classmates. (Estimate the ages, if necessary.)
    a. Find the mean age and the median age.
    b. Are the mean and median ages similar or different? Why did that happen?
2. List the names and ages of 10 family members or relatives. Try to include one very young person or one very old person (but not both). Estimate the ages, if necessary.
    a. Find the mean age and the median age.
    b. Are the mean age and median ages similar or different? Why did that happen?

3. List the courses you are taking at this time and the number of credits for each course.
    a. List the highest grade you think you will earn in each course. Then find your grade point average.
    b. List the lowest grade you think you will earn in each course. Then find your grade point average.
4. Suppose you own a gift shop. Last summer, you stocked T-shirts in five different sizes, but they took up too much shelf space. This summer, you want to order only one size. Using last summer's sales, should you find the mean size, median size, or mode size? Explain your answer.

LEARNING/STUDY STRATEGIES

1. Write a summary of the process involved in finding
    a. the mean
    b. the median
    c. the mode
2. What overall thought pattern(s) is or are used in the reading?

ON-LINE RESEARCH: STATISTICS*

Statistics are used to describe the results of surveys and other research in many different fields. Often, the "raw" data is not given in reports; instead, the researcher has already analyzed the data before presenting it to the public. The sites listed below include instances of both raw data and data that has already been analyzed. The questions, however, focus on raw data that you can analyze yourself.

1. The Media Awareness Network maintains statistics about television and other media. Visit their "Media Content: Television" page at http://www.mediaawareness.ca/eng/issues/stats/contv.htm#unreal. Find the summary titled "T.V. 'Clutter' On The Rise." read the summary to find out how much TV broadcasting time is taken up by commercials and other non-programming content. List the four time slots mentioned and the amount of time taken in each hour (given in minutes and seconds) for nonprogramming content. What is the mean amount of time for non-programming content per hour of TV content overall?
2. The Center for Science in the Public Interest, an organization that seeks to improve the safety and nutritional quality of food, includes an

article about soft drinks titled "Liquid Candy" at <u>http://www.cspinet.org/ sodapop/liquid candy.htm</u>. Scan the article to find Table 2. From the table data, determine the mean ounces per day of soda pop drunk by all teens (boys and girls together). Then find the median number of ounces per day. Finally, does the list include a mode? If so, what is it?

*If any of these sites is unavailable, use a search engine to locate a new Web site on the same topic.

16 | READING IN THE NATURAL SCIENCES

LEARNING OBJECTIVES
- ■ **To understand the scientific approach**
- ■ **To develop specialized reading techniques for the sciences**
- ■ **To learn to work with process, cause-and-effect, classification, and problem/solution patterns**
- ■ **To adapt study strategies for the sciences**

The natural sciences are divided into two categories: life sciences and physical sciences. The life sciences—biology, botany, zoology, and physiology—are concerned with the study of living organisms: how they grow, develop, function, and reproduce. The physical sciences are concerned with the properties, functions, structure, and composition of matter, substances, and energy. They include physics, chemistry, astronomy, and physical geography and geology.

THE SCIENCES: EXPLAINING NATURAL PHENOMENA

Science is built on knowledge resulting from scientific investigation. Through a process of asking well-defined, specific questions and searching for answers, science has accumulated a body of knowledge about how our physical and biological worlds function. The goal of science is to explain natural phenomena that affect our daily lives. Scientists ask questions and search for answers about any unexplained event. Consider, for example, the disease called AIDS. In scientific research that is still continuing, scientists have asked questions such as:

What causes it?

Why does it occur?

How is it transmitted?

What is its incubation period?

What are its precise effects on the immune system?

To study a problem, scientists use the scientific method. This method is also used to continually reevaluate what is known, in light of new research findings and discoveries. The operation of the scientific method was introduced in Chapter 12. In science courses, you'll be reading about research findings as well as conducting your own experiments.

Because the emphasis is on observation and experimentation, most science courses have a required weekly lab in which you are given the opportunity to observe and experiment. The lab gives you direct experience with the scientific method while reinforcing, explaining, or demonstrating theories and principles presented in the course lectures.

Why Study the Sciences?

The field of natural science investigates the physical world around us. Science addresses and attempts to answer many important questions.

- Is there extraterrestrial life?
- Why do leaves change color in the fall?
- Why do I have blue eyes when my parents' eyes are brown?

Science also explores questions essential to our well-being.

- How can cancer be cured or prevented?
- What synthetic substitutes can prevent depletion of our natural resources?
- How can water pollution be prevented?

The study of science is fun and rewarding because you come to understand more about yourself and how you interact with the physical world around you.

SPECIALIZED READING TECHNIQUES

Although most college courses present new concepts and principles, they often cover subjects in the realm of your experience. The social sciences, for example, deal with social groups and physical and emotional needs—all concerns familiar to you. Science courses, on the other hand, sometimes deal with less familiar topics—molecular structure, mutant genes or radioactive isotopes, for instance. Treatment of these topics may also be detailed and technical, involving a new and extensive vocabulary.

Because of the detailed nature of scientific material, plan to commit more time to reading and studying it than you would to studying other material—generally twice as much. Many students find that scientific study requires much greater time and effort than their other courses. Taking a science course is like taking three courses in one. You are, in a sense, taking a language course, since there is much new terminology to learn. A science course is also like a logic or philosophy course, since you must learn to work flexibly and logically with new ideas. Finally, a science course is like a graphic arts course in which you learn to draw and understand visual representations.

Reading scientific material requires specialized techniques, as does each of your other courses, but once you develop an effective approach, you will find science courses to be interesting and challenging, as well as manageable.

Use the following strategies to strengthen your approach to scientific reading.

Preview Before Reading

Because scientific material is often detailed and unfamiliar, previewing is even more important than in other courses. (Refer to Chapter 1 for a review of previewing techniques.) Your preview should include looking at problems at the end of the chapter and the chapter summary because they will provide clues about principles and formulas emphasized in the chapter.

Adopt a Scientific Mind Set

To read effectively in a science course, it is essential to adopt a scientific way of thinking. The usual concerns (such as "What is important to learn?" and "How much supporting information do I need to learn?") may be of only secondary importance. Instead, to be successful, you must adopt the scientific mind set of asking questions and seeking answers, analyzing problems, and looking for solutions or explanations. As you read, continually ask questions such as:

What does this mean? What does it *not* mean?

Does this make sense to me?

Why is this so?

How do we know this?

How does this happen?

What does this show?

Are alternative explanations plausible?

What laws govern or affect this?

To illustrate this process, Figure 16–1 shows the questions a student asked as she read a page of her chemistry textbook.

Sometimes, the questions you ask will be answered as you continue reading. Other times, you may need to seek answers yourself by referring to another chapter, by asking your instructor, or by talking with classmates. Asking and answering these questions will get you involved with the material and direct you toward scientific critical thinking.

Figure 16–1   Scientific Thinking

MARS

How far away is it?

Why?

Mars is the only planet whose surface features can be seen through Earth-based telescopes. Its distinctive rust-colored hue makes it stand out in the night sky. When Mars is near opposition, even telescopes for home use reveal its seasonal changes. Dark markings on the Martian surface can be seen to vary, and prominent polar caps shrink noticeably during the spring and summer months.

6-7   Earth-based observations originally suggested that Mars might harbor extraterrestrial life

Is it similar in other ways, as well?

The Dutch physicist Christian Huygens made the first reliable observations of Mars in 1659. Using a telescope of his own design, Huygens identified a prominent, dark surface feature that re-emerged roughly every 24 hours, suggesting a rate or rotation very much like the Earth's. Huygens' observations soon led to speculation about life on Mars because the planet seemed so similar to Earth.

In 1877 Giovanni Virginio Schiaparelli, and Italian astronomer, reported seeing 40 lines crisscrossing the Martian surface. He called these dark features *canali*, an Italian term meaning "water channels." It was soon mistranslated into English as *canals*, implying the existence on Mars of intelligent creatures capable of substantial engineering feats. This speculation led Percival Lowell, who came from a wealthy Boston family, to finance a major new observatory near Flagstaff, Arizona. By the end of the nineteenth century, Lowell had allegedly observed 160 Martian canals.

What evidence did he offer?

Why was it fashionable?

Who did this?

What causes them?

It soon became fashionable to speculate that the Martian canals formed an enormous planetwide irrigation network to transport water from melting polar caps to vegetation near the equator. (The seasonal changes on Mars' dark surface markings can be mistaken for vegetation.) In view of the planet's reddish, desertlike appearance, Mars was thought to be a dying planet whose inhabitants must go to great lengths to irrigate their farmlands. No doubt the Martians would readily abandon their arid ancestral homeland and invade the Earth for its abundant resources. Hundreds of science fiction stories and dozens of monster movies owe their existence to the *canali* of Schiaparelli.

Source: Kaufmann and Comins, *Discovering the Universe*, pp. 144–45

**EXERCISE
16–1**

*Read the following excerpt from a chemistry textbook. What questions could you
ask about the excerpt? Write them in the margin.*

COLLOIDS IN THE CAFETERIA

The next time you are in a cafeteria, look closely at the colorful gelatin dessert.
It appears to be a transparent, wobbly solid, yet it consists primarily of water.
The chocolate pudding nearby is also mainly water. Is it a solid or a liquid? When
you fill your glass with milk, can you determine whether it is a solution or a mixture? Like most foods, these are *colloids,* suspensions of particles ranging from
20 μm to 100 μm in diameter, in a solvent. Colloidal particles are much larger than
most molecules but are too small to be seen with a microscope. Colloids thus are
often classified between homogeneous solutions and heterogeneous mixtures. The
small particles give the colloid a homogeneous appearance but are large enough to
scatter light. The light scattering explains why milk is white, not transparent.

A colloid that is a suspension of solids in a liquid is called a *sol,* and a suspension
of one liquid in another is called an *emulsion.* For example, skim milk is a suspension of solids, mainly proteins, in water, so it is a sol; mayonnaise has small droplets
of water suspended in oil, so it is an emulsion. When we whip cream, milk rich in
butterfat, or beat egg whites to form meringues, we make *foams,* suspensions of a
gas in a liquid or solid. When we separate the fat from milk and churn it into butter,
we create a *solid emulsion,* a suspension of a liquid, in this case, milk, in a solid, butterfat. Gelatin desserts are a type of solid emulsion called a *gel,* which is soft, but
holds its shape.

Aqueous colloids can be classified as hydrophilic or hydrophobic. Suspensions
of fat in water, such as milk and mayonnaise, are hydrophobic colloids, because fat
molecules have little attraction for water molecules. Gels and puddings are examples of hydrophilic colloids. The macromolecules of the proteins in gelatin and the
starch in pudding have many hydrophilic groups that attract water. The giant protein molecules in gelatin uncoil in hot water. Their abundant amide groups (see
Section 11.10) form hydrogen bonds with water. When the mixture cools, the protein chains link together again, but now they enclose many water molecules within
themselves, as well as molecules of sugar, dye, and flavoring agents. The result is an
open network of protein chains that hold the water in a flexible solid structure.

—Atkins and Jones, *Chemistry: Molecules, Matter, and Change,* pp. 144–45

Learn Terminology and Notation

Physics: wave-particle duality, torque, tangential acceleration, $v = dx/dt$

Physiology: hemagglutination, ventricular diastole, myocardial infarction, DNA

Chemistry: NaCl

Astronomy: mass-luminosity relation, eclipsing binaries, bok globules

How many of these terms are familiar? They are only a few of the new terms and notations encountered in each of these courses. As you can see, you will need to spend considerable time and effort learning terminology. You must understand the meaning of specialized and technical words in order to understand the ideas and concepts being presented.

In some courses, such as physics and chemistry, formulas and notation are important as well. Symbols, abbreviations, and formulas are used to represent objects and concepts in abbreviated form. You might think of these as shorthand systems for naming elements and quantities and describing their interaction. As you read and study, avoid memorizing formulas; instead, focus on understanding what they mean and how to apply them.

A course master file, described in Chapter 3, is extremely valuable in science courses. Mapping also works well, especially in the life sciences. Finally, as you learn the meaning of each new term, also learn its correct pronunciation and spelling.

Learn Symbols and Abbreviations

Symbols and abbreviations are frequently used in the sciences. The abbreviation "g" is a shortcut expression for a unit of mass, called a gram. The symbol "g" can also stand for the gravitational constant, 9.8N/kg, for the surface of the Earth. Textbooks use different kinds of type to distinguish types of quantities. For instance, "*v*" (in italics) means speed while "**v**" (in boldface) means velocity. Watch for clues your textbook provides.

Everyday Words and Special Meanings

Scientists sometimes attach specialized meanings to ordinary words. For example, *power, pressure, force,* and *impulse* are everyday words, but they have very specific meanings to a physicist. Power, for instance, is a measure of how fast work is done or energy is transformed and is represented by the formula:

$$\text{Power} = \text{work} \div \text{time}$$

Note that its meaning in science is different from its meaning in mathematics, too, where *power* refers to a number multiplied by itself. *Pressure,* another everyday term, in physics means the amount of force per area over which the force is distributed.

Because you are familiar with these words, it is easy to overlook them when studying or to assume you already know them. Be sure to include these terms in your course master file, along with the other specialized terminology and notation.

Learn Common Prefixes, Roots, and Suffixes

As you discovered in Chapter 3, many words in our language contain prefixes, roots, and suffixes. In most science courses, you will discover a common core of these word parts that are used as the basic building blocks of a specialized terminology. In physics, for example, units of measurement take prefixes.

Prefix	Meaning
micro-	millionth
milli-	thousandth
centi-	hundredth
deci-	tenth
deka-	ten
hecto-	hundred
kilo-	thousand
mega-	million
giga-	billion

In physiology, roots and suffixes unlock the meaning of numerous frequently used terms.

Root	Word	Suffix
hem(a)—blood	hematology	-logy (study of)
	hematoma	-oma (growth, tumor)
	hemathermal	-thermal (heat)

Similarly, in chemistry, astronomy, and biology you will find sets of core prefixes, roots, and suffixes. Include these in your master file, as suggested in Chapter 3.

Read Section by Section

Chapters in science texts are usually lengthy. Because the material is so complex, try not to read an entire chapter in one sitting. Instead, divide the chapter into sections and read one portion at a time. Look for end-of-chapter problems or questions that apply to the sections you are reading. Mark them and remember to work them out after you have read the section. Be sure to make connections between sections.

Study Sample Problems

In the physical sciences, sample problems are often included in the text to demonstrate a problem-solving process. Read the sample problems carefully, alternating between the text explanation and the mathematical solution.

Next, explain the process in your own words. Doing so will solidify it in your memory. If you are unable to express the process in your own words or if you must refer back frequently to the text, this indicates that you do not fully understand the process. Don't expect to get it all the first time. These are difficult subjects, and understanding may come gradually.

Study and Draw Diagrams

Science texts contain numerous diagrams and drawings of structures and processes. These drawings often clarify a principle or concept; a diagram of a gun firing and recoiling, for example, makes the concept of conservation of momentum clear. Diagrams also are used to show forces, conditions, shapes, directions, processes, or positions. Diagrams provide a visual representation of an object or occurrence, and they increase your ability both to understand and to retain information. Diagrams are also important in answering questions and solving problems.

Many students do not pay enough attention to the diagrams included in their texts. Take time to study each drawing as you read. As you review, use the drawings to refresh your recall of key concepts and processes. Test your recall by closing the book and drawing the diagram from memory. Compare your drawing with the one in the text, noting errors, missing parts, or discrepancies. Do not be concerned if your drawings seem poor in comparison to the text; your ability to draw will improve as you practice.

You will also find diagrams useful in laboratory situations. Draw brief sketches of your equipment setup, techniques, and observations. These will help as you write your lab reports.

Brush Up on Math Skills

Mathematics is an integral part of many science courses, especially chemistry and physics. Many instructors assume you have taken algebra, which is often needed to solve equations and problems. If your math background is weak or if it has been a number of years since you studied algebra, you may need to brush up your skills. You might consider taking a review course, purchasing a skills practice book, or using computer-assisted instructional programs in the learning lab. Talk with your instructor, and ask for recommendations.

THOUGHT PATTERNS IN THE NATURAL SCIENCES

Four thought patterns are common in the sciences: process, cause-and-effect, classification, and problem/solution.

The Process and Cause-and-Effect Patterns

Many of the sciences are concerned with how and why things happen: how a tadpole turns into a frog, what makes light reflect, how the tides work, how our metabolism functions, and so forth. Process and cause-and-effect patterns are often used to explain natural phenomena. Process and cause-and-effect patterns are logically linked to each other. In a process, the steps may be linked in a cause-and-effect chain. You may find that you need to read process descriptions more than once. Read the description the first time to get an overview; then read it at least once more to understand the steps and the connections between them.

Use the following strategies to read process material.

1. *List the steps.* Either in the text margin or in your notebook, write a step-by-step summary of the process in your own words. Figure 16–2 (p. 472) shows the notes a student wrote for a physics textbook chapter on plate tectonics, explaining how islands and mountains are formed.

2. *Draw diagrams or maps.* Diagrams, maps, or flowcharts help you visualize the process and will enhance your recall as well. Chapter 10 describes several types of mapping. Figure 16–3 (p. 473) shows a diagram a biology student drew to describe how convection currents stir the air and create winds.

3. *Describe the process aloud.* Assume you are explaining the process to a friend who is not taking the course, or better yet, actually study with a friend. By forcing yourself to explain the process in a nontechnical way, you can test whether you really understand it and are not simply rephrasing the technical language used by the author.

EXERCISE 16–2

Read the following excerpt from a geology textbook which begins below and ends on page 473. Working with a classmate, one student should write a summary of the greenhouse effect while the other draws a diagram. Exchange your work, and draw a diagram based only on your partner's summary or write a summary based only on his or her diagram. Then compare the results to the whole excerpt.

CARBON DIOXIDE AND THE GREENHOUSE EFFECT

The possible relationship between carbon dioxide in the atmosphere and climate warming was proposed by Svante Arrhenius, one of the early winners of the Nobel Prize in chemistry (1903). Arrhenius knew a great deal about geology as well as chemistry, and he was familiar with the effects of glaciation on the terrain of his native Sweden. He was also aware of the growing discussion of the causes of glaciations that enlivened many geologists' meetings at the end of the nineteenth

Figure 16–2   Sample Summary

PLATE TECTONICS

Summary:

1. Earth's crust has approx. 12 large plates = lithosphere. These rest on the asthenosphere.

2. These plates spread and sink (subduction).

3. When a continental plate and an ocean plate collide, a trench and island arc will form.

4. When ocean plates collide, they create a marginal or inland sea.

5. When continental plates collide, folding and faulting of sediment and rock occurs, creating mountain ranges.

Recent ideas concerning seafloor spreading and the origin and evolution of the ocean basins are incorporated into an even more encompassing concept called **plate tectonics.** In plate tectonics theory, Earth's entire crust is composed of about a dozen large plates, up to 160 km (100 miles) thick. These plates make up the lithosphere. Each moves essentially as a rigid block over Earth's surface. The lithosphere rests upon the less rigid part of Earth called the **asthenosphere.**

The plates can be visualized as curved caps covering a large ball, or perhaps as sections of peel on an orange. Boundaries of the individual plates are usually areas of high seismic (earthquake) activity. Deformation, such as faulting, folding, or shearing mainly occurs at the boundaries between the plates. Because the surface area of Earth is essentially constant, spreading in one place must be balanced by sinking or **subduction** somewhere else.

The appearance of the edge of a continent is often influenced by its relation to areas of seafloor spreading or subduction. If a continent's edge is at the boundary of a subducting oceanic plate, a trench will form, and sometimes an **island arc** or coastal mountain range (Figure a). A **trench** is a deep, long narrow depression in the seafloor, with very steep slopes. An island arc is a curved pattern of mainly volcanic islands and a trench. It is

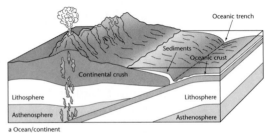

a Ocean/continent

generally curved in a convex direction (bows out) toward the ocean, with the trench on the seaward side. The Aleutian Islands and Aleutian Trench in the north Pacific is a good example of a trench-island arc system.

The subducting plate forms the trench. In the process of submerging beneath the other plate, much of its sediment is scraped off onto the landward side of the trench. This material and the subducting plate may be reheated, perhaps even melted, eventually becoming part of the continental plate and forming a coastal mountain range. These are events that occur when oceanic crust is subducted beneath lighter continental crust. A similar sequence occurs during the collision of two ocean plates. The main difference is that an inland or marginal sea may form behind an island arc (Figure b).

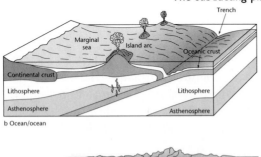

b Ocean/ocean

Results can be quite different when two plates of continental composition collide. In this case, both plates are of similar density, so neither easily overrides the other. The result is unusually intense folding and faulting of the sediments and rocks, often leading to the formation of a major mountain range (Figure c). The Himalayan Mountains are still being formed in this manner by the collision of India (continental crust) with Asia (continental crust).

c Continent/continent

Source: Ross, *Introduction to Oceanography,* pp. 51–52.

Figure 16–3   Sample Diagram

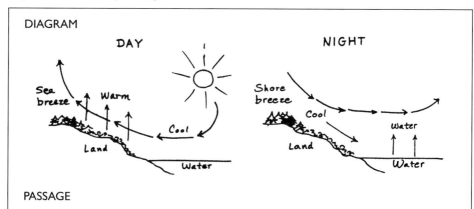

DIAGRAM

PASSAGE

Convection currents stirring the atmosphere result in winds. Some parts of the earth's surface absorb heat from the sun more readily than others, and as a result the air near the surface is heated unevenly and convection currents form. This is evident at the seashore. In the daytime the shore warms more easily than the water; air over the shore is pushed up (we say it rises) by cooler air from above the water taking its place. The result is a sea breeze. At night the process reverses because the shore cools off more quickly than the water, and then the warmer air is over the sea. Build a fire on the beach and you'll notice that the smoke sweeps inward during the day and seaward at night.

Source: Hewitt, *Conceptual Physics,* pp. 274–75.

century. He reasoned that the small amount of carbon dioxide in the atmosphere (now about 345 ppm) could affect climate because the carbon dioxide molecules strongly absorb heat rays from the Earth.

Here is how it works. The atmosphere is relatively transparent to the incoming visible rays of the Sun. Much of this radiant energy from the Sun is absorbed by the Earth's surface and then reemitted as invisible infrared heat rays. Just as a hot pavement radiates heat as it is warmed by the Sun, the Earth's surface radiates heat back to the atmosphere. The atmosphere, however, is not transparent to these infrared rays, because carbon dioxide and water molecules strongly absorb the infrared instead of allowing it to escape to space. As a result, the atmosphere is heated and radiates heat back to the surface. This is called the *greenhouse effect,* by analogy to the warming of a greenhouse, whose glass lets in visible light but lets little heat escape.

The more carbon dioxide, the warmer the atmosphere; the less carbon dioxide, the colder. Without any greenhouse effect, Earth's surface temperature would be well below freezing and the oceans would be a solid mass of ice. Geologists now have evidence that, aside from glaciations, climates ranged from warm to cool in the geological past. It is likely that some of these changes were related to changes in the amount of carbon dioxide in the atmosphere.

—Press and Siever, *Understanding Earth,* p. 348

The Classification Pattern

In the life sciences, classification is an important pattern. As a means of studying life forms or species, biologists classify them into groups or types based on shared or similar characteristics. In fact, there are seven levels of groupings altogether. Organisms are first divided into five kingdoms. Those kingdoms are subdivided into divisions called phyla, and then into classes, orders, families, genera, and species. For example, humans are classified as follows:

Category	Classification
kingdom	animalia
division	chordata
class	mammalia
order	primates
family	hominidae
genus	*Homo*
species	*sapiens*

Other examples of classification include types of cells, methods of reproduction, and types of tissues.

Classification is also used in the physical sciences. In chemistry, elements are grouped and listed by groupings on the periodic table. In physics, matter is classified into gases, liquids, plasmas, and solids.

When reading material written in this pattern, first determine what is being classified and what the types or groups are. Look for a topic or summary sentence that states what is being classified. Next, discover why or on what basis the classification was made. That is, determine what characteristics members of the group share. For example, the following excerpt from a biology textbook describes the classification of animal eggs.

TYPES OF EGGS

The three basic types of animal eggs are roughly categorized according to the amount of *yolk* they have. The amount of yolk is critical since it is the embryo's food supply, at least for a time. In some species, the embryo needs only a small supply of yolk since it soon switches to nutrients derived from the mother's blood, as is the case with humans. We only need enough to last until the embryo has implanted in the wall of the uterus. In contrast, birds leave their mother's body at a very early developmental stage, and they must carry their entire embryonic food supply with them. So, whereas a human egg is smaller than the period at the end of this sentence, it would be hard to hide an ostrich egg with this whole book.

Interestingly, both the young and the adults of these two species are about the same size.

Other kinds of animals have a moderate yolk supply. In these, the young must begin to find its own food long before it has reached its final body organization. The frog is an example. The frog egg has just enough yolk to get the developing embryo to the tadpole stage; after that, the tadpole can survive on food stored in its tail for a time, but it must soon begin to eat on its own.

—Wallace, *Biology: The World of Life*, pp. 446–47

In this excerpt, the basis of classification is directly stated in the first sentence: the eggs are classified according to the size of the yolk.

EXERCISE 16–3

Read this excerpt from a physiology textbook, and answer the questions that follow.

TYPES OF SMOOTH MUSCLE

The smooth muscle in different body organs varies substantially in its (1) fiber arrangement and organization, (2) responsiveness to various stimuli, and (3) innervation. However, for simplicity, smooth muscle is usually categorized into two major types: *single-unit* and *multiunit smooth muscle.*

Single-Unit Smooth Muscle
Single-unit smooth muscle, commonly called **visceral muscle,** is far more common. Its cells (1) contract as a unit and rhythmically, (2) are electrically coupled to one another by *gap junctions,* and (3) often exhibit spontaneous action potentials. All the smooth muscle characteristics described so far pertain to single-unit smooth muscle. Thus, the cells of single-unit smooth muscle are arranged in sheets, exhibit the stress-relaxation response, and so on.

Multiunit Smooth Muscle
The smooth muscles in the large airways to the lungs and in large arteries, the arrector pili muscles attached to hair follicles, and the internal eye muscles that adjust your pupil size and allow you to focus visually are all examples of **multiunit smooth muscle.**

In contrast to what we see in single-unit muscle, gap junctions are rare and spontaneous and synchronous depolarizations infrequent. Multiunit smooth muscle, like skeletal muscle, (1) consists of muscle fibers that are structurally independent of each other; (2) is richly supplied with nerve endings, each of which forms a motor unit with a number of muscle fibers; and (3) responds to neural stimulation with graded contractions. However, while skeletal muscle is served by the somatic (voluntary) division of the nervous system, multiunit smooth muscle (like single-unit smooth muscle) is innervated by the autonomic (involuntary) division and is also responsive to hormonal controls.

—Marieb, *Human Anatomy and Physiology,* p. 294

1. What does this excerpt classify?
2. Describe each type of smooth muscle.
3. On what basis is the classification made?

The Problem/Solution Pattern

Textbook chapters, homework, and exams in the physical sciences often contain problems. To solve these problems, you must apply the concepts, laws, and formulas presented in the chapter. Use the following steps to solve problems.

1. *Read the problem and identify what is given and what is asked for.* In word problems, mark or underline critical information. Next, restate the information using the symbols you will use as you solve the problem. Be certain not to use the same symbol to represent different quantities. For example, if there are two objects in a situation with different masses, do not use m for both masses. Use m_1 and m_2 to distinguish between the two masses.

2. *If possible, make a drawing of the problem.* Label known quantities with the correct symbols; using the symbols may suggest which equation to use in solving the problem, if you are not certain.

3. *State the principle that is related to the problem and write the general equation that embodies the principle.*

4. *Calculate the solution.* Always write the units after each number (seconds, moles, liters, etc.).

5. *Analyze your answer.* Does it make sense? Compare your solution with similar sample problems and determine whether you followed the correct procedure. Check the units as well as the numerical values.

6. *Review your solution process.* Especially if you had difficulty with the problem, pause after you solve it to figure out what you should have done or known in order to solve it more easily. Did you overlook a step or ignore a key concept? Analyzing your solution process will help you solve similar problems more easily in the future.

Here is an example of the use of this problem-solving procedure.

PROBLEM: A cat steps off a ledge and drops to the ground in $1/2$ second. What is the cat's speed on striking the ground? What is the cat's average speed during the $1/2$ second? How high is the ledge from the ground?

Steps	Example
1. Identify what is given and what is asked for	Given: drops in $1/2$ sec, $t = 1/2$ sec Asked for: 1. speed (velocity) (v) 2. average speed (average velocity) ($\bar{v}$) 3. height (distance) (d)
2. Draw a diagram	$t = 1/2$ sec
3. Determine the principle and formula	Principle: acceleration and motion of free falling bodies Formulae: $v = gt$, $d = \bar{v}t$ $g = 10$ m/s² $\bar{v} = \dfrac{\text{beginning } v + \text{final } v}{2}$
4. Calculate the solution	$v = gt$ $v = 10$ m/s² × $1/2$ s = 5 m/s $\bar{v} = \dfrac{0\text{m/s} + 5\text{ m/s}}{2} = 2.5$ m/s
5. Analyze the answer	$d = \bar{v}t = 2.5$ m/s² × $1/2$ s = 1.25 m
6. Review the solution process	Had to know acceleration of free falling bodies is 10 m/s²

—Hewitt, *Conceptual Physics*, p. 21

ADAPTING YOUR STUDY TECHNIQUES

Because of the unique content of science courses, it is especially important to adapt your study habits. Use the following suggestions for studying in the sciences.

1. *Complete reading assignments before attending lectures.* Because of the unfamiliar subject matter, you can understand lectures better if you know something about the topic. You may not understand everything you read (and it will be necessary to reread after the lecture), but you

will have an advantage during the lecture because the terms, concepts, and principles will be more familiar.

2. *Highlight your textbook selectively.* Everything looks important in scientific texts, and it is easy to fall into the habit of over-highlighting. Avoid this pitfall by reading a paragraph or section before highlighting. Then go back and mark only key terms and concepts. Do not try to highlight all useful facts. Refer to Chapter 10 for suggestions on how to highlight effectively.

3. *Use outlining.* Especially in the life sciences, many students find outlining to be an effective study and review technique. Some texts in the life sciences include chapter outlines; even though your text may have one, make your own. It is the process of making the outline that is important. Outlining forces you to decide what information is important and how it is related and then to express the ideas in your own words. Refer to Chapter 10 for specific suggestions on taking outline notes.

4. *Integrate your lab work with the text and lectures.* Most science courses have a required lab. Because the lab is scheduled separately from the lecture and has its own manual, you may fail to see the lab as an integral part of the course. The lab is intended to help you understand and apply principles and research techniques used in your course and provides you with an opportunity to ask pertinent questions. Use the following tips for handling lab work.

   - Be prepared before going to lab. Read the experiment once to understand its overall purpose and a second time to understand the specific procedures. Make notes or underline key information.
   - Ask questions before you make a mistake. Lab procedures can be time-consuming to repeat, so ask questions first.
   - Be sure you understand the purpose of each step before you perform it.
   - Analyze your results and do the lab report as soon as possible. The best time to study your results is while the experiment and procedures are still fresh in your mind. If you finish the lab work early, stay and discuss results and interpretations with other students or your lab instructor.
   - Follow the required format closely when writing your report.

5. *Use chapter problems as guides.* The end-of-chapter problems in your textbook help you determine what it is important to learn. Do the problems even if they have not been assigned by your instructor. As you read the problems, note the variables (temperature, pressure, volume, etc.) that

appear in the problems. Then be certain to learn definitions, concepts, principles, and formulas pertaining to these variables.

6. *Develop a weekly study plan.* Science is best studied on a daily basis. Devise a weekly plan that includes time every day for previewing text assignments, reviewing lecture notes, reading text assignments, preparing for and writing up labs, and—most important—reviewing in such a way as to integrate lectures, the text, and lab sessions.

7. *Prepare for exams.* Exams and quizzes in the sciences require you to learn factual information as well as develop problem-solving ability and apply your learning to practical situations. To be prepared for exams,

- Make lists of types of problems you have studied and key facts about their solution.
- Identify key laws, principles, and concepts.
- Determine where your instructor placed her or his emphasis.
- Prepare a practice test, using problems from your text, and take it as though it were an actual exam.
- Consider forming a study group with classmates.

IF YOU ARE HAVING DIFFICULTY

If the sciences are typically a difficult field of study for you, or if you suddenly find yourself not doing well in a science course, try the following survival tactics.

Use available resources. Visit your instructor during office hours to discuss your performance or to get help with particular problems. Check to see whether tutoring is available through the department office or the college's learning center.

Make changes in your learning strategies. If you are a non-science major taking your one or two required science courses, you may feel as strange as if you were in a foreign country. First, you must revise your approaches and strategies. Plan on making the changes already described in this section.

Learn from classmates. Talk with and observe the strategies of students who are doing well in the course. You are likely to pick up new and useful procedures.

Double your study time. If you are having trouble with a course, make a commitment to spend more time and to work harder. Use this added time to revise and try out new study strategies. Never spend time using a strategy that is not working.

Purchase a review book. Find a student practice manual or other learning aid and work with it regularly. Many major science texts have study guides or problem-solving guides to accompany them. Your instructor may be able to recommend specific titles. If the book you purchase does not use the same notation system as your text, be sure to note any differences.

Finally, here are some specific tips to help you "pull the course together."

1. *Review your lecture notes and text assignments frequently;* discover how they work together and where they seem to be headed.

2. *As you review, make a list of topics you do understand and a list of those you do not.*

3. *Decide whether you are experiencing difficulty as a result of gaps in your scientific background.* Ask yourself whether the instructor assumes you know things when you do not. If so, consider finding a tutor.

4. *Make a list of specific questions and ask for help from both your classmates and your instructor.*

 STUDY Tips **Preparing for Exams in the Natural Sciences**

Exams in the sciences require you to learn factual information as well as to develop problem-solving ability and apply your learning to practical situations. To be prepared for exams,

1. *Identify keys laws, principles, and concepts.* Prepare review sheets on which you summarize important information.

2. *Make lists of types of problems you have studied.* For example, in chemistry, for a chapter on gases, you might identify problem types such as pressure and volume, temperature and pressure, and temperature and volume. For each problem type, list steps in the solution.

Practice solving each problem type by using exercises in the text or by constructing your own problems.

3. *Consider forming a study group with classmates.* Quiz each other, and work through sample problems.

4. *Prepare a practice exam using problems or review questions from your text, and take it as though it were an actual exam.*

5. *Do not review by simply rereading your text and notes.* The material will look familiar, and you will think you have learned it. Instead, test yourself: Ask yourself questions and answer them. Use guide questions (see Chapter 1).

SUMMARY

This chapter describes reading strategies for the sciences. The sciences focus on asking questions about our physical and biological world and seeking answers to those questions.

Specialized techniques for reading the sciences are

- previewing before reading
- adopting a scientific mind set
- learning terminology and notation
- reading section by section
- studying sample problems
- brushing up on math skills

Four thought patterns predominate in the sciences:

- process
- cause-and-effect
- classification
- problem/solution

Suggestions are offered for adapting study techniques to the sciences.

Biology

PREREADING QUESTIONS

1. How did dinosaurs become extinct?
2. Why did other animals become extinct at this same time?

DEATH STARS AND DINOSAURS: THE GREAT EXTINCTIONS

Robert A. Wallace

1 It may be quite difficult to account for the beginnings of new species, but it is often easy to see how some species died out. We have built dams and knowingly doomed small pockets of isolated species. We have hunted other animals to extinction, as we did the dodo, the carrier pigeon, and the last common ancestor of the horse and zebra. However, other species have passed into extinction for reasons that continue to puzzle us. In particular, it is difficult to account for the massive, large-scale extinctions in which many species passed from the Earth at once. For example, why did so many species die out with the great dinosaurs at the end of the Cretaceous period?[1]

2 One hypothesis advanced to account for the die-off at the end of the Cretaceous is based on data suggesting that the temperature of the Earth dropped drastically about that time. The dinosaurs and the others, some say, simply died of the chilling effects of hypothermia. However, others have urged that the cooling of the Earth unbalanced the sex ratios of many species. They note that the sexes of many kinds of animals, such as alligators, amphibians, and some fish, are temperature dependent. That is, eggs raised in environments below a certain temperature will give rise to animals of one sex, and above that temperature, to the other sex. The argument is that as the Earth cooled below a certain critical point, all the hatchlings of some species would have been of one sex and doomed to roam the Earth without ever knowing the joys of parenthood. . . .

3 Another explanation of the great extinctions of the Cretaceous also involves a cooling episode, but this one accounts for its origins. According to the **Alvarez hypothesis,** the Earth was struck by a great asteroid that raised a cloud of dust that blocked the sun for many months and effectively impeded

[1] A period of time 65 million years ago.

photosynthesis. Any such disruption of the food chain would have led to the demise of a great many species. The evidence here is circumstantial but solid. The best line of evidence is the discovery that a rare element called iridium was deposited in a fine layer over the Earth at about the end of the Cretaceous. Iridium is uncommon in the Earth's crust, but quite common in asteroids. . . .

4   Other researchers have suggested that the Earth was struck by some heavenly body that was not an asteroid, but perhaps three or four comets. . . . The comets, they say, were from the great belt of 100 million or so comets that lazily circle the sun far beyond the reaches of the solar system. Occasionally, though, about every 26 to 30 million years, great numbers of the comets are jerked toward our sun by the passage of a companion star to the sun. The companion star has not been located or identified, but it has been named Nemesis. Journalists, with their flair for high drama, have taken to calling it the Death Star.

5   Any such companion star, if it exists, could be any of the hefty little "black stars," dense bodies with a gravitational pull so strong that not even light can escape. It has been suggested that the star has an extremely elliptical orbit that takes it far into the celestial realm—until its next deadly loop through the belt of comets. Geologists have found that the Earth has indeed been peppered every 30 million years or so by celestial objects big enough to form craters, and that the cycles roughly match the great extinctions that paleontologists tell us have taken place on our planet. Again, there is great disagreement about the existence of Nemesis and, in fact, about the periodic extinctions themselves.

6   Finally, there are those who say that about every 20 to 30 million years, the Earth passes through severe galactic storms of dark clouds and gas as the sun takes us through the plane of the Milky Way, and that these storms are responsible for the great surges of death on the planet.

7   However, on a brighter note, the sun is now passing through a clear zone, the pristine aftermath of an exploded star. So all should be clear sailing for a while . . . or so they say.

8   In summary, we have seen that, as Darwin suggested, variation in natural populations results in some organisms being better reproducers than others and that their kinds of alleles tend to increase in populations. The best reproducers, of course, will tend to be those most in harmony with the environment. Thus, populations tend to track their environment through adaptation. Evolution, then, as we understand it today, is simply a function of basic arithmetic. Those alleles that promote successful reproduction will increase in frequency.

9   Life on Earth is subject to countless pressures as it continues striving for its very existence. It must constantly react to the nature of its situation (or its predicament) and it must change. The world is a variable and changeable place,

and different life forms have evolved that are uniquely able to utilize one aspect of the Earth or another in their own ways. Put simply, life must change in order to take advantage of that part of the world available to it. In the next chapter, we will begin to explore this vast array of life and see just what the processes of natural selection have wrought.

—Wallace, *Biology: The World of Life*, pp. 191, 193–94

VOCABULARY REVIEW

1. For each of the words listed below, use context; prefixes, roots, and suffixes; and/or a dictionary to write a definition or synonym of the word as it is used in the reading.

   a. doomed (para. 1) _____

   b. extinction (para. 1) _____

   c. asteroid (para. 3) _____

   d. demise (para. 3) _____

   e. comets (para. 4) _____

   f. elliptical (para. 5) _____

   g. celestial (para. 5) _____

   h. craters (para. 5) _____

   i. paleontologists (para. 5) _____

   j. pristine (para. 7) _____

   k. alleles (para. 8) _____

   l. utilize (para. 9) _____

2. Underline new specialized terms introduced in the reading.

COMPREHENSION QUESTIONS

1. In what two ways have humans caused extinctions?
2. How could the cooling of the Earth have caused extinctions?
3. Describe one theory for the Earth's cooling at the end of the Cretaceous period.
4. Explain the "Alvarez hypothesis."
5. What is the "Death Star"?

THINKING CRITICALLY

1. Which theory of dinosaur extinction do you think is most likely to be true and why?
2. Can you think of other animals (mammals? amphibians?) not mentioned in the reading that have become extinct?
3. Do you think the writer of this selection believes in the "Death Star" theory? Why or why not?
4. Choose one of the explanations. What other evidence would you look for to confirm or refute this explanation?
5. Do you think the Earth as we know it will end? Why or why not?

LEARNING/STUDY STRATEGIES

1. Prepare a chart that summarizes the different theories that account for the extinction of dinosaurs. Use the format shown below.

THEORY	**DESCRIPTION**

2. What is the overall thought pattern used throughout this reading?

ON-LINE RESEARCH: DEATH STARS AND DINOSAURS*

The study of the evolution of species is part of many scientific fields including biology, paleontology, and geology, among others. Research some of the findings of these fields at the University of California's Museum of Paleontology (UCMP).

1. The UCMP offers an exhibit on dinosaurs, which includes a section on "What Killed the Dinosaurs? The Great Mystery." Access this part of the site by going to http://www.ucmp.berkeley.edu/diapsids/extinction.html. Scan the opening to enrich your understanding of the textbook reading: What is the technical definition of "mass extinction"? What other species died out at the same time as the great dinosaurs? Then move on to the section "Current Arguments" to get further details about the Alvarez hypothesis. What evidence is presented in support of the Alvarez hypothesis?

2. The textbook reading notes that the great dinosaurs and other species died out at the end of the Cretaceous period. Researching the Cretaceous period will help you put this mass extinction in context. For example, you can consult the UCMP's geological Web Time Machine at http://www.ucmp.berkeley.edu/help/timeform.html to find out what time period the Cretaceous covers and what era the Cretaceous period is part of. To find out what life forms were developing at about the same time as the dinosaurs were becoming extinct, go to the section on "Ancient Life." To discover where various Cretaceous fossils have been found, go to the section on "Localities." Explore the aspects of the period that interest you the most.

*If any of these sites is unavailable, use a search engine to locate a new Web site on the same topic.

17 | READING IN TECHNICAL AND APPLIED FIELDS

LEARNING OBJECTIVES

- ■ **To learn what to expect in technical courses**
- ■ **To develop specialized reading techniques for technical material**
- ■ **To learn processes and develop problem-solving strategies**
- ■ **To adapt your study strategies for technical material**

Our society has become a technological one, in which there is a heavy reliance on automation and computerization. Consequently, more technical knowledge and expertise are required. More students are pursuing degrees in a variety of technical fields, including computer information systems, environmental technology, dental technician, mechanical and electrical technology, and computer-assisted drafting. Applied fields such as EKG and X-ray technology, air conditioning and refrigeration, food service, and horticulture are other examples.

TECHNICAL FIELDS: WHAT TO EXPECT

If you are earning a degree in a technical field, you will take two basic types of courses: the technical courses in your major and required courses in related disciplines. For example, if you are earning an associate's degree in information technology, you will take numerous technical courses in programming, logic, and systems design, but you are also required to complete courses such as English composition, business communication, and physical education. Here is what to expect in each of these categories.

Technical Courses

The goal of many technical courses is to teach specific procedures and techniques that you will use on the job. These courses often present the theory and principles that govern the procedure, as well.

Grading and evaluation in technical courses is often performance-based. In addition to traditional exams and quizzes, instructors use "hands-on" exercises to evaluate your performance. In an air conditioning and refrigeration course, for example, you may be given a broken air conditioner to repair.

Work in technical fields often involves situations that require problem solving: a computer program has a "bug," a lab test produces inconsistent results, a number of landscape plantings die. Consequently, many instructors are careful to include problem-solving tasks in class, during labs, or on exams.

Many fields involve the use of instruments and equipment; others require measurement and recording of data. In either case, procedures must be followed exactly; measurements must be precise.

Although classroom lectures usually are a part of technical courses, most include some practical forms of instruction as well. Their purpose is to provide you with hands-on experience working with the procedures you are learning. As you work through lab assignments, remember that your skills are on display to your instructor just as they will be later to an employer. Develop systematic, organized routines to handle frequently used procedures and processes. Concentrate on following directions carefully. Always check and double-check your work. (Refer to Chapter 16 for additional suggestions on how to prepare and conduct lab work.) Labs also give you an opportunity to find out whether you actually understood the lecture on which the lab is based. Labs will also help you discover whether you like the career you have chosen. If you dislike labs or find them extremely difficult or too routine, you should question the appropriateness of your career choice.

Nontechnical Required Courses

Make a genuine effort to benefit from courses outside your technical field. If you are taking a required introductory psychology course, you may be the only student in the class majoring in nursing; in this case, your psychology professor can do little or nothing to relate the course to your field. As your instructor discusses various topics, you should consider how they can be applied in your field. As you learn about defense mechanisms, for example, you might consider how they might be exhibited by patients. As you study nontechnical courses, be sure to make connections and applications to your field.

READING TECHNICAL MATERIAL

Textbooks in technical fields are highly factual and packed with information. Compared to other textbooks, technical writing may seem "crowded" and difficult to read. In many technical courses, your instructor requires you to read manuals as well as textbooks. These are even more dense and, on occasion, poorly written. Use the following suggestions to help you read and learn from technical writing.

Read Slowly

Because technical writing is factual and contains numerous illustrations, diagrams, and sample problems, adjust your reading rate accordingly. Plan on spending twice as long reading a technical textbook as you spend on reading other, nontechnical texts.

Reread When Necessary

Do not expect to understand everything the first time you read the assignment. It is helpful to read an assignment once rather quickly to get an overview of the processes and procedures it presents. Then reread it to learn the exact steps or details.

Have a Specific Purpose

Reading technical material requires that you have a carefully defined purpose. Unless you know why you are reading and what you are looking for, it is easy to become lost or to lose your concentration. Previewing is particularly helpful in establishing purposes for reading.

Pay Attention to Illustrations and Drawings

Most technical books contain illustrations, diagrams, and drawings, as well as more common graphical aids such as tables, graphs, and charts. (Refer to Chapter 8 for suggestions on reading graphics). Although graphics can make the text appear more complicated than it really is, they actually are a form of visual explanation designed to make the text easier to understand.

Read the following excerpt from a building design and construction textbook describing the framing of roof rafters.

Roof Rafters

Once the ceiling joists are nailed in place, the **roof rafters** can be installed. Common sizes or roof rafters include 2 in. x 6 in., 2 in. x 8 in., or 2 in. x 10 in. members spaced 12 in., 16 in., or 24 in. o.c., depending upon the width of the house and the magnitude of the dead and live loads imposed on the roof.

The rafters from both sides are usually connected at the top to a ridge board (Fig. A). Due to the angle cut in the rafters, the ridge board must be a larger size than the rafter. The ridge board runs the entire length of the roof and helps to distribute the roof load among several rafters. The location where the rafter bears on the exterior wall is notched to form a snug fit. The notch is commonly known as a "bird's mouth." The end of the roof is known as the gable and is the location where the roof and wall join.

Collar beams (i.e., collar ties) are often required when roof spans are long and the slopes are flat. Steeper slopes and shorter spans also may require collar beams, but only between every third rafter pair. Collar beams are usually 1 in. x 6 in. or 2 in. x 4 in. members.

—Willenbrock et al., *Residential Building Design and Construction,* pp. 171–72

Figure A
Roof Rafter/Ceiling Joist
Roof Framing System

Source: Gerald E. Sherwood and Robert C. Stroh, *Wood Frame House Construction,* p. 81 (Mineola, NY: Dover Publications, Inc. 1989).

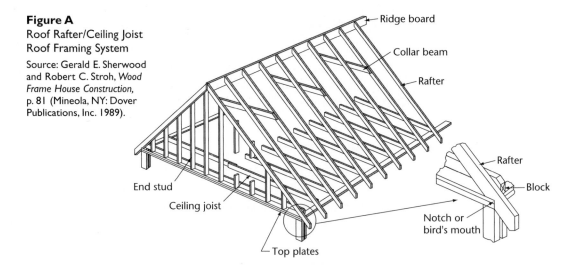

Now, study the diagram and reread the passage above. Does the diagram make the passage easier to understand?

Here are a few suggestions on how to read illustrations and diagrams.

1. *Note the type of illustrations or diagrams included in the assignment when you preview the chapter.*

2. *Look over each illustration, and determine its purpose.* The title or caption usually indicates what it is intended to show.

3. *Examine the illustration first.* Alternate between the text and the illustrations; illustrations are intended to be used with the paragraphs that refer to them. You may have to stop reading several times to refer to an illustration. For instance, when collar beams are mentioned in the preceding example, stop reading and find where they are placed in the diagram. You may also have to reread parts of the explanation several times.

4. *Look at each part of the illustration and note how the parts are connected.* Notice any abbreviations, symbols, arrows, or labels. In the example given, abbreviations are used for the north and south poles.

5. *Test your understanding of illustrations by drawing and labeling an illustration of your own without looking at the one in the text.* Then compare your drawing with the text. Note whether anything is left out. If so, continue drawing and checking until your drawing is complete and correct. Include these drawings in your notebook and use them for review and study.

EXERCISE 17–1

Read the following excerpt on ignition coils from an automotive technology textbook and answer the questions that follow.

Ignition Coils

The heart of any ignition system is the **ignition coil.** The coil creates a high-voltage spark by electromagnetic induction. Many ignition coils contain two separate but electrically connected windings of copper wire. Other coils are true transformers in which the primary and secondary windings are not electrically connected. See Figure 1.

The center of an ignition coil contains a core of laminated soft iron (thin strips of soft iron). This core increases the magnetic strength of the coil. Surrounding the laminated core are approximately 20,000 turns of fine wire (approximately 42-gauge). These windings are called the **secondary** coil windings. Surrounding the secondary winding are approximately 150 turns of heavy wire (approximately 21-gauge). These windings are called the **primary** coil windings. In many coils, these windings are surrounded with a thin metal shield and insulating paper and placed in a metal container. Many coils contain oil to help cool the ignition coil. Other coil designs, such as those used on GM's **high energy ignition (HEI)** systems, use an aircooled, epoxy-sealed **E coil** named for the *E* shape of the metal laminations inside the coil.

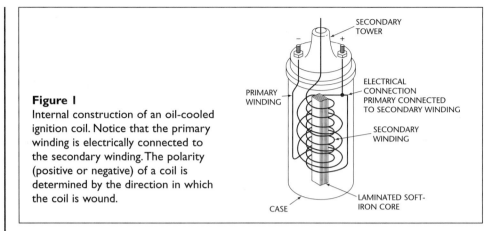

SECONDARY
TOWER

PRIMARY
WINDING

ELECTRICAL
CONNECTION
PRIMARY CONNECTED
TO SECONDARY WINDING

SECONDARY
WINDING

LAMINATED SOFT-
IRON CORE

CASE

Figure 1
Internal construction of an oil-cooled
ignition coil. Notice that the primary
winding is electrically connected to
the secondary winding. The polarity
(positive or negative) of a coil is
determined by the direction in which
the coil is wound.

—Halderman and Mitchell, *Automotive Technology: Principles, Diagnosis, and Service,* pp. 382–83

1. What is the purpose of the illustration?
2. Does the diagram make the text easier to understand? Briefly describe how.
3. Sketch a diagram of an ignition coil without referring to the original drawing.

Use Visualization

Visualization is a process of creating mental pictures or images. As you read, try to visualize the process or procedure that is being described. Make your image as specific and detailed as possible. Visualization will make reading these descriptions easier, as well as improving your ability to recall details. Here are a few examples of how students use visualization.

A nursing student learned the eight family life cycles by visualizing her sister's family at each stage.

A student taking a computer course was studying the two basic methods of organizing data on a magnetic disk: the sector method and the cylinder method. She visualized the sector method as slices of pie and the cylinder method as a stack of dinner plates.

Now read the following description of an optical disk system from a computer science textbook, and try to visualize as you read.

Optical Disks
Optical technology used with laser disk systems is providing a very high capacity storage medium with the **optical disk,** also called a **videodisk.** Videodisks will open new applications, since they can be used to store data, text, audio, and video images.

Optical disk systems look like magnetic disk systems. Each has a rotating platter and a head mechanism to record information. However, optical systems differ because they use light energy rather than magnetic fields to store data. A high-powered laser beam records data by one of two methods. With the **ablative method,** a hole is burned in the disk surface. With the **bubble method,** the disk surface is heated until a bubble forms.

The laser beam, in a lower power mode, reads the data by sensing the presence or absence of holes or bumps. The light beam will be reflected at different angles from a flat or disfigured surface. A series of mirrors is used to reflect the light beam to a photodiode, which transforms the light energy into an electric signal. The photodiode process works like the automatic doors at your local super-market. As you walk toward the door, you deflect a light beam, which signals the doors to open.

—Athey et al., *Computers and End-User Software*, pp. 122–23

Did you visualize the disks with tiny holes or bumps?

EXERCISE 17–2

Read the following passage describing a standard bumper jack. As you read, try to visualize the jack. After you have finished, draw a sketch of the jack as it is described in the passage. After you have completed your sketch, compare it with Figure 17–1 on page 495.

DESCRIPTION OF A STANDARD BUMPER JACK

Introduction—General Description

The standard bumper jack is a portable mechanism for raising the front or rear of a car through force applied with a lever. This jack enables even a frail person to lift one corner of a 2-ton automobile.

The jack consists of a molded steel base supporting a free-standing, perpendicular notched shaft. Attached to the shaft are a leverage mechanism, a bumper catch, and a cylinder for insertion of the jack handle. Except for the main shaft and leverage mechanism, the jack is made to be dismantled and to fit neatly in the car's trunk.

The jack operates on a leverage principle, with the human hand traveling 18 inches and the car only $3/8$ of an inch during a normal jacking stroke. Such a device requires many strokes to raise the car off the ground, but may prove a lifesaver to a motorist on some deserted road.

Five main parts make up the jack: base, notched shaft, leverage mechanism, bumper catch, and handle.

Description of Parts and Their Function
Base
The rectangular base is a molded steel plate that provides support and a point of insertion for the shaft. The base slopes upward to form a platform containing a

1-inch depression that provides a stabilizing well for the shaft. Stability is increased by a 1-inch cuff around the well. As the base rests on its flat surface, the bottom end of the shaft is inserted into its stabilizing well.

Shaft

The notched shaft is a steel bar (32 inches long) that provides a vertical track for the leverage mechanism. The notches, which hold the mechanism in its position on the shaft, face the operator.

The shaft vertically supports the raised automobile, and attached to it is the leverage mechanism, which rests on individual notches.

Leverage Mechanism

The leverage mechanism provides the mechanical advantage needed for the operator to raise the car. It is made to slide up and down the notched shaft. The main body of this pressed-steel mechanism contains two units: one for transferring the leverage and one for holding the bumper catch.

The leverage unit has four major parts: the cylinder, connecting the handle and a pivot point; a lower pawl (a device that fits into the notches to allow forward and prevent backward motion), connected directly to the cylinder; an upper pawl, connected at the pivot point; and an "up-down" lever, which applies or releases pressure on the upper pawl by means of a spring. Moving the cylinder up and down with the handle causes the alternate release of the pawls, and thus movement up or down the shaft—depending on the setting of the "up-down" lever. The movement is transferred by the metal body of the unit to the bumper-catch holder.

The holder consists of a downsloping groove, partially blocked by a wire spring. The spring is mounted in such a way as to keep the bumper catch in place during operation.

Bumper Catch

The bumper catch is a steel device that attaches the leverage mechanism to the bumper. This 9-inch molded plate is bent to fit the shape of the bumper. Its outer $1/2$ inch is bent up to form a lip, which hooks behind the bumper to hold the catch in place. The two sides of the plate are bent back 90 degrees to leave a 2-inch bumper-contact surface, and a bolt is riveted between them. This bolt slips into the groove in the leverage mechanism and provides the attachment between the leverage unit and the car.

Jack Handle

The jack handle is a steel bar that serves both as lever and lug-bolt remover. This round bar is 22 inches long, $5/8$ inch in diameter, and is bent 135 degrees roughly 5 inches from its outer end. Its outer end is a wrench made to fit the wheel's lug bolts. Its inner end is beveled to form a blade-like point for prying the wheel covers and for insertion into the cylinder on the leverage mechanism.

Conclusion and Operating Description

One quickly assembles the jack by inserting the bottom of the notched shaft into the stabilizing well in the base, the bumper catch into the groove on the leverage mechanism, and the beveled end of the jack handle into the cylinder. The bumper catch is then attached to the bumper, with the lever set in the "up" position.

As the operator exerts an up-down pumping motion on the jack handle, the leverage mechanism gradually climbs the vertical notched shaft until the car's wheel is raised above the ground. When the lever is in the "down" position, the same pumping motion causes the leverage mechanism to descend the shaft.

—Lannon, *Technical Writing*, pp. 419–21

Figure 17–1   Sample Diagram

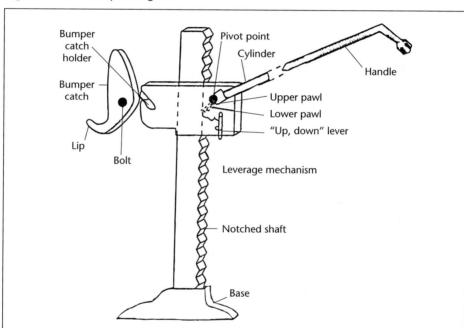

Mark and Highlight

You may find your textbooks to be valuable reference sources for lab or on-site experiences; you may also use them when you are employed in your field. Take special care, then, to mark and highlight your textbooks for future reference. Marking will also make previewing for exams easier. Develop a marking system that utilizes particular symbols or colors of ink to indicate procedures, important formulas, troubleshooting charts, and so forth. Refer to Chapter 10 for additional suggestions on how to highlight effectively.

Learn to Read Technical Manuals

Many technical courses require students to operate equipment or become familiar with computer software. Study and frequent reference to a specific manual is an additional requirement in some technical courses. Unfortunately, many technical manuals are poorly written and organized, so you need to approach them differently than textbooks. Use the following suggestions when reading technical manuals.

1. *Preview the manual to establish how it is arranged and exactly what it contains.* Does it have an index, a trouble-shooting section, a section with specific operating instructions? Study the table of contents carefully and mark sections that will be particularly useful.

2. *Do not read the manual from cover to cover.* First, locate and review those sections you identified as particularly useful. Concentrate on the parts that describe the overall operation of the machine: its purpose, capabilities, and functions.

3. *Next, learn the codes, symbols, commands, or terminology used in the manual.* Check to see if the manual provides a list of special terms. Many computer software manuals, for instance, contain a list of symbols, commands, or procedures used throughout the manual. If such a list is not included, begin making your own list on a separate sheet or on the inside cover of the manual.

4. *Begin working with the manual and the equipment simultaneously, applying each step as you read it.*

5. *If the manual does not contain a useful index, make your own by jotting down page numbers of sections you know you'll need to refer to frequently.*

6. *If the manual is overly complicated or difficult to read, simplify it by writing your own step-by-step directions in the margin or on a separate sheet.*

THOUGHT PATTERNS IN TECHNICAL FIELDS

The two thought patterns most commonly used in technical fields are process and problem/solution. Each is used in textbooks and manuals as well as in practical, hands-on situations.

Reading Process Descriptions

Testing procedures, directions, installations, repairs, instructions, and diagnostic checking procedures all follow the process pattern. To read materials written in this pattern, you must not only learn the steps but also learn them in the correct order. To study process material, use the following tips.

1. *Prepare study sheets that summarize each process.* For example, a nursing student learning the steps in venipuncture (taking a blood sample) wrote the summary sheet shown in Figure 17–2.

2. *Test your recall by writing out the steps from memory.* Recheck periodically by mentally reviewing each step.

3. *For difficult or lengthy procedures, write each step on a separate index card.* Shuffle the pack and practice putting the cards in the correct order.

4. *Be certain you understand the logic behind the process.* Figure out why each step is done in the specified order.

Figure 17–2   Sample Summary Sheet

Venipuncture

1. Wash hands, explain procedure to patient; assess patient status
2. Assemble equipment
3. Locate puncture site
4. Apply tourniquet, cleanse site
5. Place thumb distal to puncture site
6. Insert needle 30° angle, aspirate desired amount
7. Remove tourniquet, place dry compress on needle tip & withdraw
8. Remove needle from syringe and place specimen in container; label

EXERCISE 17–3

COLLABORATIVE LEARNING

Read the following excerpt describing acid rain. After you have read it, write a process summary of each stage of the acid rain process. Compare your process summary with that of a classmate.

HOW ACID RAIN DEVELOPS, SPREADS, AND DESTROYS

Introduction

Acid rain is environmentally damaging rainfall that occurs after fossil fuels burn, releasing nitrogen and sulfur oxides into the atmosphere. Acid rain, simply stated, increases the acidity level of waterways because these nitrogen and sulfur oxides combine with the air's normal moisture. The resulting rainfall is far more acidic than normal rainfall. Acid rain is a silent threat because its effects, although slow, are cumulative. This report explains the cause, the distribution cycle, and the effects of acid rain.

Most research shows that power plants burning oil or coal are the primary cause of acid rain. The burnt fuel is not completely expended, and some residue enters the atmosphere. Although this residue contains several potentially toxic elements, sulfur oxide and, to a lesser extent, nitrogen oxide are the major problem, because they are transformed when they combine with moisture. This chemical reaction forms sulfur dioxide and nitric acid, which then rain down to earth.

The major steps explained here are (1) how acid rain develops, (2) how acid rain spreads, and (3) how acid rain destroys.

The Process

How Acid Rain Develops

Once fossil fuels have been burned, their usefulness is over. Unfortunately, it is here that the acid rain problem begins.

Figure 1   How acid rain develops

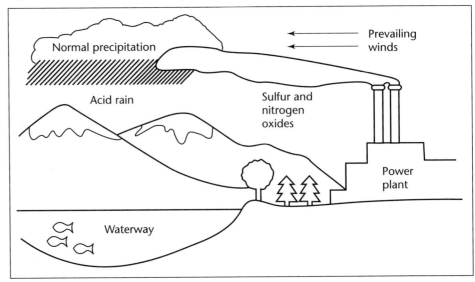

Fossil fuels contain a number of elements that are released during combustion. Two of these, sulfur oxide and nitrogen oxide, combine with normal moisture to produce sulfuric acid and nitric acid. (Figure 1 illustrates how acid rain develops.) The released gases undergo a chemical change as they combine with atmospheric ozone and water vapor. The resulting rain or snowfall is more acid than normal precipitation.

Acid level is measured by pH readings. The pH scale runs from 0 through 14—a pH of 7 is considered neutral. (Distilled water has a pH of 7.) Numbers above 7 indicate increasing degrees of alkalinity. (Household ammonia has a pH of 11.) Numbers below 7 indicate increasing acidity. Movement in either direction on the pH scale, however, means multiplying by 10. Lemon juice, which has a pH value of 2, is 10 times more acidic than apples, which have a pH of 3, and is 1,000 times more acidic than carrots, which have a pH of 5.

Because of carbon dioxide (an acid substance) normally present in air, unaffected rainfall has a pH of 5.6. At this time, the pH of precipitation in the northeastern United States and Canada is between 4.5 and 4. In Massachusetts, rain and snowfall have an average pH reading of 4.1. A pH reading below 5 is considered to be abnormally acidic, and therefore a threat to aquatic populations.

How Acid Rain Spreads

Although it might seem that areas containing power plants would be most severely affected, acid rain can in fact travel thousands of miles from its source. Stack gases escape and drift with the wind currents. The sulfur and nitrogen oxides are thus able to travel great distances before they return to earth as acid rain.

For an average of two to five days, the gases follow the prevailing winds far from the point of origin. For example, estimates show that about 50 percent of the acid rain that affects Canada originates in the United States; at the same time, 15 to 25 percent of the U.S. acid rain problem originates in Canada.

The tendency of stack gases to drift makes acid rain such a widespread menace. More than 200 lakes in the Adirondacks, hundreds of miles from any industrial center, are unable to support life because their water has become so acidic.

How Acid Rain Destroys

Acid rain causes damage wherever it falls. It erodes various types of building rock such as limestone, marble, and mortar, which are gradually eaten away by the constant bathing in acid. Damage to buildings, houses, monuments, statues, and cars is widespread. Some priceless monuments and carvings already have been destroyed, and even trees of some varieties are dying in large numbers.

More important, however, is acid rain damage to waterways in the affected areas. (Figure 2 illustrates how a typical waterway is infiltrated.) Because of its high acidity, acid rain dramatically lowers the pH of lakes and streams.

Although its effect is not immediate, acid rain can eventually make a waterway so acidic it dies. In areas with natural acid-buffering elements such as limestone, the

Figure 2 How acid rain destroys

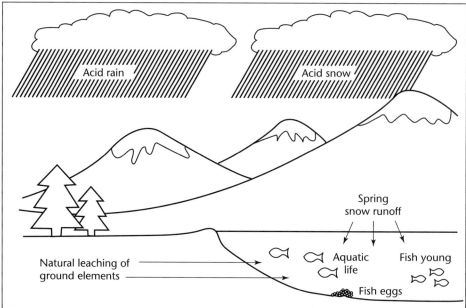

dilute acid has less effect. The northeastern United States and Canada, however, lack this natural protection, and so are continually vulnerable.

The pH level in an affected waterway drops so low that some species cease to reproduce. In fact, a pH level of 5.1 to 5.4 means that fisheries are threatened; once a waterway reaches a pH level of 4.5, no fish reproduction occurs. Because each creature is part of the overall food chain, loss of one element in the chain disrupts the whole cycle.

In the northeastern United States and Canada, the acidity problem is compounded by the runoff from acid snow. During the cold winter months, acid snow sits with little melting, so that by spring thaw, the acid released is greatly concentrated. Aluminum and other heavy metals normally present in soil are released by acid rain and runoff. These toxic substances leach into waterways in heavy concentrations, affecting fish in all stages of development.

Summary

Acid rain develops from nitrogen and sulfur oxides emitted by industrial and power plants burning fossil fuels. In the atmosphere, these oxides combine with ozone and water to form acid rain: precipitation with a lower-than-average pH. This acid precipitation returns to earth many miles from its source, severely damaging waterways that lack natural buffering agents. The northeastern United States and Canada are the most severely affected areas in North America.

—Lannon, *Technical Writing*, pp. 452–55

Problem-Solving Strategies

In technical fields, you will encounter hypothetical problems to solve that require you to apply formulas and work with procedures. More important, you will face simulated problems in labs and actual problems throughout your career. A systematic approach is helpful to improve your problem-solving abilities.

It is easy to panic when a piece of equipment fails or a procedure does not produce the expected results. Using a systematic approach to solving problems will help you in these situations. A problem is basically a conflict between "what is" (the present state) and "what should be" or "what is desired" (the goal state). For example, a medical office assistant has a problem when she cannot calm a frightened child in order to take her blood pressure. The following steps can help you attack problem situations.

Step 1: Specify the problem. Do this by evaluating the present state and determining how it differs from what is desired. The more specific you can be, the more likely that you will be able to identify working solutions. For example, if you are faced with a machine that won't function properly, decide what part or feature is malfunctioning. Don't simply say the machine won't work; instead, decide that the robot arm won't remain in position to complete the task. If your patient won't cooperate when you need to take her blood pressure, try to discover why she is unwilling.

Step 2: Analyze the problem. Analysis is a complex critical thinking skill. Begin by learning as much as you can about the problem. For instance, it may be necessary to find out why your young patient is frightened in order to be able to calm her down. To analyze a problem, it may be necessary to look beyond the obvious solution—to stretch your imagination and reach for creative options. For example, you may discover the child is frightened because you are wearing white and the child's dentist, of whom she is frightened, also wears white. When analyzing a problem, use the following suggestions.

> *Be flexible in your analysis.* Do not eliminate possibilities because they seem unlikely or never have happened in the past.

> *Brainstorm about all the possibilities.* Except for problems that must be solved immediately, spend a few minutes listing anything you can think of that is remotely related to your problem. Sort through the list later, preferably the next day. You probably will discover the seeds of a solution.

> *Talk with others about the problem.* By putting the problem into words (to a classmate or your instructor), you may hear yourself say things that will lead to further understanding.

Research problems for which you lack complete information.

Step 3: Formulate a solution path. Identify a possible solution to the problem. For some problems, such as a machine malfunction, there is only one correct solution. For others, such as an uncooperative patient, various solutions may be feasible.

Step 4: Evaluate possible solution paths. If you have identified more than one solution path, the next step is to weigh the advantages and disadvantages of each one. You will need to think through each solution path in detail, considering how, when, and where you could accomplish each. Consider the likelihood of success with each solution, and weigh both short- and long-term effects. Thinking aloud may help you realize why various solutions won't work.

Step 5: Implement the solution. If your solution does not solve the problem, analyze what went wrong and repeat the problem-solving process. A trial-and-error process may be necessary. Be sure to use a logical, systematic approach and keep track of your results for each trial.

EXERCISE 17–4

Form groups of four to five students and discuss and develop a strategy for solving each of the following problems.

1. A microcomputer will not boot the program when the disk is inserted in the second disk drive.
2. A student in a science laboratory technology course gets a different result for his lab experiment than other students conducting the same experiment.

STUDY TECHNIQUES FOR TECHNICAL COURSES

Use the following suggestions to adapt your study skills to technical courses.

Pronounce and Use Technical Vocabulary

Understanding the technical vocabulary in your discipline is essential. For technical and applied fields, it is especially important to learn to pronounce technical terms and to use them in your speech. To establish yourself as a professional in the field and to communicate effectively with other professionals, it is essential to speak the language. Use the suggestions in Chapter 4 for learning specialized terminology.

Draw Diagrams and Pictures

Although your textbook may include numerous drawings and illustrations, there is not enough space to include drawings for every process. An effective learning strategy is to draw diagrams and pictures whenever possible. These should be fast sketches; be concerned with describing parts or processes, and do not worry about artwork or scale drawings. For example, a student studying air conditioning and refrigeration repair drew a quick sketch of a unit he was to repair in his lab before he began to disassemble it. He then referred to sketches he had drawn in his notebook as he diagnosed the problem.

Reserve Blocks of Time Each Day for Study

Daily study and review are important in technical courses. Many technical courses require large blocks of time (two to three hours) to complete projects, problems, or drawings. Technical students find that taking less time is inefficient because if they leave a project unfinished, they have to spend time rethinking it and reviewing what they have already done when they return to the project.

Focus on Concepts and Principles

Because technical subjects are so detailed, many students focus on these details rather than on the concepts and principles to which they relate. Keep a sheet in the front of your notebook on which you record information to which you need to refer frequently. Include constants, conversions, formulas, metric equivalents, and commonly used abbreviations. Refer to this sheet so you won't interrupt your train of thought. Then you can focus on ideas rather than specific details.

Make Use of the Glossary and Index

Because of the large number of technical terms, formulas, and notations you will encounter, often it is necessary to refer to definitions and explanations. Place a paper clip at the beginning of the glossary and a second at the index so you can find them easily.

Preparing for Exams in Technical Courses

Exams in technical courses may consist of objective questions or of problems to solve. (For suggestions on preparing for and taking these types of exams, see the test-taking tips in Chapters 12, 13, and 15.) Other times, exams may take the form of a practicum. A practicum is a simulation, or a rehearsal, of some problem or task you may face on the job. For example, a nursing student may be asked to perform a procedure while a supervisor observes. Or an EKG technologist may be evaluated in administering an EKG to a patient. Use these suggestions to prepare for practicum exams.

1. *Identify possible tasks you may be asked to perform.*

2. *Learn the steps each task involves.* Write summary notes, and test your recall by writing or mentally rehearsing them without reference to your notes. Visualize yourself performing the task.

3. *If possible, practice performing the task, mentally reviewing the steps you learned as you proceed.*

4. *Study with another student; test and evaluate each other.*

SUMMARY

Students in technical or applied fields of study face two types of courses: technical courses and related courses in other disciplines. Specified techniques for reading in the sciences are

- reading slowly (and rereading)
- setting a specific reading purpose
- studying illustrations and drawings
- using visualization
- marking and highlighting
- reading technical manuals

Two thought patterns predominate in technical and applied fields:

- process
- problem/solution

Suggestions are offered for adapting studying strategies to technical and applied courses.

INFORMATION SYSTEMS

PREREADING QUESTIONS

1. How is data transmitted between computers?
2. Write guide questions indicating what you need to find out about each of these methods of transmitting data.

DATA TRANSMISSION

H. L. Capron

1   A terminal or computer produces digital signals, which are simply the presence or absence of an electric pulse. The state of being on or off represents the *binary* number 1 or 0, respectively. Some communications lines accept digital transmission directly, and the trend in the communications industry is toward digital signals. However, most telephone lines through which these digital signals are sent were originally built for voice transmission, and voice transmission requires *analog* signals. The next section describes these two types of transmission and then discusses modems, which translate between them.

DIGITAL AND ANALOG TRANSMISSION

2   **Digital transmission** sends data as distinct pulses, either on or off, in much the same way that data travels through the computer. However, most communications media are not digital. Communications devices such as telephone lines, *coaxial* cables, and microwave circuits are already in place for voice (analog) transmission. The easiest choice for most users is to piggyback on one of these. Thus, the most common communications devices all use **analog transmission,** a continuous electrical signal in the form of a wave.

3   To be sent over analog lines, a digital signal must first be converted to an analog form. It is converted by altering an analog signal, called a **carrier wave,** which has alterable characteristics (Figure 3a). One such characteristic is the **amplitude,** or height of the wave, which can be increased to represent the binary number 1 (Figure 3b). Another characteristic that can be altered is the **frequency,** or number of times a wave repeats during a specific time interval; frequency can be increased to represent a 1 (Figure 3c).

4   Conversion from digital to analog signals is called **modulation,** and the reverse process—reconstructing the original digital message at the other end

Figure 3 Analog signals.
(a) An analog carrier wave moves up and down in a continuous cycle. (b) The analog waveform can be converted to digital form through amplitude modulation. As shown, the wave height is increased to represent a 1 or left the same to represent a 0. (c) In frequency modulation the amplitude of the wave stays the same but the frequency increases to indicate a 1 or stays the same to indicate a 0.

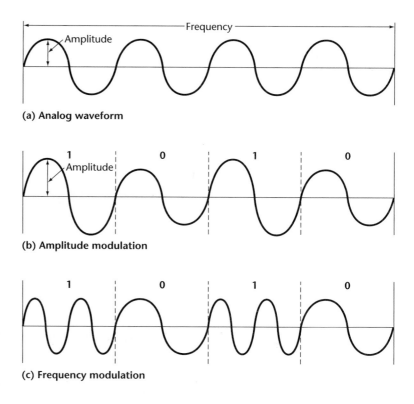

(a) Analog waveform

(b) Amplitude modulation

(c) Frequency modulation

of the transmission—is called **demodulation.** (You probably know amplitude and frequency modulation by their abbreviations, AM and FM, the methods used for radio transmission.) An extra device is needed to make the conversions: a modem.

MODEMS

5 A **modem** is a device that converts a digital signal to an analog signal and vice versa (Figure 4). Modem is short for *mo*dulate/*dem*odulate.

Types of Modems

6 Modems vary in the way they connect to the telephone line. There are two main types: acoustic coupler modems and direct-connect modems. **Acoustic coupler modems** include a cradle to hold the telephone handset. Most modems today, however, are directly connected to the phone system by a cable that runs from the modem to the wall jack.

7 A **direct-connect modem** is directly connected to the telephone line by means of a telephone jack. An **external modem** is separate from the computer (Figure 5). Its main advantage is that it can be used with a variety of computers. If you buy a new personal computer, for example, you can probably keep

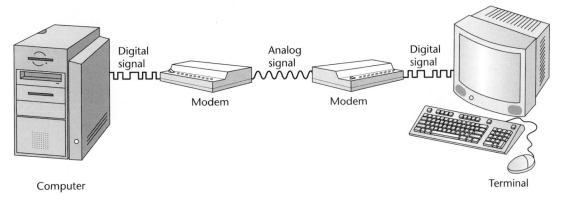

Figure 4   Modems.   Modems convert—modulate—digital data signals to analog signals for sending over communications links, then reverse the process—demodulate—at the other end.

the same external modem. For those personal computer users who regard an external modem as one more item taking up desk space, new modem-on-a-chip designs have produced a modem that is so small you will hardly notice it.

For a modem that is out of sight—literally—an **internal modem** board can be inserted into the computer by the user; in fact, most personal computers today come with an internal modem as standard equipment. As we will discuss shortly, most modems today also have *fax* capability.

8   Notebook and laptop computers often use modems that come in the form of **PC cards,** originally known as PCMCIA cards, named for the Personal Computer Memory Card International Association. The credit card-sized PC card slides into a slot in the

Figure 5   An external modem.
Source: Courtesy of 3Com Corporation

computer (Figure 6). A cable runs from the PC card to the phone jack in the wall. PC cards have given portable computers full connectivity capability outside the constraints of an office.

Modem Data Speeds

9   The World Wide Web has given users an insatiable appetite for fast communications. This, and costs based on time use of services, provide strong incentives to transmit as quickly as possible. The old—some *very* old—standard modem speeds of 1200, 2400, 9600, 14,400, and 28,800 **bits per second (bps)** have now been superseded by modems that transmit 33,600 bps. Most people today measure modem speed by bits per second, but another measure is **baud rate,** the number of times that the signal being used to transmit data changes. At

Figure 6   A PC card modem.   This PC card modem, although only the size of a credit card, packs a lot of power: transmission at 56,000 bytes-per-second. The card is slipped into a slot on the side of the laptop keyboard. Look closely at the right end of the modem and you can see the pop-out jack. So, in this order: slide in the card, pop out the jack, and snap in the phone card.

Source: Courtesy of 3Com Corporation

lower modem speeds, each signal change represents one bit being sent, so bits per second and baud are the same. At higher speeds, more than one bit may be sent per signal change, so bits per second will be greater than the baud rate.

10   Since modems work over the phone lines, which are designed to carry tones of different pitches, the limited number of pitches holds the top modem speed to about 30,000 pbs—or so it was thought. Now, using compression techniques, modems can send data at an astonishing 56,000 bps. This speed is limited to one direction, from the Internet to the user, but that fits perfectly with what users usually do—download files from the Internet. Note the transmission time comparisons in Table 1.

Table 1 Data transfer rates compared	
Rate (bps)	**Time to transmit a 20-page single-spaced report**
1,200	10 minutes
2,400	5 minutes
9,600	1.25 minutes
14,400	50 seconds
28,800	25 seconds
33,600	30 seconds
56,000	12.5 seconds

ISDN

11   As noted earlier, communication via phone lines requires a modem to convert between the computer's digital signals and the analog signals used by phone lines. But what if another type of line could be used directly for digital transmission? That technology is called **Integrated Services Digital Network,** but it is usually known by its acronym, **ISDN.** The attraction is that an **ISDN adapter** can move data at 128,000 bps, a vast speed improvement over any modem. Another advantage is that an ISDN circuit includes two phone lines, so a user can use one line to connect to the Internet and the other to talk on the phone at the same time. Still, ISDN is not a panacea. Although prices are coming down, initial costs are not inexpensive. You need both the adapter and phone service and possibly even a new line, depending on your current service. Also, ongoing monthly fees may be significant. Furthermore, ISDN is unavailable in some geographic areas.

—Capron, *Computers: Tools for an Information Age*, pp. 164–65

VOCABULARY REVIEW

1. For each of the words listed below, use context; prefixes, roots, and suffixes; and/or a dictionary to write a brief definition or synonym of the word as it is used in the reading.

    a. binary (para. 1) _____

    b. analog (para. 1) _____

    c. coaxial (para. 2) _____

    d. modulation (para. 4) _____

    e. connectivity (para. 8) _____

    f. constraints (para. 8) _____

    g. superseded (para. 9) _____

    h. insatiable (para. 9) _____

    i. compression (para. 10) _____

    j. download (para. 10) _____

2. Underline new specialized terminology introduced in the reading.

COMPREHENSION QUESTIONS

1. Is digital or analog transmission the more commonly used type of transmission? Why?
2. How can a carrier wave be altered to produce a digital signal?
3. What does a modem do?
4. What are the two ways that a modem can connect to a telephone line? Which type is used more today?
5. Explain the difference between an external and an internal modem. Why do some users prefer external modems?
6. Describe two ways in which modem speeds can be measured.
7. How fast are the highest-speed modems? How is this accomplished?
8. Explain what an ISDN, is and name two advantages it has over modems.

THINKING CRITICALLY

1. Give three examples of digital and/or analog signals that are common in everyday life. Why are these signals incompatible with each other? What method(s) can be used to overcome these incompatibilities?

2. If cost were no object, what electronic device(s) would you employ to access outside information with a computer? Explain the advantage(s) these devices would offer over cheaper solutions.

3. Why is the baud rate of a modem sometimes equal to and sometimes not equal to the bits per second of the same modem?

LEARNING/STUDY STRATEGY

Draw a conceptual map showing the various methods of data transmission.

ON-LINE RESEARCH: DATA TRANSMISSION*

In technical and technological fields of study, the ability to locate and apply information is important. The Internet may prove to be one of your most important resources for finding information, and your course work will teach you how to apply what you find.

1. Suppose you have connected a new 56K modem and you want to find out how quickly you are downloading data. Consult Modem Central's "56K Modem Troubleshooting Guide" at http://www.56k.com/trouble/#known, and then write a brief description of the process.

2. *PC World Online* published an article titled "What to Do When 56K Is Not OK" in February 1998. Read the article at http://www.pcworld.com/hardware/communications/articles/feb98/1602p049.html. List five problems that can prevent a 56K modem from transmitting data at 56K bits per second. If you want, access the troubleshooting guide from question 1 above to find information about how to solve these problems.

*If any of these sites is unavailable, use a search engine to locate a new Web site on the same topic.

CREDITS

Photo Credits

Page 34: Mary Kate Denny/Photo Edit; **93:** Bob Daemmrich/The Image Works; **219 (left):** © Michael Mix; **219 (right):** © Michael Mix; **242:** Peter Weit/Corbis Sygma; **243:** Charles Caratini/Corbis Sygma; **249:** Rick Reinhard/Impact Visuals 1993; **313:** © Charles D. Miller, III; **378:** Flip Schulke/Black Star; **424:** *Dorothea Lange, Migrant Mother, Nipomo, CA, 1936.* Courtesy of the Dorothea Lange Collection © 1982. The Oakland Museum, The City of Oakland, California; **426:** *Charles White, Preacher, 1952.* Collection of Whitney Museum of American Art. Purchase 52.25. Photograph © 2000. Whitney Museum of American Art, New York; **507:** Courtesy of 3Com Corporation; **508:** Courtesy of 3Com Corporation.

Text Credits

Chapter 1 Page 16: Josh R. Gerow, from *Psychology: An Introduction*, Fifth Edition, pp. 217–219. Copyright © 1997 by Addison-Wesley Educational Publishers, Inc. Reprinted by permission. **17:** Richard L. Weaver II, from *Understanding Interpersonal Communication*, Seventh Edition, pp. 423–426. Copyright © 1996 by HarperCollins College Publishers, Inc. Reprinted by permission of Addison-Wesley Educational Publishers, Inc. **20:** Bruce E. Gronbeck, Kathleen German, Douglas Ehninger, and Alan H. Monroe, from *Principles of Speech Communication*, Twelfth Brief Edition, pp. 38–39. Copyright © 1995 by HarperCollins College Publishers, Inc. Reprinted by permission of Addison-Wesley Educational Publishers, Inc. **27:** Frank Schmalleger, from *Criminal Justice Today: An Introductory Text for the Twenty-First Century*, Fifth Edition, p. xviii. Copyright © 1999. Reprinted by permission of Prentice-Hall, Inc., Upper Saddle River, NJ. **28:** Weaver II, *Understanding Interpersonal Communication*, Seventh Edition, pp. 226–227. **29:** Jerry A. Nathanson, P. E., *Basic Environmental Technology*, Third Edition, p. 351. Upper Saddle River, NJ: Prentice-Hall, Copyright © 2000. **34:** Josh R. Gerow, from *Psychology: An Introduction*, Third Edition, pp. 654–656. Copyright © 1992 by HarperCollins College Publishers, Inc. Reprinted by permission of Addison-Wesley Educational Publishers, Inc.

Chapter 2 Page 40: Leon Baradat, from *Understanding American Democracy*, p. 163. Copyright © 1992 by HarperCollins Publishers, Inc. Reprinted by permission of Addison-Wesley Educational Publishers, Inc. **41:** Josh R. Gerow, from *Psychology: An Introduction*, Fifth Edition, p. 553. Copyright © 1997 by Addison-Wesley Educational Publishers, Inc. Reprinted by permission. **41:** Joseph A. DeVito, from *Human Communication: The Basic Course*, Seventh Edition, p. 182. New York: Addison-Wesley Educational Publishers, Inc., 1997. **42:** Josh R. Gerow, from *Psychology: An Introduction*, Third Edition, p. 700. Copyright © 1992 by HarperCollins College Publishers, Inc. Reprinted by permission of Addison-Wesley Educational Publishers, Inc. **42:** Robert A. Wallace, from *Biology: The World of Life*, Sixth Edition, p. 283. Copyright © 1992 by HarperCollins Publishers, Inc. Reprinted by permission of Addison-Wesley Educational Publishers, Inc. **43:** James William Coleman and Donald R. Cressey, from *Social Problems*, Sixth Edition, p. 277. New York: HarperCollins College Publishers, Inc., 1996. **43:** William Keefe, Henry J. Abraham, William H. Flanigan, Charles O. Jones, Morris S. Ogul, and John W. Spanier, from *American Democracy*, Third Edition, p. 178. Copyright © 1990 by Harper & Row Publishers, Inc. Reprinted by permission of Addison-Wesley Educational Publishers, Inc. **43:** Gerow, *Psychology: An Introduction*, Third Edition, p. 250. **44:** Karen C. Timberlake, from *Chemistry: An Introduction to General, Organic, and Biological Chemistry*, Sixth Edition, p. 30. Copyright © 1996 by HarperCollins College Publishers, Inc. Reprinted by permission of Addison-Wesley Educational Publishers, Inc. **44:** Michael C. Mix, Paul Farber, and Keith I. King, from *Biology: The Network of Life*, Second Edition, p. 532. Copyright © 1992 by Michael C. Mix, Paul Farber, and Keith I. King. Reprinted by permission of Addison-Wesley Educational Publishers, Inc.

44: Keefe et al., *American Democracy*, Third Edition, p. 186. **45:** Gerow, *Psychology: An Introduction*, Third Edition, p. 319. **45:** Baradat, *Understanding American Democracy*, pp. 99–100. **47:** Samuel L. Becker, from *Discovering Mass Communication*, Third Edition, p. 159. Copyright © 1992 by HarperCollins College Publishers, Inc. Reprinted by permission of Addison-Wesley Educational Publishers, Inc. **48:** Gerow, *Psychology: An Introduction*, Third Edition, pp. 554–557. **58:** Ralph Nader, from *Time Dollars*, 1992 (Rodale Press, Inc.). Reprinted by permission of Edgar Cahn, Ph.D., J.D.

Chapter 3 Page 64: Pocket Dictionary, "Dilemma": Philip D. Morehead, *The New American Webster Handy College Dictionary*, Third Edition, p. 197. New York: Signet, a division of Penguin Books USA, Inc., 1995. **64:** Collegiate Dictionary, "Dilemma": Copyright © 1996 by Houghton Mifflin Company. Reproduced from *The American Heritage Dictionary of the English Language*, Third Edition. **65:** Entry #541.12 from *Roget's International Thesaurus*, Fifth Edition by Peter Mark Roget. Copyright © 1992 by HarperCollins Publishers, Inc. Reprinted by permission of HarperCollins Publishers, Inc. **68:** J. Ross Eshleman, Barbara G. Cashion, and Laurence A. Basirico, from *Sociology: An Introduction*, Fourth Edition, pp. 34–35. Copyright © 1993 by HarperCollins College Publishers. Reprinted by permission of Addison-Wesley Educational Publishers, Inc. **68:** Walter S. Jones, from *The Logic of International Relations*, Seventh Edition, p. 379. Copyright © 1993 by Walter S. Jones. Reprinted by permission of Addison-Wesley Educational Publishers. **69:** J. Ross Eshleman and Barbara Cashion, from *Sociology: An Introduction*, Second Edition, p. 380. Copyright © 1985 by HarperCollins College Publishers, Inc. Reprinted by permission of Addison-Wesley Educational Publishers, Inc. **72:** Jack Levin and James L. Spates, from *Starting Sociology*, Fourth Edition, pp. 251–252. Copyright © 1990 by Jack Levin and James L. Spates. Reprinted by permission of Addison-Wesley Educational Publishers, Inc. **80:** Thomas C. Kinnear, Kenneth L. Bernhardt, and Kathleen A. Krentler, from *Principles of Marketing*, Fourth Edition, pp. 57–58. Copyright © 1995 by HarperCollins Publishers. Reprinted by permission

of Addison-Wesley Educational Publishers, Inc. **81:** Michael C. Howard, from *Contemporary Cultural Anthropology*, Fifth Edition, pp. 12–13. Copyright © 1996 by HarperCollins College Publishers. Reprinted by permission of Addison-Wesley Educational Publishers, Inc. **87:** Richard L. Weaver II, from *Understanding Interpersonal Communication*, Sixth Edition, pp. 230–233. Copyright © 1993 by HarperCollins College Publishers. Reprinted by permission of Addison-Wesley Educational Publishers, Inc.

Chapter 4 Page 94: Thomas C. Kinnear, Kenneth L. Bernhardt, and Kathleen A. Krentler, from *Principles of Marketing*, Fourth Edition, p. 301. Copyright © 1995 by HarperCollins Publishers. Reprinted by permission of Addison-Wesley Educational Publishers, Inc. **97:** Gini Stephens Frings, *Fashion: From Concepts to Consumer*, Sixth Edition, p. 11. Upper Saddle River, NJ: Prentice-Hall, Inc., 1999. **98:** Philip G. Zimbardo and Richard J. Gerrig, from *Psychology and Life*, Fourthteenth Edition, p. 501. Copyright © 1996 by Philip G. Zimbardo, Inc. and Richard J. Gerrig. Reprinted by permission of Addison-Wesley Educational Publishers. **98:** Donald C. Mosley, Paul H. Petri, and Leon C. Megginson, from *Management: Leadership in Action*, Fifth Edition, p. 555. Copyright © 1996 by HarperCollins Publishers, Inc. Reprinted by permission of Addison-Wesley Educational Publishers, Inc. **100:** Arlene S. Skolnick, from *The Intimate Environment: Exploring Marriage and the Family*, Sixth Edition, p. 224. Copyright © 1996 by Arlene S. Skolnick. Reprinted by permission of Addison-Wesley Educational Publishers. **103:** Robert A. Wallace, from *Biology: The World of Life*, Sixth Edition, p. 754. Copyright © 1992 by HarperCollins Publishers, Inc. Reprinted by permission of Addison-Wesley Educational Publishers, Inc. **105:** Arthur H. Purcell, "Trash Troubles" from *The World & I*, November 1998, Vol. 3, No. 11. Reprinted with permission from The World & I, a publication of The Washington Times Corporation, Copyright 1998. **108:** Dr. Kenneth R. Fehrman and Cherie Fehrman, from *Color: The Secret Influence*, pp. 82, 83. Copyright © 2000 by Prentice-Hall, Inc. Reprinted by permission of Prentice-Hall, Inc., Upper Saddle River, NJ. **110:** Nick Fiddes, from

Inc. **368:** Gerow, *Psychology: An Introduction*, Fifth Edition, pp. 305–306. **370:** Eshleman et al., *Sociology: An Introduction*, Fourth Edition, pp. 356–358. **375:** William E. Thompson and Joseph V. Hickey, from *Society in Focus: An Introduction to Sociology*, Second Edition, p. 81. Copyright © 1996 by William E. Thompson and Joseph V. Hickey. Reprinted by permission of Addison-Wesley Educational Publishers, Inc. **378:** Eshleman et al., *Sociology: An Introduction*, Fourth Edition, pp. 487–490.

Chapter 13 Page 386: Lawrence J. Gitman, from *Principles of Managerial Finance*, Ninth Edition, pp. 581, 582. Copyright © 2000 by Lawrence J. Gitman. Reprinted by permission of Addison Wesley Longman. **388:** Robert C. Nickerson, from *Business and Information Systems*, pp. 263–265. Copyright © 1998 by Addison-Wesley Educational Publishers, Inc. Reprinted by permission of Prentice-Hall, Inc., Upper Saddle River, NJ. **391:** Thomas C. Kinnear, Kenneth L. Bernhardt, and Kathleen A. Krentler, from *Principles of Marketing*, Fourth Edition, p. 278. Copyright © 1995 by HarperCollins Publishers. Reprinted by permission of Addison-Wesley Educational Publishers, Inc. **392:** William M. Pride, Robert J. Hughes, and Jack R. Kapoor, from *Business*, Fifth Edition, pp. 386–387. Copyright © 1996 by Houghton Mifflin Company. Reprinted with permission. **395:** Gitman, *Principles of Managerial Finance*, Ninth Edition, p. 8. **395:** David Van Fleet, from *Contemporary Management*, Second Edition, p. 251. Copyright © 1991 by Houghton Mifflin Company. Used with permission. **396:** Nickerson, *Business and Information Systems*, p. 40. **397:** Van Fleet, *Contemporary Management*, Second Edition, p. 270. **398:** Nickerson, *Business and Information Systems*, p. xvii. **401:** Kinnear et al., *Principles of Marketing*, Fourth Edition, pp. 300-303.

Chapter 14 Page 409: "Mirror" from *Crossing the Water* by Sylvia Plath. Copyright © 1963 by Ted Hughes. Originally appeared in the *New Yorker*. Reprinted by permission of HarperCollins Publishers, Inc. and by Faber and Faber Ltd. **411:** Sharon Curtin, from "Aging in the Land of the Young," *Nobody Ever Died of Old Age*. Boston: Little, Brown and Company, 1972. **412:** Martin Luther

King, Jr., "Letter from Birmingham Jail" from *Why We Can't Wait*, p. 363. New York: Harper & Row Publishers, Inc., 1964. **415:** "The Negro Speaks of Rivers" from *Selected Poems* by Langston Hughes. Copyright © 1926 by Alfred A Knopf, Inc. and renewed 1954 by Langston Hughes. Reprinted by permission of the publisher. **417:** "Dream Deferred" from *The Panther and the Lash: Poems for Our Times*, pp. 383–384, by Langston Hughes. Copyright © 1951 by Langston Hughes. Reprinted by permission of Alfred A. Knopf, Inc. **417:** "Because I Could Not Stop for Death" by Emily Dickinson. Reprinted by permission of the publishers and the Trustees of Amherst College from *The Poems of Emily Dickinson*, Thomas H. Johnson, ed. Cambridge, MA: The Belknap Press of Harvard University Press. Copyright © 1951, 1955, 1979, 1983 by the President and Fellows of Harvard College. **420:** Kate Chopin, "The Story of an Hour," 1894. **427:** Vivian Pollack, *Dickinson: The Anxiety of Gender*, p. 191. Ithaca, NY: Cornell University Press, 1984. **428:** Charles R. Anderson, from *Emily Dickinson's Poetry: Stairway to Surprise*, pp. 245–246, 1996. Reprinted by permission of Nations Bank, Trustee for Dr. Charles R. Anderson. **433:** Lloyd Schwartz, "Leaves" from *Goodnight, Gracie*, 1992. Reprinted by permission of the author.

Chapter 15 Page 439: Margaret Lial, John Hornsby, and Charles Miller, from *Introductory Algebra*, Sixth Edition, pp. 163–164. Copyright © 1998 by Addison Wesley Longman, Inc. Reprinted by permission of Addison Wesley Longman. **441:** Margaret Lial and Diana Hestwood, from *Prealgebra*, First Edition, p. 87. Copyright © 1999 Addison Wesley Longman, Inc. Reprinted by permission of Addison Wesley Longman. **442:** Charles D. Miller and Stanley A. Salzman, from *Business Mathematics*, Fourth Edition, p. 373. Copyright © 1987 by Scott, Foresman and Company. Reprinted by permission of Addison-Wesley Educational Publishers, Inc. **443:** L. Murphy Johnson and Arnold Steffensen, from *Elementary Algebra*, p. 178. Copyright © 1985 by Scott, Foresman and Company. Reprinted by permission of Addison-Wesley Educational Publishers, Inc. **450:** Margaret Lial, Stanley Salzman, Diana Hestwood, and Charles Miller, from *Basic College Mathematics*, Fifth

INDEX